Praise for *Davos Man*

"Powerful. . . . Goodman's repor[...] funny. . . . *Davos Man* shows us th[...] inextricably linked to a great crime, perhaps [...] this century: the hijacking of our democracy."

—*Washington Post*

"A meticulously researched, clearly reported and truly infuriating history of the way the top 1% of the world has systematically arranged the way societies operate in order to become even richer, all to the detriment of the rest of us. . . . The book serves as a call to arms and an invitation to fight back against the continued unabashed pillaging of all economies by those who least need it." —*San Francisco Chronicle*

"Excellent. . . . An angry, powerful look at the economic inequality that's been brought into sharp relief by the COVID-19 pandemic. . . . A powerful, fiery book, and it could well be an essential one." —*NPR*

"A biting, uproarious yet vital and deadly serious account of the profound damage the billionaire class is inflicting on the world. Peter S. Goodman guides the reader through the hidden stories and twisted beliefs of some of the titans of finance and industry, who continually rationalize their bad behavior to themselves."

—Joseph E. Stiglitz, recipient of the
Nobel Prize in Economic Sciences

"Unflinching and authoritative, Peter Goodman's *Davos Man* will be read a hundred years from now as a warning, bellowed from the blessed side of the velvet rope, about a slow-motion scandal that spans the globe. Deliciously rich with searing detail, the clarity is reminiscent of Tom Wolfe let loose in the Alps in search of hypocrisies and vanities."

—Evan Osnos, National Book Award–winning author of
*Age of Ambition: Chasing Fortune, Truth, and Faith in the
New China* and *Wildland: The Making of America's Fury*

"Well-written and well-reported. . . . A passionate denunciation of the mega-rich."
—*Economist*

"One of the great financial investigative journalists, Peter S. Goodman delivers a meticulously detailed account of how the billionaire class has hijacked the world's economy, feasting on calamity, shirking taxes, all the while spouting bromides about compassionate capitalism. I so wish this tale of limitless greed and hypocrisy were a novel or a miniseries and not the truth about the world in which we live. Reader, prepare to be enraged."
—Barbara Demick, author of *Nothing to Envy: Ordinary Lives in North Korea* and *Eat the Buddha: Life and Death in a Tibetan Town*

"*New York Times* global economics correspondent Goodman mounts a scathing critique of the greed, narcissism, and hypocrisy that characterize those in 'the stratosphere of the globe-trotting class.' . . . An urgent, timely, and compelling message with nearly limitless implications."
—*Kirkus Reviews* (starred review)

"Impressively detailed. . . . Very readable, extensively reported. . . . A well-researched and lively explanation of how the global economy works, and the turning points that have enabled profiteering by the ultra-rich while undermining societal and democratic institutions."
—Charter

"The *Times*'s global economics correspondent profiles five billionaires (along with workers and migrants across the world) to show how their exploitation of the pandemic has exacerbated inequality across the globe."
—*The New York Times Book Review*

"Goodman is a skilled reporter whose stories of private affluence and public squalor are filled with detail and human interest."
—*Wall Street Journal*

DAVOS MAN

HOW THE BILLIONAIRES
DEVOURED THE WORLD

PETER S. GOODMAN

MARINER BOOKS
New York   Boston

HarperCollins books may be purchased for educational, business, or sales promotional use. For information, please email the Special Markets Department at SPsales@harpercollins.com.

A hardcover edition of this book was published in 2022 by Custom House, an imprint of William Morrow.

FIRST MARINER BOOKS PAPERBACK EDITION PUBLISHED 2023.

Designed by Lucy Albanese

Library of Congress Cataloging-in-Publication Data

Names: Goodman, Peter S., author.
Title: Davos man : how the billionaires devoured the world / Peter S. Goodman.
Description: First edition. | New York, NY : Custom House, [2022] | Includes bibliographical references and index.
Identifiers: LCCN 2021045346 (print) | LCCN 2021045347 (ebook) | ISBN 9780063078307 (hardcover) | ISBN 9780063078314 (trade paperback) | ISBN 9780063078321 (ebook)
Subjects: LCSH: Billionaires. | Capitalism—Moral and ethical aspects. | Wealth—Moral and ethical aspects. | Democracy.
Classification: LCC HC79.W4 G66 2022 (print) | LCC HC79.W4 (ebook) | DDC 305.5/234—dc23
LC record available at https://lccn.loc.gov/2021045346
LC ebook record available at https://lccn.loc.gov/2021045347

ISBN 978-0-06-307831-4

22 23 24 25 26 LBC 5 4 3 2 1

For Leah, Leo, Mila, and Luca

CONTENTS

Part III: Resetting History

"THEY WRITE THE RULES FOR THE REST OF THE WORLD"

For most of us, 2020 was a year of prolonged torment. Its very numerals seem likely to endure as shorthand for mass death, fear, isolation, shuttered schools, threats to livelihood, and countless more mundane forms of misery from the worst pandemic in a century.

But one select group—a species of human known as Davos Man—thrived like never before. The wealthiest, most powerful people on earth used their money and influence to separate themselves from the pandemic, riding it out in their oceanfront estates, mountain hideaways, and yachts. They feasted on calamity, snapping up real estate, shares of stock, and other companies at distressed prices. They applied their lobbying muscle to turn gargantuan, taxpayer-financed bailout packages into corporate welfare schemes for the billionaire class.

They seized on the pandemic—a disaster worsened by their plundering of public health care systems and stripping of government resources—as an opportunity to take credit for rescuing humanity. In a year that exposed the fatal consequences of decades of tax evasion by the world's billionaires, the same people who engineered this monumental grift demanded adulation for their generosity.

"In the pandemic, it was CEOs in many, many cases all over the world who were the heroes," said Marc Benioff, founder of Salesforce, a Silicon Valley software giant. "They're the ones who stepped forward with their financial resources and their corporate resources, their employees, their factories, and pivoted rapidly—not for profit, but to save the world."

Benioff was speaking in late January 2021 at the annual meeting of the World Economic Forum, the ultimate gathering place for the most affluent people on the planet. The pandemic had forced the cancellation of the usual in-person event in the Swiss Alps resort of Davos. In place of the white geodesic dome where Benioff held a lunch that included pop stars like Bono and Will.i.am, he and his fellow panelists convened on a clunky video-conferencing platform. The snow-covered peaks that formed the backdrop to Davos were replaced by drapes and bookcases glimpsed behind the speakers in their home offices. Instead of the free-flowing conversation of the Forum, participants engaged in halting discussion marred by connectivity issues.

But one key attribute endured despite the awkward refashioning of Davos: the lofty pledges for change voiced by the people most invested in preserving the status quo.

Benioff was on a panel discussing so-called stakeholder capitalism, the idea that businesses were no longer ruled solely by the imperative to enrich shareholders, but answerable to a broader array of interests—employees, the environment, local communities. His message was self-congratulatory: mission accomplished.

He and his fellow CEOs had banded together to secure protective gear like face masks and gowns for hospitals. Pharmaceutical companies had developed COVID-19 vaccines in record time. Bankers had unleashed credit, preventing bankruptcies.

"CEOs stepped up this year," Benioff said. "We would not be

where we are in the world today without the outstanding leadership of many, many CEOs who did heroic work all over the world, to basically save their communities."

Given the wretched state of the world at that moment, Benioff's depiction was breathtaking, a striking form of self-aggrandizement served up as social concern. It highlighted the gap between the billionaire class and the rest of humankind, one that stretched beyond the decimal places required to convey their fortunes. Benioff and his fellow corporate chieftains were effectively inhabitants of a separate reality—the realm of Davos Man.

Around the world, the pandemic had killed more than 2 million people while threatening hundreds of millions with poverty and hunger. The actual culprit was the coronavirus, but its lethal impacts and economic ravages had been magnified by the actions of the sorts of CEOs who flocked to Davos.

Private equity magnates like Stephen Schwarzman, who once described a proposed tax increase on the wealthy as an act of war—"like when Hitler invaded Poland"—had extracted profits from his investments in hospitals, excising costs while contributing to a systemic diminishing of American health care. Jamie Dimon, overseer of the biggest bank in the United States, had helped secure tax cuts for people who lived in Park Avenue penthouses, paid for by a weakening of government services. Larry Fink, the world's largest asset manager, broadcast his putative concern for social justice while squeezing poor countries to pay impossible debts in the midst of the pandemic.

The richest man on earth, Jeff Bezos, had added to the colossal scale of his e-commerce empire while failing to provide warehouse workers with protective gear, instead bestowing a valiant sounding title: they were essential workers—a label that condemned them as dispensable, rendering the virus an illegitimate reason to stay home.

If the agony of 2020 had demonstrated anything it was how

the rich could not only prosper but profiteer off everyone else's suffering.

By the end of the year, the collective wealth of billionaires worldwide had increased by $3.9 trillion, even as their philanthropic contributions fell to their lowest level in nearly a decade. Over the same year, as many as 500 million people descended into poverty, with their recovery likely to take a decade or more.

The pharmaceutical companies had indeed displayed mastery in concocting COVID-19 vaccines. But they had priced most of humanity out of the market for their lifesaving medicines.

Inside his oceanfront estate in Hawaii, Benioff preferred to exult in his triumphs while using the pandemic as an opportunity to impugn government. Davos Man championed stakeholder capitalism as a means of preempting government regulation; as a substitute for the public making use of democracy to fairly distribute the gains of capitalism. In taking a bow on behalf of corporate executives, Benioff was implicitly advancing the idea that the government need not tax billionaires, because they could be entrusted to fix life's problems out of their own beneficence.

"CEOs are gathering every week to figure out how we can improve the state of the world and get through this pandemic," he said, contrasting that against what he described as "the dysfunction of governments" and nonprofit organizations. "They were not the ones who saved us," Benioff said. "So the public is counting on CEOs."

Benioff was revealing himself as a choice specimen of a species that we must understand if we are to make sense of what has happened to humanity over the last half century. Widening economic inequality, intensifying public anger, and threats to democratic governance have all resulted from the depredation of Davos Man—an unusual predator whose power comes in part from his keen ability to adopt the guise of an ally.

Over recent decades, the billionaire class has ransacked governments by shirking taxes, leaving societies deprived of the resources needed to combat trouble. In the midst of a public health emergency, Davos Man was pointing to the resulting weakness of government as justification for depending on his generosity.

"We have to say it," Benioff said. "CEOs are definitely the heroes of 2020."

The term *Davos Man* was coined in 2004 by the political scientist Samuel Huntington. He used it to describe those so enriched by globalization and so native to its workings that they were effectively stateless, their interests and wealth flowing across borders, their estates and yachts sprinkled across continents, their arsenal of lobbyists and accountants straddling jurisdictions, eliminating loyalty to any particular nation.

Huntington's label referred directly to anyone who regularly made the journey to Davos to attend the Forum, their inclusion in the proceedings validating their standing among the winners in modern life. But over the years, *Davos Man* has grown into a catchall used by journalists and academics as shorthand for those who occupy the stratosphere of the globe-trotting class, the billionaires—predominantly white and male—who wield unsurpassed influence over the political realm while promoting a notion that has captured decisive force across major economies: when the rules are organized around greater prosperity for those who already enjoy most of it, everyone's a winner.

Davos Man and his hired guns—lobbyists, think tanks, battalions of public relations people, and obsequious journalists who prize access to power over truth—have resolutely perpetuated this idea, even in the face of overwhelming evidence to the contrary.

My mission is to help you understand Davos Man as a species. He is a rare and remarkable creature—a predator who attacks without restraint, perpetually intent on expanding his territory and seizing the nourishment of others, while protecting himself from reprisal by posing as a symbiotic friend to all.

Nowhere is this mode more vividly displayed than at the annual meeting of the Forum in Davos.

On paper, the Forum is just another multiday seminar devoted to steadfastly tackling the problems of the day, with earnest discussions on climate change, gender imbalance, and the digital future. Lest one fail to grasp its high-minded mission, it is spelled out boldly—"Committed to Improving the State of the World"—these words embossed on banners draped from streetlights, on every wall in every meeting room, and on the computer bags carried home as tokens of power by working journalists.

This mantra gives away the central incongruity of the enterprise. The collective fortune of the 2020 attendees was estimated at half a trillion dollars. The people who gather in the Alps are, by any measure, the world's ultimate winners. Their stupendous fortunes, their brands, and their social standing are intimately intertwined with the economic system as constituted, rendering dubious their commitment to improvement—a word that connotes change.

Behind the scenes, the Forum is a staging ground for business deals and strategic networking, a schmooze fest underwritten by financial behemoths and consulting firms, and an opportunity for everyone present to congratulate themselves on making it to the right side of the human divide.

"That is the magic of Davos," a former Forum executive told me. "It is the largest lobbying operation on earth. The most powerful people gather together behind closed doors, without any accountability, and they write the rules for the rest of the world."

The history of the last half century in Europe, North America, and other major economies is in large part the story of wealth flowing upward. Those reared in the most exclusive communities, educated at the fanciest schools, and intertwined in the most elite social networks have leveraged their privileges to secure unfathomable wealth, shuttling in their private jets between their beachfront villas and their mountain redoubts, buying their children passage to Ivy League universities, while stashing their holdings on Caribbean islands and other territories beyond reach of the tax collector.

Meanwhile, hundreds of millions of working people grapple with the impossible math of managing bills with paychecks that have shrunk.

The bare facts of this story are now so familiar that they may seem preordained. Books and magazines have dissected how the internet, globalization, and automation have reshaped modern life, rewarding urban-dwelling, educated professionals while punishing the lesser-skilled. Yet much of the literature tends to treat these shifts as beyond our control, like natural phenomena no more subject to human design than the wind and the tide.

The shape of our economies is not the product of happenstance. It is the result of deliberative engineering by the people who constructed the system in the service of their own interests. We are living in a world designed by Davos Man to direct ever-greater fortune toward Davos Man.

The billionaires have financed politicians who champion the uplifting of the already stratospherically uplifted. They have deployed lobbyists to eviscerate financial regulations, permitting banks to lend and gamble relentlessly, while depending on public largesse to cover their losses. They have defenestrated antitrust authorities, clearing the way for mergers that have enriched investment banks and shareholders, while bestowing oligarchic control upon large companies. They have squashed the power of labor movements, shrinking paychecks and handing the savings to shareholders.

Davos Man will tell you that he has earned his wealth by being smarter and more innovative than the next guy. He disdains taxes as a punitive insult to his skill and slavish work ethic. He is fine with handing over a little of his money, but on his terms alone, through branded philanthropic efforts, and especially if it puts his name on a hospital wing, or yields a photo of himself surrounded by grateful children in some wretched country made slightly less wretched by his generosity.

Through official pronouncements, Davos Man tends to dismiss money as incidental to the meaningful enterprise: Improving the State of the World. His social media platforms and technology "solutions"—algorithms and devices that give companies Godlike knowledge about customers and employees—are, in the mythology of Davos, expressions of his yearning to foster community. His financial derivatives, the complex instruments that played a central role in producing the 2008 global financial crisis, are a manifestation of his fervor to allow the marketplace to liberate humanity from small-minded minutiae like arithmetic.

You already know that the billionaires have triumphed comprehensively, amassing unprecedented wealth along with defining influence over the course of modern life. What we need to understand is how they have pulled it off—by warping the workings of democracy. Davos Man's monopolization of the fruits of global capitalism is no accident. He has insinuated into our politics and culture what we may call the Cosmic Lie: the alluring yet demonstrably bogus idea that cutting taxes and deregulating markets will not only produce extra riches for the most affluent, but trickle the benefits down to the lucky masses—something that has, in real life, happened zero times.

The history of capitalism is full of wealthy people applying their riches toward securing power, crafting the rules toward furthering their interests. Davos Man's most cunning innovation is how he has successfully cast himself as a concerned global citizen, while pervading the idea that his continued victories are a requirement for society to achieve any wins at all.

The Robber Barons of the late nineteenth century—

industrialists like Andrew Carnegie, and financiers like J. P. Morgan—were by and large satisfied with their wealth as an end in itself. Davos Man's appetite for affirmation operates on a different level. He is not content with owning homes the way that most people own socks. He pretends that his interests are the same as everyone else's. He seeks gratitude for his exploits, validation as the product of a just system in which he is a guardian of the public interest, even as he devours all the sources of sustenance. He argues that his own prosperity is a precondition for broader progress, the key to vibrancy and innovation.

This is how Davos Man has managed to turn every crisis into an opportunity for his further enrichment, finding in dire public health emergencies and financial conflagrations a justification for public relief, and implanting in every bailout a mechanism that steers public money his way.

To some degree, we have been titillated by Davos Man's exploits. We enjoy our billionaire porn—his outlandish birthday parties, glimpses of his trophy real estate, details of his divorce settlements. We watch shows like *Billions* and see him sweating through the plot twists, and, along the way, we buy into the implicit notion that he has earned his perch.

But now Davos Man's gluttony is threatening our entire ecosystem. His extreme overconsumption has undermined faith in governance, giving rise to rage among the other creatures in the biosphere.

In this book, I will argue that Davos Man's relentless plunder is the decisive force behind the rise of right-wing populist movements around the world. Typically, journalists explain such political shifts by pointing to recent events that have been exploited for electoral gain by fearmongering politicians who tap into nostalgia and nationalist sentiments—an influx of immigrants, the loss of status for a privileged group. But the full causes are deeper, stemming from grievances that have built up over decades as Davos Man has pillaged the gains of capitalism, depriving regular people of basic economic security. This has laid the ground for politicians who weaponize fear and foment hate, while prescribing incoherent solutions to legitimate social problems.

Davos Man's domination of the gains of globalization is how the United States found itself led by a patently unqualified casino developer as it grappled with a public health emergency that killed more Americans than those who died in World War I, World War II, and the Vietnam War combined. Davos Man's marauding explains why the United Kingdom was still consumed with Brexit—an elaborate act of self-harm—at the same time that it was failing to get a handle on the pandemic. It explains how France became roiled by a ferocious protest movement, and how even Sweden, a supposed bastion of social democracy, now seethes with anti-immigrant hate.

This is not how history was supposed to unfold.

Only a generation ago, a triumphant chorus was proclaiming the effective end of class conflict. The West, led by an all-powerful United States, had won the Cold War, punctuated by a Hollywood ending. The euphoric masses that tore down the Berlin Wall seemed to certify that Communism was dead, leaving capitalism as the universally acclaimed economic blueprint.

Francis Fukuyama famously pronounced "the end of history," as if the elements that had defeated authoritarianism—free speech, free trade, democracy, liberalized markets, unbridled consumerism—would prove the template for civilization going forward.

Fukuyama was properly ridiculed for applying the gloss of academic authority to a shallow narrative in which the United States would supposedly remain the guiding light for eternity. But his conception aligned with the conventional wisdom that liberal democracy was indeed the most evolved state of social organization, the recipe that would protect civil liberties and enable prosperity, with each reinforcing the other.

Instead, in some countries—among them India, the Philippines, and Hungary—democracy has devolved into the mechanism for the pursuit of tribal vengeance, the means through which popular movements wield tyrannical power, attacking liberalism itself.

How did the supposedly permanent triumph of the free market and the liberal democratic order curdle into the venomous disorder of right-wing hate?

And how did a deadly pandemic—the sort of danger that might have once bolstered a collectivist response—become another moment for profiteering by the richest people on earth?

This, in a nutshell, is what happened.

Davos Man emerged from the triumph of the Cold War to loot the material advances of the peace, depriving governments of the resources needed to serve their people.

The greatest beneficiaries of global capitalism applied their winnings toward the ultimate hostile takeover: They captured the levers of democratic governance. They bankrolled accommodating politicians, and then wielded their influence to tilt the workings of capitalism in their favor.

They demonized government and embraced privatization as the solution, placing public goods in the hands of profit-making companies.

They sold austerity as a virtue and imposed it on government spending, cutting education, housing, and health care. Then they funneled the spoils of this liquidation to themselves through tax cuts. They spread the idea that the world's wealthiest countries could not afford to furnish health care, education, and reliable public transportation to their people.

They forged international trade deals that generated magnificent opportunities for the professional ranks, while refusing to share the winnings with the rest of the populace. They assaulted labor unions and transferred work to low-wage countries, stifling wages while downgrading full-time jobs to itinerant gigs.

They deregulated banking, boosting their compensation, while triggering a global financial crisis. Then they bailed themselves out and sent the bill to ordinary citizens.

All the while, they poisoned the political conversation with the Cosmic Lie—the fatuous idea that showering the wealthy with tax cuts would trickle benefits down to all.

For the first three decades after World War II, American-led capitalism spread the gains of economic growth widely and progressively. But the capitalism since hijacked by Davos Man is not really capitalism at all. It is a social welfare state run for the benefit of the people who need it least; a sanctuary for billionaires in which systemic threats are extinguished with taxpayer money, while commonplace calamities like joblessness, foreclosure, and the absence of health care are accepted as the rough-and-tumble of free enterprise.

The usual measures of extreme inequality are at once familiar and astonishing.

Over the last four decades, the wealthiest 1 percent of all Americans has gained a collective $21 trillion in wealth. Over the same period, households in the bottom half have seen their fortunes diminish by $900 billion.

Since 1978, corporate executives have seen their total compensation explode by more than 900 percent, while wages for the typical American worker have risen by less than 12 percent.

Worldwide, the ten richest people are collectively worth more than the economies of the poorest eighty-five countries combined.

To take in such numbers is to reckon with the reality that Davos Man's refashioning of the global economy amounts to a historic act of larceny.

Had income in the United States continued to be distributed in the same fashion as during the first three decades after World War II, the bottom 90 percent of earners would have received an additional $47 trillion. Instead, that money flowed upward, enriching a few thousand people while jeopardizing American democracy itself.

And that was before COVID-19.

In the aftermath of the pandemic, the global economy appears likely to emerge with an even more pronounced tilt toward the needs of Davos Man. As publicly financed emergency relief schemes are withdrawn, some working people will find themselves in desperate straits, their savings depleted, making them so eager for jobs that they will be even more vulnerable to exploitation. Racial and class divides will widen.

In the United States and Europe, Davos Man is positioned to gain greater advantage over smaller businesses, many of which will disappear. A future economy dominated by the goliaths will be even more rewarding to shareholders and tougher on workers.

The developing world, short of medical care and teeming with people lacking basics like clean water, may slip further behind. A billion people are at risk of falling into extreme poverty by 2030.

The strife and inequality will create more opportunities for political movements that employ scarcity as a springboard to hate, stoking fear of ethnic and religious minorities as an electoral strategy.

But none of this is inevitable. Like every crisis, the pandemic presents an opportunity for the public to mobilize in pursuit of broader interests.

When historians one day look back at this moment, they will, with any luck, recognize an inflection point, a moment when the dire consequences of inequality became so inarguably grave that they triggered a full-on reckoning with the structural deficiencies of the global economy.

This book is aimed at encouraging that outcome. It contemplates how we might adapt to the profound injustices of the global economy, reviving the sort of capitalism we knew before, in which societies gained the virtues of the market system—innovation, dynamism, and growth—along with functioning mechanisms that fairly apportioned the gains.

A public health emergency has laid bare the vulnerabilities at work around the globe, creating an opportunity for the public to override the usual machinations of Davos Man.

In the United States, Joe Biden's defeat of Donald Trump in November 2020 brought renewed attention to relief for the jobless and others cut down by the economic downturn. The new president filled his administration with economists who had spent their careers focused on the struggles of working people. He quickly helped deliver a $1.9 trillion relief package aimed at ordinary households, redoubled efforts to reduce the monopoly power of giant technology companies like Amazon, and unleashed a campaign to increase taxes on corporations and the wealthiest people to finance government programs for everyone else.

But Biden owed his election in part to campaign contributions from Davos Men, whose interests were amply represented in the ranks of his government. He swiftly dispatched the popular notion that he would hew to his traditional centrist confines, surprising jaded Washington observers with his willingness to challenge the corporate establishment. Biden used the budget process to pursue a significant restructuring of the American economy—one that could reverse decades of raiding by the wealthiest people on earth. He catalyzed an international effort to eradicate tax havens and impose a worldwide minimum rate of corporate taxation. He lent American support to a global campaign to set aside patents toward making COVID-19 vaccines available to countries that could not afford to pay what pharmaceutical companies demanded.

But whether Biden will ultimately deliver is in no way certain, just as efforts at tackling inequality in other countries confronts the reality that those with the most wealth are adept at using it to protect their interests

The billionaires retain a formidable apparatus to fight off attempts to rewrite the rules. They are skilled at striking the pose of responding to societal outrage while protecting an order in which their privileges remain sacrosanct.

Taking on Davos Man requires an understanding of the beast.

Consider this book a guided safari through Davos Man's unbounded terrain.

We will track five key specimens—Bezos, Dimon, Benioff, Schwarzman, and Fink—while paying special attention to the United States, the United Kingdom, Italy, France, and Sweden. This study does not fully encompass the world, focusing by design on the United States as the largest economy and the primary architect of (what is left of) the liberal democratic order, along with its leading postwar allies and an oft-celebrated social democratic paragon: Sweden. Today, the ranks of the billionaire class are well represented from China to India to Brazil. Some of these characters are to be found in these pages, along with ordinary people around the globe—migrant workers from Bangladesh, African immigrants in Sweden, itinerant laborers in Argentina, steelworkers in Illinois, and refugees from Afghanistan.

We will also observe other creatures that play a symbiotic role in preserving Davos Man's dominance—the Forum's founder, Klaus Schwab; the former American president Bill Clinton; the French president, Emmanuel Macron; Trump's Treasury secretary, Steven Mnuchin; Mitch McConnell, the Republican Party leader in the American Senate; and George Osborne, the former overseer of the British treasury, whose imposition of austerity laid the ground for Brexit. Each of these figures has aided Davos Man in pursuit of fresh prey while helping himself to choice morsels.

We will examine Davos Man's evolutionary forebears—the Robber Barons in the United States, and Italian magnates who pioneered outlandish forms of tax evasion.

And we will explore the invasive species that has thrived in the aftermath of Davos Man's destruction of the human habitat—right-wing populists like Italy's Matteo Salvini and Donald Trump, who claimed power by feigning an attack on Davos Man, while actually advancing his supremacy.

We will see how Davos Man has captured more than wealth and power. He has seized control of the very language that we use to describe what has happened to the world, limiting our expectations for our own societies by convincing us that we cannot afford change. Davos Man presents his own story as the narrative of human progress, rendering efforts to force him to share the wealth as attacks on freedom. He has employed the mechanisms of democracy to sabotage democratic ideals.

PART I

Global Pillage

The disposition to admire, and almost to worship, the rich and the powerful, and to despise, or, at least, to neglect persons of poor and mean condition is the great and most universal cause of the corruption of our moral sentiments.

—ADAM SMITH, *The Theory of Moral Sentiments*, 1759

I believe there are more instances of the abridgement of the freedom of the people by gradual and silent encroachments of those in power, than by violent and sudden usurpations.

—JAMES MADISON, speech at the U.S. Constitutional Convention, 1787

CHAPTER 1

"HIGH UP IN THE MOUNTAINS"

Davos Man in His Native Habitat

<u>JANUARY 2017</u>

Days before Donald Trump was to be inaugurated president of the United States, a parade of extravagantly wealthy people descended on a village perched high in the snow-encrusted peaks of the Swiss Alps.

As they approached the Congress Centre in the middle of Davos, many fresh from the cabins of private jets, they confronted an impediment to their customary freedom of movement: a security check.

There was Eric Schmidt, the former executive chairman of Google, surrendering his Android phone for inspection. Jack Ma, whose Chinese e-commerce company, Alibaba, had yielded a personal fortune worth some $22 billion, was emptying his pockets before entering the complex.

Michael Dell, whose company once revolutionized laptop computers, plunked his device onto a conveyor belt that rolled it into an X-ray machine, just like the schmucks flying commercial out of LaGuardia.

Jamie Dimon, chief executive of JPMorgan Chase, whose

toxic investments brought minimal scrutiny from regulators before the last financial crisis, submitted to an obligatory inspection of his overcoat.

This exceedingly privileged slice of humanity had arrived in Davos for an annual five-day pilgrimage known as the World Economic Forum.

The Forum is overseen by a nominally nonprofit organization that has made it an essential assembly place for those most consumed with making money.

In its half century of existence, the Forum has turned itself into an indispensable stop on the traveling circuit of the global elite—corporate executives, heads of state, management consultants, venture capitalists, hedge fund managers, and public intellectuals—plus a handful of Hollywood celebrities, musicians, and artists, along with academics, activists, and teeming hordes of journalists. Every January, a crowd numbering about three thousand jams the town, displacing the skiers who normally predominate. Attendees roam from earnest seminars on climate change and the future of work held inside the Congress Centre to dinners and cocktail parties thrown at surrounding hotels by global banks and technology giants.

This year, Davos Man was grappling with an unfamiliar sensation—not fear exactly, but a soupçon of concern that people on the rest of the planet were increasingly prone to questioning the justice of his station. What had begun nearly two decades earlier as an inchoate movement against globalization, a series of unruly protests dominated by young people decrying the World Trade Organization, had burgeoned into a multigenerational revolt against the establishment in countries far and wide.

Trump was the most obvious manifestation of the uprising. Though the billionaires in Davos were quietly salivating over the wealth-enhancing implications of American democracy coming under the control of one of their own—or, at least, someone who played a billionaire on television—they were also cognizant that his ascension reflected public outrage over what they represented: a gluttonous cabal that had seized the gains of globalization while leaving most people poorer and increasingly anxious.

The United States was the primary architect of the post–World War II liberal democratic order, which had worked magnificently for the sorts of people who flocked to Davos. In entrusting the presidency to a reality television star famed for groping women, dog whistles to white supremacists, multiple bankruptcies, and open contempt for international institutions and trade agreements, the American electorate had effectively mandated the destruction of the status quo. Trump was promising to blow up globalization, avenging the long-term marginalization of enraged white men in the middle of America whose living standards had slumped.

The people who mattered most in Davos—the corporate chieftains and finance masters—generally saw through Trump's displays of nationalist brio as a political charade, while focusing on the tax cuts and other perks attainable under his presidency. But they betrayed a smidgen of concern that the active empowering of angry people who blamed the wealthy for their troubles was a story that could play out unpredictably, with potentially unpleasant consequences.

Britain was six months into its fractious divorce with the European Union. Brexit, as this bewildering process was known, represented an assault on another pillar of the global economy and the liberal democratic order. Many of the same forces that had put Trump in the White House had helped produce Brexit.

As the Forum began, the organizers had taken these developments as the cue to educate participants on the pitfalls of widening economic inequality.

The bare facts of Davos Man's triumph were impossible to dismiss.

A half century earlier, the chief executive officer of the typi-cal publicly traded American company had earned twenty times as much as the average worker. In the years since, the gap had widened exponentially, lifting the CEO's compensation to 278 times that of the rank-and-file.

Tax policies written by Davos Man for his own benefit had enhanced the divide.

A pair of University of California at Berkeley economists, Emmanuel Saez and Gabriel Zucman, tallied up all the taxes that Americans paid, from federal, state, and local income taxes to sales taxes and capital gains on investments. They had con-cluded that the richest four hundred Americans, whose average wealth was $6.7 billion, had seen their effective tax rate cut by more than half since 1962—from 54 percent to 23 percent. Over the same period, those in the bottom half, who earned about $18,500 a year, had seen their tax burden *increase,* from 22.5 per-cent to 24 percent.

The occupants of executive offices were surrendering a smaller slice of their incomes to the tax authorities than the people who scrubbed their palatial private bathrooms.

In Britain, the average worker was earning less than they had a decade earlier.

The official theme for this year's Forum was "Responsive and Responsible Leadership." If the agenda was any indication, Da-vos Man had become aware that his propensity to rig the system had caused ill feelings. There were sessions on "Ending Corrup-tion," "Ending Executive Pay," and "Inclusive Growth." Sheryl Sandberg, chief operating officer of Facebook—the social plat-form whose algorithms and pursuit of advertising revenues had turned it into a mass purveyor of fake news that fueled social fury—was to take part in a panel discussing "A Positive Narra-tive for the Global Community."

Generally, Davos Man was not big on introspection that conflicted with the bottom line. He was mostly annoyed that inequality was even a topic, given that it clashed with his favorite sort of tale—the ones where everyone lived happily ever after so long as the unfettered pursuit of wealth was sacrosanct.

What Davos Man supposedly cared most deeply about was channeling his intellect and compassion toward solving the great crises of the age. He might have retreated to his mountain-top palace in Jackson Hole or his yacht moored off Mykonos, but he was too obsessed with rescuing the poor and sparing humanity from the ravages of climate change.

So he was here—paying fees reaching several hundred thousands of dollars a year for a Forum membership, plus another $27,000 per head to attend the meeting—posing for photos with Bono, congratulating Bill Gates on his philanthropic exploits, tweeting out inspirational quotes from Deepak Chopra, and still finding time to buttonhole that sovereign wealth chieftain from Abu Dhabi in pursuit of investment for his luxury-goods mall in Singapore.

This was my seventh year attending Davos as a journalist, though I still felt out of place. Throughout my prior career—working first as a freelancer in Southeast Asia, then as a junior reporter in Alaska, later as a Shanghai-based correspondent for the *Washington Post,* and eventually as a national economic writer for the *New York Times*—I have centered my reporting on people who have suffered the consequences of Davos Man's depredation. I have written about families who have lost their homes to foreclosure in Florida and California, workers whose wages have eroded from Ohio to England, landless laborers enduring feudal poverty in the Philippines and India. I am used to operating in places where CEOs are scrutinized as potential sources of harm—a stark contrast to Davos, where billionaire executives are celebrated as benevolent agents of progress, with journalists frequently complicit in the narrative.

But in 2010, I accepted an offer to oversee business and technology coverage at the Huffington Post, which then seemed poised to overtake legacy media. Its founder, Arianna Huffington, gravitated toward any buzzy gathering that included billionaires who might finance her next venture. She brought me along to Davos to project the sense that she was the vanguard of journalism, having poached an old-school newspaper guy from the *Times*.

When I jumped to another digital upstart in 2014 as the global editor in chief, I continued going to Davos as an exercise in brand building. And when I returned to the *Times* in 2016, moving to London, where I became a roving global economic correspondent, I carried on with the Forum, because I had reluctantly come to see it as journalistically useful. Amid the preening and virtue signaling were people—potential sources—who were intimately involved with issues of consequence.

If you were willing to break decorum and pose pushy questions, you could learn things of value, even if much of it was off the record. I talked to the Iraqi president about the future of ISIS, and pressed central bankers and Treasury secretaries on matters of economic policy. I buttonholed Jamie Dimon and provoked his laments about the tax code. I attended a dinner with Peter Gabriel, who revealed that he was making music with monkeys.

More than anything, I gawked at the spectacle, at once horrified and mesmerized. The contrast between the Forum's noble packaging and its crude reality was surreal.

I saw billionaires engage in simulations of the Syrian refugee experience—led around in the dark while blindfolded, as angry officials demanded papers—before savoring truffles at dinners thrown by global banks. Outside conference rooms featuring discussions on human trafficking, I watched venture capitalists fist-bumping over having scored invites to the bacchanal thrown by a Russian oligarch who flew in prostitutes from Moscow.

Pharmaceutical industry executives began their mornings

in meditation sessions led by mindfulness guru Jon Kabat-Zinn before retiring to private suites to plot their next merger engineered toward lifting drug prices.

A loose and informal hierarchy was at work. The ultimate Davos Men like Schwarzman and Fink rarely appeared in the main areas of the Congress Centre, where the panel discussions were held, generally confining themselves to exclusive lounges for corporate members or private suites at hotels scattered around town. Heads of state would occasionally sweep through the building accompanied by their security details.

Second-tier Davos Men—corporate executives and investment managers whose net worth was confined to the mere tens of millions of dollars—tended to meet one another and journalists in hotel lobbies, while popping up at cocktail parties hosted by consulting and accounting firms. Finance and trade ministers from Europe, Australia, and Latin America huddled in the hallways with economists, executives, and journalists.

Prominent writers and intellectuals wandered about. Nobel laureate economists Joseph Stiglitz and Robert Shiller were perennials. Former government officials turned lobbyists were well represented, using Davos as a central venue for networking. Al Gore was somehow everywhere.

The peasantry of the proceedings—bleary-eyed journalists, bespectacled academics, anxious entrepreneurs relentlessly pitching their start-up companies, the working stiffs of the diplomatic corps, and activists affiliated with human rights and environmental organizations—could generally be found in the bowels of the Congress Centre, in lounge areas outside the meeting rooms, occupying uncomfortably round-backed chairs upholstered in dull tones of brown and tan. There, some loitered in a grown-up game of musical chairs, perpetually looking out for an unused power outlet so we could charge our smartphones. We journalists scanned for people worth talking to, while deleting some of the hundreds of emails sent by overeager PR flaks seeking to connect us with the venture-funded company that had pioneered a way to sell our dream lives to advertisers or turn recycled potato chip bags into couture dresses for refugee children.

Everyone stole glances at one another's badges, which were helpfully color-coded in a hierarchical identification of worth: white for standard grade participants, platinum for senior government officials, and orange for regular working press, who were denied entry to many events while stuffed into a spartan media tent that reinforced their lack of status.

My own white badge gave me free reign to wander as I desired, attending all sessions and approaching other participants, or positioning myself strategically to overhear conversations between Davos Men. I was an outsider with insider privileges.

Every now and again, some master of the universe in an especially well-cut suit would appear briefly, invariably in a hurry, donning a badge embossed with a hologram. This was like spotting a unicorn. We regular badge holders speculated over what cosmically important doors they might open.

Indeed, for most participants, much of the Davos experience consisted of not really grasping what the hell was going on, while nursing the sense that more interesting things were surely happening to more connected people somewhere else. We scrutinized one another's faces for some flicker of recognition, looking past and around the useless masses in pursuit of someone plugged-in, or the odd celebrity—the actors Matt Damon and Forest Whitaker were wandering around this year—all while trying not to be stampeded by the battering ram of a security detail escorting Israeli prime minister Bibi Netanyahu.

On my first night in town, I dropped my bag at my rented apartment and trudged through the snow to the Belvedere Hotel, a colonnaded white fortress towering over the main street.

I was attending an "executive dinner forum" featuring a discussion about the pushback to globalization. The event was a joint production of the *Financial Times,* the salmon-tinted newspaper that was required reading among the globe-trotting tribe, and Wipro, an Indian consulting firm. The published agenda promised an exploration of appropriate responses to the "turbulent mix of uncertainty and complexity" roiling the global economy.

If Davos Man had come to dinner hoping to be reassured that the story would end happily, he was in for a bummer.

Ian Goldin, a professor of globalization at Oxford University, warned attendees that they were at risk of wasting the potent virtues of the modern economy—the connectedness, the convenience, the technological advancements that had rescued humanity from disease, poverty, ignorance, and boredom.

"There's never been a better time to be alive, and yet we feel so glum," Goldin said. "So many people feel anxious. So many people feel that this is one of the most dangerous times."

Goldin had coauthored a prescient book that highlighted one especially potent danger that could derail the global economy: a pandemic that shut down supply chains. The world had become so dependent on goods transported across oceans that trouble in any one place could quickly spread everywhere. Major companies had been ruled by an imperative to stay lean as a way to cut costs and reward shareholders, leaving them little margin for error once such a scenario unfolded.

Goldin rattled off a list of other alarming developments. Trump appeared likely to yank the United States from a global pact aimed at limiting climate change. Britain's abandonment of the European Union risked splintering the bloc.

"You can't stop managing an entangled environment by disconnecting," Goldin said. "The idea that somehow we can forge our future in an insular way, even for the biggest countries like the U.S., is a fantasy."

This was all globalization boilerplate. But then Goldin artic-
ulated the tricky part for Davos Man. He was going to have to
make sacrifices, Goldin said, or the world could be in for a re-
play of the Renaissance. That celebrated period of extraordinary
scientific progress, commercial growth, and artistic creativity in
Europe ended in revolution. The gold leaf adornments to Tuscan
cathedrals were glittering statements of the era, but they did
not put food on the tables of the peasantry. The spices landing
in Mediterranean ports from Asia were at the center of a lucrative global trade, yet they were too expensive for most people
to enjoy. By the eighteenth century, angry mobs turned on the
Medicis, the family that ruled Florence, sending the clan fleeing.

"We need to learn these historical lessons," Goldin concluded.
"We need to make the choices to ensure that globalization is
sustainable, that connectivity is sustainable, that we deal with
the intractable problems that are worrying people."

When the members of a panel took their seats to discuss how
to proceed, it quickly became clear that Davos Man was not especially inclined toward sacrifice.

Abidali Neemuchwala, Wipro's chief executive, had advice
for workers threatened with redundancy: get some job training.
"People have to take more ownership of upgrading themselves
on a continuous basis," he said.

My former boss, Arianna Huffington, who had just launched
a wellness site that aimed to vacuum up sponsorships from spa
resorts, offered her antidote to capitalism's shortcomings. It involved comfier pillows, more sleep, and meditation.

I spent the next few days surveying proposed solutions to
inequality. At a panel inside the conference center, Ray Dalio,
founder of the American investment firm Bridgewater Associates, suggested that the key to reinvigorating the middle class
was to "create a favorable environment for making money." This
left the impression that the current environment was somehow
not conducive to moneymaking, a curious argument coming

from a person whose net worth was pushing $19 billion. Dalio touted the "animal spirits" that could be unleashed by stripping away regulations.

At another panel discussion entitled "Preparing for the Fourth Industrial Revolution," the Indian magnate Mukesh Ambani scoffed at the idea that government ought to attack poverty by transferring wealth from the richest people. Ambani was the chairman of the petrochemicals colossus Reliance Industries. He was hailed as the wealthiest person in Asia, with a net worth exceeding $73 billion. His prescription for easing poverty was to let technology dispense new forms of credit.

"Embrace the free market for creation of wealth," he said.

Seated to his left, Marc Benioff perked up. His company, Salesforce, had turned itself into a global behemoth on the strength of software used by businesses to track customer details and leads about future sales.

"Artificial intelligence will create digital refugees," Benioff said. "People will be displaced from jobs, tens of millions of people across the planet, because technology is moving forward so rapidly, creating much lower cost, much easier to use and more capable work environments."

Among the actors creating "more capable work environments" was Salesforce itself. The company's promotional literature listed the key elements of its software, including "more personalized outreach with automation," and "chatbots and other automated messaging."

Yet on this panel, Benioff presented himself not as the billionaire CEO of a company whose revenues were derived from replacing human hands, but as a concerned citizen.

"Are we going to be committed to supporting and improving this state of the world?" he said. "Or are we just going to kind of let it go as it is?"

The moderator, Ngaire Woods, dean of Oxford's Blavatnik School of Government, was refreshingly unwilling to let this

question pass as just another rhetorical demonstration of Davos
Man sensitivity.

"You've just painted a picture of hundreds of millions of people who will no longer have jobs," she said. "What is it that you
think leaders should be doing?"

A trustee of the Forum, Benioff reached deep into the well of
Davos concepts.

"We really need to be mindful of, and start having these very
serious conversations," he said. "Multistakeholder dialogues,
honestly."

The event at which he was speaking had itself been billed as
a *very serious conversation*. Yet the solution to the problem of his
own company threatening untold numbers of jobs was, apparently, more talking.

Not just any kind of talking, though. Stakeholder dialogues.

The word *stakeholder* is a talisman for Davos Man, its usage ev-
idencing high-minded principles. It is a demonstration that the
speaker cares about loftier matters than the crude enrichment
of shareholders. They empathize with their workers and their
workers' children. They worry about the vitality of the communities down there, in the shade of their skyscraper headquarters.
They would prefer that polar bears not succumb to heatstroke,
and that homeless people be housed somewhere.

Benioff has literally written the book on this—*Compassionate
Capitalism: How Corporations Can Make Doing Good an Integral
Part of Doing Well*.

That Benioff has emerged as a leading proponent of such
principles is ironic, given that he frequently cites Larry Ellison,
the founder of the software giant Oracle, as his mentor. Ellison
has no truck with the idea that business is about anything more
than adding zeros to his net worth. In an exchange in the dot-
com era with my colleague Mark Leibovich, Ellison pantomimed

gagging in disgust as he derided technology chieftains who describe their undertakings as moral crusades.

"Oh, well, the reason we're doing software here at Oracle is because someday children will use this software, and we wouldn't want to leave a single child behind," Ellison said in a tone of theatrical sarcasm. "What I really care about is making the world a better place." Then he gagged himself again.

He was talking about people like Marc Benioff.

Reared in San Francisco, Benioff speaks in a vernacular that is equal parts Silicon Valley proselytizer and Davos disciple.

"I've always believed that technology holds the potential to flatten the world in wonderful ways; to foster a more diverse, trusting and inclusive society while creating once-unthinkable opportunities for billions of people," he wrote in his memoir, whose title encapsulated Davos Man philosophy—*Trailblazer: The Power of Business as the Greatest Platform for Change.*

Benioff is an apostle of a faith with no shortage of adherents in the technology realm—the now-clichéd admixture of bohemian mysticism and ruthless entrepreneurialism that connected the venture capitalists of Sand Hill Road to the naked hordes at Burning Man.

"I have been very fortunate to have met a lot of what I would call gurus," he once said. "I'm probably the only person to use Larry Ellison and the Dalai Lama and Neil Young in the same sentence."

Partial to Hawaiian shirts, Benioff frequently celebrates the concept of *ohana,* a Hawaiian term that loosely translates to "family," and that supposedly formed the central organizing principle governing Salesforce—a spirit of kinship connecting its tens of thousands of employees.

"We love being together as one *ohana*" is a phrase he has uttered on conference calls with Wall Street stock analysts. During corporate retreats in Hawaii, he led his executive team into the surf as they dug their feet into the sand and joined hands for a group blessing ceremony. In Davos this year, he would host a Hawaiian themed party inside a nightclub featuring a performance by the Black Eyed Peas.

At six foot five, Benioff wandered the *ohana* floor at Salesforce's sixty-one-story San Francisco headquarters—the tallest building in the city—in the company of his golden retriever, who bore the title Chief Love Officer. He was rhapsodic about Dreamforce, the four-day Salesforce gathering that began as a way to showcase new products but had evolved into a mini-Davos by the Bay, featuring concerts by Stevie Wonder and U2. The days began with meditation sessions led by Buddhist monks. "It's a four-day opportunity to consider big ideas and pursue better versions of ourselves," he wrote in his memoir.

Benioff's father had owned a chain of dress shops in the San Francisco Bay Area. As a child, Benioff rode along in the family Buick as his father hauled bolts of fabric and dresses among his six shops.

"During those endless Sundays in the station wagon," Benioff wrote, "I was struck by my father's work ethic and unwavering integrity. There was no funny business whatsoever with the financials or inventory."

He was also struck by the haphazard way that his father managed information—what was selling best and where, which fabric was needed when. His father did the books by hand, a process that kept him leaning over the kitchen table late into the evening.

By the time he was a teenager, Benioff was dismantling and rebuilding rudimentary computers. He taught himself to code while producing his own video games. He persuaded his father to allow him to build him a customer database. This was the inspiration for what would become Salesforce, a dominant player in the software niche of customer relationship management, a company that would eventually be worth more than $200 billion.

As Silicon Valley origin stories go, this one traced the usual route: technologist recognizes a problem, develops a solution, gets wildly rich, the end. But Benioff presented Salesforce less as a vehicle for profit than a way to generate social impact.

He had joined Ellison's company, Oracle, fresh out of the University of Southern California. Less than four years later, when he was only twenty-six, he had reached the vice president ranks. He enjoyed a special relationship with the boss, sailing on Ellison's yacht in the Mediterranean. But then Benioff suffered a crippling loss of morale, prompting him to take a three month sabbatical. In southern India, he met a woman known as "the hugging saint."

As Benioff recounted the experience years later, he told her about his business interests and how they seemed "in some way connected to the existential confusion" that consumed him. Through a cloud of incense, she gazed at him intently. "In your quest to succeed and make money," she told him, "don't forget to do something for others."

This, Benioff later wrote, was how Salesforce took shape.

From its incorporation in 1999, he pledged that it would devote 1 percent of its equity and product to philanthropic undertakings, while encouraging employees to dedicate 1 percent of their working time to voluntary efforts. Salesforce employees regularly volunteered at schools, food banks, and hospitals. They joined the relief efforts in the aftermath of Hurricane Katrina, and ranged as far as the Tibetan plain to work in refugee camps.

"There are very few examples of companies doing this at scale," Benioff told me. "The example they always gave was Ben and Jerry's Ice Cream." He said this with a chuckle, amused by any comparison to the aging Vermont hippies who had brought the world Cherry Garcia. "Most companies in our industry have never really given back at scale."

This was not about public relations, Benioff insisted, but a product of societal demand.

"Doing well by doing good is no longer just a competitive advantage," he wrote. "It's becoming a business imperative."

Benioff was by many indications a true believer, not just idly parroting Davos Men talking points. When the state of Indiana proceeded with legislation that would have allowed businesses to discriminate against gay, lesbian, and transgender employees, Benioff threatened to yank investments in the state, forcing a change in the law. He had shamed Facebook and Google for abusing the public trust and called for regulations on search and social media giants.

"I'm trying to influence others to do the right thing," he told me during an interview in the middle of 2020. "I feel that responsibility."

I found myself won over by his boyish enthusiasm, and his willingness to talk at length without preconditions, and absent public relations minders—a rarity for Silicon Valley.

Benioff's philanthropic efforts had been directed at easing homelessness in San Francisco, while expanding health care for children. He and Salesforce would collectively contribute $7 million toward a successful 2018 campaign for a local ballot measure that levied fresh taxes on San Francisco companies like his own in an effort to stem homelessness, a stance that put him crosswise with other technology CEOs.

"As SF's largest employer we recognize we are part of the solution," he declared on Twitter (a platform he at one point considered buying). The new taxes were likely to cost Salesforce $10 million a year.

That sounded like a lot of money, ostensible evidence of a socially conscious CEO sacrificing the bottom line in the interest of catering to societal needs. But it was less than a trifle alongside the money that Salesforce withheld from the government through legal tax subterfuge.

The same year that Benioff backed the special levy to address homelessness in his hometown, his company recorded revenues exceeding $13 billion while paying the modest sum of zero in federal taxes. Salesforce deployed fourteen tax subsidiaries scattered from Singapore to Switzerland, moving its money and assets around in a masterful display of accounting hocus-pocus that made its taxable income vanish.

Benioff did not invent this tax avoidance contrivance. He inherited it from his Davos Man forebears, who, over decades, deployed hordes of lobbyists to turn the United States into their refuge.

During the Clinton administration, the Treasury opened up a loophole that enabled executives at multinational corporations to engage in large-scale chicanery without risk of seeing the inside of a penitentiary. They were permitted to set up subsidiaries in foreign countries that beckoned with low taxes—Ireland was a popular choice—and then legally transfer their intellectual property there. Their new international outposts charged the rest of the corporation exorbitant licensing fees to use the intellectual property. The net effect: on their American earnings statements, the wealthiest corporations looked like money losers, paying taxes accordingly.

In the decade and a half after Clinton's Treasury bestowed this gift on American corporations, their effective tax bills plunged from over 35 percent of their revenues to 26 percent. So-called profit shifting has been costing the American Treasury $60 billion a year in lost taxes.

Compared to this legalized form of tax evasion, the $10 million that Benioff had helped secure to attack homelessness in San Francisco amounted to a rounding error. Benioff's individual compensation the following year would exceed $28 million, most of it in stock grants and stock options. These sorts of pay packages were a key driver for the astronomical housing prices of the San Francisco Bay Area, a primary cause of the very homelessness that Benioff was intent on eliminating.

Benioff and his wife, Lynne, appear genuinely concerned

about the state of American education and children's health.
They have demonstrated their concern with their checkbook.
But what happens to programs like Medicaid and Head Start—
key sources of health care and early childhood education for
low-income Americans—when the largest companies pay no
federal taxes? What happens to mass transit, to job training, to
roads and highways, to public-health research?

Benioff's version of compassionate capitalism airbrushed key
"stakeholders" out of the picture: The government was missing.
His endless talk of the *ohana* did not include labor unions. At
the center of his vision for his company—at the core of Davos
Man thought in general—was the assumption that the wealthiest people could be relied upon to do the right thing, sharing
the fruits of their success. The occasional flinging of a few gold
coins would protect their palaces from any mobs showing up at
the gates.

Under Davos Man's logic, the wealthy are magnanimous,
so unions are an unnecessary intrusion on business, and taxes
represent money seized by the government; money that could
otherwise be showered on the fortunate people who would benefit from his philanthropic undertakings. This was an idea that
went back to Carnegie and the rest of the Robber Barons, whose
grandiose public works projects—libraries, museums, concert
halls—were proffered as societal compensation for their lopsided share of the economic gains, and their violent suppression
of labor uprisings.

Davos Man had updated this logic by denigrating government. Public sector bureaucrats would predictably squander
taxpayer dollars through inefficiency and lack of discipline, the
billionaires argued. Whereas they could efficiently target their
philanthropic pursuits at clearly defined missions. Having earned
their money through the rough-and-tumble of the competitive
marketplace, they were tightly organized and nimble, making

them better able to engineer impact with their money. Through this framing, Davos Man deftly rendered his discretionary dollops of generosity as recompense for grand-scale tax evasion.

Benioff had derived his wealth by helping make the world more unequal, arming the largest corporations with a tool kit that helped them enrich their shareholders. He relished his identity as a digital disrupter intent on turning business into the driver for social transformation. But his philanthropy, his genuine likability, and his empathy obscured the central reality of his enterprise: he was an enabler, a beneficiary, and a reinforcer of the world as it was.

If Ellison was his main guru in the early stage of his career, Benioff had more recently gravitated toward the teachings of Klaus Schwab, the founder of the World Economic Forum.

Benioff credited Schwab with introducing him to "stakeholder theory," calling it "one of the greatest intellectual contributions to the world of business."

Schwab was the master of ceremonies at Davos. A dour economist with ramrod-straight posture, he spoke forcefully and slowly, in a thick German accent bordering on farcical, as if every word were among the most meaningful uttered in history.

Born in 1938, Schwab had come of age in Europe's postwar reconstruction. He was steeped in the principles of social democracy, endorsing the notion that government should play a central role in the marketplace, protecting workers against joblessness while providing universal health care and pensions. He was an unwavering devotee to the project of European integration and the dream of a continent mobilized through collective action. During a graduate sojourn at Harvard in the late 1960s, Schwab became enamored of the corporate management theories in vogue in the United States. He sketched out stakeholder theory as the means to express what he came to portray as the optimal arrangement—business and government working cooperatively to promote higher living standards.

This was the spirit that animated what Schwab first called the European Management Forum, a gathering of academics, business executives, and government officials that he organized in 1971, when he was only thirty-three.

He picked Davos as the venue because the remote and placid setting seemed conducive to a focused interchange of ideas. A compact though oddly charmless village, Davos sat in a valley surrounded by arresting peaks. In Victorian times, it had served as a sanitorium for people suffering tuberculosis, and later as a haven for intellectual debate. Einstein had given a presentation on relativity there. "High up in the mountains," Schwab wrote, "in this picturesque town known for its clean air, participants could exchange best practices and new ideas and inform each other of pressing global social, economic, and environmental issues."

The first iteration drew 450 participants from more than two dozen countries. Over the years, as heads of state increased in number, security intensified, reinforcing the sense of achievement in simply making it in. Davos attendees became increasingly global, and the Forum expanded, launching regional meetings in China, Africa, the Middle East, India, and Latin America. To better reflect its wider scope and identity, the organization adopted a new name: since 1987, it has called itself the World Economic Forum.

Today, the Forum regularly convenes panels of experts and executives while producing a blizzard of reports—on digital transformation, on the future of health care, on advanced manufacturing, on seemingly everything.

But the meeting in Davos remains the center of the Forum's orbit.

The Forum long ago outgrew its Davos confines, exhausting

the meager supply of hotel rooms, and forcing grown professionals to share glorified dorm spaces in bare-bones chalets for upward of $400 a night, or otherwise commute from neighboring villages while relying on Forum shuttle buses, whose schedules appear as closely guarded as the North Korean nuclear launch codes.

Despite the outward appearances of glamour, attending the Forum has become a supreme and unending torment of logistical hassles, astonishing costs, and physical deprivation—exhaustion, dehydration, hunger, and angst. But this is also central to the experience, a feeling of overwhelming befuddlement tinged with elation that you are somewhere that is supposed to signify your own importance in the momentous sweep of history—a ridiculous yet highly effective means of motivating people to keep showing up.

"The anxiety of exclusion pervades," the journalist Nick Paumgarten once described it. "It is the natural complement to the euphoria of inclusion. The tension between self-celebration and self-doubt engenders a kind of social electricity."

Because the most powerful people on earth regularly attend, other powerful people feel a compulsion to come, which reinforces the Forum's intrinsic value. This is Schwab's keenest insight into the human condition, his understanding of the magnetic pull of power itself. He has constructed a happening that demands space on the calendars of the most overscheduled people, an event where the interests of Bill Clinton, Mick Jagger, and Greta Thunberg all somehow intersect in time and space.

As the Forum has grown, so have Schwab's entrepreneurial inclinations, operating alongside the idealistic pursuit that first inspired the gathering. Like most Davos Men, Schwab has mastered the art of holding two irreconcilable positions at once, unencumbered by the typical constraints of rank hypocrisy. He blithely disregards the obvious contradictions between the pristine values he publicly champions—inclusion, equity, transparency—and the unsavory compromises that he makes in wooing people with money and influence. He has leveraged shameless dedication to canoodling the powerful into an extraordinarily lucrative enterprise whose product is access to the people the Forum convenes.

Schwab's movements through the Congress Centre unfold like military exercises, a coterie of agitated minions accompanying him everywhere. On his travels, he demands the privileges of a visiting head of state, complete with welcoming delegations at the airport.

At the Forum's headquarters in Switzerland—a glass-fronted campus looking out on Lake Geneva—a hallway connecting two wings is lined with photos of Schwab posing with world leaders. When a Forum employee who was late for a meeting once pulled into Schwab's spot in the parking lot, aware that the boss was overseas, he caught wind of it, and insisted that she be fired, relenting only after senior staff intervened to save her.

Schwab has frequently told his colleagues that he anticipates receiving a Nobel Peace Prize. In the mid-1990s, when the Forum convened a gathering in South Africa, Schwab delivered a speech in front of Nelson Mandela at the closing plenary in which he cribbed from Martin Luther King Jr. "I have a dream," he said dramatically.

"Several of us almost threw up," recalled Barbara Erskine, who then ran the Forum's communications.

But if Schwab is something of a ludicrous character, he is also begrudgingly admired as a savant. "He has a knack, an incredible knack to smell the next fad and to jump into it," said one former colleague.

He recognized early on that the Forum had to distinguish itself from the run-of-the-mill business conferences, where people sat around talking about money. In defining a high-minded mission—"Improving the State of the World"—Schwab turned attendance into a demonstration of social concern.

He reinforced the value proposition through relentless networking, making Davos an indispensable venue for business. He enticed multinational corporations to pay hundreds of thousands of dollars a year for the privilege of serving as "strategic partners," securing access to exclusive lounges and private conference rooms inside the Congress Centre. There, executives encounter one another along with heads of state, investors, and other people capable of improving the state of their balance sheets.

Schwab choreographs bilateral meetings at which heads of global banks and energy companies can personally beseech presidents of countries for preferential tax treatment and access to promising oil fields. Consulting giants and software companies make plays for government contracts by speaking directly with the decision-makers. Top executives can fly in and meet a dozen heads of state in the course of four or five days, sitting across tables in soundproof rooms, beyond the purview of securities regulators, journalists, and other hindrances.

The core activities of the Forum—the sober speeches and panel discussions—have long been eclipsed by the extracurricular events that dominate Davos outside its official auspices.

Regular participants at the Forum boast about having attended zero panels and never setting foot inside the Congress Centre—a cynical mark of sophistication.

Schwab feigns unhappiness, bemoaning the supposed dilution of the experience as Davos fills with private parties. "We do not welcome them," he once said. "They detract from what we are doing." But he does not complain about the attendant perks.

Despite the Forum's status as a not-for-profit organization, Schwab and his wife, Hilde Schwab—the organization's cofounder—have adeptly positioned themselves to benefit from the gusher of money moving through it. Audi has long served as the Forum's exclusive shuttle partner, using Davos as a showcase for its newest vehicles, while supplying the Schwabs with cars at steep discounts. The Forum budget covers his globe-trotting, and the catering and security services at his palatial home in the Cologny neighborhood of Geneva—the Beverly Hills of Switzerland—where Schwab frequently hosts extravagant dinners.

Over the years, the Forum has spent almost 70 million Swiss francs (nearly $80 million) to purchase land in the area, including two parcels bridging Schwab's home and the Forum headquarters, making them contiguous. Even in the 1990s, when the Forum employed only a few dozen staff, Schwab's salary was tied to the pay for the secretary general of the United Nations, supplying him roughly $400,000 a year.

But Schwab was not satisfied by ordinary wealth. He entrusted his nephew, Hans Schwab, with the construction of a series of for-profit businesses, tapping the Forum as his personal venture capital fund.

His nephew had been overseeing the logistics of the Forum's events when, in the mid-1990s, he joined forces with a contractor to create a new company, Global Events Management. The Forum supplied about half of the startup capital. From inception, the new business enjoyed a contract from the Forum to manage all of its events, a deal worth several million dollars a year.

Klaus Schwab was so delighted by the success of the business that he told Hans that he was entitled to 5 percent. His nephew asked if he should prepare a legal document making this official. His uncle waved him away. "We're family," he said.

Schwab was cognizant that running a for-profit company on the side of a nonprofit could bring unwanted scrutiny from the authorities. Yet he was so proud of his entrepreneurial exploits that he pressed Barbara Erskine, the communications chief, to write about the events business in the Forum's annual report. When she balked, suggesting that this would constitute an admission that the Forum was taking liberties with its nonprofit status, Schwab was not grateful for her counsel.

"He was furious," Erskine told me. "He sat me down and said, 'Look, I want to be regarded as a businessman.'"

Schwab soon dispatched his nephew to Boston to run his new obsession—Advanced Video Communications, a startup that was building a videoconferencing system. At Schwab's direction, the Forum had invested roughly $5 million into the venture.

For two years, Hans Schwab oversaw the refining of the product while raising more funds. He brokered a deal under which a publicly traded technology company, USWeb Corp., purchased the video startup, handing over stock that valued it at about $16 million. The company elevated Klaus Schwab to its board while awarding him stock options worth as much as $500,000.

As USWeb's shares soared in value, the Forum's initial $5 million investment became worth at least $20 million. Just before the merger closed, Klaus Schwab called his nephew and demanded a last-minute change. The Forum's shares in Advanced Video Communications had been transferred to a new entity— the Schwab Foundation for Social Entrepreneurship. The foundation was to receive the proceeds.

Hans Schwab was taken aback. A last-minute change of ownership threatened to derail the transaction. But his uncle was adamant.

"He said, 'This needs to get done right now,'" Hans Schwab told me. "I had never heard of the Schwab Foundation, and I suddenly had to change all of the contracts. I knew it was his little thing that he was cooking up. Suddenly, in the last hour, he could see that there was going to be huge sums of money involved, the sort of money that he had never seen before, and he wanted to put it in a structure over which he had 100 percent control."

According to its website, the foundation was Hilde Schwab's undertaking. The organization promotes small-scale enterprises that address issues of social importance—extending the reach of clean water and electricity in the developing world, and creating opportunities for women. Where the money has gone is effectively unknowable. Swiss authorities require minimal disclosure.

The same year of the USWeb deal, Publicis Group, a French advertising and public relations giant, purchased the events business in a deal that fetched 6 million Swiss francs. Hans Schwab approached his uncle to ask about his promised 5 percent.

"He said, 'We can't do that,'" the younger Schwab recalled. "It doesn't look good."

Schwab's ultimate talent, say those who have worked with him, is an ability to cater to the narcissistic tendencies of the powerful. He displays faith in the veracity of his statements, even when they are at odds with reality and the ethos of the Forum. This has allowed Schwab to celebrate authoritarian leaders as champions of the public good, while raking in partnership revenues from companies hungry for access to the markets they rule.

This particular year, Schwab had scored an especially monetizable coup. He had persuaded China's president, Xi Jinping, to attend Davos and deliver a keynote speech.

Xi's speech was the highlight of the 2017 meeting. Jack Ma occupied a front-row seat in the auditorium. So did the outgoing American vice president, Joe Biden, nursing regrets that he had not run against Trump.

Xi used his turn at the podium to lay claim to credentials as the ultimate defender of the rules-based international trading system, a committed devotee to international cooperation.

That the president of China could portray himself this way underscored the astonishing extent to which the traditional order had been upended. China had long been accused of subsidizing state industries, exploiting its workers, and dumping its products at unfairly low prices on world markets. Xi ruled not by dint of having won an election, but in accordance with the dictates of the Chinese Communist Party. On his watch, Beijing had mounted a brutal crackdown on dissent.

Thrilled by Xi's participation, Schwab bestowed the one currency he could pay—laundered legitimacy.

"In a world marked by great uncertainty and volatility, the international community is looking to China to continue its responsive and responsible leadership," Schwab declared as he introduced the Chinese leader.

In a central irony of the Forum, the founding Davos Man was hosting an event crammed with lectures about transparent governance while bowing to a Chinese dictator, all the while running his own operation in a fashion uncomfortably akin to a Chinese state-owned enterprise.

None of this was new. To attend Davos and dip into its various currents has always involved participating in a none-too-subtle form of stagecraft.

But this year, with the world listing toward illiberalism, Davos Man and his annual celebration of himself felt especially unmoored from reality.

Inside a fondue restaurant, at a cozy dinner organized every year by the writer Anya Schiffrin and *Financial Times* columnist Rana Foroohar, I decompressed with journalist and economist friends. We were fellow adventurers, huddled around the campfire to relate our sightings—Davos Man in his native habitat.

Joe Stiglitz, the economist, was respected enough to gain entree to gatherings of billionaires, yet grounded in the troubles of wage earners, making his impressions valuable. We compared notes on the Forum. So much talk of inequality. So little discussion of policies that could shift wealth from Davos Man to everyone else.

Stiglitz rattled off what a reasonable approach might include: bolstering the power of workers to bargain for better wages, and redistributing wealth through progressive taxation.

"More rights to bargain for workers, that's the part where

Davos Man is going to get stuck," Stiglitz said. "The stark reality is that globalization has reduced the bargaining power of workers, and corporations have taken advantage of it."

This was a point that Stiglitz had been making for years. The global economy was not some product of random events. Its beneficiaries had engineered it to serve their interests.

People often discussed globalization like it was so complex that no one was really in charge, while presenting it as an all-or-nothing proposition: We could have global supply chains and modern medicine, or we could go back to sleeping on cave floors and eating grubs. We could accept widespread economic inequality as the unavoidable price that society paid for wonders like iPhones and air-conditioning, or we could wind up like Venezuela.

Davos Man was not the originator of this formulation. More than a century earlier, Robber Barons like Carnegie had portrayed inequality as the inevitable by-product of human progress.

"We cannot evade it," Carnegie wrote in 1889. "It is best for the race, because it ensures the survival of the fittest in every department. We accept and welcome, therefore, as conditions to which we must accommodate ourselves, great inequality of environment; the concentration of business, industrial and commercial, in the hands of a few."

But Davos Man had advanced the idea from a defensive justification for his station to an offensive weapon in pursuit of more wealth. Here was the central component of the Cosmic Lie, the argument that innovation only thrived when the rewards were dramatic, as if winner-take-all marketplaces were a requirement for any wins at all.

"The way we have managed globalization has contributed significantly to inequality," Stiglitz said. "But I have not yet heard a good conversation about what changes in globalization would address inequality."

That night, a handful of major American financial executives gathered for cocktails at a private event. The conversation turned to Trump and his unorthodox approach to governance. Were they worried about a trade war? About confrontation with Iran or North Korea? About the breakdown of the liberal democratic order?

They shrugged. They were not thrilled about Trump's proclivity to bully people on Twitter, threatening American companies that invested overseas. They could live without his talk of renouncing American public debt, as if the United States Treasury were a giant Trump casino staring down a creditor. But they were delighted by the elevation of a man who valued what they valued: money. Trump had promised to deliver tax cuts, and he was poised to deliver, given that Republicans were in charge of both chambers of Congress. Like everything else in Trump's world, they would be amazing, huge, unprecedented.

Inequality was a subject for panel discussions. Privately, Davos Man was anticipating the ineluctable feeling of more money landing in his accounts, beyond the purview of any pain-in-the-ass tax collector.

CHAPTER 2

"THE WORLD THAT OUR FATHERS IN WORLD WAR II WANTED US TO LIVE IN"

How Davos Man Poisoned Globalization

As a sixth grader in Houston, Jeff Bezos designed a student survey to assess the effectiveness of the teachers at his school, yielding a graph of their relative performance. Years later, as a single twentysomething in New York City, he took ballroom dancing classes on the assumption that it would increase his "women flow," breaking down dating the way that investment bankers analyze deals.

Stories about Bezos's obsessive analytical tendencies are so numerous that they constitute their own genre. They resonate as the explanation for how a nerdy kid from American suburbia took a simple idea for how to sell books and grew it into an empire so vast that it has refashioned modern life.

More than any other Davos Man, Bezos is the embodiment of success in an age defined by innovation, iconoclasm, and net worth. Budding entrepreneurs mine his biography with cultish reverence. Bezos has played along, serving up anodyne "Jeff-isms" that are embraced by the business world as the secrets to effective management. ("The keys to success are patience, persistence, and obsessive attention to detail.") He touts Amazon's leadership principles, including "Customer Obsession," "Hire and Develop the Best," and "Insist on the Highest Standards."

Amazon's dominance surely reflects its founder's formidable skills of execution, but the company's statement of principles is missing key elements that have been integral to its rise. The complete list would have to include amassing monopoly power and applying it to crush competitors; relentlessly squeezing workers for productivity; and gaming the tax system to avoid surrendering money to the government.

These are the less celebrated ingredients that have allowed Bezos to capture an outsized share of the gains from globalization, amassing a personal fortune exceeding $200 billion, including the trophies of the Davos Man lifestyle: a triplex penthouse with two swimming pools on Manhattan's Fifth Avenue, a $165 million mansion in Beverly Hills—the most expensive property ever sold in California—a 27,000-square-foot home in the nation's capital, along with a $66 million Gulfstream jet and a custom-built 417-foot-long yacht worth $500 million. Bezos constructed a miraculously efficient marketplace and distribution network, connecting factories around the world with millions of consumers. Along the way, he bestowed once-unimaginable convenience on humanity while erasing the traditional limits of time and space, pervading the sense that virtually anything can now be purchased nearly everywhere. But the benefits of this grand accomplishment have flowed overwhelmingly into Bezos's own pocket, while the costs have been borne by laborers around the globe, whose wages and working conditions have been relentlessly pressured by Amazon.

The magnitude of Bezos's winnings may be an outlier, but his mode is representative. This is how Davos Man looted an American economy that once lifted fortunes for everyone, capturing wealth that previously flowed to ordinary people.

And this is how many American workers—especially the white working class—became so enraged by globalization that they came to see trade as a conspiracy, embracing a president who threatened to blow the whole thing up.

Amazon's astonishing scale reflects its unrivaled success in utilizing crucial elements of the global economy—not least, the explosion of international trade in the decades after World War II. But Bezos's near-limitless wealth alongside the desperation of his workers provides a potent illustration of why globalization has come to be depicted as a malevolent force in many countries, a sentiment exploited by political movements offering fake solutions to very real problems.

The erosion of faith in international trade is a dangerous development, a threat to a vital legacy. Trade has been central to rising living standards across major economies for generations. And trade has proved a crucial component of a world order that has discouraged armed conflict.

At the end of World War II, as the victorious powers engineered a new order, they leaned heavily on the notion that communities whose livelihoods are dependent on trade have an abiding interest in peace. They turned lethal combatants into lucrative business partners, creating jobs, lifting incomes, and diminishing the appeal of nationalism.

This is what Davos Man has threatened by hogging the bounty of globalization.

The descent into World War II had been hastened by trade hostilities.

In 1930, as the United States confronted the Great Depression, the Republican-controlled Congress unleashed the infamous Smoot-Hawley Tariff Act to insulate American factories and farms from foreign competitors. The law imposed steep tariffs on hundreds of products, from sugar to iron.

Outraged international trading partners responded with their own tariffs on American-made goods. Tit became tat, and world trade collapsed, intensifying the Depression globally.

When the Democrats took over Congress two years later, they repealed the law, but Britain, France, Germany, and other European countries maintained their tariffs, entrenching the nationalist animosity that exploded into war.

Some 85 million dead later, the soon-to-be victorious Allies gathered at a hotel in Bretton Woods, New Hampshire, in July 1944 to plot the postwar order. They emerged three weeks later with an agreement designed to avoid the reawakening of nationalistic hostilities. They would make their currencies freely exchangeable. They formed the International Monetary Fund to aid countries facing financial duress. And they embraced a proposal for an organization that would promote international commerce.

"The peoples of the earth are inseparably linked to one another by a deep, underlying community of purpose," declared the head of the American delegation, Treasury Secretary Henry Morgenthau. "A revival of international trade is indispensable if full employment is to be achieved in a peaceful world and with standards of living which will permit the realization of men's reasonable hopes."

Successive American administrations would champion open trade as a magnanimous vehicle of liberty for people around the world—an easy sell during the Cold War, when the repressive Soviet-style system could be depicted as the inevitable alternative. But no small measure of self-interest guided the policy. The United States had emerged from the war as a superpower. Its economic output had roughly doubled as its factories produced the armaments for battle. Half of the world's manufactured wares were produced inside American plants. Its financial reserves were second to none. If money and goods were allowed to move freely around the globe, no country would prosper more than the United States.

The three decades that followed the end of World War II did not eradicate deep-seated racial and gender discrimination in the United States. They included a disastrous war in Vietnam and extreme social ferment. Yet within those thirty years, the United States saw broad economic advancement. Tax rates exceeding 70 percent for the wealthy coincided with robust economic growth that averaged 3.7 percent a year. That translated into jobs and rising wages for virtually every slice of the population—whites, Blacks, Latinos, Asians; men and women; people with high school educations and those with advanced degrees. The benefits were far from equal, but the old dictum that a rising tide lifts all boats had operative force.

The trade organization conceived at Bretton Woods was abandoned in 1950, as the United States objected to its rules taking precedence over domestic policy. But it was replaced by a more limited yet enduring entity known as the General Agreement on Tariffs and Trade, a broad pact to reduce barriers to commerce. By 2000, the volume of trade between members of the GATT and its successor institution, the World Trade Organization, had swelled to twenty-five times the volume of the half century earlier. The result was a consumer windfall, and an expanded array of export opportunities for businesses around the world, generating jobs.

In previous centuries, countries generally looked abroad only for items that they could not produce at home. Oceans were vast and full of pirates, tempests, and other terrors.

Transportation was expensive and prone to mishaps, while communication was plagued by misunderstanding. But the advent of so-called container shipping—which put finished wares inside standardized crates that were easily transferred to trucks and rail—dramatically accelerated the pace of loading and unloading. The emergence of global banking and the internet further shrank the globe.

With the risks of trade tamed, multinational brands were

supplied a compelling opportunity to reduce their costs by making their goods in low-wage countries.

Regional trade blocs expanded the options. President Clinton signed into creation the North American Free Trade Agreement in 1993, turning the United States, Canada, and Mexico into a massive zone for duty-free commerce. From that moment forward, workers in American factories were competing with counterparts south of the border. At the same time, American factories could buy components made in Mexico and use them to produce finished goods—a boost to domestic competitiveness.

The net effect of this expanded competition diminished the bargaining power of American workers. Any drive for greater pay or improved working conditions confronted the threat that the executives might close up shop and decamp to Mexico.

At the same time, another force was transforming the workings of American capitalism: shareholders were mounting an insurrection, taking over companies and tossing out managers who failed to provide satisfying returns.

The economist Milton Friedman set the revolution in motion in 1970 with an essay in *The New York Times Magazine* whose title distilled its essential content: "The Social Responsibility of Business Is to Increase Its Profits."

To Friedman, the market was sacred. Left to its own devices, it would determine the best use for investment more efficiently than any bureaucrat or do-gooder interest group. He laid down the intellectual infrastructure for Davos Man, deploying the parlance of economic theory to give license to unmitigated greed. Executives could justify no end of abominable behavior—poisoning the air, accelerating climate change, firing American workers, and moving production overseas—on the grounds that not doing these things amounted to ripping off shareholders.

Maximizing profit was not merely okay; it was a moral imperative.

Friedman's formulation encouraged a crop of corporate raiders, who pioneered new forms of riskier debt known as junk bonds to purchase lumbering old companies. The new investors installed their own managers, employing a playbook engineered to lift stock prices: shrink the workforce and shutter less profitable operations. Given that executive compensation was increasingly tied to share prices, managers had a powerful incentive to strip out costs like paychecks, knowing that their own pay would rise in response.

The era of shareholder maximization gathered force through the 1980s and into the following decade as Wall Street tapped new sources of money. Pension funds directed the retirement savings of workers into the stock market. Mutual funds pooled the savings of ordinary people. The internet allowed regular people to buy and sell stocks on a whim, while competition brought down transaction costs.

By the mid-1990s, amid the burgeoning dot-com era, Americans were exchanging stock tips as dinner party conversation. Chief executives like Bezos struck heroic poses on the covers of glossy magazines, alongside Hollywood stars and athletes.

As stock prices soared in the United States, Friedman's influence went global, injecting shareholder maximization into economic policy in much of the developed world.

Students at business schools were marinated in management strategies aimed at optimizing shareholder value. Graduates forged careers in finance, where clever people dreamed up fresh accounting gimmicks and takeover tactics that could produce what the markets rewarded—a jump in earnings—without increasing sales or producing anything of intrinsic value. The archetype was Jack Welch, who took over General Electric, a company known for making light bulbs and toasters, and turned it into a collection of financial portfolios.

Steve Schwarzman graduated from Harvard Business School two years after the publication of Friedman's essay. Jamie Dimon graduated from the same institution a dozen years later.

They rose through the ranks at a time when the shareholder was the center of the economic universe.

This was the cardinal principle at the heart of globalization as engineered by Davos Man.

The trading system shaped by Morgenthau and his contemporaries at Bretton Woods was not built for the kind of globalization propelled by Friedman's doctrine.

It had especially not been designed for a global economy that included China, the most populous nation on earth. Its Communist Party government actively courted Davos Man and his money, offering access to virtually unlimited numbers of easily exploited workers.

The postwar order hashed out at Bretton Woods had assumed that trading partners were more similar than not—the world as described by classical economics. England made clothing and Spain made wine, so their trade would be mutually beneficial. But when China joined the ranks of the World Trade Organization in 2001, nearly every manufacturer on earth was supplied a cheaper way to make products: they could shift production to an authoritarian country teeming with people who were desperate for jobs and barred from organizing for better pay.

Under the terms of its entry, China promised to open its marketplace to multinational companies in exchange for the right to sell its exports around the planet. For multinational corporations, this kicked off a modern-day gold rush. Home to 1.3 billion people and counting, China was potentially the largest untapped consumer market, as well as an increasingly enticing venue for manufacturing.

China gained inclusion in the global trading system in no small measure because of Davos Man and his relentless lobbying in Washington. For corporate executives, China beckoned as a means of furthering the mission to enrich shareholders, in accordance with the principles laid down by Milton Friedman. Chinese factories were able to make a widening array of products—from blue jeans to auto parts to industrial chemicals—at prices a fraction of those in wealthy countries. For manufacturers in North America and Europe, the mere threat of shifting production to China forced unions to swallow pay cuts.

The year after China joined the WTO, Walmart, the American discount retailing giant, moved its global procurement center to the Chinese boomtown of Shenzhen, relying on surrounding factories to fill its stores with thousands of items, from electronics and Christmas ornaments to office furniture and tools. As Walmart's sales grew, its stock price soared, turning its founders, the Walton family, into the richest clan in the United States, boasting a fortune estimated at more than $136 billion.

Major American automakers would eventually sell more cars in China than in the United States. The bulk of the world's apparel industry steadily concentrated its operations in China, lowering costs and rewarding executives at leading brands like Zara, H&M, and Nike.

Bezos's fortune multiplied as Amazon's stock gained value, in part because of the company's success in tapping Chinese factories for low-priced goods.

Global banks like Jamie Dimon's JPMorgan Chase followed their customers to China, establishing branches. Private equity magnates like Schwarzman tapped China's prodigious savings as a source of investment, bolstering their share prices.

Along the way, Davos Man's lobbying pushed corporate taxes lower in the United States, while reducing individual tax rates on income and estates. The billionaires employed teams of accountants who indulged perfectly legal strategies to keep their growing wealth beyond reach of the tax authorities.

In one single year, 2007, Amazon's stock price doubled, increasing Bezos's total fortune by nearly $4 billion. That same year, Bezos paid no federal income taxes, according to documents seen by ProPublica. He and his then wife, MacKenzie Scott, listed income of $46 million for the year. Through the magic of clever accounting—losses on investments, interest paid on loans, and nebulous special items—they made their liabilities disappear.

Amazon and other American companies were able to rely on Chinese factories because of the internet—an elemental piece of infrastructure created through publicly financed research. Corporations moved parts, raw materials, and finished products around the country in pursuit of profit thanks to highways, ports, and airports maintained by the government. These costs were socialized and covered by taxpayers as a spur for job creation. In sidestepping the tax collector, Davos Man effectively privatized the gains of the Chinese bonanza, while sharing the proceeds with his fellow shareholders through dividends and soaring stock prices.

In the fourteen years after its entry into the WTO, China's exports swelled from $266 billion per year to nearly $2.3 trillion. The beneficiaries of this surge included nearly anyone who ever set foot inside a shopping mall or purchased anything online.

But trade produces losers along with winners. The upside tends to get spread thin; the losses are often concentrated and profound, shaking communities whose factory jobs are undercut by cheaper imports.

This is what happened to Granite City, Illinois.

Granite City occupies the eastern bank of the Mississippi River, just across the water from St. Louis. A pair of German immigrants erected a steel mill there in 1878. Over the next century, the town grew as the steelworks expanded.

The complex of factories provided paychecks that enabled generations of men to buy modest bungalow homes on squares of lawn. They distributed their earnings throughout the community, sustaining hardware stores, a movie theater, restaurants, barbershops, and a bowling alley.

"This was like a family business," said Dan Simmons, who started working at the mill in 1978, when he was eighteen, joining his father and his twin brother. "If I came in hungover and fucking off, my dad knew about it. If you got behind on bills or had a kid going off to college, you could find a little overtime. We were the poster children for the middle class."

But when I visited Simmons in the summer of 2016 at the headquarters of the United Steelworkers Local 1899, where he was in charge, he had become a de facto social worker. Only 375 of the 1,250 workers he represented at the Granite City mill were actually working. The rest were furloughed, laid off, early retired, long-term disabled, or some other bureaucratic jargon for *unemployed*.

Simmons greeted those who arrived seeking help. One man did not know how to operate a computer and needed instruction in how to search job listings. Some confided that they did not have the cash to adequately feed their families. Simmons led them into a windowless storage room lined with shelves, inviting them to take donated boxes of pasta and loaves of bread.

In the center of a town built on steel production, the union hall was doubling as a food pantry. "These are some proud steelworkers," Simmons said. "It's difficult for them."

The night before, he had received a call from the niece of a high school classmate, a laid-off mill worker. The man had shot himself to death, leaving behind two children.

All around the headquarters was palpable evidence of a community in terminal decline. Supermarkets had been traded in for Dollar Stores. Hardware stores and restaurants were boarded up, replaced by payday lenders and pawnshops. The bowling alley was abandoned.

Simmons and his fellow union workers had a ready explanation for what had happened. Steel mills in China were operating around the clock, producing far more steel than the global economy needed, dumping their wares on markets from Europe to North America.

"They don't care what the price is, because they are doing it to employ their people," Simmons said. "China is ramping up, producing more than they ever have. They're taking over."

China's steel industry was dominated by state-owned companies that enjoyed access to virtually unlimited credit. They breached labor and environmental rules with impunity. Over the previous decade, China's share of world steel production had grown from less than one-third to half, while its exports had more than quadrupled. That surge was pushing down prices worldwide. Steel mills in the United States were limiting production in a bid to stem losses.

Similar forces were decimating American furniture makers and textile mills in the Carolinas, auto parts factories in Michigan and Ohio, and electronics plants in California.

Between 1999 and 2011, the shock inflicted by Chinese imports eliminated nearly one million American manufacturing jobs, and roughly twice that number if you considered the ripple effects—the restaurants and taverns closed as factories shuttered, the truck drivers not needed, the carpenters who lost work as their neighbors lost jobs.

In communities suffering the impacts of surging Chinese imports, wages and employment remained depressed for a decade and longer.

Still, depictions of a Chinese juggernaut running roughshod over American workers were incomplete. From China's perspective, the nation was simply catching up to Western economies that had gotten rich through colonial plunder, including the iniquities of the opium wars. China was harnessing its advantages in the global economy—not least, its enormous, low-wage workforce. Whatever one had to say about globalization, a full assessment had to include the fact that it had lifted more than 300 million Chinese people out of poverty.

China's laborers were vulnerable to the same bottom-up transfer of wealth that was playing out in the United States. A new crop of Chinese magnates amassed riches by seizing land from farmers and then sharing a piece of the action with local Communist Party officials. The well-connected were turning wheat fields into golf courses and rice paddies into science parks, while using their winnings on jaunts to five-star pleasure palaces in Macau.

The People's Republic of China—still nominally dedicated to the Marxist revolution that had founded it—was becoming nearly as unequal as the United States. Between 1978 and 2015, the top tenth of Chinese households saw its share of national income climb from 27 percent to 41 percent. Over the same period, earnings for the bottom half dropped from 27 percent of national income to 15 percent—just a tad more than the 12 percent brought home by their American counterparts.

But in Granite City, people were too consumed with securing groceries to gain the full measure of what was happening on the other side of the planet.

Union members in the United States traditionally voted for the Democratic Party. Yet by July 2016, some of the people in Simmons's union were embracing the unusual figure who had captured the Republican nomination for president. Most knew little to nothing about Donald Trump's tendency to lead his companies into bankruptcy. Some wrote off as political correctness the outrage over the insults Trump hurled at women, Mexican immigrants, Muslims, the disabled, and even the parents of a decorated Marine who had died on a foreign battlefield.

The steelworkers in Granite City knew this much about Trump: He was rich and famous, and he was promising to destroy the carefully concocted plans of the political establishment. He would crash his way into the White House, halt globalization, and bring jobs home.

Among some who had worked at the mill, Trump had tapped into something else as well, a tacit understanding among the predominantly white workforce that their race was supposed to confer inoculation against indignities like worrying about whether you could make your mortgage payment. Joblessness, visiting food pantries, and feeling powerless—these were supposed to be problems for other people.

"If we keep eliminating the top paying jobs with benefits and send the jobs to the third world, we'll be what the third world is now," said Jim Phelps, who grew up in Granite City, and whose father worked at the mill for forty-two years. "I will vote for Donald Trump. He says almost everything out loud that I think in my mind and don't say."

A lot of this rhetoric related to building a wall along the Mexican border to bar the hordes of immigrants who were, as Phelps understood it, streaming into the country to steal what was left of the American Dream.

"As a white American born here, I want to see the borders closed," he said.

Black unemployment had long been stuck at roughly twice the rate for white Americans, at levels the political class would surely have treated as a national emergency had they afflicted everyone. Once the scourge of joblessness reached white communities, growing numbers of white voters were inclined to declare a systemic crisis.

This was something that Trump understood viscerally. The tariffs he would eventually impose on Chinese imports would increase prices for a vast range of goods in the United States, effectively shrinking the paychecks of tens of millions of ordinary American workers—especially women, Blacks, and Latinos whose labors were concentrated in service industries. Trump would increase costs for businesses, weakening their international competitiveness. In exchange for this widespread harm, Trump's trade war would bolster prospects for a bare smidgen of the national labor force—the 16 percent of workers without college degrees employed in manufacturing.

In short, overwhelmingly white, male factory workers in towns like Granite City would gain a measure of protection at the expense of communities with lower incomes and higher rates of long-term joblessness.

"The fetishization of manufacturing jobs is hardly a neutral policy," wrote the economist Adam Posen. "The image of men doing dangerous things to produce heavy stuff seems to resonate with nostalgic voters in a way that women providing human services does not."

For his part, Simmons disdained Trump as a fraud. Still, he understood why Trump was gaining support. His way of describing the forces shaping industrial towns rang true. In Granite City, as in hundreds of similar communities, a basic American bargain had long held, the idea that anyone willing to set an alarm clock and go off to work could count on a reasonably comfortable existence. That understanding was inoperative.

"When you can ship stuff halfway around the world and you can buy it cheaper than we can make it here, something's wrong," said Dan Drennan, who had worked at the mill in Granite City for thirty-eight years before he was laid off. "This isn't the world that our fathers in World War II wanted us to live in."

But indicting trade and globalization for the deprivations in American factory towns was like blaming the weather for tearing the roof off your house, rather than the contractor who had built it with shoddy materials. The ultimate culpability fell on Davos Man. He had rigged the system to ensure his further enrichment, while depriving working people of a commensurate share of the gains.

U.S. Steel, the conglomerate that owned the Granite City mill, declared a loss of $440 million in 2016. Still, the company paid out $31 million in dividends to its shareholders. It provided a $1.5 million salary to its president and CEO, Mario Longhi, plus stock-based compensation and other benefits that swelled his total pay beyond $10.9 million.

This was how capitalism worked in the United States. When trouble arose, the consequences fell on working people in the form of joblessness, bankruptcy, and depression. Corporate overseers found a way to add to their coffers no matter what happened.

Some economists warned early on that allowing China into the global trading system posed perils for manufacturing towns everywhere else.

Washington's assent "will signal to the world that the United States has, in effect, abandoned the cause of putting worker rights and environmental standards on the agenda of international trade," declared the economist Jeff Faux in 2000.

But such talk was drowned out by exuberant cheerleading from Davos Man and his collaborators. Investing in China was not just good for shareholders, they said, but good for the world. It would tether China's fortunes to the global economy, which would force its leaders to embrace the values of its trading partners. Davos Man was not exploiting China for cheap labor; he was championing civil liberties.

Bill Clinton embraced this formulation as he campaigned for China's inclusion into the WTO—along the way vacuuming up hefty campaign contributions from the multinational companies eager to get a crack at the Chinese market.

"China is not simply agreeing to import more of our products, it is agreeing to import one of democracy's most cherished values, economic freedom," Clinton declared in 2000. "It is likely to have a profound impact on human rights and political liberty."

Five years later, Clinton accepted an invitation from China's most prominent Davos Man, Jack Ma, the founder of the e-commerce company Alibaba, to give a keynote address at a

Chinese internet conference. It was hosted in Ma's hometown, the lakefront city of Hangzhou. Yahoo, the web portal, then owned 40 percent of Ma's company.

A Chinese journalist who had used a Yahoo email account to leak information to an international human rights organization had just been sentenced to ten years in prison. Yahoo had identified him to Chinese authorities, claiming that it had to comply with local laws. Human rights groups were urging Clinton to use his presence to call attention to this episode, but he said nothing about it in his speech, which celebrated the internet as a force for human liberation.

When I tried to ask Clinton afterward how he squared his talk of freedom with the jailing of a journalist handed over by the people paying for his junket, he grinned, motioned that he could not hear the question, and melted into a security cordon.

Far from changing China, Western businesses were themselves changed by China. JPMorgan Chase handed out internships to the children of Chinese Communist Party officials, whose parents subsequently developed an appreciation for the company's investment banking services.

Schwarzman's private equity company, Blackstone, sold tens of billions of dollars' worth of real estate to Chinese companies, including the Waldorf Astoria hotel in New York. A Chinese sovereign wealth fund, the State Investment Company of China, invested $3 billion in Blackstone's initial public offering, taking a nearly 10 percent stake in the company. The deal gained the swift blessing of China's leadership.

Schwarzman promoted his most passionate cause, the Schwarzman Scholars program, as a crucial source of progress. Modeled on the Rhodes scholarship, it brought students from Harvard, Yale, Cambridge, and other prestigious campuses to study at China's Tsinghua University in the name of boosting international understanding.

The Blackstone chief delighted in the ceremonies celebrating the young scholars backed by his fortune. He typically ducked questions about the role of senior Chinese Communist Party leaders in selecting the applicants. Tsinghua University "oversees the process of selecting Chinese Scholars," Blackstone said in a written statement, in response to questions I posed to Schwarzman. "Since the founding of the program, the intention has always been for China to identify its future leaders for participation." He was also not keen to discuss how the Schwarzman Scholars had invited as a graduation speaker the CEO of a Chinese company that built artificial intelligence used in the surveillance of the ethnic minority Uyghurs, who had been forced into concentration camps in western China. "The program chose as a speaker a recognized global leader in Artificial Intelligence, given the relevance and importance of the topic for future leaders," Blackstone's statement continued. "Your broader charge that hosting a campus speaker represents full involvement in or endorsement of all their alleged activities is absurd. Such a view is fundamentally at odds with long-running academic tradition and common sense."

The Blackstone statement boldfaced and underscored one sentence: "We fundamentally reject your premise that canceling cultural exchanges between young student leaders who will help set future policy is the best path to create a more peaceful world." That was, in fact, not my premise. I lived in China for almost six years. Schwarzman and I once spent three days at the same high-level conference in Beijing, during which we met with President Xi Jinping. In knocking down this straw man, Blackstone was highlighting Davos Man's tendency to present false binary choices as a defense of the status quo. We could either have American billionaires cozying up to China's leaders while extracting investment or we could cut ties.

The workers in Granite City were not wrong in their obsession over China. Chinese competition was a menace to their living standards. But the ultimate culprit for their deteriorating fortunes was in their own country—in boardrooms in New York and Silicon Valley, and in government offices in Washington, where Davos Man wrote the rules.

In some places, especially Scandinavian countries, those harmed by trade saw the damage limited and repaired by government programs. The state trained workers for new careers when they lost jobs while helping them with their bills while they were out of work. But in the United States, spending on social safety net programs had been gutted as Davos Man shrunk his tax bill.

In Denmark, when the typical breadwinner in a family of four lost their job, they could count on 88 percent of their previous income six months later, thanks to unemployment benefits and other social programs. In the United States, the same family had to find a way to survive on 27 percent of their previous income.

Denmark collected taxes worth about 45 percent of its annual economic output. In the United States, the government was operating with tax revenues worth less than 25 percent of its economy.

It was not globalization that was to blame for the despair in Granite City. It was the way the gains had been apportioned—not by accident, but willfully and meticulously, as a means of directing more treasure to Davos Men like Bezos.

Amazon was, on the surface, a minor player in Granite City. It operated a warehouse that employed workers cast off by the steel mill. Same as everywhere, its trucks navigated local streets, dropping off packages. But its real impact was foundational. As much as any company, Amazon had altered the balance of power between employees and employers.

With a workforce nearing 1.3 million, Amazon has risen into the second-largest private employer in the United States, behind only Walmart. It has applied its scale toward downgrading wages while squeezing additional productivity out of every hour of labor.

In short, Amazon has helped sort the contemporary world into winners and losers—those positioned to enjoy the utility of its unparalleled distribution network, and those harmed by its market supremacy.

The Robber Barons amassed their dominance in an age when steel was central to industry. Bezos constructed his empire in a time in which internet bandwidth was a crucial commodity, allowing him to set his sights on the globe while insinuating his services into nearly every area of modern commerce.

Bezos was both a beneficiary of the international trade regime constructed in the decades after World War II, and a primary actor in perverting its workings to divert most of the gains to billionaires like himself.

Raised in upper-middle-class comfort, Bezos was a serial achiever who was not shy about sharing this information.

"I have always been academically smart," he once said.

At Miami Palmetto Senior High School, he let everyone know that he would be the valedictorian, and then achieved it. Then he enrolled at Princeton, the only college that interested him. ("Einstein was there for goodness' sake," he said.)

He graduated summa cum laude in 1986, took a job at a telecommunications startup, passed through banking, and then landed in the hedge fund world, working for David E. Shaw, a legendary investor who was early to the technique of employing mathematical algorithms to ferret out profitable trades. It was there that Bezos hatched the idea that would become Amazon— what he and Shaw referred to as "the everything store."

It was the middle of the 1990s, and the internet was about to reshape the business world. Shaw tasked Bezos with figuring out what products could be most profitably sold online. Books were a counterintuitive example—the internet appeared poised to destroy print media—but Bezos cracked the code. There were

3 million books in print. That was more than any brick-and-mortar superstore could ever stock, supplying an online marketplace an immediate advantage.

Bezos hired people whose brains were wired like his. Job interviews entailed Socratic interrogations—*How many gas stations are there in the United States?*—allowing Bezos to observe how the subject broke down the problem.

He emulated Walmart's dominance, poaching its executives and embracing its frugality. He made a show of getting his loyalty card stamped at the coffee kiosk at Amazon's headquarters in Seattle. He had chosen the city as his base in part to limit Amazon's exposure to sales taxes: they were due only on orders delivered to people in states where the company had physical operations, and Washington was home to relatively few people. Employees had to pay for parking.

Bezos favored the word *relentless*. Every minute of every day was required if Amazon was to achieve Bezos's mission of market domination. When a female employee asked him about the possibility of a healthier work-life balance, Bezos was withering.

"The reason we are here is to get stuff done," he said. "If you can't excel and put everything into it, this might not be the place for you."

Nearly everyone respected him as the smartest person in every room, even as they struggled to square his intensity with his preposterous laugh. Its sound was variously described as that of "a jackass gargling bumblebees," or "a cross between a mating elephant and a power tool." The uninitiated could easily have misinterpreted it as a cry for emergency medical attention.

Laugh notwithstanding, Bezos was the source of abject fear among those assigned to present their ideas to him. He didn't suffer fools, and he found them everywhere.

"We need to apply some human intelligence to this problem," he once said after an employee laid out a proposal that did not win the boss's favor. "Are you lazy or just incompetent?" he snapped at another underling.

For an Amazon executive, nothing was more alarming than a customer service complaint forwarded to them by Bezos with his addition of a single character at the top—a question mark.

In a transformation that is now well-known yet decisive, Amazon grew into the central clearinghouse for a vast array of products—clothing, office supplies, electronics, toys, and, eventually, groceries. By 2019, its international distribution network was delivering 3.5 billion packages a year, or one for every two people on earth.

It expanded into video streaming and then turned itself into a major player in Hollywood, producing movies and television shows. It earned the lion's share of its revenues through a dominant hold on the business of hosting and transporting computer data, operating like the railway system for the digital age. Bezos was also pursuing his childhood fascination with life beyond Earth, launching satellites and pursuing a commercial space exploration business.

As the journalist Franklin Foer put it, "If Marxist revolutionaries ever seized power in the United States, they could nationalize Amazon and call it a day."

In culture and composition, Bezos's company reflected the traditional power configuration of the society that produced him. By late 2019, the seventeen executives who comprised Bezos's senior team included precisely zero African Americans and one woman. Still, he insisted that Amazon was a meritocracy, disdaining the word *diversity* as synonymous with a lowering of standards.

During the late 1990s, in the midst of the dot-com boom, Bezos had been a star draw at the Forum. Like many of his fellow participants, he cast his personal success as a form of societal triumph, validation for the system that had allowed him to turn a good idea into a jackpot. He and the other billionaires in Davos projected an understanding that their success was the result not of a rigged system, or racial privilege, or inclusion in Ivy League social networks, but of simply having worked harder. The wealth they commanded was their just reward, as if the only thing separating Bezos and the people laboring in his warehouses was their failure to cram as hard for the test.

Davos Man deployed this idea as a prophylactic against profit-diluting regulation. Bezos's intelligence and work ethic were beyond reproach, but his astonishing wealth was not the result of purely market forces: he had applied his money and savvy toward warping the marketplace in his favor.

Amazon's success rested on international trade. Bezos constructed an intuitive website and a sophisticated logistics operation, but he depended on factories around the world to make what he was delivering. This was the concept for "the everything store" that he had dreamed up with Shaw.

"The idea was always that someone would be allowed to make a profit as an intermediary," D. E. Shaw said in 1999. "The key question is: Who will get to be that middleman?"

Amazon actively recruited Chinese suppliers to sell to its customers, producing a surge of products that did not arrive as advertised, or violated federal safety standards, according to a *Wall Street Journal* investigation. By 2019, nearly 40 percent of Amazon's most active accounts were based in China (though the company disputed this).

Bezos had long dodged criticism about his company—his shoddy treatment of warehouse workers, his ruthless undercutting of independent booksellers and other competitors—by positing himself as a canny beneficiary of changes that were essentially inevitable, borne by technology, and beyond the powers of earthlings to contain.

"Amazon isn't happening to the book business," he once said. "The future is happening to the book business."

But Bezos had deliberately shaped that future. Amazon had

financed lobbying efforts to fight off sales taxes that threatened to encroach on its business. States that contemplated collecting sales taxes found themselves bullied by Amazon, as the company threatened to bolt for more hospitable jurisdictions. Amazon applied its muscle toward rolling back corporate taxes—a campaign that came to fruition when Trump took office.

By 2018, Amazon was employing twenty-eight lobbyists in Washington, more than any other technology business, plus one hundred more retained on contract. This formidable apparatus included four former members of Congress.

Beyond the United States, the company tangled with unions, especially in France and Germany, drawing accusations that it was seeking to Americanize the workforce—a synonym for lowering pay.

Amazon had also proven a prime beneficiary of years of corporate lobbying that had defenestrated American antitrust law, enabling Bezos to swallow up scores of companies in amassing greater market share. Amazon had been allowed to marshal unprecedented volumes of data about the buying habits of its customers, and then use that knowledge to sell more in a fashion that was in no way transparent. It had leveraged its status as the decisive marketplace for everything from ballpoint pens to dishwashing liquid to steer customers to its own products. Part of why Bezos had assembled a fortune larger than the annual economic output of Kuwait was because his customers were unwittingly paying a premium.

This was ironic given that Amazon was, above all, a beneficiary of decades of corporate lobbying that weakened antitrust law through a decisive claim: Big businesses were more efficient, which made them better for consumers.

This was the same argument that Davos Man's forefathers had deployed to dismantle the protections against corporate abuses that went back to the New Deal of the 1930s. This was how large companies fended off enforcement for their exploitation of labor and their predatory treatment of smaller businesses. Anything that yielded lower prices was to be applauded as consistent with the public interest. Amazon was a monument to the success of that formulation.

Even as Amazon raised pay for five hundred thousand of its workers to a minimum of $15 an hour in April 2021—its response to reports of dangerous conditions inside its warehouses—the move resonated more as a way to harm competitors than to redress unfair treatment. By lifting wages, Amazon ensured that rivals like Walmart would struggle to hire enough workers. Amazon could then capture more of the e-commerce market, reinforcing its dominance.

Trade and globalization had worked as the Bretton Woods forebears had envisioned, turning adversaries into trading powers, generating jobs and economic growth, and delivering a profusion of affordable products to shops around the globe. But Davos Men like Bezos had seized most of the gains.

This is how Michael Morrison, a longtime steelworker in Granite City, found himself so desperate for a paycheck that he reluctantly went to work at an Amazon warehouse, earning a fraction of his previous wages.

Morrison had started working at the steel mill in 1999, when he was thirty-eight—a father with three young children, suddenly contemplating the long haul.

"I felt like I had finally gotten into a place that was so reliable I could retire there," he said.

He began at the lowest rungs, performing the sweaty work of shoveling slag out of the furnaces, before working his way up to one of the most prized positions—crane driver. From inside a cockpit tucked in the rafters, he operated the controls, guiding a 350-ton ladle that spilled molten hot iron.

It was a difficult job that required finesse and perpetual focus given that a simple mistake could prove expensive or even deadly. He earned $24.62 an hour, allowing him to pay his mortgage. He bought a truck and a boat for fishing trips.

Morrison wanted his three children to penetrate the white-collar world, so he worked as many overtime shifts as he could, salting away savings for college. His daughter completed her master's in epidemiology. His son enrolled at a nearby private college, McKendree University.

Then, in the fall of 2015, U.S. Steel began slowing production in Granite City. Two days before Christmas, Morrison finished his regular shift at the plant and went into the break room.

"Everybody was standing there like zombies, looking at the bulletin board," he told me. A list of names was tacked there, his among them. Those on the list were to clean out their lockers.

"I've worked since I was twelve," he said, struggling to comprehend this turn. He had started with a paper route, then taken a job as a cook at his brother's taco joint.

A blue Steelworkers Union T-shirt hugged his burly frame. His calloused hands attested to years of physical labor. But his $2,000 biweekly paycheck had become a $425-a-week unemployment check. And then the money stopped. He had reached the six-month limit for unemployment benefits.

"I had to tell my son that he can't go back to McKendree for his junior year," Morrison said, as he struggled to maintain composure. "He has to go to community college."

He swallowed hard, tears escaping from the corners of his eyes. "It just crushes you," he said. "I didn't get to go to college. I wanted my kids to succeed."

He had recently interviewed for a job as a supervisor at an Amazon warehouse, but it required computer skills that he lacked. So he took a lower-level job there as a "fulfillment associate"—one of the grunts who wandered the aisles of the warehouse pulling products off shelves and putting them in boxes. It paid $13 an hour, barely half his wages at the steel mill.

On his first day, the supervisors lined up the associates for a preshift team-building exercise. "They said, 'We're gonna clap three times, and then we're gonna yell, "Go shipping floor!"'" Morrison recalled.

He did not comply, bringing the attention of his Amazon bosses.

"A guy came up to me and he goes, 'We noticed you weren't clapping,'" Morrison said. "I said, 'Yeah I'm not into that. That's not my thing.' He goes, 'Well, that's kind of how we form unity here.' And I says, 'Well, I've been a union member for over thirty years, and I've never clapped once.' It just made me feel degraded."

He finished his shift and never returned, eventually landing at another warehouse where he worked nights for $17.50 an hour.

Like most of his fellow steelworkers, Morrison had been a Democrat all his life. And, like many of his union brethren, he was won over by Trump—by his promise to take on China; by his focus on the immigrants who were, in the central mythology of the Trump campaign, stealing jobs.

Morrison found the videotape in which Trump was caught saying that he grabbed women in the crotch to be distasteful, but he figured that was how many politicians behaved. When I asked him whether he accepted Trump's praise for neo-Nazi marchers and white supremacists, Morrison took a long breath.

"I don't consider myself a racist in any way," he said, though he made clear that he bought the central idea of the Trump candidacy—that white people were confronting an existential threat. "The illegal aliens are coming across."

He wound up not voting for Trump in 2016, swayed by Simmons, who beseeched him to honor his union. But enough others voted with their sympathies to send Trump to the White House. In a nation accustomed to thinking of itself as a land of opportunity, Trump exploited downward mobility combined with lies about immigrants as a pathway to power.

Contrary to the insta-analysis of the moment, Trump did not win simply because he captured white working-class votes. Less than a third of his support in 2016 came from that group. Davos Men like Schwarzman embraced Trump as a way to secure tax cuts and deregulation. White voters broadly flocked to Trump for the same reason that they had tended to vote Republican for a generation—in homage to lean government and low taxes, an implicit rebuke of the welfare state that many white Americans were inclined to see as handouts for minorities, even though whites were the most numerous recipients.

But 60 percent of white working-class voters pulled the lever for Trump in 2016, furthering a steady, long-term shift toward Republicans. The counties that had absorbed the greatest pressure from imports from China and Mexico showed the largest increases in support for the Republican presidential candidate.

Seven decades after Morgenthau had proclaimed the advent of an age governed by international cooperation, Trump delivered a bellicose inaugural address that could be boiled down to two words: "America First." He repeated it, as if taunting those who still believed in globalization.

"We must protect our borders from the ravages of other countries making our products, stealing our companies and destroying our jobs," he said.

By 2020, Morrison was back at his old job at the steel mill, crediting that turn with the tariffs Trump applied to Chinese products. He voted for Trump that year.

"The way I feel, the Republicans were for jobs, and the Democrats were for unions," Morrison told me. "And if you don't have jobs, you don't need unions."

By then, he had come to blame the media for the destruction of middle-class life. He blamed the Democrats, immigrants, social media—everyone but Davos Man, whose plundering was so comprehensive as to be effectively invisible.

CHAPTER 3

"SUDDENLY, THE ORDERS STOPPED"

Davos Man's Forebears

To study the evolution of *Homo sapiens*, we need to examine chimpanzees. If we want to understand Davos Man's progression, we must go to Italy.

As much as anywhere, wealthy Italians have mastered the art of stashing their money beyond reach of the government. Tax evasion sometimes seems to rival soccer as the national sport—a reality that has bred cynicism within the populace, undermining governance, while making politics noisy, fractious, and prone to elevating incompetent opportunists.

Decades before Davos Man pursued his global pillaging, his forebears were perfecting the technique in Italy. Their looting of the public coffers has weakened the state's ability to respond to crises like the pandemic, while limiting investment that could produce a more vibrant economy.

One company stands out as an especially pungent example of the Italian elite's perversion of capitalism for its own benefit. Over generations, Italy's most powerful people have exploited Fiat, stripping the giant automaker for personal enrichment at public expense.

No one played the con more aggressively than Gianni Agnelli, known throughout Italy as *L'Avvocato*—the Lawyer.

Born in the northern Italian city of Turin in 1921, Agnelli commanded popular fascination throughout his life. His grandfather founded Fiat, whose rise was emblematic of Italy's miraculous recovery from the devastation of World War II. The company and the country had grown wealthy in tandem, applying their design and engineering prowess to produce objects that the world coveted.

Agnelli assumed control of the company in 1966. Fiat prospered as the middle class grew, supplying reliable and affordable cars. Its marketing wrapped itself in the flag: The company was Italian in the same way that Ford was American. By 1970, Fiat was making more than 1.4 million vehicles a year in Italy while employing one hundred thousand people.

"Agnelli is Fiat," went a popular slogan, "Fiat is Turin, and Turin is Italy."

The Agnellis were known as the Kennedys of Italy—their wealth, glamour, fame, brushes with tragedy, and tendency toward scandal operating in equal measure. Gianni favored escapades to the French Riviera behind the wheel of sports cars, and in the company of starlets. In a nation uniquely dedicated to fashion, he was an icon who flouted conventions. "He wore his tie askew and his watch atop his cuff to suggest *sprezzatura*— the Italian art of appearing not to care about one's appearance— and to disconcert his rivals," *Esquire* declared as it enshrined Agnelli on a list of "Best Dressed Men in the History of the World."

He married another famous tastemaker, a half-American, half-Italian with a title attesting to her noble provenance— Donna Marella Caracciolo dei Principi di Castagneto. An art collector and a fabric designer, she was a frequent presence in fashion magazines. Their marriage was the subject of ceaseless gossip, enhanced by Agnelli's dalliances with the socialite-cum-diplomat

Pamela Harriman and Jackie Kennedy Onassis, the widow of the former American president John F. Kennedy.

At the height of his powers, Agnelli was celebrated as the king of Italian industry and the nation's richest man, with a fortune estimated at more than $2 billion. His enterprises comprised more than one-fourth of the value of Italy's stock markets while employing 360,000 people. He owned two of Italy's most significant newspapers as well as one of the country's most formidable soccer teams, Juventus. He acquired a controlling stake in Ferrari, a national icon, and led Fiat on a global expansion.

When he died of prostate cancer in 2003, two months shy of his eighty-second birthday, Agnelli's funeral was broadcast live on national television. More than one hundred thousand people thronged Fiat's headquarters for a final glimpse of his body before it was carried to Turin's main cathedral.

Italy's then prime minister, Silvio Berlusconi (a fellow billionaire), attended the ceremony. Pope John Paul II released a statement celebrating Agnelli as "an authoritative protagonist of some of the most important moments of Italian history."

But six years after his death, Agnelli was revealed to be something else—a tax cheat of monumental proportions.

This came to light in 2009, as Agnelli's daughter, Margherita Agnelli, filed a lawsuit against her own mother and several of her legal and financial advisers, accusing them of having hidden part of her father's assets. The legal machinations pulled back the curtain on a secret that shook Italy. For years, Agnelli had salted away pieces of his fortune overseas.

The impressive haul was estimated at 1 billion euros, including luxury apartments scattered around the world, six in Paris alone. Agnelli had hidden his holdings in a tangle of foreign vehicles—a foundation in Liechtenstein, three companies chartered in the British Virgin Islands, and a pair of Swiss entities that contained holding companies in Amsterdam, Luxembourg, and Delaware.

Revered for supplying Italy with cars and paychecks, Agnelli had been quietly enriching accountants and lawyers tucked in every tax haven on earth.

Italian authorities went after Agnelli's widow and daughter for tax evasion. They eventually settled with the state, though Margherita would again find herself having to account for wealth stashed overseas following the release of the Panama Papers— the trove of leaked documents that revealed how the world's wealthiest people had hidden their treasure. The papers exposed that she, too, had established her own holding company in the British Virgin Islands, stocked with 1.5 billion euros.

By then, Italy had devolved from a shining example of post-war success into Europe's most hapless major economy. Corruption festered as the Mafia retained its force. The country's banks were stuffed with loans that would never be repaid, in part because they had been lent in support of dubious ventures run by politically connected overseers. Alarming levels of government debt—a hangover from a public spending binge in the 1980s—limited the state's capacity to invest in education, health care, and infrastructure.

As a founding member of the European Union, Italy had adopted the euro currency in 1999, gaining the stability and discipline of a monetary system dominated by the debt-averse Germans. But the strict rules of the currency limited deficits, preventing the government from spending to promote growth.

Italy had never recovered from the 2008 global financial crisis—the result of Davos Man's reckless gambling in the casino den of international banking. Grand-scale tax evasion and European prohibitions on deficit spending combined to starve the economy of capital, yielding stagnation.

As youth unemployment soared—exceeding 40 percent by 2013—young people fled, decamping for Britain and France in search of jobs. Many moved back in with their parents, deferring plans for careers and starting families, and contributing to a stark drop in the Italian birth rate. This itself deepened the cause for despair: as the population aged, that spelled fewer working-age people whose taxes could finance pensions and health care for retirees. These grim truths seeped into the Italian vernacular, prompting talk of lost decades, lost generations, lost dreams.

In the south of Italy, where an unremitting sense of economic depression was palpable, I met a twenty-nine-year-old named Elio Vagali, who had sustained himself by cleaning homes and picking tangerines—nearly always under the table, and without the protection of a full-time job. The measure of his desperation was reflected by his most fervent aspiration. He was eager for a job at the Ilva steel mill, a rusting complex in the city of Taranto, on the Ionian Sea. It had been implicated for a cancer cluster in the surrounding community. Vagali was willing to risk his health for a paycheck that would allow him to move out of his parents' apartment. And still there was no position.

"You either know somebody, or you don't get in," Vagali told me when I met him in February 2018. "There's nothing here for me."

In the rest of Europe, Davos Man tended to exploit Italy as a cautionary tale as he battered away at union power and urged "fiscal restraint"—his favored term for spending cuts to finance tax cuts for himself. Davos Man would tell you that Italy was what happened when a government disregarded budget constraints while lavishing generous pensions on workers. The near impossibility of firing workers undermined Italy's efforts to attract investment.

There was truth to these depictions. Italy's labor protections were extraordinarily bureaucratic, limiting the growth of businesses. Its court system was hopelessly slow, a major reason that banks could not work out their bad debts: they often found it impossible to collect on the collateral. But much of what was wrong with Italy came down to a lack of growth and a shortage of government resources. And Italy's lack of vigor and perpetually bleak finances were in large part the result of Davos Man's depredations.

Technocrats in Rome had assented to demands for budget cuts from the European Union under the rules of the bloc. Austerity and tax evasion had combined to leave Italy perpetually short of funds. This helped explain why roads, bridges, and railroads were decaying, and how a sophisticated health care system would buckle in the face of the pandemic. Executives used political connections to gain public support for private companies and then pocketed the proceeds.

Faced with high debts and budget shortfalls, the government focused on improving tax collection to close the gap. In 2009, Prime Minister Silvio Berlusconi—later brought down himself by a tax evasion scandal—introduced a so-called tax shield that invited Italians who had hidden their money overseas to bring it home legally while surrendering a mere 5 percent to the government.

The scheme proved enticing for wealthy people operating in the shadows, and costly for the Italian state. The authorities dropped major investigations into tax evasion that might have netted substantial returns. They surrendered 700 million euros alone in ditching a case against Italians who had deposited their money in the coffers of HSBC's banking operations in Switzerland.

Subsequent Italian administrations intermittently threatened war against tax evaders while proffering amnesty. Italy's debts rose, its infrastructure deteriorated, and bitterness festered as the poor and middle class watched the country grow increasingly unequal.

By 2014, evasion of European value-added taxes alone was costing the Italian treasury upward of 37 billion euros, according to an estimate from the European Union.

Along the way, Fiat traced Italy's decline, losing money, shedding jobs, and producing cars unwanted by consumers.

Its engineering skill had been supplanted by another talent—
dexterity in pulling political strings to secure public largess.

Agnelli was briefly succeeded at Fiat by his brother Umberto.
When he, too, died the following year, the company installed
Sergio Marchionne as CEO.

Blunt, brash, and singularly devoted to the bottom line, Marchionne eschewed suits, favoring casual attire. He took over a
company that was losing 5 million euros a day. Marchionne fired
managers and slashed unprofitable businesses. He revealed himself as a Davos Man par excellence, displaying a knack for using
crises to extract money from the government.

In August 2005, while most of Italy was at the beach, Marchionne paid a visit to Berlusconi at his residence in Rome. Fiat
was considering shuttering its remaining factories in Italy, Marchionne warned, a step that would eliminate tens of thousands
of jobs. The only alternative was a public rescue. Marchionne demanded an immediate infusion of cash—more than 130 million
euros—plus government subsidies for research and development programs, and tax incentives for consumers to buy its cars.
Otherwise, Berlusconi would find himself having to explain why
Italy's hallmark company was Italian no more.

Berlusconi agreed. By October 2005, Fiat was profitable again,
and paying out dividends to shareholders. Emboldened by this
success, Marchionne repeated the gambit, threatening layoffs to
secure public aid. He persuaded the government to take responsibility for the bulk of paychecks at a Fiat plant outside Naples.
Italy even handed the company money to expand abroad. Despite
public assistance, Fiat shuttered a factory in Sicily, spelling layoffs for 1,500 workers.

Marchionne's most consequential undertaking was a merger
that would reorient Italy's place in the global economy: Fiat took
over Chrysler, one of the Big Three automakers in the United
States. From the moment that deal was completed in 2014, Fiat's
shares began trading on the New York Stock Exchange, giving

global investors greater influence over wage and working conditions at Italy's most prominent company. At the same time, Fiat formally ditched Italy, legally establishing itself in the United Kingdom.

Agnelli had been known to remark that the *I* and the *T* in Fiat's name were a testament to the company's unbreakable bond with Italy. But those ties could not withstand the allure of lower taxes in Britain, especially on capital gains, which enabled the company to hand out fatter dividends to shareholders.

The combination of Italian state aid and diminished wages was supposed to have made Fiat more competitive, generating jobs and future tax receipts. But the move to Britain meant that Fiat would pay the bulk of its taxes there.

In the decade after Marchionne assumed the helm, Fiat's Italian workforce shrunk from more than 44,000 to about 23,000. Half of the remaining workers were covered by a special state-regulated system in which Fiat was able to pay them below their contractual rate.

One employee was prospering, however. Marchionne became the highest-paid CEO in Italy, collecting more than 46 million euros in total compensation in 2017, including stock grants and a bonus. That package was a reward from the people whose interests he had diligently served—shareholders.

Fiat's fate signaled that Italy had been conquered by Davos Man. Years of taxpayer rescues and support schemes had subsidized a multinational corporation that now distributed its bounty to shareholders in London, New York, and other faraway centers of affluence, while abandoning the communities and workers that had nurtured it.

Davos Man's comprehensive pillaging of Italy and the country's loss of vibrancy played out gradually over decades. The country's decline eroded faith in institutions and the governing elite. By 2019, 77 percent of Italians described the economic situation as bad, according to a survey by the Pew Research Center, while 73 percent said the country's elected leaders were not concerned about the situation for ordinary people. This opened a path for cynical politicians who pinned the blame for Italy's troubles not on the insiders who had looted the country, but on faceless outsiders.

Much as Trump's ascent in the United States had been propelled in part by deepening anger among the white working class, right-wing extremists in Italy exploited the dearth of economic opportunities as they rode to power. And just as Trump drew votes by stirring up baseless fears of immigrants, the Italian right drew strength by blaming migrants from Africa for home-cooked problems.

As growing numbers of migrants began landing on Italian shores in 2014, Matteo Salvini, leader of a party called the League, used the influx as a springboard to prominence. His simplistic prescription for Italy's challenges—stop immigration—and his racist appeals to cultural chauvinism ignored the root causes of popular distress: corruption, tax evasion, and austerity. He spared Davos Man blame, while training his wrath on foreigners.

The effectiveness of his pitch rested on the enduring appeal of tribalism in a country in which the economy had long ceased functioning for many working people. Salvini and other right-wing extremists prospered by offering a seemingly coherent, if bogus, narrative for what had happened to the Italian middle class.

You could see this transformation in places like Prato, a city in the central region of Tuscany, where voters had long supported the political left, but were suddenly lurching right.

Prato was a textile town in the same way that Granite City was a steel town. Edoardo Nesi possessed a commanding view over the whole works. His villa perched in the hills above the city looked directly down on the source of his family's wealth—the textile mill started by his grandfather.

Nesi spent his days running the textile business and his nights penning novels. The walls of the family villa were lined with bookshelves crammed with poetry, art volumes, and leftist explorations of economics. His father had been a lover of Beethoven, literature, and timely accounts payable. He bestowed on his son a lucrative arrangement that comprised three-fourths of the business. They sent wool to overcoat manufacturers in Germany that paid unfailingly, ten days after delivery.

"My father said, 'Go to school and then come to work for me and everything will be good,'" Nesi told me. "'We have always had success. You will have it, too.' He kept telling me how simple it was, just deliver good quality in time. That was the secret. We lived in a place where everything had been good for forty years. Nobody was afraid of the future."

Over centuries, Prato had amassed wealth as a center of high-end textiles. It had a network of canals that had been laid down by the Romans, allowing the waters of the Bisenzio River to be diverted as needed.

After World War II, people poured into the mills from the surrounding countryside. At first, the local plants churned out inexpensive woolen blankets. Then they shifted to fabrics of varying heft and texture, adding synthetics that stretched and shimmered. By the 1980s, the fashion houses of Milan were sending designers to Prato to collaborate on new fibers, as the local mills yielded fabric for Armani, Versace, Dolce & Gabbana, and other icons of the realm. Local entrepreneurs watched runway models wearing their creations on catwalks in Paris and felt indomitable.

"We thought we were the best in the world," said Nesi. "Everybody was making money."

The fruits of Prato's wealth were shared widely because of the dominance of the Communist Party. Despite its Marxist trappings and solidarity with the Soviet Union, the party was not oriented to overthrow capitalism. It was leftist in the same way as Nordic countries like Denmark, its leaders intent on parceling out the gains of economic growth to ensure that everyone could afford a home, a steak on the grill, a car. Local unions ensured high wages and comfortable working conditions. The Communists used their power over the purse strings to deliver public works, including a library and a textile museum.

But by the 1990s, Nesi's German customers were purchasing cheaper fabrics woven in the former East Germany, Bulgaria, and Romania. Then, they began buying fabric from China, where similar material could be procured for less than half the price of Prato's.

By 2000, Nesi's business was struggling to break even. The following year, China entered the World Trade Organization. "Suddenly, the orders stopped," he said.

Prato experienced a punishment that it had previously meted out to others. In the middle of the nineteenth century, the city's artisans had begun importing used woolen clothing from around the world and respinning it into fresh yarn that was much cheaper than alternatives, allowing them to undercut competitors in France and England.

But the scale and ambition of China's rise was unprecedented. Factories in coastal cities like Shanghai and Guangzhou were buying the same German-made machinery used by the mills in Prato. They were hiring Italian consultants who were instructing them on the modern arts of the trade. Prato's 6,000 textile companies shrank to 3,000. A textile workforce that had reached 40,000 plunged to 19,000.

Just as in Granite City, the ensuing misery prompted angry talk about globalization and the impossibility of competing with China. But China was merely the means by which Davos Man realized the maximization of profits for his own gain. The squeeze was coming from multinational businesses that dominated the apparel trade.

Nesi's German customers faced relentless pressure to drop their prices as a new breed of retailer took over their industry—companies that answered to shareholders. Enormous brands like Zara and H&M were increasingly using low-wage factories in Asia to make their goods.

Zara had been founded by a reclusive Spaniard named Amancio Ortega, who forged a conglomerate called Inditex that would become the world's largest collection of clothing retailers. Born in 1936 in the northwest of Spain, Ortega had worked as a delivery boy for a store that sold men's shirts, and then as an assistant to a tailor, before launching his own clothing outlet, catering to the wealthy. By 1975, he had opened his first Zara store and was pioneering a concept known as fast fashion: he employed a team of trendspotters who scoured fashion runways for promising new looks and then copied them, rushing cut-rate versions into stores only weeks later. Zara sold its wares in sleek, elegant stores strategically located near luxury brands like Gucci and Chanel, using proximity to capture their allure.

Though Inditex kept much of its production in Spain, its growing reliance on factories in China kept its wages low. This is how Ortega turned himself into the richest person most people had never heard of, a man who supposedly favored eating in the company cafeteria, even as he accrued a fortune estimated at $55 billion.

H&M was the world's second largest clothing retailer and another fast-fashion icon. Launched in Sweden in 1947 by a man named Erling Persson, it began as a women's clothing retailer. By the early 1980s, the founder's son, Stefan Persson, was in charge and leading the company on a global expansion. Its foreign dealings brought disclosures of exploitation—workers allegedly passing out in the face of chemical fumes at a factory making clothes in Cambodia, child laborers found in the company's Myanmar plant. Not coincidentally, the profits were vast, supplying Persson with wealth estimated at $13.5 billion.

Back in Prato, Nesi's sales evaporated. He even tried his hand at making clothes for Zara, but was exasperated by the ceaseless demands for lower prices.

"You started to work on how to pervert your own quality in order to sell it to Zara," Nesi said. "It had to be something that looks like your quality without actually being it. That's more or less a description of what they wanted our life to become—something that looks like your life, but is of lesser quality."

He sold the business in 2004, ahead of what seemed an inevitable collapse, in order to spare his father from "an old age full of shame."

As he recounted the story fifteen years later over plates of pasta at his dining room table, his sadness over the ending remained palpable.

"My father was my idol," Nesi said. "I used to think that my father made his temple and I ruined the temple, because I couldn't find a way to sell. Then I realized how my problem was very common. Many other companies were not able to sell their fabrics anymore."

Down in the flatlands of Prato, Roberta Travaglini, a sixty-one-year-old mother of two grown boys, had become dependent on handouts from her parents' pensions to buy groceries. She had also developed a passion for the Italian right, and a tendency to explain her loss of station with racist jeremiads about the people she blamed—the Chinese workers who had set up shop in the failed textile mills, the African immigrants who loitered at a park strip outside her apartment.

Travaglini and nearly everyone in her family had worked in the local textile factories, and had been unwavering supporters of the political left. She had fond memories of the boisterous

Communist Party rallies her father had taken her to as a child, the gatherings amid music, dancing, and free-flowing wine.

But when I met her in Prato in the spring of 2019, Travaglini had been out of work for three years. She was cadging odd jobs fixing clothes for people in her neighborhood, using the workshop on the ground floor of her parents' apartment. She was disgusted by the influx of Chinese immigrants and the success of their businesses. They were importing fabric from China, stitching up clothes, and selling their finished wares at street fairs in Paris, capturing premium prices by affixing a valuable label—Made in Italy.

Products with that label should be made by Italians, she hissed, and Chinese people would never be included in that identity. Not even the children of immigrants, who were born and educated in Prato, spoke native Italian, and were increasingly expanding from garment sewing into sophisticated design work, launching their own brands.

There were jobs to be found in the Chinese-owned factories, but Travaglini had not bothered to apply. "I don't think it's fair that they come to take jobs away from Italians," she said. "Ideologically, I fight against this, so I can't go to work there."

This was nonsense. Before the influx of Chinese immigrants, Prato's failed factories had sat empty. Now they were full of the sound of clattering sewing machines. Far from preying on Prato, the immigrants were an engine of revival.

"We are doing jobs that Italians are not willing to do," said Sang Wei, who had arrived fourteen years earlier from Anhui, one of China's poorest provinces, opening a restaurant that sold takeaway containers of rice and vegetables. "We work harder. We get up first thing in the morning every day, seven days a week, and we are here from 6 A.M. until 8 P.M. Italian people are not going to do this."

Prato was by many estimates home to the largest community

of Chinese in Europe. Travaglini patronized their businesses, buying discount clothes at a boutique near her apartment. But she spoke of immigrants as a symptom of Italian decay—of globalization gone awry, of her own vulnerability in an age in which national leaders no longer cared about people like her. In the previous year's national elections, she had cast her vote for Salvini's party.

In the years after the global financial crisis, the party Salvini headed—then known as the Northern League—swept into power in Prato. It launched a crackdown on the Chinese-owned factories. It used nighttime raids on the plants to harass workers, while decrying "illegal immigration" as the source of economic decline.

In its current incarnation, the party was focused on the latest arrivals—immigrants landing on Italian beaches from North Africa, fleeing wars in Syria, Afghanistan, and Somalia. Salvini pointed at their Muslim faith and warned that Europe was in danger of becoming "an Islamic caliphate." He described migration as an "invasion" that threatened Italians with "ethnic cleansing." Like Trump, he presented himself as a corrective to global integration, an unapologetic nationalist who would rescue the dispossessed from what had become of the Italian left, long since metamorphosed into a distant elite.

To Travaglini's ear, Salvini was offering an accounting of what had happened to her life. "We are in the hands of the world elites, who want to keep us poorer and poorer," Travaglini told me. "When I was young, it was the Communist Party that was protecting the workers, that was protecting our social class. Now, it's the League that is protecting the people."

Salvini had already secured a place in the government, in an ill-fated coalition headed by the spectacularly inept Five Star movement. Then he overreached, bringing the government down on the bet that this would trigger elections. Instead, Five Star had found another coalition partner, leaving Salvini an outsider. Still, he remained a force, biding his time until the next elections.

Tuscany, Umbria, Marche, and Emilia-Romagna—four Italian provinces that had elected Communists as recently as the 1980s, and then reliably supported center-left candidates—were more recently elevating far-right parties.

The abandonment of the left could be read as a sign that its program worked only so long as there were gains to distribute. When lean times came—when there were no paychecks to share—the left had no answer, opening an opportunity for the right.

But why were there not enough jobs?

It had nothing to do with Chinese immigrants filling Prato. They were creating jobs.

It had nothing to do with migrants from North Africa, whose arrival came years after Italy descended into a moribund state.

The imprints of Davos Man were everywhere—tax evasion, financial shenanigans, the looting of the system by the powerful.

The extreme right hardly talked about these things. Its prescriptions for lifting living standards were minimal and incoherent. It gained influence by playing on fear and promising to revive a comforting image of Italy's past, centered on halting the influx of outsiders.

It had forged an emotional connection with the dispossessed, people who could be reached with nativist rhetoric. Those who earned their living with their hands understood that their lives and security were shaped by forces beyond national borders. Salvini projected the illusion of being able to restore control.

Looking down on his family's former textile factory from above Prato, Nesi was pained by this turn. He disdained the extreme right as a regressive turn. But he understood that this was precisely their appeal.

"It's the power of nostalgia," he told me.

The year after he sold the mill, Nesi's daughter, then ten, dragged him into H&M, eager to buy an overcoat.

"The shop was fantastic," he recalled. "Very well lit, beautiful people inside, and the clothes were beautiful. But I was seeing them from thirty meters away. And every step I was taking, I was seeing something wrong.

"Then I touched the clothes," Nesi continued. "The fabric was very bad. Then you looked at the price, and you could see that it's less than half of what you would pay in any other shop, and you could see that the Western world is finished."

But that takeaway was merely a high-grade version of the cultural arrogance that prevented Italy from reckoning with its problems. Nesi's family business had not been taken down by "the East" or globalization, or other nebulous terms that really meant unfair competition from China. Zara and H&M were, in fact, European companies. It was not their provenance that explained Prato's torment, but rather the way in which these companies were organized—as a means of maximizing returns to shareholders above all other considerations.

Nesi's diminished legacy did not reflect the supposed failure of Western civilization. It was a testament to how one select group had monopolized the gains. Prato had been decimated by Davos Man.

The nostalgia Nesi identified as fuel for the extremist right reflected a popular yearning for a time when Italians could take their middle-class station for granted. The people who had taken that away were not across an ocean. They were all around—in government offices in Rome, in elegant villas in next-door Florence, and in the other redoubts for Davos Men, who diverted the labors and savings of Italians into their private bank accounts.

Nostalgia was politically potent, a way to mobilize people far beyond Italy. On the other side of the English Channel, a renegade faction of Davos Men used it to sabotage Britain's place in the global economy for personal gain.

"OUR CHANCE TO FUCK THEM BACK"

Davos Man and Brexit

George Osborne was not inclined toward seeking popular affirmation. In bearing and elocution, he presented like someone accustomed to deference by dint of his standing as a member of the English aristocracy.

He was the eldest son of the seventeenth baronet of Ballintaylor, a hereditary title that traced its lineage back to 1629. He attended St. Paul's, an elite boarding school whose London campus occupied a stretch of the River Thames that included a boathouse and seven cricket pitches. Then he enrolled at Oxford University, the ivy-draped nesting ground for the ruling class.

Over the course of a meteoric political career, Osborne had gained a reputation as a shrewd tactician, as well as someone not reluctant to share his cleverness with the rest of humanity. In 2010, when he was only thirty-eight, Osborne had assumed control of the national treasury, becoming Britain's youngest ever chancellor of the exchequer in a government headed by his fellow Oxford alumnus—and drinking society member—David Cameron. He had used that perch to assault the nation's vaunted social safety net, imposing cuts to a vast array of government programs in the name of fiscal rectitude.

The tabloid papers portrayed him as ruthless in his ideological crusade for a smaller government unburdened by the needs of the poor, the infirm, the decrepit, and the disabled. Osborne appeared to regard such characterizations as a badge of honor, evidence that he was taking on important fights shirked by less heroic figures. He had once supposedly warned his eight-year-old son that he would hear unkind words about his father.

"I sat him down and said there were things he needed to know about what Daddy does," Osborne recounted. "He needed to understand that Daddy might not always be very popular, and that there might be people who don't like Daddy."

But on this day in June 2016, as he stood in the atrium of an office building in Bournemouth, a modest city on the southern coast of England, Osborne found himself uncharacteristically seeking the favor of several hundred people gathered around him.

He and Prime Minister Cameron confronted a situation that risked enshrining them as two of the most disastrous public servants in the history of their nation. In a mere three weeks, the United Kingdom would go to the polls to vote on a colossal question: whether to abandon the European Union.

Cameron had put this option before the people in the form of a referendum, with every expectation that they would vote to remain, affirming Britain's central place in Europe and its lucrative free trade zone. The prime minister had called the vote in the hopes of putting down a seething insurrection inside his governing Conservative Party, where a rogue faction had long used Britain's inclusion in the European Union to stir up support among noisy nationalists. Once voters rejected Brexit—as the exit option was known—this electoral ploy would be defused forevermore. Conservative leaders could safely carry on without fear of ambush from Union Jack–waving opportunists.

Except voters were not playing along. The polls were uncomfortably tight, which put Cameron's and Osborne's political futures in grave doubt along with the sanctity of their nation. Scotland was threatening to bolt the union if Brexit passed. The referendum also posed monumental risk to the British economy, which was largely dependent on unimpeded trade across the English Channel.

At the center of concern was finance, an industry integral to Osborne's job as the overseer of the treasury and, as it happened, his personal fortunes in what would become the post-Brexit phase of his career.

The story of the modern British economy was deeply entwined with the rise of finance, and especially the global expansion of American banking.

Back in the 1980s, Britain's Iron Lady, Prime Minister Margaret Thatcher, had courted investment by stripping away rules limiting trading, a course that had elevated London into a global financial center rivaled only by New York.

Every business day, people on trading floors in London completed transactions involving the exotic financial instruments known as derivatives that were collectively worth nearly $1 trillion, or roughly three-fourths of the total for the globe. Almost one-fifth of the world's banking transactions were consummated somewhere in the United Kingdom, while $2.4 trillion's worth of foreign currencies was exchanged daily.

As an industry, finance employed more than 1.1 million people in Britain, while generating annual revenues exceeding a quarter of a trillion dollars.

Brexit threatened to upend a substantial portion of this business. As much as one-third of the financial transactions in Britain involved clients based somewhere in continental Europe. If Britain really left Europe, no one knew what rules would apply going forward, which was reason enough for people in charge of money to stash it somewhere else.

To underscore the stakes and urge voters to reject Brexit,

Osborne had come to Bournemouth to visit the offices of one of the primary actors in Britain's rise to financial dominance— JPMorgan Chase, the largest American bank.

"The answer to the challenges we face in this world is not to withdraw the drawbridges and think you can seal yourself off," Osborne declared. "We can't afford to build a wall around Britain. And we've succeeded by engaging."

He nodded reverentially at the star of the day's festivities— Jamie Dimon, the bank's chairman and chief executive officer, whose very presence on British soil amounted to the essential message: Brexit was not merely a domestic political question, but a threat to the global economy. The potential consequences were disturbing enough to have provoked the attention of a man running a bank then stocked with $2.5 trillion in assets.

In contrast to Osborne, Dimon carried himself like a person who was used to being liked. His raffish charm, wry grin, and shock of gray hair tended to disarm those he encountered with what felt like genuine warmth.

Other CEOs suffered stiff interactions with their underlings, dispensing canned jokes and pretending to care about people's lives outside the enterprise of making money. Dimon—known to all as Jamie—was a figure who conjured familiarity even among those who barely knew him.

But on this day, with the referendum swiftly approaching, Dimon was not trying to make people feel comfortable. He was aiming for fear. He made the requisite show of not interfering in another sovereign nation's election. "I cannot and will not tell the British people how they should vote," he said, before warning his employees that voting for Brexit would be like setting their money on fire.

"It's a terrible idea for the British economy and jobs," he said.

Dimon's bank employed roughly sixteen thousand people in the United Kingdom, some four thousand in Bournemouth alone. Those jobs were there in large part because of Britain's inclusion in the European Union. The bank used its British hub to serve clients across the European continent.

If Britain voted to leave, it would set in motion a process of dissolution so tedious and intricate that some likened it to un-scrambling an omelet. It would generate years of expensive, commerce-impeding uncertainty over the regulations that would govern future dealings with the twenty-seven remaining coun-tries of the European Union. No one knew how it would play out.

Dimon's bank would not be able to wait and hope that a deal would emerge preserving the current setup. He would be forced to assume the worst and commence planning for it immedi-ately, anticipating an era in which his bank's operations in Brit-ain would be separated from its European clients by a freshly revived border. He would be compelled to start moving jobs to the other side of the Channel to ensure that it could continue to serve clients there without interruption, come what may.

"I don't know if it means 1,000 jobs, 2,000 jobs," he said. "It could be as many as 4,000."

Davos Man was generally aghast at Brexit, viewing it as a dis-ruptive reordering of the geography of global commerce. Over the decades, London had become a preeminent center of finance in large part because of Britain's place in the European single market—a free trade zone stretching from Cyprus to Ireland, holding half a billion of the wealthier people on earth.

When a Spanish utility needed cash to build a new power sta-tion, it came to London to sell its bonds. Danish pork exporters used London to buy derivatives to hedge risks of fluctuations in currency markets. Pension funds across Europe relied on Lon-don to manage their money.

Brexit put much of this business in play. The European Union was already threatening to require that trading in the euro, the currency used by nineteen of its members, be restricted to the Continent.

In matters of regulation, Davos Man preferred to ingratiate

himself with a single, central authority. Brexit would require that bank executives spend time figuring out who mattered inside regulatory dens scattered from Estonia to Malta, wooing and flattering tiny people suddenly handed giant powers to disrupt global flows of money. This would necessitate ego-stroking dinners, internships for unemployable children, and familiarity with domestic arcana. It was certain to be a profit-diluting, time-wasting pain in the ass.

It was also historically retrogressive. Ever since Thatcher deregulated finance, turning London into a speculator's paradise, the global banks had steadily centralized their operations there. They had pulled people out of Milan, Frankfurt, and Amsterdam and brought them into burgeoning headquarters in London, turning former docklands in East London into a thicket of skyscrapers known as Canary Wharf. Brexit was going to roll history backward, forcing the banks to move people back to the Continent.

Beyond crude considerations of money, Brexit posed an existential challenge to the European Union—another piece of the firmament in the liberal democratic order forged at the end of World War II. It had been conceived by the victorious Allies as a means of promoting trade and replacing nationalism with a broader solidarity.

The E.U. was a haphazardly constructed organization whose contours and processes beggared comprehension. The end of the Cold War had brought in former East Bloc countries that swelled its ranks, including Hungary and Poland, whose governments displayed keen interest in European development money and less concern for the rule of law.

Famously bureaucratic and prone to philosophical dickering over its mission, the E.U. typically took forever to make decisions, even in the face of dire emergencies. It was like an air traffic control center still debating what radio channel to use as a jumbo jet plunged toward the ground. The bloc had subjected Greece to years of torment after the country slid into insolvency, ultimately administering a bailout that protected creditors— chiefly, German banks—while condemning ordinary Greeks to years of desperation. The leadership had endlessly debated how to respond to the waves of migrants landing on Mediterranean beaches in the summer of 2015—how many to admit, and where to shelter them—before doing essentially nothing, leaving national governments to blame one another and erect fences, deflecting the misery toward their neighbors.

Reforming the E.U. was a perennial cause for think-tank gatherings and dissertations, though its inscrutable processes and penchant for technocratic jargon appeared beyond alteration. In Britain the political right had long detested the bloc as an incursion on its cherished sovereignty, a stubborn weed growing in the garden of national vanity. The right-wing tabloid press was full of mostly made-up stories about overreaching European rules that supposedly governed absurd details, like the acceptable curvature of a banana. The left abhorred the E.U. as a neoliberal vessel dedicated to flattening national rules as a means of opening Europe to the depredations of multinational corporations.

Yet there was little question that the project of European integration had been one of the conspicuous successes of the postwar era. The E.U. had presided over decades that had been largely defined by peace, rising prosperity, and the forging of a collective European identity. The single marketplace at the center of the bloc had proved durable and bountiful. Companies could treat it like one giant country, without encountering border controls, customs checks, and other hindrances to commerce.

"The European Union, I really do believe, is one of the greatest human endeavors of all time," Dimon said in Bournemoth. "For this continent to come together and try to live in peace after not a century but one thousand years of war, and it's worked so far. It's not perfect. It needs some leadership, which is more reason to stay in."

Dimon was correct in his assessment about Brexit—a fact that would only clarify in the years following the referendum. Unrelenting political acrimony played out as Britain struggled to arrange its future dealings with Europe, against a backdrop of economic decline. British exporters sold nearly half of their wares to members of the European Union. Whatever sort of Brexit resulted, some of this commerce was certain to be impeded. In the meantime, tortuous negotiations scared off investment and slowed growth.

Little examined was how the Brexit campaign was the work of a rogue subset of Davos Men in the hedge fund world who aimed to escape Europe as a means of getting out from under regulations. They were willing to undermine the national interest in pursuit of their own gains.

Though Dimon's message was legitimate, the overseer of America's largest bank lacked standing to opine on what was best for the British people. Moreover, his tribe, the Davos Men who ran global finance, were responsible for the anger that had set Brexit in motion: publicly financed bailouts that spared bankers from the consequences of their disastrous speculation, followed by budget austerity for all. Dimon's warning that Brexit would damage the British economy collided with the fact that British workers had been absorbing damage for decades, suffering wage stagnation and declining living standards, under policies that Davos Man collaborators like Osborne had designed to woo the investment of people like Jamie Dimon.

Osborne's role as the architect of austerity undermined his use as a public emissary in pursuit of votes for almost anything. His pedigree, his blue suits, his air of smug superiority, and his trademark smirk made him easily lampooned for his abiding sense of entitlement.

"He looks permanently pink and facetious," a member of Parliament from the Labour Party had once remarked, "as though life is one big public-school prank."

This was not a helpful trait for a politician who had earned distinction as the man perpetually demanding sacrifice from others. Osborne had slashed spending on social welfare programs and support for local governments, forcing communities to shutter facilities. He had withheld funds for the nation's national health care system. And he had cut corporate taxes, while indulging the Cosmic Lie.

In short, he had traded the economic security of ordinary Britons for the enrichment of Davos Man.

And as he stood next to Dimon in Bournemouth, Osborne claimed that everything had worked out magnificently. "I'm proud of the way we've turned things around in the last five or six years," Osborne said. "We've succeeded by engaging in the world."

Which made the case against Brexit sound like an endorsement for a continuation of national trauma.

When Jamie Dimon was nine years old, his father asked him what he wanted to be when he grew up.

"I want to be rich," he replied.

This was less an aspiration than a wish to maintain the life into which he had been born.

His grandfather had arrived in New York from his native Greece in 1921, starting out as a busboy, before forging a career as a stockbroker. He taught the business to Dimon's father, who in turn initiated his own son. Somewhere along the line, the family name, Papademetriou, was traded in for Dimon, in a traditional act of American assimilation.

Even as he was quick to advertise his Greek immigrant roots and his links to the New York City borough of Queens—land

of regular people, across the river from patrician Manhattan—
Dimon spent most of his youth on Park Avenue. His family home
was just down the street from the apartment that he would purchase as an adult. He and his two brothers attended the nearby
Browning School, an all-boys private institution whose alumni
included several members of the Rockefeller clan.

He spent weekends at the family country house in Greenwich,
Connecticut, whose very name was synonymous with extraordinary wealth and power. There, he got to know Sandy Weill, the
brokerage chief who would become his mentor, launching him
on a career that would reach the heights of finance.

It was not a chance encounter. His father had worked for
Weill for three decades. Their homes in Greenwich were close by,
and the two families regularly socialized. Weill had grown up in
the blue-collar world of Flatbush, Brooklyn, a Polish Jew whose
family had been part of the great wave of European immigrants
landing in New York in the first decades of the twentieth century.

The Weills and the Dimons shared the sense that the United
States was a land of boundless opportunity in which anyone
could prosper. They also illustrated a less celebrated truism:
American success frequently involved the effective harnessing
of elite social networks. After Dimon's sophomore year at Tufts
University, Weill offered him a summer job at his firm. Following business school, Dimon again worked for Weill, who had just
sold his company, Shearson, to American Express.

Dimon followed Weill on to his next adventure, overseeing
a series of increasingly audacious mergers that turned a small-
time Baltimore-based lending operation into what would become
Citigroup, one of the largest financial conglomerates in history.

Dimon was widely viewed as the heir apparent to take over.
But he impatiently pushed Weill to execute the transition sooner,
angering his mentor. Not ready to retire, Weill denied Dimon a
place in the banking operation before firing him.

It was 1998, the middle of the dot-com boom. Dimon flirted with taking a job at a startup company called Amazon.com, but opted instead to remain in finance. He took over Bank One, a Chicago-based lender, where he doubled the company's value in only four years. He persuaded JPMorgan Chase to buy the bank for $58 billion in 2004. The next year, he became CEO of the combined entity.

Dimon's ascent was typically attributed to his extraordinary work ethic and his meticulous fretting over details. On Wall Street, he was celebrated as a truth-teller and irascible wiseass.

"Don't do anything stupid," he once told an executive who worked for him. "And don't waste any money. Let everybody else waste money and do stupid things. Then, we'll buy them."

In an unusual break with protocol that earned him no love from the bank's lawyers, Dimon had admitted in 2007—a year before the global financial crisis—that Wall Street had been gorging on debt and gambling on increasingly risky investments. "We do not yet know the ultimate impact of recent industry excesses," he declared in his annual letter to shareholders.

But his company was in fact profiting from those excesses. Dimon appeared to be looking away from danger signs as he allowed his people to carry on with hazardous bets that lifted the bank's share price.

JPMorgan Chase had provided banking services to Bernard Madoff as he operated what would prove to be the largest Ponzi scheme in American history, bilking investors out of $19 billion. Within the bank, numerous people had for years warned that Madoff's books appeared to be doctored. His numbers were "possibly too good to be true," one employee wrote, while an executive actually used the P word, suggesting that Madoff's returns "are speculated to be part of a Ponzi scheme."

The bank shielded management from the threat of criminal culpability by arguing that it was too woefully disorganized to have acquired a coherent understanding of the Ponzi scheme operating under its roof. It agreed to pay $2.1 billion in fines to federal authorities without admitting wrongdoing.

Dimon had also been in charge as JPMorgan Chase played a central role in delivering the global financial crisis. The American finance industry had written mortgages to nearly anyone in possession of a signature. Banks bundled millions of loans into bonds, paid ratings agencies to vouch for them as solid investments, and then peddled the product to suckers around the globe.

A fall in housing prices spoiled trillions of dollars' worth of investments tied to mortgages. By the fall of 2008, institutions that had traded aggressively in such securities lurched toward collapse. The George W. Bush administration, Congress, and the Federal Reserve operated on the understanding that they had to overwhelm markets with money or watch another Great Depression unfold.

Dimon huddled with Bush's Treasury secretary, Hank Paulson, engineering JPMorgan Chase's takeover of the first major casualty of the crisis—the teetering investment bank Bear Stearns. Here was a classic example of the cozy ties between Davos Man and his putative regulatory authorities. Paulson was the former chief of another investment banking giant, Goldman Sachs. He was tapping his Davos Man network, using Dimon to remove Bear and its toxic pile of mortgage-related investments from the marketplace, limiting the threat of cascading failure through the financial realm. Paulson helped arrange for the Federal Reserve to put up $29 billion in public money to cover further losses within Bear's portfolio. Dimon walked away with the remains of a rival plus a taxpayer-financed rescue.

Paulson soon rushed to Capitol Hill bearing a three-page "plan" that demanded authorization to spend $700 billion however he deemed necessary, no strings attached. After a brief performance of scrutiny, Congress complied, adding only token requirements that the money be spent on things other than paying bonuses to the very executives who had nearly blown up the world.

JPMorgan Chase received a $25 billion federal bailout, though Dimon insisted that his bank did not actually need the money, taking it only at Treasury's urging. (He left out the fact that, absent federal action, many of the companies that owed his company money would have disappeared.) Amid the chaos, JPMorgan Chase also took over the retail operations of Washington Mutual, another failed lender. It was all about good citizenship, not money, Dimon insisted.

"Counter to what most people think, many of the extreme actions we took were not done to make a profit," Dimon said a decade later, in a memo to his employees. "They were done to support our country and the financial system."

But the actions Dimon oversaw made his already enormous bank even bigger, which boosted its value. By 2019, the five largest banks in the United States controlled 46 percent of all bank deposits, up from only 12 percent two decades earlier. Investors understood that these institutions were Too Big to Fail, meaning systemically important enough that the government would always come running to save them. This allowed them to borrow at cheaper rates, boosting their profitability, lifting share prices, and putting money in the pockets of Davos Men like Jamie Dimon.

Paulson's old firm, Goldman, recouped $12.9 billion in trading losses from taxpayers via the $182 billion bailout of the giant insurance company, American International Group. AIG also tapped some of the money to pay bonuses to its top executives. And less than a week after the company received the first $85 billion in rescue funds, it took its executives on a retreat to a luxury beach resort in Southern California, spending more than $440,000, including $23,000 on spa treatments. That episode enhanced the sense that American capitalism had become a grifter's paradise. Corporate overseers could engineer a cataclysm that wiped out nearly $8 trillion in wealth, while destroying jobs for tens of millions of people, and then use their rescue money to pay for massages and chocolate-dipped strawberries at a pleasure palace by the sea.

As Barack Obama took office in January 2009, he delivered an $800 billion package of public spending measures aimed at stimulating the economy. He also summoned Dimon and the CEOs of other major banks to the White House for a stern chat.

Obama assembled them in the state dining room, where they sat around a long mahogany table, provided with only glasses of water. There, the president admonished the bankers for continuing to dispense enormous pay packages. When the participants protested that they were merely paying what the market required to hang on to their talent, the president cut them off.

"Be careful how you make those statements, gentlemen," Obama said. "The public isn't buying that. My administration is the only thing between you and the pitchforks."

As it turned out, Obama's administration proved a more than adequate buffer protecting Davos Man from any bloodlust for accountability. His Justice Department failed to send a single executive to prison for their role in the financial crisis, opting instead to negotiate a series of mild settlements.

Obama also refused to administer meaningful relief to American homeowners. His Treasury secretary, Timothy Geithner—a creature of Wall Street who would go on to head a private equity company—shot down proposals for direct relief for homeowners, even as foreclosures soared along with attendant problems like bankruptcy and homelessness. He argued that forgiving mortgage debt would amount to "moral hazard," a happy ending for reckless borrowers who had used their addresses like ATMs, using lines of credit to finance vacations and new cars.

Some people had borrowed in such fashion, but more had fallen into arrears because their wages had been stagnating and declining for decades, while the costs of housing, health care, and education all climbed. Because Davos Men like Benioff were using their stock-based pay to amass real estate, sending prices skyward, ordinary people were forced to pay more for their own homes. If they wanted to put their children in high-quality schools, they had to pay what it cost to live in the best districts. People had taken out second mortgages to come up with the money to send children to college, to cover the costs of emergency medical care. These were the realities that drove many homeowners to borrow too much.

Still, Geithner and Obama would not budge. They offered distressed borrowers weak relief schemes that merely extended their repayment terms and dropped interest rates, then looked the other way while lenders sabotaged such programs. This policy failure condemned homeowners to the loss of their properties while guaranteeing voluminous inventory in distressed real estate for opportunistic investors like Steve Schwarzman.

Meanwhile, the Fed snapped up trillions of dollars in bonds, keeping borrowing costs low and allowing corporations to binge on debt. They exploited their access to free credit to enrich shareholders while declining to invest or hire aggressively.

In the decade following the financial crisis, the companies that made up the S&P 500, a broad swath of the American stock market, spent $5.3 trillion—or more than half their profits—to buy back their stock, sending their share prices higher. They spent another $3.8 trillion on handing out dividends. Over the course of those ten years, the wealth of American billionaires increased by more than 80 percent. Meanwhile, the vast majority of Americans were still waiting for recovery.

Dimon's company ultimately submitted to a settlement with American regulators that included a $13 billion fine along with a public acknowledgment that it had fleeced the institutions that purchased its loans. Much of the mischief had been the handiwork of Bear Stearns and Washington Mutual before Dimon's bank assumed control, but some had transpired on his watch.

The deal, struck in 2013, was supposedly a chastening moment for the bank. But the fine was a trifle for an institution that possessed more than $2 trillion in assets. Dimon's compensation nearly doubled that year, reaching $20 million.

Even so, in Davos the following January, he complained that the unsavory depictions of his bank had been very upsetting.

"I think a lot of it was unfair," Dimon said, "but I am not going to go into the details."

When the American Congress responded to the financial crisis with regulations that forced banks to set aside more dollars in reserve against future fiascos, Dimon and his lobbying minions strenuously sought to prevent the Obama administration from making the rules applicable to foreign subsidiaries. He complained about international rules that threatened to impose surcharges on banks that did not sufficiently boost their reserves. In a heated exchange behind closed doors with Mark Carney—then the governor of Canada's central bank, and later the head of the Bank of England—Dimon called the rules "anti-American."

Dimon's protestations about supposed regulatory overreach seemed especially disingenuous the following year, as JPMorgan Chase disclosed that its London trading floor had been used as the venue for a series of shockingly unsuccessful bets, yielding losses that exceeded $6 billion. The trader responsible for this recklessness became known as the London Whale.

Dimon had been telling anyone who would listen that the bad eggs who had produced the financial crisis were gone, so it was time for the government to relax and let bankers be bankers. The London Whale debacle provided a poignant reminder that huge banks were still concocting wild schemes that their own leaders either tacitly approved or did not grasp.

None of this unfortunate history prevented Dimon from offering his counsel to Britain on the imprudence of Brexit.

Brexit's very existence was itself an outgrowth of this unsavory history.

In the worst of the Great Financial Crisis, in December 2009, British taxpayers had been on the hook for nearly £1 trillion of guarantees to the country's teetering banks. The bailouts had been delivered by a Labour Party government. As a new coalition government headed by the Conservatives assumed power in May 2010, it used the disaster as an opportunity to advance a long-running offensive against what remained of Britain's social welfare state.

The financial crisis had ravaged the ledger books. Britain's annual budget deficit had ballooned from some £10 billion to £100 billion, lifting the total national debt to about £1 trillion. Osborne, the incoming chancellor of the exchequer, crafted an emergency budget promising liberation through collective pain. Government spending in nearly every area of life would be slashed by roughly one-fourth over the next four years, and more in the years ahead. Programs for the poor, disabled, and jobless would be streamlined, while people would be encouraged to trade welfare checks for paychecks. Corporate taxes were lowered as a supposed means of luring investment.

Osborne delivered this grim arithmetic by casting himself as the sober adult in a room full of drunken teenagers who had gotten hold of Dad's credit card.

"The truth is that the country was living beyond its means when the recession came," he told Parliament. "Today, we have paid the debts of a failed past, and laid the foundations for a more prosperous future."

He and Cameron portrayed austerity as part of a noble refashioning referred to as the Big Society. Once Britain hacked away at the bloated government bureaucracy, grassroots organizations, charities, and private enterprise would step to the fore, reviving struggling communities and taking over the work of administering to people in need of help.

To a degree, a spirit of volunteerism did flow from austerity. Public libraries came to depend on the donated labors of concerned citizens, who eventually outnumbered paid staff. Schools began serving breakfast as well as lunch, cognizant that students in poor households were showing up unfed. Parents swapped hand-me-down school uniforms. But celebrating this sort of collectivism as part of the Big Society was akin to setting your house on fire and then reveling in the community spirit as your neighbors came running to help extinguish the blaze.

The government slashed spending on law enforcement, road maintenance, and care for the elderly. Courts struggled to attend to their business. Prisons saw an outbreak of violence and suicide amid overcrowding and a reduction of staff.

More than an exercise in budget math, austerity seeped into the national identity, diminishing expectations about the future.

This was most palpable in the north of England, which was full of struggling towns and cities dispossessed by industry. In these communities, modern history tended to be told in the cadence of lamentation, their story one of intermittent neglect and plunder. Thatcher's name was an epithet, owing to her campaign to subjugate organized labor in the 1980s. "There is no such thing as society," she had famously declared. She crushed striking miners as she privatized the mines. She diminished government programs that helped people facing duress.

A quarter century later, Osborne's austerity was absorbed as an effort to complete Thatcherism.

"It's clearly an attack on our class," said Dave Kelly, a sixty-year-old retired bricklayer in the town of Kirkby, on the outskirts of Liverpool. "It's an attack on who we are. The whole fabric of society is breaking down."

During World War II, Kirkby had been built around a munitions factory. After the war, it prospered as a hive of industry. Kelly's father was a crane driver. His mother had worked as an inspector at a frozen foods factory. He and his brother and sister had grown up in a three-bedroom house with a garage. They played table tennis at a local community center, and swam in a public pool across the street from their house.

But by early 2018, as Kelly led me on a morbid tour, the factory where his mother had worked had been dismantled. The swimming pool had been shut years earlier, when the local council ran out of money. The dance hall Kelly had helped build had become a center where laid-off workers came to file paperwork seeking disability payments. At the youth club where he and his own children had gathered, a sticker on the front window advertised one of the primary reasons people arrived now: "Money Managing & Debt Advice. Housing Advice. Rent Arrears."

"It's a tragedy," Kelly said. "The town is in terminal decline."

A few miles south, in the town of Prescot, residents had been horrified to learn that a popular park had been included on a list of assets that the local council was considering selling to developers in a frantic bid to raise money. They had already seen their library sold and refashioned into a glass-fronted luxury home. The local museum had receded into town history. The police station was gone, replaced by a mostly unstaffed desk in a new government building. Now they were threatened with the loss of Browns Field. The park sat in the town center, containing a playground and soccer fields.

"Everybody uses this park," said Jackie Lewis, who had raised two kids in town and was walking her dog across the lush grass. "This is probably our last piece of community space. It's been one after the other. You just end up despondent."

People swapped conspiracy theories about how the soon-to-be-deposed head of the council for the surrounding borough of Knowsley, Andy Moorhead, had opted to sell Browns Field. When I dropped in on Moorhead, he did not look the part of an austerity villain. Then sixty-two, he had spent most of his working years in services for poor children. He was a career member

of the Labour Party, with the everyday bearing of a genial deni-
zen of the corner pub.

"I didn't become a politician to take things off of people," he
said. "But you've got the reality to deal with."

The reality was that the government in London was phasing
out grants to localities, forcing them to pay for services using only
housing and business taxes. "It's ideological," he said. "No one
should be doing this, not in the fifth wealthiest country in the
whole world."

In Liverpool—a handsome if gritty waterfront city that was
home to half a million people—local officials had seen their
budget cut by roughly two-thirds since the advent of austerity.

The Merseyside Fire and Rescue Service, whose domain en-
compassed Liverpool, had been forced to shutter five fire stations and shrink its force from about 1,000 people to 620.

"These cuts certainly aren't making anyone safer," said the
fire chief, Dan Stephens.

He recalled a blaze three years earlier. An elderly couple had
been trapped in their home in the middle of the night. The first
engine got there within six minutes, but the second did not arrive until four minutes later because it had to come from another station.

"One lived, and one died," he said. "If we could have gotten
out there faster, chances are both would have lived."

Individual budgetary problems were combining to make the
result worse than the sum of the parts. Austerity had eliminated
home health care, which meant that growing numbers of elderly
people were being left at home unattended. The city had cut
mental health services, so fewer staff were on hand to check on
hoarders, who tended to amass stacks of old newspapers. Poor
people were losing cash grants and falling behind on their electric
bills, resorting to candles for light during hours of darkness.

Most of these concerns were not the fire chief's problem.
Collectively, they yielded an alarming increase in fire risk. Un-

attended elderly people plus piles of newsprint plus candles: no great powers of imagination were required to imagine wailing sirens.

"There are knock-on effects all the way through the system," Stephens said. A few weeks later, he quit and moved to Australia.

Much as the United States took the Great Depression as the impetus for the New Deal during the 1930s, forging government programs like Social Security, Britain had produced defining social schemes, anchored by its National Health Service. The establishment of the medical system had been celebrated as a turning point, the moment when Britain sought to move past its historical legacy—its colonial barbarity, its role as a financial and logistical hub for the slave trade—applying its wealth and ingenuity toward more honorable pursuits.

"We as a country said, 'We have been cruel. Let's be nice now and look after everyone,'" said Simon Bowers, a general practitioner at a medical center in Liverpool. "The NHS has everyone's back. It doesn't matter how rich or poor you are. It's written into the psyche of this country."

When I visited him in 2018, Bowers's clinic was packed with people waiting for hours for the chance to see a doctor. He saw the fingerprints of austerity on the stress-related ailments he was increasingly encountering—high blood pressure, heart problems, sleeplessness, anxiety.

This was not the result of reasoned health policy.

"It's a political choice, to move Britain in a different way," he said. "I can't see a rationale beyond further enriching the rich while making the lives of the poor more miserable."

As British voters went to the polls in June 2016 to decide whether to remain in the European Union, austerity was not on the ballot, but its impacts framed the question.

The Leavers claimed that a hidebound, rule-obsessed government in Brussels was preventing Britain from achieving its destiny as a swashbuckling global power. They promised that the country would forge trade deals with faster-growing nations like China, India, and the United States. Trade with these countries was unlikely to rise to more than a fraction of commerce with Europe, but symbolism had greater currency than math.

In calling the vote, Prime Minister Cameron was betting that, following a noisy campaign, Britons would back the sensible option to remain. But he and Osborne did not grasp the extent of the loathing that much of the electorate felt for their kind. They were creatures of the elite, Davos Man collaborators who had both been members of Oxford's notorious Bullingdon Club, a private, male-only dining society with a reputation for excessive drinking, public vandalism, and other consequence-free hijinks reserved for people of extraordinary privilege. They had used their power to make Britain hospitable to people like Jamie Dimon.

Their miscalculation became apparent on the night of the vote, as the BBC began reporting the returns. The first results came from Sunderland, a city in the north of England whose largest employer was Nissan, the Japanese automaker. Nissan made cars in Sunderland and then shipped them across Europe duty-free, an arrangement imperiled by Brexit. The company's CEO had publicly expressed a "preference as a business" that Britain remain within Europe. Surely, worries about paychecks would trump other considerations.

Instead, Sunderland voted heavily in favor of bolting Europe.

Months later, I took a train to Sunderland to try to understand what had happened. By then, the permutations of the Brexit vote were clear. Britain was headed into years of wrangling over its future relationship with Europe. Investment was slowing. Whatever damage resulted would surely hit Sunderland as hard as anywhere.

Why had people there voted for this?

I huddled with Nissan workers and talked to a restaurateur who had voted for Brexit as a way to limit welfare payments and was already experiencing "Regrexit" as he struggled to hire dishwashers. The Eastern European immigrants who typically took such jobs were abandoning England. But the truest thing I heard—and pardon the foreign correspondent cliché—came from a taxi driver.

"No one here really understood what Brexit was, or what would happen if we voted for it," he told me. "We just knew that people in London had been fucking us for as long as we could remember. Thatcher fucked us. Then Cameron and Osborne fucked us. And then Cameron and Osborne came up here and asked us to help them by voting against Brexit. We weren't voting with that lot. It was our chance to fuck them back."

There were many other reasons why voters sent Britain toward the European exits. The Leave campaign catered to fears of terrorism, displaying photos of Muslim refugees arriving in Europe. They promoted Brexit as the means of shutting the door on immigrants. The campaign lied about the money that Britain would supposedly save by leaving the E.U., enabling spending on domestic priorities like the National Health Service. They withheld the fact that Britain received funds from the European bloc and would see its own coffers diminished by a hit to trade.

But the argument ultimately boiled down to whether voters bought into what Britain had become—an important component of a larger European bloc, increasingly multicultural, and integrated with the world—or preferred to chase visions of what the nation had been long ago: a stand-alone imperial power.

The Leavers coalesced around the mantra that Brexit was about taking back control. It was a cynical play for nostalgia pressed by a renegade faction of Davos Men who ran hedge funds and gambled on real estate. They waved the Union Jack in pursuit of control over one area that was of unique benefit to them—financial regulation. Their nostalgia was a yearning for a time when they could draw on English social networks to write the rules without the intrusions of European bureaucrats.

"We want out of burdensome, unnecessary regulation," Richard Tice, a London property magnate who cofounded the Leave campaign, told me when I went to see him a month before the vote. The economy would be in for "a bit of bumping and boring" in the years ahead, he acknowledged. "Life's not just about money," he said.

Tice's firm managed a hoard of real estate worth in excess of $750 million. He filled out a double-breasted blue suit as he occupied a bench above the lobby of the upscale May Fair Hotel, where a two-bedroom suite ran $4,300 a night. "It's like an extension of my office," he said. Waiters raced fearfully, bearing trays laden with flutes of champagne. A red Maserati sat parked in front of the entrance.

European Union regulators had responded to the financial crisis with rules that restricted the operations of hedge funds. They were subject to a blizzard of paperwork, required to disclose their reserves, limited in their borrowing, and forced to adhere to curbs on their compensation. Most ominously, they could sell only to "professional investors," with retail customers walled off for their own protection.

These new rules posed a threat to the pursuit of the next chateau. Brexit offered a way out, a return to the golden age in which hedge fund managers could run their operations however they desired.

One hundred executives from within British finance signed a letter backing the Leave campaign. "We worry that the EU's approach to regulation now poses a genuine threat to our financial services industry," it declared.

Among the most prominent signatories was the hedge fund manager Crispin Odey, whose wealth was estimated at £825 million. He had once sunk £130,000 into outfitting his country estate with the world's most indulgent chicken coop, a Palladian-style gray zinc temple adorned with an Athenian statuette that was soon known as "Cluckingham Palace." He had also contributed nearly £900,000 to the Leave campaign. Another signer was the hedge fund manager Paul Marshall, possessor of a fortune estimated at £630 million.

These were the people financing a campaign that was saturating Britain with bombastic talk of reclaiming sovereignty, ending the indignity of European marginalization, and returning money to the people.

The real story of how Brexit came to dominate British life was similar to how Trump had ridden the anger of steelworkers into the Oval Office, putting him in position to shower billionaires with tax cuts. It was a rebellion of the dispossessed against Davos Man, whose gluttony had yielded austerity, one fomented by a subset of Davos Men who sought the freedom to resume the recklessness that had started all the trouble.

Brexit would prove hazardous to its overseers, a witches' cauldron whose poisonous fumes wafted unpredictably over the landscape.

The day after the mortifying rebuke of the Brexit referendum, an ashen-faced Prime Minister Cameron resigned. He was replaced by the politically hapless Theresa May, who had publicly opposed Brexit during the 2016 campaign, yet inherited the unenviable job of making it reality.

May suffered through three years of ritualized parliamentary torture in a failed effort to craft something that could technically qualify as Brexit without disrupting important elements like membership in the single market, all the while menaced by rebellions from within her party. After a lifetime's worth of humiliation, she handed the unfinished business of Brexit to her successor, Boris Johnson.

Johnson was another product of posh English society—a classmate of Cameron's at Eton College, the elite school that had yielded no fewer than twenty British prime ministers. He was a political cartoonist's dream, with a globular face fringed by a mane of studiously wayward hair, and a physique that attested to intimate familiarity with the inside of a steakhouse. He had started his career as a journalist, making his name in Brussels with a series of factually creative attacks on the E.U. He took power with a mandate to "get Brexit done." Conventional wisdom had it that he would be devoured like May.

But Johnson possessed the advantage of being unburdened by any definable set of beliefs. He appeared beholden only to his desire to continue in residence at 10 Downing Street. And he was bestowed a magnificent political gift: his opposition party interlocutor, Jeremy Corbyn, was as beloved as wet socks.

Stylistically and politically stuck in another era, Corbyn had served as a member of Parliament since 1983. He had long nursed antipathy to the E.U. from the left. This undermined his party's potential appeal as a gathering place for the growing number of citizens who were appalled by Brexit. Even as a majority of voters shifted to thinking that Brexit was a mistake, Johnson capitalized on Labour's weakness to wrest an overwhelming majority in national elections in December 2019.

Johnson's triumph signaled the end of the first phase of the civil war. Brexit was going to happen. Would it happen via a deal with Europe, or in a chaotic plunge into uncharted waters? No one knew. But some version of Brexit lay ahead.

Yet Johnson's victory was tempered by recognition that the path forward was perilous. He owed his office in large part to communities in the north of England, where traditional Labour voters had flipped Conservative. If he wanted to hang on to their support, he was going to have to liberate them from austerity. He had to unleash spending on rail lines and roads to put people to work. He needed to dramatically increase funding for the National Health Service. All of this would require money.

But Johnson also owed a debt to his Conservative Party base, which demanded a real Brexit. Not the soft kind that May had tried to finesse, but a clean break with Europe. That was going to take away money by disrupting trade.

Johnson either could deliver on his mandate to take Britain out of the European orbit, or he could expand the economy to come up with funds to make life less miserable in the industrial communities that had embraced him. It was difficult to see how he could do both.

Decades of economic strife for ordinary people had produced Brexit. The messy process of negotiating Britain's separation from Europe threatened to stretch on indefinitely toward Brexiternity. Which perpetuated the economic strife.

After months of histrionics and threats to walk away from the negotiating table without any sort of trade deal, Johnson finally struck a minimal agreement with Europe in December 2020 preserving key aspects of commerce across the Channel. But the deal pointedly left out finance, prompting Dimon to envision a day when his bank might abandon Britain altogether.

"Paris, Frankfurt, Dublin and Amsterdam will grow in importance as more financial functions are performed there," Dimon wrote in a letter to shareholders released in April 2021. "We may reach a tipping point many years out when it may make sense to move all functions that service Europe out of the United Kingdom."

On the other side of the English Channel, another Davos Man collaborator eyed the discord in Britain and saw an opportunity to entice some of its bankers to decamp for Paris.

CHAPTER 5

"IT HAD TO EXPLODE"

Davos Man's President

In a nation famous for its sneering hostility to business, Emmanuel Macron—a former investment banker with starstruck eyes for billionaires—centered his presidency on the proposition that gratifying the wealthy would yield greater opportunities for France.

"For our society to get better, we need people who succeed," he said in 2017, in the first months of his tenure. "We shouldn't be jealous of them. We should say 'fantastic.'"

Macron's allegiance to the Cosmic Lie both shaped his policies and imperiled his tenure. He slashed taxes on the wealthy, and then affixed a new levy on gasoline, enraging working people and provoking the furious protests known as the Yellow Vest movement.

As he reconfigured the national pension system, Macron treated one billionaire like an oracle—BlackRock chairman Larry Fink, the Davos Man who managed more money than anyone, and whose counsel influenced the French approach to retirement savings. When the public learned about Fink's involvement, Macron absorbed withering accusations that he was selling out the interests of the French populace for the pleasure of billionaires.

In seeking to turn France into a refuge for Davos Man, Macron threatened the habitat for all.

Macron had spent most of his life marinated in the thinking and social conventions of the wealthy. He had worked in the investment banking division at Rothschild, a company uniquely intertwined with the history of globalization, having financed the construction of railway lines across Europe, and the British government's military adventures.

Nakedly ambitious, Macron had prepared to lead France all his life. He had written an undergraduate thesis on Machiavelli and then secured a master's degree from Sciences Po, a breeding house of the French elite, whose alumni included seven French presidents and thirteen prime ministers. Then he trained for a career in the civil service at another preparatory ground for the ruling class, the National School of Administration. It had been founded by his hero and role model, Charles de Gaulle, the leader of French forces against the Nazis, and the dominant national figure during the first decades of the postwar era.

Macron's self-assurance, English fluency, chic suits, and admiration for billionaires put him in good stead at the World Economic Forum, where he projected a sense of representing an updated version of France long before he captured the presidency.

His election was celebrated among the moneyed as a signal that France was shaking off decades of antipathy toward business.

"We believe that this presidency is favorable for France and above all Europe," Larry Fink said in June 2017. "France will energetically change its economy."

At a gathering to promote Paris as a financial center, Jamie

Dimon said Macron would prove a spur for "entrepreneurship, growth and jobs," laying out the welcome mat for the affluent.

"It's nice to be wanted," Dimon added.

At a mere thirty-nine years of age, Macron was the youngest president in the history of the republic. He was well versed in the realities of the digital age, a seeming curative for the antiquated state of French life, which was too often romanticized as respect for tradition.

He had captured office by distinguishing himself as the least objectionable alternative to the doomed candidates presented by the French establishment. The Socialist Party had imploded. Its standard-bearer, the incumbent president Francois Hollande, was too unpopular to even muster a run for reelection. Macron had served as Hollande's economy minister before bolting as the party careened toward irrelevance. The center-right was rife with internal discord.

Macron had run as a technocrat who would pragmatically fix what needed fixing. He built a new party from scratch, En Marche, deploying it as evidence that he was beholden to no camp. He raised a campaign war chest of nearly 16 million euros, an astonishing haul that was proffered as evidence of a popular groundswell.

But this missed the point. From inception, Macron cultivated power by extending himself as a Davos Man collaborator.

Nearly half of his campaign funds were harvested from a mere eight hundred donors. Far from a popular revolt storming the Bastille, he represented the palace court elevating one of its own. Macron's fund-raising operation was run by a former executive of BNP Paribas, a major French bank. It included Emmanuel Miquel, a former senior leader at JPMorgan Chase. A Rothschild director, Philippe Guez, hosted a fund-raiser at his Paris apartment, offering a venue for other bank executives to meet with Macron. The bank's managing partner, Olivier Pecoux, organized a fund-raiser on the Champs-Élysées.

During Macron's turn as economics minister, he and his wife, Brigitte—his former literature teacher—regularly entertained France's wealthiest people at their Paris apartment, which overlooked the Seine. Sometimes, they hosted two dinners in a single night.

Nearly every week, they dined with Bernard Arnault, the chairman and chief executive officer of Moët Hennessy Louis Vuitton, the world's largest maker of luxury goods. His company's empire of brands included Christian Dior, Bulgari, and Givenchy. Catering to people willing to spend $150,000 on a piece of luggage had supplied Arnault with a fortune estimated at more than $100 billion, making him one of the three wealthiest people on earth.

Arnault's yacht, *Symphony,* was longer than a football field and boasted six decks, including a dance floor, a golf practice range, a heliport, and an outdoor cinema. Its glass-bottom swimming pool was fed by a waterfall. He owned a villa in the seaside resort of St. Tropez, a private island in the Bahamas, a palatial home in Paris, and a world-famous winery in Bordeaux, Château d'Yquem, whose rich and honeyed dessert wines inspired poetry. His collection of modern art included works by Picasso, Andy Warhol, and Jeff Koons.

Among Arnault's passions were playing the piano, wandering the flower gardens of his estates, and conjuring new ways to avoid paying taxes. He quickly surmised that Macron could prove useful in the latter pursuit.

As economy minister, Macron had opposed Hollande's failed effort to impose a 75 percent levy on incomes above one million euros, warning that this would make France "like Cuba without the sun." Arnault had been so alarmed by this proposal that he had applied for a Belgian passport to avoid the tax, provoking accusations of treason.

Arnault used a newspaper that he owned, *Les Echos,* to publish an op-ed endorsing his friend's candidacy. "Emmanuel Macron's program is built on the conviction that private enterprise is the only effective lever for sustainable, healthy and massive job creation in France," Arnault wrote. "A company that is not hindered in its development, that is not distracted from its desire to grow by unreasonable taxation or bureaucratic procedure, has no other agenda than to invest, innovate and create sustainable jobs."

Arnault did not appear hindered. He was a master at the art of avoiding taxation. His yacht was worth about 130 million euros, making it liable for wealth taxes of about 2 million euros a year. Arnault's accountants had made that bill disappear by putting *Symphony* under the official control of a shell company that was registered in the tax haven of Malta. The shell company graciously leased the vessel back to its purchaser for the exclusive enjoyment of Bernard Arnault.

When journalists suggested that this arrangement made Arnault a less than wholesome source of counsel on economic policy, Macron defended his dining partner. "What you call tax fraud is not criminally punishable by law," he told a television interviewer.

For Macron, Arnault's savvy and wealth were the very point of his endorsement. It validated Macron's relevance as a candidate, inspiring other rich people to contribute to his campaign. His fund-raising targeted bankers, entrepreneurs, lobbyists, and influencers, promising liberation from taxes.

Macron focused special attention on reversing the exodus of wealthy French people. He set the tone with a fund-raising dinner in October 2016 in a villa outside Brussels owned by Marc Grossman, founder of Celio, a popular French menswear brand. There, the future president promised attendees that he would ax wealth taxes. He took several trips to London, which was home to three hundred thousand French citizens, securing donations from expatriates working in international finance.

In a runoff election, Macron extinguished the noisy insurrection of the National Front, the extremist-turned-mainstream party led by Marine Le Pen, whose growing popularity and shrill denunciations of Muslim immigrants were heightening alarm over Europe's tilt toward right-wing populism.

Macron could be easily lampooned for grandiloquence. He had famously likened the French presidency to Jupiter, the king of all gods in Roman mythology. (Even Trump, who made no secret of his envy for the earthly powers of Vladimir Putin and Xi Jinping, had not reached to the heavens for authority.) But no one could accuse Macron of lacking vision. Far beyond France, he inspired hope as an antidote to the forces of nationalism and illiberalism.

At Davos in January 2018, he packed the main auditorium for his keynote address. Macron presented himself as the remaining guardian of liberal democracy, casting French revival as central to the preservation of the post–World War II order. He prescribed greater European solidarity as the requisite response to Brexit, Trump, and the debasing of democracy.

"If we want to avoid this fragmentation of the world, we need a stronger Europe, it's absolutely key," Macron told the Forum. "France is back at the core of Europe, because we will never have any French success without a European success."

He was intent on delivering the one thing required to undercut the appeal of Le Pen and other hate-spewing opportunists: economic growth. He would root out the lethargy that had seeped into the national identity, with the unemployment rate stuck near 10 percent. He would boost education while enhancing research in areas like artificial intelligence to inculcate the skills needed to prosper in a modern economy. He would invest in technologies that could transform France into a world leader in attacking climate change. The best and the brightest French minds would return from London, New York, and Silicon Valley, turning France into a hotbed of innovation. Growth would inoculate the nation against the anger that was poisoning democracies around the globe.

"If I cannot explain to people that globalization is good for them, and that it will help them develop their own lives, then they will be the nationalists, the extremists who want to get out of the system," he said in Davos. "And they will win in every country."

Key to this refashioning was unshackling businesses from the strictures of archaic rules that discouraged risk-taking.

Macron's first undertaking—a major refashioning of French labor law—put him directly at odds with the country's trade unions. Though they represented less than 10 percent of the French workforce, they had long proved their ability to mobilize the masses, unleashing strikes that could bring the country to a standstill. Macron was seeking to rewrite a famously obtuse collection of French labor rules that filled out 3,324 pages.

Firing workers in France was costly and time-consuming, involving lengthy severance and legal processes. This made hiring employees akin to marrying them. If the relationship proved unfulfilling, divorce entailed expensive agony, giving French employers commitment phobia. They increasingly tended to rely on contract and temporary workers, which kept joblessness high and wages low.

Over the previous two decades, legitimate full-time jobs—the kind that could enable a person to buy a home and plan a life—had remained flat, at about 1 million, while the number of contracts lasting less than a month exploded from 1.6 million to 4.5 million.

Macron's reform rested on a logical premise: If firing workers became easier, employers would take the plunge and hire. People with better jobs would spend more, boosting economic growth.

Macron was aided in his mission by the fact that the largest

French unions were themselves removed from the broader interests of the populace, functioning as a privileged club for their members. They were mobilized in defense of the continued employment of the predominantly white, middle-aged, native-born French who filled out their ranks.

One in five young people under twenty-four was unemployed. The *banlieue*—the grim, distant suburbs ringing major cities—were full of African immigrants who had never known formal employment. The full extent of the crisis was unknown, because measurements of racial disparity were all but forbidden in France—a vestige of the Nazi past, and a testament to the French fantasy of equality for all.

The unions were almost comically disinterested in discussing how to create jobs. When I posed the question to Manu Blanco, a board member of the CGT, one of France's largest unions, he suggested that the workweek be shortened from its current thirty-five hours so that more people could share in the existing labor. Only in France could a union boss suggest that the solution to not enough work was to work less.

Street demonstrations predictably greeted Macron's refashioning of the labor rules, but he divided the unions, winning measured support with promises of additional severance. He packaged his alteration as sensitive to French social mores. This was not American-style capitalism, in which Jeff Bezos ran his warehouses like gulags, but a gentler variant, like Nordic-style free enterprise. Within months, the strikes dissipated. The reforms became law.

But then Macron overreached, staking his political capital on bestowing a handsome gift to Davos Man. He delivered on his promise to eviscerate the wealth tax, effectively lowering it by 70 percent—a measure that was expected to cost the state 10 billion euros over the first three years.

He maintained that this generosity toward billionaires

would attract investment from overseas and spur businesses to expand.

The resulting anger was immediate, intense, and unrelenting.

France seemed an unlikely venue for a sustained outpouring of civil unrest. Economic inequality was nowhere near the levels in the United States or Britain. France delivered comprehensive national health care to every citizen. Only Denmark, Sweden, and Belgium spent a larger share of their economies on social welfare programs for working-age people.

But the gap between the affluent and everyone else had been widening for decades. Between 1983 and 2015, the wealthiest 1 percent of French households had seen their average incomes double, while the rest of France—the bottom 99 percent—saw their incomes climb by only one-fourth.

And the big picture masked extreme forms of inequality— between people in cities and those in towns and villages; between those with full-time jobs and the growing ranks of temporary workers; between the old and the young, who were largely excluded from government programs.

Equality had special currency in France. The ideals of the French revolution—*liberté, egalité, fraternité*—functioned as more than words engraved above the entranceways of government buildings. They were a covenant between the state and the people.

In previous eras, disaster had proved a leveler. The years between the start of World War I and the end of World War II saw a dramatic reduction in inequality by destroying the wealth of those who controlled most of it. For the next two decades inequality widened. Then came the explosive strikes and occupations at universities and factories in May 1968, a quaking revolution that was cultural as much as political—a backlash to the conservatism of de Gaulle, to traditional sexual mores, to the American war in Vietnam, to capitalism itself.

Laying down the template that Macron would deploy a half century later, de Gaulle boosted the minimum wage to appease the demonstrators. The result was greater spending power for the poor, closing the inequality gap.

But the 1980s began the reversal. Much as Thatcher slashed social programs in Britain, and as Ronald Reagan led the revolt against government in the United States, successive French administrations nullified wage increases for the poor while reducing unemployment benefits.

By 2014, barely 20 percent of national spending on social programs was being directed at households in the bottom fifth of French incomes—a smaller share than in the United States. Funds that had previously gone to the poor were going to people like Arnault.

For those drawn to the Yellow Vests, Macron represented not some new outrage, but the final straw.

The wealth tax had been designed to soften the impact of the country's broader refashioning. It had been instituted in 1982 by France's first Socialist president, François Mitterand, as a means of bolstering social programs. Ever since, it has served as a prop in depictions of France as antagonistic to affluence, exhibit A in the stereotype that France was run by beret-wearing beatniks who saw anyone donning a gray suit as an enemy of the people.

Macron argued that scrapping the tax on everything except real estate would advertise that France was eager to welcome foreign capital. It was a message tailored in part to encourage people like Jamie Dimon to contemplate Paris as a sanctuary for the bankers that JPMorgan Chase would pull from Britain as Brexit unfolded.

In another play for London business, Macron pledged to slash the tax rate on private equity profits from 75 percent to 30 percent—a direct sweetener for executives like Steve Schwarzman.

Once in office, Macron moved slowly, lest he disrupt his

primary objectives, especially the labor reforms. But Macron's most loyal base—Davos Man—was impatient for the bonanza. The wealthiest people in France had been incensed by a speech from Prime Minister Edouard Philippe in the summer of 2017 in which he delivered the news that the wealth tax would remain in place for another two years. Three days later, at an annual economic forum held in the city of Aix-en-Provence, executives let it be known that they were nursing feelings of betrayal. The organizers of the forum, a neoliberal think tank called Cercle des Economistes, demanded that Macron immediately eviscerate the wealth tax.

Members of a powerful collection of French companies, the French Association of Private Enterprises, secretly met the president at the Élysée Palace to express their displeasure over the delay. Among the members of the association was Arnault's company. Shortly after the meeting, Macron's Finance Ministry announced that the tax would be gone the following year, 2018.

Lifting the wealth tax did entice wealthy people to move to France. But it produced no discernible boost to investment. A report from the French Senate Finance Committee later concluded that the tax reduction saved the one hundred wealthiest people in France an average of 1.2 million euros a year. They did not use this money to expand factories, launch new businesses, or hire people. They bought cars, shares of stock, and added to Arnault's fortune by snapping up Louis Vuitton luggage and cases of Dom Pérignon champagne.

"There is no trickle down effect," the chairman of the committee told the panel. "This is a considerable gift made to the rich."

The year before its abolition, the wealth tax had applied to 351,000 French households in a country of 67 million—the richest one-half of 1 percent. Among the beneficiaries of the cut were the president and his wife, who owned a home in Le Touquet, a seaside playground for wealthy Parisians.

Macron had delivered to his base, but at the cost of reinforcing his hold on an unwanted moniker—President of the Rich.

It was a title he had earned one revelation at a time.

First came word that, during his first three months in office, Macron had racked up a 26,000-euro bill for makeup services. For his fortieth birthday, Macron threw himself a party at the Château de Chambord—a multispired estate with no less than 282 fireplaces, set in a game reserve in the Loire Valley—prompting accusations that he was cavorting about like a monarch. This notion was only enhanced by the disclosure that Macron had ordered a new set of 900 dinner plates and 300 side plates for the Élysée Palace, at a cost potentially reaching 500,000 euros, followed by news that Macron was seeking to install an opulent new swimming pool at his presidential hideaway on the Côte d'Azur.

Macron's expensive tastes coincided with his penchant for whining about bloated state budgets and the stubborn refusal of the commoners to make themselves rich—as if their neglecting to upgrade their own swimming pools reflected a failure to prioritize.

The government "spends a truckload of cash on social programs," Macron said in one especially disastrous turn on television, "but the people are still poor." He had lectured workers aggrieved about a factory closure in a rural area, telling them to "stop messing around" and simply move somewhere that had jobs.

These episodes could not be dismissed as gaffes. They revealed Macron's core identity as someone marinated in the worldview of Davos Man, with a sense of entitlement to some of the spoils.

This was the backdrop in the fall of 2017, as Macron made the decision that would define his presidency. Having slashed the tax bill for friends like Arnault, he increased taxes on gasoline, arguing that this was needed to encourage the transition to green energy.

Across France, protestors donned yellow safety vests—the uniform of the working class—and brought the country to a halt.

Paris, where Macron resided, had an efficient network of public transportation—a comfortable subway system, and ubiquitous public buses to go along with a network of bicycle paths. Nearly everywhere else in France, people relied heavily on cars to get to jobs, schools, and stores.

In many communities, people viewed the gas tax as proof that their struggles were irrelevant in Macron's calculation. His justification was especially galling. His pursuit of a greener France would play well in places like Davos, while they were forced to pay for it. As one popular Yellow Vest slogan put it, "Macron is concerned with the end of the world. We are concerned with the end of the month."

The gas tax turned Virginie Bonnin, a forty-year-old single mother of three, into a foot soldier in the rebellion that shook the country. She lived in Bourges, a city of sixty thousand people in the heart of the country. Bourges was centered around a Gothic cathedral, its warren of narrow streets giving way to drab suburbia, with big-box retail shops and auto lots extending into the surrounding fields.

Once a hub of munitions factories and textile plants, Bourges had seen many of its jobs disappear. The plants that remained were increasingly inclined to hire temporary workers.

"We are disposable," said Bonnin, who had spent most of her working life in local auto parts plants.

She was earning 1,900 euros a month. She had to wait until Thursday night to learn her hours for the coming week, making it difficult to manage her parenting responsibilities. This sort of lament was familiar for Americans, who associated it with Walmart workers, but it was increasingly the reality in France, too.

When Bonnin's jobs ended, unemployment benefits typically sustained her. "I have enough to get to the end of the month, but it's tricky," she said. "In those times, I will not eat meat so that the kids can eat meat."

The gas tax landed atop months of increasing fuel prices.

"You put fuel in the tank to go to work," she said, "and then you work to be able to buy fuel."

Her Facebook feed filled with angry posts and calls for action. People planned to gather at a highway on-ramp south of the city. They would put on their yellow vests and block trucks and cars.

On the first day the movement convened, a chilly gray morning in November 2018, Bonnin was among the several hundred people who showed up. As they stood on the pavement, physically preventing France from carrying on with its business, most of the drivers stuck in the ensuing traffic jam tooted their horns in solidarity.

"Everyone is fed up," Bonnin said. "It had to explode."

The Yellow Vest movement soon disrupted nearly every city in France. Protestors flooded Paris, smashing the windows of banks and shops, setting fire to cars, and even vandalizing the Arc de Triomphe. They tangled with the police, who unleashed rubber bullets and tear gas to quell the fury.

Macron, who usually appeared unflappable, looked besieged. After several weeks, he reversed course and suspended the gas tax. It was an extraordinary concession in the face of violent opposition. It was also too late.

The protests were no longer about a single policy, or even about what Macron had come to represent. The Yellow Vests had captured favor as an expression of outrage over the violation of the central idea of France; the understanding that social harmony would flow from equality. Macron could scrap the gas tax, but he could not take back the injury he had inflicted on the national psyche, the sense that he had trashed France's moral code.

The protests went on, destroying Macron's aura of technocratic calm, and pushing his approval rating as low as 23 percent. Five months in, he held a series of town halls around the country to listen to the complaints, then submitted to the first press conference of his presidency.

"One can always do better," he said. "We haven't always put the human at the heart of our project. I've given off the feeling of always giving orders. Of being unfair." He committed to "a profound reorientation of the philosophy I believe in—more human, more humanist."

Macron promised 5 billion euros' worth of tax cuts for the middle class. He vowed to stop closing hospitals, cease shuttering rural schools, and even banish to history the National School for Administration, the elite institution where he had trained for the civil service.

But money was of limited use in a conflict now propelled by a sense of unfairness. Bonnin's family lived in an affordable apartment paid for in part by a government housing subsidy. What had drawn her to the Yellow Vests was less a feeling of desperation than a deepening sense of grievance.

"Having to make sacrifices while rich people aren't paying taxes anymore," she said. "There's a sense of despair, as well as a sense of social injustice."

The Yellow Vests congregated inside a crude tent they had fashioned on the southern edges of Bourges, in the field of a sympathetic farmer, near the traffic roundabout that had been their first point of mobilization.

Inside, a dozen people occupied wooden benches, drinking instant coffee and passing around cigarettes. Some stood outside in a drizzle, huddling around a makeshift firepit—a pile of burning construction pallets.

An older man lamented that his pension did not cover his bills. A twenty-year-old woman named Coralie Annovazzi complained that she was still living with her parents as she bounced from one temporary waitressing job to the next. People her age were excluded from government benefits like cash grants for those with low incomes.

Her hatred for Macron was visceral, yet nothing provoked harsher words than a group of people much closer at hand—

refugees from Afghanistan, Sudan, Sierra Leone, and other war-torn countries, who were living in a former motel alongside the highway. To Annovazzi, their presence constituted proof that she and her people had been displaced.

"These migrants, they have gotten the latest sneakers, the latest smartphones, and all of that is paid for by the state," she said.

Another woman, Claudine Malardie, leapt up to offer support. The refugees were "constantly sexually assaulting local women," she said. "If you're French, you don't get any assistance, and if you're foreign, you do," she continued. "Give me a pot of black paint and I'll paint my face in black, and then I will get benefits."

When I pressed her to justify this racist depiction, Malardie let slip that she did in fact receive benefits—an 860-euros-a-month disability payment. She lived in public housing, paying only 300 euros a month in rent for a state-subsidized apartment.

She did not know anyone who had actually had contact with the refugees. As for the claim that the men were assaulting local women, Malardie acknowledged that she was just repeating something she had heard. "I read it on Facebook," she said.

The notion that the refugees explained the troubles of the French working class did not endure even minimal scrutiny. The ninety-nine mostly young men stuck in the former motel were sitting quietly in their rooms when I went over to have a look. They were not allowed to work while they waited for their asylum claims to be processed, so they were using a collection of weathered schoolbooks to study French, or texting with friends and relatives back home. There were no shops within walking distance, so they rode the bus downtown to buy groceries, trying to stretch out the 200 euros a month they received in public support.

If these were the people who had stolen French prosperity, they were keeping it well hidden.

But the migrants provided an opening for the opportunistic far right. As she campaigned for European parliamentary elections in early 2019, Marine Le Pen laid claim to representing the Yellow Vests.

"The battle is now between nationalists and globalists," she declared. Her party emerged with the highest vote total.

Despite the rebuke from the Yellow Vests, Macron was not finished with his project to refashion France. In the fall of 2019, he embarked on his restructuring of the French pension system.

France was spending 14 percent of its economic output on pensions, compared to an average of 8 percent in the world's most developed nations. The typical French worker was retiring at sixty. The system comprised forty-two separate pension schemes, each with its own convoluted rules and boondoggles secured by one union or another.

Macron had been so bludgeoned by the Yellow Vests that he began the mission by promising not to raise the retirement age or diminish what the government spent on pensions. He merely aimed to impose order. He would take the tangle of separate pension programs and reconfigure them into one unified system.

The unions smelled a ruse. As they saw it, spending lots of money on pensions should be considered a point of national pride—the hallmark of a civilized society—not a problem demanding reform.

Under the existing pension system, people were generally entitled to retire at a standard matching the average of their twenty-five best years of earnings. Macron was proposing to replace this with a setup in which people earned points during their careers, with their final total determining their pension payments. The certainty of a state-furnished retirement would be ditched for something that looked like lotto. Some people were going to lose.

One figure had positioned himself to land among the ultimate winners—a Davos Man who had, over decades, quietly amassed unrivaled influence over the movement of money around the planet: Larry Fink had gained Macron's attention and was deftly using it to help refashion the French retirement system, transforming it from a walled-off refuge mostly beyond reach of the global financial services industry into an enticing frontier.

Fink was among the most consequential figures in finance, yet curiously unknown outside his realm. His company, Black-Rock, had successfully wandered the globe, persuading pension systems, university endowments, health care networks, and other institutions to entrust it with managing their portfolios, taking control of more than $7 trillion. Along the way, Fink had become a billionaire, and a Zelig-like figure in global capitalism, a behind-the-scenes adviser to presidents, central bankers, and fellow Davos Men.

He had proven especially adept at winning the trust of the most deep-pocketed client of all, the United States government.

"He's like the Wizard of Oz," the former investment banker turned financial journalist William D. Cohan once remarked. "The man behind the curtain."

Raised in the sprawl of the San Fernando Valley, north of Los Angeles, Fink headed east after business school, launching a career on Wall Street.

He landed at First Boston bank, in what was then a sleepy preserve of American finance—bond trading. Fink helped turn it into a raging profit center, developing a new kind of bond called mortgage-backed securities. By buying individual mortgages, pooling them together, and then selling the resulting bonds to investors, home loans were transformed into the raw materials for a wildly lucrative investment vehicle.

Fink's innovation was initially progressive, diminishing the risks of mortgage lending and promoting home ownership. But

Wall Street's excessive gambling on mortgage-backed securities would emerge as a leading cause for the global reckoning of 2008.

Fink built his reputation as a master of the intricacies of complex corporate restructurings. At the age of only thirty-one, he had reached the status of managing director, the youngest in First Boston's history. But in 1986, he committed a grievous error that cost the firm $100 million, a bad bet on a rise in interest rates. That mistake—which Fink blamed on the analytical systems he had relied on—destroyed his career at the bank. It also marked the beginning of his obsessive interest in harnessing the computing power used to process data.

Two years after that episode, Fink left the bank and joined Steve Schwarzman's firm, Blackstone, running a bond-trading venture under a boutique arrangement they called BlackRock.

It was extraordinarily profitable, but Fink and Schwarzman possessed too much ego and bravado to peacefully coexist. They clashed over how to distribute the winnings, prompting Schwarzman to sell the unit to a bank in Pittsburgh for a mere $240 million, a rare atrocious transaction for one of Wall Street's master dealmakers.

Fink's company swallowed up competitors in a slew of mergers, and sold its shares to the public in 1999. It expanded from bonds into every sphere of finance—stocks, real estate, hedge funds.

BlackRock's scale supplied a unique perspective on the global marketplace. This itself became the source of its most substantial line of business. Chastened by his costly error at First Boston, Fink had overseen the development of a computer-driven risk management system that scoured portfolios for unseen perils, simulating the effects of abrupt changes in market sentiments, shifts in interest rates, and other consequential developments. The advanced system, known as Aladdin, gave BlackRock the capacity to identify risks lurking in the markets. In the mid-1990s, Fink figured out that he could sell Aladdin to other financial institutions as a service. Jamie Dimon's bank was using it. So were more than one hundred other financial institutions.

Aladdin is what positioned the company to win the business of the ultimate investor, Uncle Sam.

As Washington unleashed bailouts amid the financial crisis in the fall of 2008, the government took control of vast portfolios of bonds and other securities. Someone would have to manage all these investments. Larry Fink got the job.

He was in prime position, because he was an insider's insider. In the months before the crisis, BlackRock had worked for nearly every major player in the unraveling—the insurance giant AIG, Lehman Brothers, and the two government-backed mortgage companies, Fannie Mae and Freddie Mac. His team of data experts had probed their portfolios, supplying him intimate knowledge of the risks.

As U.S. Treasury Secretaries Hank Paulson and Timothy Geithner formulated the federal rescue response, they relied on Fink's counsel. When legal questions nearly derailed JPMorgan Chase's emergency takeover of Bear Stearns—specifically, whether the Treasury had the authority to cover losses incurred by the Fed in serving as guarantor—Fink settled the issue. He told Paulson and Geithner that BlackRock could supply the Fed a letter attesting to the minimal risk of further losses.

Fink had been wrong about some not-insignificant details. Even after Bear's collapse, he had counseled his clients to make larger bets on riskier investments in pursuit of greater rewards. And he publicly vouched for the solidity of Lehman Brothers before the giant investment collapsed, sending waves of terror across the financial landscape.

But Fink possessed something invaluable—the confidence of the people running the system.

Under its arrangement with the United States government, BlackRock assumed control of taxpayer-owned portfolios stuffed with the detritus of disastrous trading positions forged by its clients—Fannie and Freddie, AIG, and Bear Stearns, by then under Dimon's control.

This presented a gaping conflict of interest. BlackRock was at once influencing the prices of distressed debt and trading in it.

Fink scoffed at such talk. "Our clients trust us," he said.

There was truth to that assertion. With his unremarkable clothes, balding pate, nervous energy, and old-school wire-rim spectacles, Fink's brand was that of a details-fretting nerd. His leisure time was spent not on gargantuan yachts but at his home in Colorado, where he was partial to fly-fishing. Arnault could wax poetically about the magnificence of Sauternes. Fink was a devotee of In-N-Out Burger.

Of course, he was also a regular at San Pietros, the Italian restaurant in midtown Manhattan that functioned like a private club for connected money people, drawing bank chiefs, the head of the New York Stock Exchange, and even Bill Clinton. He was a reliable attendee of the World Economic Forum, later taking a seat on its board of trustees. This gave Fink a perch from which to ingratiate himself with the Davos Man collaborator running France.

In June 2017, less than a month after assuming office, Macron hosted Fink at the presidential palace. Later that month, Macron's economics minister, Bruno Le Maire, traveled to New York to court Wall Street investment. His schedule included a dinner with Fink. Four months after that, Macron's government convened a panel of thirty experts to formulate plans for the pension reform, including the head of BlackRock France.

BlackRock helped organize a summit convened at the presidential palace with nearly two dozen investment firms featuring discussion of emerging opportunities in France, including pension reform. Fink signed a note that was sent to participants and marked "Confidential—Not for Distribution." It described the summit as a chance for "unique and dynamic conversations" with the top leaders of the nation. "We will spend all day discussing the transformative vision of President Macron with representatives of his cabinet."

Fink attended the summit. He brought with him another Davos Man collaborator—George Osborne, the former British chancellor of the exchequer, and architect of austerity. A year after the debacle of the Brexit referendum, which had cost Osborne his job, he had reinvented himself as an instrument of the financial services industry.

Osborne's calamitous oversight of the treasury had helped produce Brexit, while turning him into a villainous figure in his own country. But the experience had also supplied him with an inside understanding of the interaction between finance and government—a valuable commodity for which Davos Man was willing to pay.

Osborne was pleased to sell. In the months after the Brexit referendum, he collected more than £600,000 for a series of speeches to financial services firms including Citibank and BlackRock.

Osborne was also working for HSBC, a notorious bank that was frequently being probed in one European country or another for its willingness to help clients with their tax evasion needs.

In 2015, when he was still running the treasury, Osborne had cut a special bank tax in an effort to persuade HSBC to keep its headquarters in London. Brexit prompted HSBC to reconsider those plans. In Davos in January 2017—six months after the Brexit referendum—HSBC's chief executive said the bank was considering moving perhaps one thousand jobs to Paris. That same year in Davos, HSBC threw a private event for twenty clients, featuring a talk from Osborne.

A few days later, Fink announced that he had hired Osborne in an advisory role. "At the center of our mission is helping people around the world save and invest for retirement," Fink said in a statement. "George's insights will help our clients achieve their goals."

Osborne would work only four days a month for BlackRock, for which he pulled down £650,000 a year. Now, in late October 2017, he was devoting one of those days to counseling Fink on how to extract profits from retirees in France.

At the summit in Paris, Osborne made a presentation titled "Geopolitics and the Market." It was followed by a series of talks from Macron's cabinet officers—on the pension and labor reform plans, investments in French transportation, and opportunities for international finance.

As the French press would later note, none of the ministers entered these meetings into their official diaries, hiding them from public view. The summit ended with a reception with Macron.

Two years later, as Macron began the push to reconfigure the pension system, BlackRock had insinuated its aims into the government's own proposals.

According to a BlackRock analysis published in October 2019, France beckoned like a gold mine for international asset managers. The French were sitting on mountains of savings entrusted to cash and conservative government bonds. Only about 5 percent of French savings were in stocks as compared to 34 percent in the United States.

BlackRock urged the government to promote the adoption of private retirement accounts in which ordinary people could invest in a basket of stocks.

These details garnered little attention among the French public until January 2020, when Macron conferred the ultimate distinction on the president of BlackRock France, Jean-Francois Cirelli, elevating him into the ranks of the country's Legion of Honor. The head of the local branch of the world's largest asset management company was now officially a national hero.

The pension reform plan had already stirred up a vociferous protest movement. On the barricades, the public acclaim for the BlackRock chief appeared to validate every suspicion about

Macron: he was a tool for international finance; the President of the Rich selling out the public interest by funneling national savings to Davos Men.

Nearly one hundred protestors stormed BlackRock's office in Paris, accusing the company of a conspiracy to seize public wealth. They spray-painted anticapitalist slogans on the walls and carpets before the police arrived to make arrests.

BlackRock protested that it was an innocent bystander. "We deplore the fact that our company continues to be caught up in an unfounded controversy driven by political objectives," the company said in a statement. "We reiterate that BlackRock has never been involved in the current pension reform project and does not intend to be."

But whether and how BlackRock had lobbied for pension changes notwithstanding, Fink's company was certain to benefit from any shift of French savings into the stock market by dint of being the largest money manager on the planet. Buying almost anything in the global marketplace—stocks, bonds, mutual funds—presented the likelihood that BlackRock would capture a piece of the action.

Davos Man had won the day. Macron's party had the power to institute his pension alteration, histrionics aside.

Despite his perpetual humiliations, the taunting names, and the accusatory slogans, Macron had produced no less than a revolution: France was now governed by the same principle that had spurred upward mobility for billionaires from the United States to Britain—the idea that the key to national salvation was making life more rewarding for people like Larry Fink.

The Cosmic Lie had so comprehensively captured the globe that it was even shaping economic policy in the ultimate bastion of social democracy—Sweden.

CHAPTER 6

"EVERY STONE I LOOKED UNDER WAS A BLACKSTONE"

How Davos Man Conquered Utopia

As a special rapporteur on housing for the United Nations, Canadian human rights lawyer Leilani Farha traveled the world, documenting the impacts of financial players trading housing like fungible commodities—the evictions and foreclosures, the trauma for families forced to abandon homes and neighborhoods, the rootlessness and despair.

In Prague, Farha learned of a building full of Roma, a vulnerable minority group long subject to extreme discrimination. They were being pushed out by a new development and threatened with imminent homelessness. Farha was surprised to discover that an American company was an investor in the project. She soon encountered the same firm in Germany, Spain, and the United States.

"Every stone I looked under was a Blackstone," Farha told me. "They were ubiquitous."

Blackstone was the world's largest private equity firm. It was in control of an unrivaled global collection of real estate—a landlord mercilessly devoted to the extraction of profit. Over the years, Blackstone's cofounder, Stephen A. Schwarzman, had applied his inexhaustible drive to assemble a business empire like no other.

Through a series of holding companies and joint ventures, Schwarzman's firm had taken control of apartment blocks, houses, and office buildings in cities around the world, employing the same basic playbook: Buy cheap, in communities where tenants were vulnerable. Raise rents, impose fees, and flip the assets to someone else.

It was a model that had proved bountiful to Schwarzman's shareholders and traumatic to the communities in which he operated.

Blackstone was present even in Sweden, the supposed paragon of enlightened social democracy. The company had invested with a local partner in a low-income community on the outskirts of Stockholm, where tenants were outraged about diminished service, exponentially higher rents, and evictions.

Farha found this astounding. Sweden was by reputation the sort of country that seemed engineered to prevent the predation of billionaire landlords.

But that notion was fast becoming out-of-date.

Like nearly everywhere else, Davos Man had captured the upper hand in Sweden, persuading the government to slash taxes for the wealthy. Economic inequality was widening. Public services were stretched, sowing popular unhappiness. This had created an opportunity for a right-wing party with roots in the neo-Nazi movement, the Sweden Democrats. The movement was gaining support by blaming Sweden's problems on immigrants. Much like in France, Italy, and the United States, this formulation proved highly effective in capturing votes, but its explanatory power was misdirected. It provided a reprieve to the real culprits for Sweden's troubles—Davos Men like Schwarzman.

Among the sources of unhappiness in Sweden was the

difficulty of finding affordable housing—a reality that reflected how Schwarzman and other billionaires had upended the real estate market.

In March 2019, Farha and another U.N. special rapporteur focused on human rights wrote a letter addressed to Schwarzman personally.

"The financialization of housing is having a grave impact on the enjoyment of the right to adequate housing for millions of people across the world," their letter declared. "As one of the largest real estate private equity companies in the world, with $136 billion of assets under management, operating in North America, Europe, Asia and Latin America, your practices are significantly contributing to this."

The letter directly cited a neighborhood Farha had visited in Sweden, where tenants had been pushed out by higher rents. It accused Blackstone of applying "significant resources and political leverage to undermine domestic laws and policies"— specifically, stripping away rent control laws.

Blackstone defended itself with impeccable Davos Man logic. Its real estate ventures were not the cause of distress. They were, in fact, the solution.

"We share your concern about the chronic undersupply of housing in major metropolitan centers around the world," the company wrote, "and are proud that Blackstone has contributed to the availability of well managed rental housing by bringing significant capital and expertise to the sector."

There comes a point in nearly any conversation about economic inequality where someone starts talking about Sweden.

Among those in favor of government playing an active role in tackling social problems, Sweden serves as shorthand for an ideal approach. It operates on the so-called Nordic Model, the economic setup that prevails throughout Scandinavia, enjoying exalted status among many economists as a proven means of softening the rough edges of capitalism. The model retains the virtues of market forces—innovation and competition—while putting a floor beneath society, preventing homelessness and destitution.

The key has been a shared willingness among Sweden's people to pay some of the highest taxes on earth in exchange for generous public services. Health care and education are universally available and furnished by the state. When a baby is born in Sweden, the parents are guaranteed 480 days of leave, to be divided between them. That policy, combined with government-provided childcare, has enabled Swedish women to work at higher rates than in nearly any other country.

Unions sit down with employer's associations to hash out contracts that establish basic pay scales, with everyone clear that workers are entitled to a representative share of the profits. When people lose their jobs, they gain comprehensive unemployment benefits and access to a remarkably effective job training program.

Americans tend to view our own winner-take-all system as the genuine form of capitalism, while dismissing the Nordic variant as nanny state socialism. But this is backward. Capitalism as practiced in the United States has been hobbled, not promoted, by the nation's minimalist social safety net. How many laid-off steelworkers might be able to train for more productive careers if a year of college did not cost as much as a BMW? How many startup companies never come into being because Americans are dependent on employers for health care, making people afraid to try something new?

In Sweden, government officials like to say that they protect people, not jobs. They allow the markets to sort out which businesses succeed and which fail, while ensuring that workers are cushioned against the consequences.

In 2017, I visited a mining operation in the center of Sweden, where truck drivers were slated to be replaced by self-driving vehicles. Crews that used to journey into the frigid mineshaft, inhaling dust and exhaust fumes, had been superseded by a handful of workers who sat inside, using joysticks to control robots that physically extracted silver and nickel.

In much of the world, automation was a source of terror for working people, a direct threat to their paychecks. Robots never got sick and had no interest in spending time with their families. "Frugality drives innovation," Bezos had once said. He was putting that principle to work in developing drones to replace delivery drivers and robots to take over from warehouse workers. In many countries, unions were mobilizing in resistance to automation.

Not in Sweden. The miners put stock in the Nordic Model. They expressed faith that if their company gained greater flexibility to proceed with automation, that would lift profits, and they would wind up sharing the gains.

But that faith rested on the assumption that the Nordic Model would itself endure. And that proposition was confronting a stiff test in the form of Europe's largest per capita influx of refugees.

The refugees were arriving from some of the most troubled places on earth—Syria, Somalia, Afghanistan, and Iraq. They bore physical and emotional scars. They required housing, health care, mental health counseling, and job training. Their children needed schools. All of these things cost money.

The traditional willingness of Swedes to finance extensive public services had long rested on a basic understanding: everyone had to work.

Many of the newcomers would face difficulty forging careers in Sweden. They didn't speak Swedish, and often lacked education.

"People don't want to pay taxes to support people who don't work," said Urban Petterson, who held a seat on the local governing council in the town of Filipstad, in the lake country west of Stockholm. "Ninety percent of the refugees don't contribute to society. These people are going to have a lifelong dependence on social welfare. This is a huge problem."

These sorts of stereotypes were common among Petterson's party, the Sweden Democrats. Its members tended to write off migrants as lazy parasites, despite the fact that most were busily studying Swedish and training for careers. The party was exploiting the migrants as an opportunity for a needed makeover. It was recasting its racist rejection of multiculturalism as a form of fiscal rectitude.

As we sat in a cafe in the center of town in June 2019, Petterson spoke of budget math in describing his opposition to immigration. But the longer we spent together, the more he betrayed his basic discomfort with the presence of Somali women pushing shopping carts on the streets of his town.

"These groups don't have the same language," Pettersson said. "They have different religions, different ways of life. If there's too many differences, it's hard to get along. It's interesting to meet someone from another country for half an hour. But if you're going to live together it's tough."

The Sweden Democrats had emerged from the political wilderness to capture mainstream status. The party had run third in national elections in 2019 on the strength of the message that integrating refugees was a drain on the treasury.

In Filipstad, the local government had initially embraced the refugees as a solution to a budget problem. Surrounding iron ore mines, once a major employer, had been shuttered in the 1970s. The town's population had been halved from twenty thousand to ten thousand, as people left in search of work. Those who remained tended to be older, requiring expensive health care. Looking after senior citizens was a core responsibility of municipal governments. With the tax base shrinking, who would pay to take care of the grandparents?

In the designs of the government, the refugees would fill the gap. Most of the people arriving needed public support, but their children would grow up speaking Swedish. They would be educated in Swedish schools, making them fully capable of forging careers. Their taxes would finance needed services.

"This doesn't shake the Swedish welfare model in any way," Claes Hultgren, the municipal manager in Filipstad, told me. "Rather, when we have succeeded with these people, they will be a huge resource."

Decades of Swedish experience suggested this was true. The problem was that the government was not following through with the needed support.

The first refugees began arriving in Filipstad in the 1980s, mostly from the Balkans. The current wave had begun in 2012, cresting in 2015, when 160,000 people applied for asylum. Sweden was a country of 10 million. This was the equivalent of 5 million people arriving in the United States in a single year.

The national government bused them en masse to Filipstad, taking advantage of the availability of empty housing. When municipal officials expressed concerns about the costs of integrating so many, the government sent money covering the first two years. After that, the cash stopped on the understanding that the refugees would by then be ready for work.

But that was delusional. The first arrivals had included doctors and other skilled professionals, who were easy to integrate. The later arrivals were far more challenging. As I visited in 2019, the town held 750 working-age refugees. Five hundred had never completed high school, and 200 were illiterate.

"The state keeps saying we need to prepare people fast," said Hannes Fellsman, who ran the municipal training programs. "That's impossible. You have to educate them."

In my meetings with Sweden Democrats, every conversation about immigration seemed to begin with careful talk of government allocations before veering to their revulsion over Sweden becoming a more diverse society.

Another member of the Sweden Democrats on the Filipstad council, a bus driver named Johnny Grahn, groused about the cuts the town had been forced to make as it expended more on the refugees. It had eliminated a coordinator for activities at a senior center. People were enduring interminable waits for dental care.

"There is almost a collapse in the system," he said. "All of these cuts are made to balance the budget, which is right now being dominated by welfare. When there are so many people arriving who don't work, the whole thing falls apart."

Then he told me about the mosque that had been constructed in town. The early morning call to prayer was waking longtime residents, Grahn complained. Preschools were "inundated" with refugee children, he said. Violent crime was increasing.

"We are talking about people who don't want to learn Swedish, and don't want to enter society," he said. "Integration isn't just about us helping them. They have to want it."

This sort of nonsense collapsed upon meeting nearly any migrant who had endured the journey here.

In the south of Sweden, I spent an afternoon with a refugee from Afghanistan named Babak Jamali. Six years earlier, when he was only thirteen, he had fled the war in his native Afghanistan, riding in the trunk of a car through Pakistan and into Iran. There, he found construction jobs for $2 a day, while he squatted in half-finished apartment blocks. Lacking legal papers, he was perpetually vulnerable to police who would shake him down for bribes. He hired a smuggler to truck him into Turkey, and then to Greece. He rode buses up the Balkan peninsula and eventually to southern Germany. Another Afghan refugee told him life would be easier in Sweden, so he caught a train to the city of Malmo.

For the last year, he had been living with an artist outside the town of Horby, in an old brick house that lacked plumbing. By law, he could not work while his asylum case was pending, so he was studying Swedish, attending classes six days a week in the hopes of eventually training to become an electrician. To get to class, he walked fifteen minutes up a dirt road—even in subzero winter temperatures—and then waited for a bus to town. One driver refused to pick him up, forcing him to wait for the next bus. Sometimes, passing drivers hollered at him, telling him to go home.

In the pie charts assembled by officials tasked with managing refugees, Jamali presented as the worst-case scenario—the sort of person most likely to draw indefinitely on the beneficence of the taxpayer. He had not completed middle school and spoke very little Swedish. But that profile masked the reality that he had navigated terrifying obstacles to get here, and was intent on working toward a career. Surely this was testament to intelligence and drive.

"I want to live the way other people live," he told me.

The racism that infused the Sweden Democrats was not incidental to their view of public finances. It was the driver of a growing aversion to paying taxes, a sentiment that threatened the Nordic Model. The spirit of collectivism began fraying once the beneficiaries of community largess included large numbers of people who were different from the majority.

A similar erosion of solidarity was fundamental to understanding the antitax rebellions in the United States, beginning in the 1980s. Racial integration prompted the white power structure to dismantle public works.

In the American South, the ending of racist Jim Crow laws in the 1960s had begun the exodus to the suburbs by white families seeking distance from Black communities. Dependent on their minivans for transportation, professional-class white families balked at paying taxes that financed services like public transportation.

By the 2010s, as the United States sought to escape from the Great Recession, unemployment offices in cities like Atlanta and Nashville were full of African American men who could not reach available jobs. Many lived downtown, while work had gravitated to the suburbs. The public bus did not bridge the divide.

Once Black people secured equal rights on public transportation, white taxpayers starved the system of finance. Rosa Parks had gained the right to sit wherever she liked on the bus. Except now there was no bus.

Sweden was supposed to be more compassionate. But Sweden was one of the most homogeneous societies on earth. As native-born Swedes confronted the fact that their taxes were financing the settlement of people who looked different and prayed to different gods, some refused to go along.

The framing of the argument over immigration and the impact on public resources spared one central actor of scrutiny: the billionaires whose success in shedding their tax burden had forced decades of budget cuts.

Sweden was indeed struggling to maintain its traditionally generous public services. But this was not because newcomers had arrived, constructing cacophonous houses of prayer and monopolizing dental care.

It was because Davos Man had added Sweden to the confines of his refuge.

When he died in January 2018 at the age of ninety-one, Ingvar Kamprad, the founder of IKEA, was celebrated as a national icon. Along with the inevitable jokes about whether his coffin had required assembly from a flat pack, his passing afforded an opportunity to recount Sweden's version of the Horatio Alger story.

Kamprad had launched his first business as a five-year-old on his family farm, buying matches in bulk and selling them retail to his neighbors. Soon, he was hawking Christmas decorations, ballpoint pens, and watches. By the time he was seventeen, he had his own mail order catalogue, using a milk van to deliver his wares to the local train station. Then, he moved into furniture. People liked the sleek, angular look of what he was selling, and they especially liked the prices. That formula would turn IKEA into the largest retailer of furniture on earth.

Kamprad famously disdained the typical trappings of a tycoon, flying economy class. He drove an old Volvo—a requisite detail in every profile (though he also drove a Porsche). He wore secondhand clothes that he purchased at flea markets, and he made a point of getting haircuts when he was in low-wage countries like Vietnam. He had a habit of showing up unannounced at IKEA stores around the world and pretending to be a customer to test out the experience. In his bearing and demeanor, he looked like just another guy snagging a cheap bookcase before grabbing a plate of meatballs.

Not all of the details of his biography were endearing. Kamprad had been forced to acknowledge his participation in a fascist group that had been sympathetic to the Nazis. He had a legendary temper that he would train on unfortunate subordinates. But mostly he displayed a composite of traits that Swedes were inclined to see in themselves—hardworking, resourceful, innovative, and willing to travel great distances in advance of a good idea.

Yet if Kamprad was Sweden's most celebrated entrepreneur, he was also a symbol of a more dubious achievement—the triumph of Sweden's wealthiest people in lowering their tax bills.

In 1973, he abandoned Sweden to get out from under its hefty taxes, which then reached as high as 90 percent, moving to Denmark, and then to Switzerland. In 1982, he transferred control of IKEA to a foundation registered in the Netherlands, a legal ruse that allowed the company to pay minimal taxes.

"His philosophy throughout the years has been that IKEA should at all costs avoid paying taxes," Kamprad's longtime assistant wrote in a memoir. "Ingvar does not for reasons unknown to anybody but himself, want to see taxes go to the general well-being of people. Health service, schools and social care are, so to speak, not part of the Kamprad vocabulary."

He made contributions to charities, "but only symbolic sums," his assistant wrote, accusing IKEA's founder of bearing "an avarice so limitless that it is difficult to understand for any ordinary taxpayer."

In 2013, following the death of his wife, Kamprad returned home to Sweden. Over the four decades of his absence, the country had made itself more hospitable to people of spectacular means, in part to dissuade future Kamprads from leaving.

It had dropped its top income tax rate to 57 percent while eliminating many levies on property, wealth, and inheritance. It had cut corporate taxes. The net effect was a reduction in government revenue equivalent to 7 percent of national economic output (though some 40 percent was recovered by closing loopholes and broadening other taxes).

Sweden paid for this reduction by slashing public spending from about 65 percent of its overall economy to just above 50 percent. It privatized government services, including care for elderly people.

Much of the refashioning reflected how Swedish policymakers were, like their counterparts almost everywhere, embracing the thinking of economists like Milton Friedman. On university campuses, in think tanks, and in policy journals, some economists began to portray the state as less the solution to social problems than an obstacle to national dynamism.

"It's like fashion," said Torbjörn Dalin, chief economist at Kommunal, a Swedish trade union. "You don't think that you're following fashion. You're not interested in that. But when you look back at the picture, you can see that, 'Okay, I am following it, even if I don't understand it.' Of course you're following it. It's like a mindset that is coming from everywhere."

True to form, economists warned that Sweden's generosity toward workers was unsustainable. Economic growth fueled by government spending had rendered joblessness largely unknown for the Swedish populace, with the average rate of unemployment just above 2 percent between 1960 and 1994. But business leaders complained that the government was subsidizing industries that were not internationally competitive. As wages rose, inflation spread through the Swedish economy.

By the fall of 1992, Sweden's central bank lifted interest rates as high as 75 percent to choke off inflation, while preventing a plunge in the value of the currency, the krona. The economy contracted violently. By the following year, the unemployment rate was above 8 percent.

As Sweden pursued the goal of joining the European Union, gaining admission in 1995, the government slashed public sector jobs to comply with the bloc's limits on debt. Sweden reduced job training and unemployment benefits. It curtailed spending on childcare, added fees to the national health care system, and diminished care for the elderly.

Sweden's largest companies used global expansions to push wages lower, employing a threat recognizable to their unions in the United States: work more for lower pay or watch production get moved overseas.

And as Sweden's government gratified wealthy people with tax cuts, its ministers parroted the Cosmic Lie that they would pay for themselves by prompting investment.

Some of the funds Sweden spent on world-class social programs were given to people like Stefan Persson, scion of the founder of H&M.

In the years following Sweden's elimination of the wealth tax, he did indeed increase investment—in the English countryside. He purchased an 8,700-acre country estate, an entire English village complete with medieval chapel and a cricket pitch, plus another 8,500-acre manor where he meandered the grounds shooting partridge and pheasants like a lord.

Incomes in Sweden were widening faster than any wealthy economy on earth. Those ensnared in poverty doubled to 14 percent of the population between 1995 and 2013.

Meanwhile, those at the top were raking it in—especially as the value of real estate soared.

Throughout the country, one in four young adults was living at home with their parents, in large part because the cost of housing was beyond them. People were waiting fourteen years for apartments at rents regulated by the state.

The situation was especially dire in Stockholm, where the vacancy rate was about 1 percent, as compared to 3.8 percent in that bastion of affordable housing, New York City.

Among those responsible for driving housing prices higher was Steve Schwarzman.

Like every Davos Man, Schwarzman wielded his origin story as protection against those inclined to scrutinize the injustice of one man ending up with so much.

"I grew up in the middle-class suburbs of Philadelphia, absorbing the values of 1950s America: integrity, straightforwardness, and hard work," he wrote in his memoir.

As a teenager, he chafed at having to spend his weekends working in his father's store, Schwarzman's Curtains and Linens. Instead of attending high school dances, he was stuck measuring drapes.

The United States was in the midst of the post–World War II construction boom. Millions of soldiers freshly returned home were raising families, driving explosive demand for new housing. Schwarzman implored his father to turn the store into a national chain.

"We could be like Sears," he told him.

But his father was guilty of an emotion Schwarzman would never grasp—contentment.

"Steve," he told his son, "I'm a very happy man. We have a nice house. We have two cars. I have enough money to send you and your brothers to college. What more do I need?"

Schwarzman needed more.

Near the end of his senior year at Yale, he exploited his inclusion in the secret society Skull & Bones to seek counsel from another member, W. Averell Harriman, the diplomat who had done a turn as governor of New York. Harriman invited him for lunch at his home on the Upper East Side of Manhattan.

When Schwarzman confided that he entertained thoughts of a political career, Harriman, then nearing eighty, posed a question: "Young man, are you independently wealthy?"

"No," Schwarzman replied.

"Well," Harriman told him, "that will make a great difference in your life. I advise you, if you have any interest in politics whatsoever, to go out and make as much money as you can. That will give you independence if you ever decide you want to go into politics. If my father wasn't E. H. Harriman of the Union Pacific Railroad, you wouldn't be sitting here talking to me today."

Schwarzman forged a career on Wall Street. He started at the lowest rungs of the investment bank Donaldson, Lufkin & Jenrette, occupying a cockroach-infested, fourth-floor walk-up apartment on Manhattan's Lower East Side. When an older colleague invited him to dinner at her family's Park Avenue apartment, where the library displayed de Kooning paintings, Schwarzman recognized a superior way of living.

He landed at Lehman Brothers, where he made partner in only six years, and cultivated a bond with the company's then-CEO, Peter G. Peterson, who had served as secretary of commerce in the Nixon administration.

When Peterson was forced out of Lehman in a purge, he and

Schwarzman joined forces to start their own shop. Blackstone, launched in 1985, took its name as an amalgam of its founders— *schwarz*, which means "black" in German, plus *stone*, derived from the Greek meaning of "Peter."

The business they pursued, so-called private equity, was a sanitized term that replaced its disgraced predecessor, the leveraged buyout industry. Its corporate raiding techniques had been a hallmark of the 1980s and its poster child, Michael Milken, the financier who spent nearly two years in prison for securities fraud. The outlines of the strategy were unchanged: borrow astronomical sums of money, buy companies, slash costs (often through mass firings), and extract huge dividends before flipping the assets.

Bank robbers plotted getaways; private equity magnates pursued exits.

The key to the formula was leverage. If you paid $10 for an asset and sold it for $11, that spelled a $1 profit, a mere 10 percent return. But if you borrowed nine of the ten dollars, putting down only one, the same $1 gained became a 100 percent profit.

Peterson and Schwarzman persuaded pension funds to entrust them with their savings. They tapped university endowments and medical institutions. They enticed well-heeled international players to invest, courting sovereign wealth funds stuffed with Persian Gulf oil fortunes.

One select group prospered alongside Blackstone's executive ranks: tax lawyers, accountants, and lobbyists employed to keep the grubby hands of the government off the spoils.

Schwarzman and the rest of Blackstone's executive ranks treated their slice of the winnings as so-called carried interest— accountant vernacular for income taxed at barely half the rate as that paid by suckers in other trades.

Blackstone expanded, launching a hedge fund that profited from volatility in the global marketplace. It started another fund to invest in real estate.

Schwarzman's personal real estate portfolio grew in tandem. In 2000, he paid $37 million for a thirty-five-room apartment spread over three floors of a New York Art Deco landmark that had once been owned by John D. Rockefeller—740 Park Avenue. His neighbors in the building included Steve Mnuchin, the former Goldman Sachs executive who would become Treasury secretary in the Trump administration, and John Thain, the CEO of the ill-fated investment house Merrill Lynch.

Three years later, Schwarzman paid nearly $21 million for a 13,000-square-foot British Colonial–style mansion in Florida. It was designed by the Palm Beach architect Maurice Fatio and designated a historic landmark, but Schwarzman had it dismantled and reassembled in larger form, much to the consternation of local preservationists. Three years after that, he spent $34 million for a place in the Hamptons, adding it to a collection of beach houses that included an estate in St. Tropez and a waterfront spread in Jamaica.

"I love houses," he once said. "I'm not sure why."

Blackstone would soon tap the stock market, filing the paperwork for an initial public offering in early 2007. The process required that the firm open its file cabinets for public perusal, revealing it had $78 billion in assets on its balance sheet.

The world soon learned what the IPO was worth for Schwarzman—$677 million in cash, plus 24 percent of the stock, for a stake valued at $8 billion. He and the other beneficiaries harnessed the power of creative accounting to shield $3.7 billion in income from taxation.

By then, the zeitgeist had moved against him, casting Schwarzman as a symbol of the excesses of the age. The press hailed him as the new king of Wall Street, especially as Blackstone closed the largest private equity deal in history, paying $39 billion for a trophy case of American commercial real estate. His executive chef in Florida confided to the *Wall Street Journal* that entertaining Schwarzman for a weekend entailed spending $3,000 on groceries, including stone crabs that ran $40 a claw. Schwarzman had once interrupted his poolside sunbathing to complain that an employee was not wearing the requisite black shoes with his uniform.

Peterson, displaying his political savvy, tried to warn his younger partner to avoid ostentatious displays of wealth. But that advice was overwhelmed by Schwarzman's visions for his sixtieth birthday.

He and his wife, Christine Hearst Schwarzman, rented a brick-fronted armory that occupied an entire block on Manhattan's Upper East Side. They decked it out with orchids and palm trees, while adorning the walls with replicas of Schwarzman's private art collection, including a full-length portrait of the birthday boy. They hired the comedian Martin Short and the pop star Rod Stewart. The soul artist Patti LaBelle sang "Happy Birthday." The guests included a real estate magnate named Donald Trump, the billionaire and New York mayor Michael Bloomberg, and several Wall Street CEOs, among them Jamie Dimon. The cost of the party was estimated at somewhere between $3 million and $5 million. Schwarzman would later describe it as "a celebration with six hundred people we cared about."

A century earlier, a New York socialite, Cornelia Martin, had left her own mark on the Gilded Age with a notorious soiree at the Waldorf Hotel. The guest list ran to almost eight hundred, the ruling elite of the time decked out in homage to the icons of affluence among their European forebears. More than one attendee dressed up as Marie Antoinette, whose lavish spending had helped lead the nation into insolvency—and her neck to the guillotine. The revelers did not present their comforts as a sign of a just society. "We are the rich," one guest declared. "We own America. We got it. God knows how, but we intend to keep it."

Schwarzman and his fellow Davos Men were not satisfied

with mere wealth. They demanded that society ratify their privilege as morally sound. Schwarzman enjoyed the hedonistic pleasures of a maharajah while claiming standing as an everyman.

"I don't feel like a wealthy person," he once said. "Other people think of me as a wealthy person, but I don't."

Others certainly did. Shortly after Blackstone's stock offering, the Senate Finance Committee introduced a bill that sought to dramatically increase taxes on private equity firms. It diminished the carried interest bonanza. Nicknamed "the Blackstone bill," its four bipartisan cosponsors included a young senator from Illinois named Barack Obama. Another bill in the House produced similar results, threatening to increase Blackstone's tax rate from 15 to 35 percent, while providing the Treasury with an additional $26 billion over the next decade.

Schwarzman stayed true to the plan that he had hatched decades earlier with Harriman. He had amassed wealth as a means of wielding influence. Now, he used his influence to protect his wealth.

He joined with other industry players and formed a trade association, the Private Equity Council. The council and its member companies unleashed a battalion of twenty lobbying firms. Blackstone alone would spend nearly $5 million on lobbying in 2007.

They trained their attention on Senator Chuck Schumer, a Democrat from New York, the state that was, not incidentally, home to Wall Street. Schumer deployed a novel means of pretending to champion public interest regulation while guaranteeing the maintenance of the status quo: he recast the bill to broaden its reach, making it applicable to real estate, which guaranteed wider opposition. The bills died.

Even in victory, Schwarzman did not stand down. He bolstered his armor by hiring Washington insiders drawn from Republican and Democratic administrations alike. Between 2011 and 2020, Blackstone and its employees donated nearly $54 million to candidates for federal offices and their so-called super PACs, pools of campaign cash stocked with corporate proceeds.

Meanwhile, Schwarzman pursued a fresh obsession. The American economy was sinking into the most punishing recession in seventy years. Millions of households were falling behind on their mortgages. As the new Obama administration failed to marshal meaningful relief, a tsunami of foreclosures resulted—a magnificent opportunity.

Blackstone dispatched purchasing teams to auctions held on courthouse steps. By late 2014, Schwarzman's company had spent $7.8 billion—most of this borrowed money—to amass some forty-one thousand homes scattered across more than a dozen American cities, with the bulk concentrated in the Sun Belt states of California, Florida, Arizona, and Georgia. Its portfolio was focused on neighborhoods with large numbers of African American and Latino families.

Eventually, Blackstone's investments in foreclosed homes would swell to $10 billion. The company created a new entity to manage its kingdom of distressed real estate: Invitation Homes.

In Schwarzman's telling, his mass purchase of foreclosed homes was an act of civic righteousness, a moment when he helped his country recover from an epic disaster.

"Millions of Americans were now looking to rent instead of buy," he wrote in his memoir, as if the foreclosure crisis represented a sudden change in consumer preferences. His company hired electricians, plumbers, and construction workers. They repaired neglected homes and hacked away at rodent-infested jungles of weeds and overgrown lawns.

"Once we fixed up the houses and leased them out to families, we saw these neighborhoods come back to life, their social fabric restored," Schwarzman wrote.

You could almost hear the soundtrack for a life insurance commercial, as an adorable toddler romped with a golden retriever puppy on the lawn of a freshly painted Colonial. But the story of Invitation Homes was less wholesome. Tenants complained of vermin, leaks, mold, and sewage backups while waiting endlessly for someone to help. Invitation invited them to pay much higher rents or pack up, while sticking households with late fees even when their lateness was the result of the company's frequently malfunctioning Web portal.

When I reached out to Schwarzman to explore these complaints, the company declined to arrange an interview, though a team of spokespeople provided statements attesting to the excellence of Invitation Homes, the falsity of reports to the contrary, and Blackstone's dedication to the public good.

Strikingly, Blackstone claimed that the company had not profited from the foreclosure crisis, because it had not owned single-family homes before the financial crisis. But the company certainly presented itself as a savvy beneficiary in its dealings with investors. In October 2013, Blackstone raised $479 million by selling bonds backed by more than three thousand distressed homes. Schwarzman celebrated the bond issue with a party for three hundred people held inside the Waldorf Astoria hotel, the same property used for the Gilded Age soiree a century earlier.

By the time it sold off the last of its stake in Invitation Homes in late 2019, Blackstone had taken in about $7 billion—more than doubling its initial stake.

American housing prices had recovered dramatically, but the gains did not flow into the blue-collar and middle-class households whose communities had been decimated. Private equity magnates, led by Schwarzman, pocketed most of the bounty.

Sweden was merely one small component of Blackstone's strategy to reap profits from real estate around the world. As the financial crisis went global, so did Blackstone's pursuit of distressed housing—a moment that Schwarzman had anticipated.

"As we look at the current situation in Europe, we're basically waiting to see how beat up people's psyches get, and where they're willing to sell assets," Schwarzman had told a Goldman Sachs conference in 2010. "You want to wait until there's really blood in the streets."

Blackstone had been active in Sweden since the mid-1990s, when it joined forces with a leading Swedish investment bank, Enskilda Securities, to pursue a buying spree across Scandinavia. Its Swedish partner included among its executive ranks a familiar presence in Davos, Jacob Wallenberg, whose family dynasty held stakes in major European companies.

In 2016, Blackstone plunked down $287 million for just less than a third of Sweden's largest publicly traded real estate company, D. Carnegie & Co., which owned and managed sixteen thousand apartments, primarily in Stockholm. It eventually upped its stake to 61 percent.

This was how Eva Kaneteg and her family got an up close look at Davos Man.

Kaneteg had lived in the same three-bedroom apartment in the Stockholm suburb of Husby for more than four decades. She had raised her two sons there. The apartment was spacious, bright, and affordable on her salary as a city bus driver.

When she moved in, the complex had been owned by the municipality. Workers promptly handled repairs. But in the early 1990s, the complex was privatized, changing hands several times.

In 2017, Blackstone effectively became her landlord.

The first sign of change was at the local customer service office, where Kaneteg arranged needed repairs. It had previously been open five days a week. Suddenly, it was open only two days a week, and then for only two hours. Kaneteg was invited to call a telephone hotline, but that typically required that she sit on hold for up to an hour.

Her apartment had not been improved for forty-four years, but Kaneteg knew she could not ask for a renovation. Her rent was determined through negotiations between the Blackstone-owned subsidiary, known as Hembla, and the tenant's association, protecting her from increases. If the landlord renovated an apartment, they were freed to negotiate individually with tenants, permitting dramatic rent increases.

"They are taking every chance they can to evict tenants," Kaneteg told me.

She was paying 8,400 kroner a month—about $950—including utilities. One of her neighbors, Binta Jammeh, was paying more than that for a mere one-bedroom apartment that had been renovated. She and her husband had moved in in November 2017. Barely six months later, Hembla had increased their rent while demanding that they pay for water and electricity—a total increase of roughly one-fifth.

Jammeh's family had moved to Sweden from Gambia twenty years earlier, when she was eight. She spoke fluent Swedish and understood her rights. She fought the increase, winning a slight reduction. But her parents and friends in the African immigrant community lacked the resources to protest, suffering from clear discrimination in her view.

"Most of our people don't want to be a problem," she said. "They just accept it as it is."

In the fall of 2019, Blackstone sold its stake in Hembla to a German residential property firm, collecting $1.26 billion. The return affirmed the company's "unwavering focus on its tenants," Blackstone's head of real estate for Europe declared.

Kaneteg was astonished by the transaction. It underscored how her home—the place where she had spent most of her sixty-four years—was just a financial play for distant powers.

"People living here got nothing," she said. "I can't fathom that one of the world's biggest private equity companies is able to dictate conditions for us and make this enormous gain without doing anything for us.

"We've never experienced this before in Sweden," she continued. "The one place that we must feel safe and secure, our homes, and we don't anymore."

What did any of this have to do with the endurance of the Nordic Model? Everything and nothing.

Davos Man's plunder, the public spending cuts, privatization, and the skyrocketing cost of housing had all played out over decades, forming the backdrop to life. The refugees had arrived in a conspicuous wave. You could see the newcomers at train stations, on shopping streets, and in parks. For the Sweden Democrats, immigrants were a useful vehicle for rallying patriotic fervor, a definable if bogus explanation for what had happened to the country.

That history could play out this way even in Sweden meant that it could happen virtually anywhere.

The grift was accelerating, and especially in the United States.

CHAPTER 7

"THEY ARE NOW LICKING THEIR LIPS"

The Donald Does Davos

As President Trump arrived in Davos for the World Economic Forum in January 2018, conventional wisdom had it that his presence was akin to the owner of a topless barbecue joint crashing a gathering of Talmudic scholars.

A year into his presidency, Trump had more than lived up to his "America First" mantra. He was attending an event premised on the importance of international cooperation—the theme of this year's meeting was "Creating a Shared Future in a Fractured World"—though he derided multilateralism as the province of suckers. Trump denied climate change and mocked anything that he placed under the rubric of "political correctness," from gender equality to racial justice—causes that the Davos crowd supposedly cared about passionately.

Yet the notion that Trump's war on the global elite set him up for a hostile reception at the Forum mistook Davos Man's animating priorities. Trump had arrived in the Alps having dramatically improved the part of the world that mattered most to billionaires—their bulging piles of money.

Little more than a month before flying to Davos, he had signed into law what he called a "big, beautiful" package of tax cuts worth $1.5 trillion. Artfully entitled the Tax Cuts and Jobs Act, it was heavy on the cuts and dubious on the rest, a fact evident to anyone paying even minimal attention to the orgy of lobbying that Davos Man had unleashed in pursuit.

The billionaires had walked away with much of the bounty in a deft bit of economic redistribution—from the bottom up.

The centerpiece of the package was a slashing of the corporate tax rate from 35 percent to 21 percent. Three-fourths of the benefits of that reduction would be vacuumed up by shareholders, with the wealthiest 1 percent of all households capturing the largest gains.

Middle-class people gained a taste of tax relief, but it disappeared after eight years, giving way to increases. A host of accounting gimmicks boosting the wealthiest people and corporations would last indefinitely.

By 2027, Americans earning between $40,000 and $50,000 per year would find themselves paying a collective $5.3 billion more in taxes, while people earning $1 million and more would still be savoring cuts reaching $5.8 billion.

"When you put all these pieces together, what you're left with is we are squandering a giant sum of money," the late Edward D. Kleinbard, a former chief of staff at the Congressional Joint Committee on Taxation, told me. "It's not aimed at growth. It is not aimed at the middle class. It is at every turn carefully engineered to deliver a kiss to the donor class."

Never one to allow principle to stand in the way of an opportunity to ingratiate himself with power, Klaus Schwab lauded Trump for his signature accomplishment.

"On behalf of the business leaders here in the room, let me particularly congratulate you for the historic tax reform package passed last month," Schwab said as he introduced Trump.

He credited the tax cuts with "fostering job creation, as well as stimulating economic growth in the United States, and also providing a tremendous boost to the global economy."

Schwab even issued Trump what sounded like a blanket exoneration for his astonishing breaches of decency—his racist attacks, his derision of women, his writing off much of Africa as "shithole countries."

"I am aware that your strong leadership is open to misconceptions and biased interpretations," Schwab told Trump. "Therefore, it is so essential for us in the room to listen directly to you."

Trump's embrace at Davos laid bare the sham at the heart of the Forum, the idea that it was dedicated to the noble concerns filling out its mission statement—"the global public interest," "the highest standards of governance," and "moral and intellectual integrity"—rather than the self-interested aspirations of the people paying the bills.

The Forum was a prop in the service of Davos Man as he pursued greater wealth and power. Everything else was artifice.

From his first day in office, Trump had distinguished himself as a man singularly hostile to the agenda that Schwab and his organization were supposedly pursuing.

He had yanked the United States out of the Paris climate agreement. He questioned the relevance of NATO, the military alliance that had prevailed in Europe since the end of World War II. Not least, Trump was readying a full-blown trade war, while issuing imperial edicts that American companies abandon China.

Trump was operating under the guidance of his chief trade adviser, Peter Navarro, an economist derided as a charlatan by many of his peers, yet celebrated in Trumpland as a truth-telling warrior. Navarro had coauthored a book called *Death by China*, which traded in the fatuous idea that American economic problems were the result of decisions made in Beijing, rather than Davos Man's manipulation of Washington.

Trump was threatening to blow up the North American Free Trade Agreement. He was mulling whether to walk away from the World Trade Organization, the linchpin of the rules-based international trading system. In the Trumpian calculus, the institution was a gratuitous impediment to American muscle-flexing. As the world's largest economy, the United States possessed the authority to dictate the rules in its own interest rather than submitting to the designs of globalist wonks in Geneva.

Trump had not been bluffing. He was serious about wrecking the postwar liberal order forged by Morgenthau and American allies in the previous century. If the rhetoric of the Forum had any meaning, Davos Man was supposed to be appalled by this historical turn, which made Trump's arrival at the Forum a source of titillating anticipation.

Much of the corporate world was indeed uneasy about Trump's tendency to call out multinational companies that had set up factories outside the United States—a clear play for support in places like Granite City. The trade war would prove debilitating to many American companies, menacing the very American manufacturing jobs it was supposed to preserve. The tariffs disrupted American factories by raising the cost of components and parts they brought in from China.

Trump would eventually impose tariffs on steel, even from stalwart allies like Europe, Canada, and Japan, while citing a justification that amounted to the nuclear option: He claimed the tariffs were necessary to address a threat to national security. In the age of America First, buying coils of metal from Ontario was akin to hiring ISIS to run security at Disney World.

Trump's trade war would cause a downturn across American manufacturing. The steel tariffs were especially damaging. Major companies like Caterpillar, which made tractors and construction machinery, were slowing production as steel prices climbed. In Michigan, factories that had resisted moving production to Mexico were suddenly contemplating that step as the steel tariffs increased their costs.

Trump was delivering on his mandate to attack China on behalf of working-class Americans. The results added injury to the people whose votes had proved crucial in putting him in office. Yet Trump remained popular in industrial communities, a testament to his genius in the one area of life in which he had inarguably succeeded—reality television. In his presidency, imagery outweighed policy.

More than seven times as many Americans worked at factories that made cars compared to those employed by steel mills. Trump's steel tariffs were damaging the competitiveness of the former to gratify the latter. But Trump understood that—as television content—a small number of people resuming work was vastly more powerful than larger numbers of people keeping their own jobs. You could point a camera at the former; the latter was a footnote in a Commerce Department report. He flew out to Granite City, donned a hard hat, and mugged for the photographers alongside beaming steelworkers as the mill reopened. Their gratitude was the defining reality.

Davos Man hoped the trade war would prove a momentary bit of theater before Trump moved on to something else. Schwarzman was alarmed by the talk of "decoupling" from China, as if the two largest economies on earth were a pair of bickering spouses. Behind the scenes, he worked both sides, using his access to Trump and President Xi to try to ratchet down the tension and prevent an expensive rupture.

Fink also served as a go-between as he pursued Beijing's blessing to operate the first foreign-owned mutual funds business in China.

Dimon fretted that a trade war was foolhardy. "There may be retaliation," he told a television interviewer. "It kind of opens up a whole Pandora's box of additional problems. It could escalate. It could hurt growth."

Every time Trump threatened fresh trade action or claimed that trade wars were winnable, the stock market retreated in horror. Though Trump portrayed any product made in another country and sold in the United States as Americans getting ripped off, investors understood global supply chains. They could calculate the hit when factories in Michigan were separated from plants that made crucial parts in China. Some hoped Mnuchin would intercede and wean the president from Navarro's wealth-destroying counsel. There were moments of ceasefire and, later, an interim deal, but major tariffs proved an unchanging feature of the Trump presidency.

This was the cost of the performance that Trump staged for blue-collar Americans—a satisfying if empty demonstration of American machismo.

Meanwhile, he gave Davos Man something solid and enduring. He handed out money.

Like Bernard Arnault in France, Steve Schwarzman was intent on cashing in on the utility of having a Davos Man collaborator in high office.

Schwarzman dined frequently with Trump at his Florida estate, Mar-a-Lago, which sat near his own waterfront mansion. Though Schwarzman had not contributed to Trump's 2016 campaign, he made up for it with a $250,000 gift to his inauguration committee.

Trump picked Schwarzman to chair a "Strategic and Policy Forum" that was supposed to advise him on economic matters. The panel also included Dimon and Fink. And as he filled out his administration, Trump surrounded himself with men (they were nearly all men) who gave Schwarzman a comfortable feeling, having dipped their beaks in the milk-and-honey of private equity.

The Commerce secretary, Wilbur Ross, had started his own private equity firm. The chairman of the Securities and Exchange Commission—the cops of finance—hailed from a Wall Street firm, Sullivan & Cromwell LLP, which touted its work for private equity as a core expertise. Trump entrusted the Treasury to Mnuchin, Schwarzman's Park Avenue neighbor and fellow foreclosure enthusiast.

Right after Trump's inauguration, Schwarzman threw another landmark birthday party, his seventieth. If the hullabaloo over his sixtieth had left him reluctant to further his reputation as the face of the New Gilded Age, this was not apparent from the extravaganza he unleashed at his Four Winds Estate in Florida. Two camels wandered the sands. A twelve-minute fireworks display exploded into the night. The pop star Gwen Stefani sang "Happy Birthday" before taking Schwarzman for a sashay across a dance floor inside a two-story tent, where acrobats leapt. The cake came sculpted in the shape of a Chinese temple complete with a dragon. This was what $9 million could buy a person intent on not letting their birthday pass without the appropriate revelry.

The guests included Trump's daughter and son-in-law, Ivanka Trump and Jared Kushner. Mnuchin was there, too. Their presence underscored the role that Trump was expected to play in ensuring that Schwarzman's eighth decade would be safe from any assaults on his storehouses of money.

Jamie Dimon was also eager to exploit the presence of a transaction-minded friend of plutocrats in the White House.

In addition to running America's largest bank, Dimon was overseeing the Business Roundtable, an association of chief executive officers. He had assumed its chairmanship in January 2017, taking over an organization that had been a less than central player in Washington. Dimon was keen to boost the Roundtable's influence by building consensus. He settled on an issue that everyone in the corporate ranks could quickly get behind: tax cuts.

He brought in Joshua Bolten, who had been White House chief of staff under George W. Bush, to serve as president of the organization. Bolten had actively campaigned against Trump, suggesting that a frequently bankrupt real estate magnate might not be the best fit for the Oval Office. But nothing makes people in Washington lose their memories faster than the smell of free money.

"That was then, this is now," Bolten said. "I'm excited about the opportunity generated by the Trump administration and Republican Congress for enactment of hugely beneficial pro-growth policies."

Pro-growth was one of those magic terms in Washington, a thing that no one could oppose. Seasoned veterans of the federal process shamelessly used it to describe practically anything—agricultural subsidies enjoyed by a handful of megacorporations, trade protections that jacked up the cost of something real for millions of consumers (snow tires, lumber) to spare a handful of political donors from competition.

But the Trump tax cuts took the masquerade to another level. The Washington ritual of handing fresh billions to billionaires required that they be presented as a tonic for the ailing middle class. The Business Roundtable unleashed a television advertising campaign that was a tour de force of cynical manipulation.

"Millions of Americans drop out of the workforce," a narrator intoned in an ad aired in August 2017 (when the unemployment rate sat below 5 percent). A camera panned across a packed line in an unemployment office, followed by a desolate business office, and then past a shuttered factory with broken windows before landing at the culprit in this exploration of decline: the headquarters of the Internal Revenue Service.

"America's outdated tax system has produced slow economic

growth," the narrator continued. "Good jobs are disappearing." The solution? "Tax reform."

Reform was another beloved piece of Davos Man nomenclature, a means of making anything sound like progress, from eliminating retirement benefits to taking money from schoolteachers and giving it to Jamie Dimon.

Trump wrapped his tax cuts in the Cosmic Lie. Corporations would invest and hire. The wealthy would spend. The money would land in the pocketbooks of waitresses and car dealers and dry cleaners.

"Not only will this tax plan pay for itself, but it will pay down debt," Treasury Secretary Mnuchin said in urging congressional passage.

That declaration provoked near-universal derision. The University of Chicago surveyed thirty-eight prominent economists across the ideological spectrum. Only one pronounced faith that the cuts would produce substantial economic growth.

Pressed by Congress to substantiate his claim, Mnuchin's Treasury produced a single-page memo that imagined fantastical rates of economic growth, yielding enough revenue to cover the cuts.

"We acknowledge that some economists predict different growth rates," the statement read—Washington argot for "This will happen right after we extract oil from Saturn."

Two years after the tax cuts took effect, corporate investment was lower than before. Rather than buying equipment and hiring people, companies used their windfall to purchase a record $1 trillion's worth of their own shares over the course of 2018, enriching shareholders. They also paid out a record $1.3 trillion in dividends that year.

Wages rose less than 3 percent in the first year after the tax cut, even as the unemployment rate dropped. The budget deficit widened by more than a third, making a mockery of Mnuchin's claim that the cuts would pay for themselves.

But the tax cuts worked perfectly as a perk for the people who mattered—Jamie Dimon and his fellow CEOs at the Business Roundtable. JPMorgan Chase reported record high earnings of $32.5 billion for 2018. In his annual letter to shareholders, Dimon acknowledged that $3.7 billion came via the reduction in corporate taxes.

Dimon took home $31 million in compensation for the year, while Wall Street paid out a collective $27.5 billion in bonuses—a sum more than triple the total earnings of every full-time, minimum wage worker in America.

Marc Benioff's company lobbied directly for the drop in the corporate tax rate. Benioff would credit the tax cuts for a jolt in investment.

"The economy is ripping," he would say later in 2018. "I can tell you emphatically that I've talked to, personally, hundreds and hundreds of CEO's—not just in this country but all over the world—and all of them have consistently said that the reason they are investing more is because of the confidence they have from the tax breaks."

The tax cuts would add to the American federal debt, already in excess of $20 trillion. Eventually, Republicans and conservative Democrats would take such numbers as the impetus for budget cutting, training their attention on programs for the most vulnerable people—Medicare and Medicaid, which delivered health care for older and low-income people, food stamps, housing aid, and cash grants for the poor.

Republicans liked to present themselves as guardians of the public purse, soberly acting out of fiscal propriety in contrast to Democrats, whom they accused of showering money on people who preferred welfare to jobs. Trump's tax cuts revealed the hollowness of this pose.

Republicans sounded the alarm about deficits when the conversation centered on elements of no interest to the Davos Men who financed their campaigns. Public debt was presented as the reason that the United States could not possibly afford the same sort of national health care that was somehow manageable in nearly every other developed democracy. Yet there always seemed to be plenty to spend on tax cuts for billionaires.

Among the more earnest participants in Davos—high-minded members of nongovernmental organizations, human rights groups, and environmental advocates—Trump's presence indeed registered as disturbing.

At a dinner he hosted annually on the sidelines of the Forum, George Soros, the financial trader and democracy advocate, warned that Trump was part of a wave of authoritarian rulers. "The survival of our entire civilization is at stake," Soros said, citing "the rise of leaders like Kim Jong-un and Donald Trump."

But within the community that spent the most, and threw the most lavish parties, Trump was the man who had just made the skies rain money.

The panel of CEOs Trump had convened to advise him at the beginning of his term, headed by Schwarzman, had been abruptly disbanded, after the president expressed sympathy for white supremacists and neo-Nazis who had marched in Charlottesville, Virginia. The business leaders could not countenance the optics of counseling a president who had described as "very fine people" the participants in a violent parade that had featured displays of swastikas and chants of "Jews will not replace us."

The tax cuts had erased such unpleasantness from the memory banks.

"There are companies all around the world who are looking at the U.S. now and saying, 'This is the place to be in the developed world,'" Schwarzman declared during a panel discussion. Privately, Schwarzman defended Trump from accusations of bigotry. "There's not a racist bone in his body," Schwarzman said frequently as he made the rounds at the Forum.

Trump threw a private dinner in Davos, inviting the chiefs

of a dozen major European companies. He walked around the table, patting the executives on the back and urging them to invest in the United States, conducting himself like a one-man economic development authority.

The next day, he took his turn at the podium in the Congress Centre to deliver his keynote address.

Trump's speech was brief, uncharacteristically mild, and even restrained. He tossed a peace offering to the internationalists, declaring that "America first does not mean America alone." Mostly, he stumped for American business, cheerleading for foreign investment.

I later ran into Nobel Prize–winning American economist Joseph Stiglitz. He had been meeting with finance people.

"They are now licking their lips," he told me. "Davos Man has been able to overlook Trump's 'America First' rhetoric, his anti-climate change action, his protectionism, nativism, racism, bigotry, narcissism, misogyny, for the lucre that seems to be the true motivating force behind Davos Man."

It would take the pandemic to reveal the full dimensions of Davos Man's voracious appetite.

PART II

Profiteering Off a Pandemic

Chaos isn't a pit. Chaos is a ladder.

—PETYR "LITTLEFINGER" BAELISH,
Game of Thrones

Protestors Criticized for Looting Businesses Without Forming Private Equity Firm First

—HEADLINE IN THE SATIRICAL NEWSPAPER
THE ONION, May 28, 2020

CHAPTER 8

"THEY ARE NOT INTERESTED IN OUR CONCERNS"

Davos Man Decimates Health Care

Ming Lin could see the danger mounting.

It was March 2020, and growing numbers of patients were turning up with flu-like symptoms at the hospital where he worked as an emergency room doctor in Bellingham, Washington.

Dr. Lin was a seasoned veteran of the emergency room. Raised in Texas, he had worked in New York during the terrorist attacks of September 11, 2001, at one of the closest hospitals to the World Trade Center. He had moved to the Pacific Northwest with his family in 2003, taking a job at the hospital in Bellingham, a small city on the Puget Sound, about one hundred miles north of Seattle. Seventeen years later, he was rooted there.

Dr. Lin's parents and his wife hailed from Taiwan, where the government had distinguished itself for early vigilance against COVID-19. He had been following the spread of the virus in Asia, making him especially attuned to the threat bearing down on the United States. The pandemic had already infected one hundred thousand people worldwide. Cases had been confirmed in Oregon, California, and in the state of Washington, where the governor had recently declared a state of emergency. Yet even as patients began arriving at Dr. Lin's hospital in March 2020, administrators seemed not to be taking the menace seriously.

People were arriving with high fevers and hacking coughs, and then left to sit in waiting rooms without social distancing. The greeters at the reception desk were not provided protective masks. When some brought their own, they were told not to wear them for fear of alarming patients.

Because of shortages, nurses inside the operating room were being supplied one surgical mask per shift, not the N95 variety that afforded greater protection. They were forced to reuse that mask as they moved from patient to patient, a disturbing breach of basic hygiene.

Dr. Lin proposed that the hospital set up an outdoor triage center, allowing doctors to assess the needs of incoming patients while limiting the risks of spreading the virus. Management ignored him. Ditto his suggestion that patients arriving for treatment should be screened with questionnaires and temperature checks: the administration worried about upsetting people arriving for lucrative outpatient surgeries.

He urged that the hospital move faster to test staff for the virus, using a local laboratory that could provide results within a day, rather than relying on its usual provider, which entailed waits of longer than a week. But the hospital's regular lab charged only $50 for a test, one-fourth as much as the quicker option—a no-go.

Dr. Lin was technically an employee of TeamHealth, a national staffing company that provided doctors to emergency rooms. When he complained to his supervisors that the hospital was jeopardizing his safety along with public health in a country of more than 300 million people, they opted not to press for changes. That might anger managers at the hospital—the paying client.

Dr. Lin was horrified that considerations of profitability were outweighing concerns about a pandemic that would eventually take the lives of more than half a million Americans. But he was not shocked. His employer, TeamHealth, was owned by Blackstone.

Steve Schwarzman had a knack for gravitating toward money. In the twenty-first century, in the largest economy on earth, money was increasingly in health care.

Americans spent $3.8 trillion on medical care in 2019 alone. That was more than double the level of two decades earlier, and an amount larger than the annual economic output of Germany. The money was changing hands in a fashion that was especially attractive to Davos Man—through transactions that were often unavoidable, and almost never transparent.

Schwarzman's real estate success had demonstrated his dexterity at exploiting the vulnerable. American health care beckoned as the ultimate opportunity. Hardly anyone understood the complexities of their health insurance policies, making medicine a rewarding sphere for price gouging. Medical care was an industry nearly impervious to economic downturns.

Hospital emergency rooms were uniquely attractive. Nearly half of all health care services were furnished there. The customer was frequently in no state of mind to haggle over costs or consider the financial consequences of submitting to care.

"A few times in every investor's life, an immense opportunity appears," Schwarzman wrote in his memoir.

One of those arrived in 2016, as Blackstone paid $6.1 billion to take control of Dr. Lin's employer, TeamHealth.

That deal was a milestone on private equity's aggressive march into American health care. Over the last two decades, the industry has invested more than $833 billion into more than seven thousand deals—$100 billion in 2018 alone.

Private equity players purchased entire medical practices (while establishing sham structures that kept doctors legally in control to avoid tripping state prohibitions). The industry focused on expensive specialties like plastic surgery, dermatology, and cardiac surgery. It captured ambulance services.

As in everything that private equity touched, health care found itself subject to intensifying demands for profit. The new owners of hospitals and clinics slashed costs, which typically involved diminishing care. They consolidated facilities and raised prices, while unleashing lobbyists and lawyers to deactivate traditional antitrust concerns. They shuttered institutions that failed to yield adequate returns.

As the logic of profit maximization gained influence—competing with the traditional imperatives of medicine—managers limited their purchases of protective gear and ventilators, undermining American readiness for future disasters. They introduced metrics that encouraged doctors to operate like units of business, focusing on enhancing revenue rather than prioritizing health.

Preparedness was subordinated to efficiency. In an era ruled by shareholder interests, a hospital room that sat unused was no different than a vacant hotel suite or an unsold car. It was capital wasted, an expenditure best skipped to free up cash to return to shareholders via dividends.

Some experts warned that entrusting vast swaths of American health care to Davos Men like Schwarzman was dangerous.

"It's the same value-extraction strategy private equity specializes in," the economist Eileen Appelbaum wrote in 2019, "only this time it's quite literally a matter of life and death."

The following year, the magnitude of the risk became inescapable, as a novel coronavirus swept across the United States and the world.

TeamHealth was one of the two largest players in the emergency room staffing industry. The biggest was Envision Healthcare, which had been purchased for nearly $10 billion by another private equity giant, KKR. Collectively, the two companies employed roughly one of every three medical personnel working inside American emergency rooms.

The two companies were masters of the idiosyncrasies of the American health care system—a uniquely confusing tangle of competing insurance companies affiliated with separate networks of doctors, all governed by varying rates of reimbursement and regulated by rules that differed from state to state. They exploited the fact that people with private insurance—as opposed to government-run programs like Medicare—paid wildly differing amounts for the same treatments depending on their health coverage. They also benefited from the reality that even healthy, clear-thinking people, to say nothing of those rolled into emergency rooms on stretchers, were frequently bewildered by the particulars of their policies.

One of the key things that most patients did not grasp was that they could go to a hospital that was solidly part of their insurance network, operating on the reasonable assumption that they would receive care at the lowest rate, only to be treated by an emergency room doctor who was outside of the network, triggering often-exorbitant bills.

Long before the pandemic, this practice was facing scrutiny from congressional panels that were investigating so-called surprise medical billing. The surprise was not of the happy variety. More than a fifth of the time that patients visited the emergency room of a hospital that was within their insurance network, they later discovered that an out-of-network specialist had administered treatment. This resulted in charges that frequently ran as much as seven times what Medicare would have allowed. People in low-wage jobs, who lived paycheck to paycheck, often found themselves hassled by collection agents for unaffordable bills. Surprise billing was at the center of the story of how medical crises were pushing Americans into bankruptcy.

A 2017 paper by a team of researchers at Yale University described surprise billing as an organized assault on American health care and an affront to the free market system. "These higher payment rates, caused not by supply or demand, but rather by the ability to 'ambush' the patient, represent a transfer from the consumer to physicians," the paper asserted.

By the summer of 2020, TeamHealth was facing a class-action lawsuit filed in California that accused the company of systematically preying on unwitting emergency room patients. A Blackstone spokesman rejected as "completely false" allegations that TeamHealth had engaged in surprise billing. But the Yale paper found that, in the first months after TeamHealth took over an emergency room, the share of patients billed at out-of-network rates soared from less than 10 percent to more than 60 percent. The same paper found that TeamHealth's arrival at a hospital emergency room was soon followed by a roughly one-third increase in its out-of-network billing rates.

Surprise billing had become such a rewarding practice that TeamHealth and Envision spent more than $28 million on a 2019 advertising campaign that defeated congressional efforts to ban the practice.

The ads produced as part of their effort—the handiwork of a group named Patient Unity—were masterworks of misdirection. In one widely broadcast spot, a blond mother peered into the camera with a look of grave concern "A surprise medical bill can be traumatic, especially after a trip to the E.R," she said. But the legislation being proposed was being advanced by "big insurance companies," she warned. They were seeking to burnish their "record profits" with "a scheme called government ratesetting." If they succeeded, the result would be "doctor shortages and hospital closures."

Not for the first time, Davos Man sought to preserve his ability to take advantage of customers by provoking fear of the very mischief he was engaged in, while spinning the proposed regulatory fix as the source of the treachery.

The spread of the virus had exposed the extent to which Dr. Lin's hospital, like much of commercial life, had been ruled by an excessive compulsion to stay lean as means of rewarding shareholders.

Multinational companies had overdone it on "just-in-time-manufacturing," sparing themselves the costs of stocking warehouses with backup parts while relying on the web to order what they needed in real time. As electronics manufacturers locked down in China, factories from South Korea to Michigan suffered shortages of Chinese-made components. The world could endure a delay in the availability of the iPhones or auto parts, but the consequences of shortages in health care were profound. The lack of protective gear at Dr. Lin's hospital, and at medical facilities around the world, were in part an outgrowth of this "just in time" mentality.

The most serious manifestation of the embrace of going lean was a grave shortage of hospital beds.

In the United States, the previous decade had seen the completion of 680 hospital mergers, which had been almost wholly unchallenged by federal antitrust authorities. The new corporate owners tended to view people coming in the door less as patients than as customers. They sought to minimize their dealings with patients covered by government programs like Medicare and Medicaid—which were regulated by revenue-limiting restrictions on pricing—while maximizing their treatment of more affluent patients bearing private insurance. They shuttered hospitals in lightly populated and low-income communities, given the relative dearth of revenues to be harvested.

Rural areas alone saw 170 hospitals shuttered in the fifteen years before the pandemic. Over the same span, rural American counties suffered drops in the availability of a range of services, from surgery to obstetric care—a trend exacerbated by cuts to Medicare.

Corporate owners ran their hospitals as suppliers of services that had to be managed against demand. Too much capacity would yield downward pressure on prices. Shutting hospitals and consolidating their operations to reduce beds secured the same advantages that airlines gained in limiting flights: the ability to charge more.

By the time the pandemic arrived, the United States had 924,000 hospital beds, down from nearly 1.5 million in the mid-1970s. In the twenty-five metropolitan areas that had absorbed the greatest consolidation, the price of a hospital stay had increased by as much as half.

In New York City, eighteen hospitals had closed since 2003, resulting in the loss of more than twenty thousand beds, and leaving the nation's most populous metropolitan area exposed during a surge in demand for medical care.

By late March 2020, the city was resorting to the construction of an emergency field hospital in Central Park. Local morgues had run out of space, with bodies stored in refrigerated trailers, while exhausting the supply of body bags.

As a second wave built in December 2020, with the United States suffering more than two hundred thousand new COVID-19 cases a day, patients were stuck for hours on gurneys stashed in hospital corridors awaiting care for lack of available beds. Hospitals that served more than 100 million Americans—a third of the populace—were in a critical state, having filled at least 85 percent of their intensive care beds.

Years before the coronavirus, Dr. Lin had noticed the subtle manifestations of practicing medicine under the employ of the world's largest private equity company. At his hospital, Blackstone's purchase of TeamHealth had tilted the balance slightly yet perceptibly away from patient interests and toward bottom-line imperatives. The concerns of emergency room doctors on a range of medical questions—from proper protocols for stroke victims, to testing for bacterial infections—now competed for primacy with the dictates of hospital management, which had an interest in treating patients faster.

Half the staff meetings were about treating patients; the other half were about how to extract more income from each patient. Schwarzman's company paid its emergency doctors based on how many Relative Value Units (RVUs) they generated—a measure of revenue per patient. At the meetings, TeamHealth supervisors reminded doctors that some tests, like electrocardiograms, generated additional RVUs. The implication was clear: order more profitable tests, and be sure to document them.

TeamHealth reinforced this imperative by distributing spreadsheets listing every doctor's name, and ranking their performance by RVU, making clear who was delivering, and who had to try harder.

Dr. Lin saw upsides to this approach. At hospitals that paid emergency room doctors by the hour, some people sat around doing very little. No one sat around inside Dr. Lin's hospital, because their pay was directly tied to how many patients they treated.

But the downside was also evident. Doctors were incentivized to view patients as profit streams.

Dr. Lin also recognized the severity of surprise billing. Sometimes, people arrived at the emergency room in serious trauma, suffering heart attacks or blunt force injuries, and expressed fears of being admitted, given the size of the bills that their previous visits had generated. Lying on gurneys and in pain, people fretted about what their insurance would cover.

But this process of change had played out gradually. The pandemic swiftly revealed acute dangers.

Dr. Lin asked why the people at the reception desk were not wearing masks and was told that the hospital did not want to frighten patients. Some were arriving for elective procedures like colonoscopies, knee and hip replacements, hernia repair, and back surgeries—a major source of revenue.

This was a fault line running through the American health care system. The federal government, acting on the warnings of epidemiologists, was calling for the cancellation of elective procedures. But hospitals controlled by corporate entities that answered to shareholders resisted such moves as a threat to their bottom lines. At hospitals that did scrap elective procedures, many slashed pay and even eliminated staff in response to the hit to their revenues.

The University of Pittsburgh Medical Center had swallowed up other providers in a series of mergers, capturing 41 percent of the market for health care in Western Pennsylvania. With $20 billion in annual revenues, its president and CEO, Jeffrey Romoff, had netted more than $8.5 million in total compensation the previous year. The company was refusing to comply with an order from Pennsylvania's governor to scrap elective procedures. At the same time, the system's chief medical and scientific officer, Dr. Steven Shapiro, was publicly dismissing the threat from the pandemic and urging the authorities to reopen the economy— an obvious conflict of interest. If life got back to normal, his hospital stood to make more money.

In Bellingham, Dr. Lin argued that only surgeries that were required to address life-threatening ailments should be taking place. But elective procedures were the bread-and-butter of the industry. They continued uninterrupted.

Dr. Lin was especially incensed to see the nurses inside the operating room working without proper protective gear even as the hospital told the local newspaper that it had more than ample stocks. He approached his TeamHealth manager, complaining that employees' lives were being imperiled. This yielded no action. TeamHealth did not want to jeopardize its relationship with the hospital by complaining about its management.

Frustrated, Dr. Lin took to Facebook to sound the alarm.

Previously, he had been an infrequent visitor to the site, going months without posting anything. He did not stand out as a promoter of any particular cause. His profile photo was a shot of himself surrounded by his three children in a swimming pool. He had previously shared a picture of an Elvis impersonator, and a photo of his wife playing the violin. On March 16, Dr. Lin posted a note he had sent to his manager detailing his worries about the dangerous conditions inside the hospital. It was "so far behind when it comes to protecting patients and the community," he wrote, "but even worse when it comes to protecting the staff."

TeamHealth's human relations department spotted his Facebook post and arranged a phone call the following day among Dr. Lin, the company's executives, and hospital administrators. After an hour on the phone, Dr. Lin was in no way reassured.

"The impression I get is that they are not interested in our concern," he wrote on Facebook. "If bars and restaurants and non-essential stores are closed, so should elective procedures."

Dr. Lin's direct supervisor, Worth Everett, called him and urged him to take down his Facebook post and apologize to TeamHealth's CEO. He said it was inappropriate for Dr. Lin to criticize his employer. TeamHealth's business was by then struggling with "low volume," Dr. Everett told him, because fewer people were coming to the emergency room. He accused Dr. Lin of worsening this trend by scaring people.

Dr. Lin refused to comply. He was a doctor whose loyalties were to patients, colleagues, and public health—not to maximizing revenue. COVID-19 cases were then rising inside the hospital.

His Facebook feed filled with support from around the country. People called him a hero. Other health care workers reported that they, too, were laboring with inadequate protection. Some offered to donate masks. Dr. Lin organized a collection effort, directing people to drop off items at a nearby health center.

Then the CEO of the hospital was quoted in the local paper offering assurances that none of the hospital caregivers who had contracted the coronavirus had gotten it via exposure to patients.

Dr. Lin was irate. He ridiculed the claim on Facebook.

The same day—twelve days after his initial post—another supervisor sent him a text: "You need not show up for work, your shift has been covered."

Dr. Lin texted Dr. Everett to confirm this. His supervisor's reply eliminated all doubt: he had been fired. He later filed a wrongful termination lawsuit against the hospital.

Dr. Everett did not respond to repeated messages left on his voice mail. When I reached out to Blackstone to ask about the issues that Dr. Lin surfaced, a spokesman for TeamHealth—working for a corporate communications company called Narrative Strategies DC—emailed a statement.

"From the very beginning of the COVID-19 pandemic, Team-Health took every possible step to support our clinicians doing heroic work," the statement said.

TeamHealth had not terminated Dr. Lin, according to the statement. Rather, he had been "removed" from his position by the hospital. "We repeatedly offered to place him at another contracted hospital anywhere in the country so he could do the important work of caring for patients during an ongoing global pandemic," the statement read.

This was a typical Davos Man attack maneuver—hit back harder. Confronted with testimony that TeamHealth prioritized profits over public health, the company was essentially accusing Dr. Lin of dereliction in a disaster.

A few weeks after Dr. Lin's departure, TeamHealth reduced hours for its emergency room doctors in the face of declining revenues.

By then, Schwarzman and his fellow Davos Men had a fresh opportunity to exploit. The pandemic had become a dire threat to the economy. Governments around the world were readying monumental rescue packages, with scant oversight.

Davos Man had been here before. He knew what to do.

CHAPTER 9

"THERE'S ALWAYS A WAY OF MAKING MONEY"

Davos Man Never Wastes a Crisis

As a casino magnate, Donald Trump had specialized in racking up debts he never paid back. As president of the United States, he found himself on the other side, handing out public money to the wealthiest people on earth.

Trump's tax cuts were supposed to be his ticket to reelection. The strategy might very well have worked, if not for the coronavirus. Though they achieved little for the real economy, they yielded exuberance in the stock market.

Between late December 2017, when Trump signed his tax cuts into law, and early February 2020, the S&P 500—a widely watched index of stocks—soared more than 20 percent, yielding more than $3 trillion in gains. Trump crowed about every record, presenting the stock market as the gauge of his excellence, a flashing indicator of American revival.

Roughly half of all American households owned not a penny's worth of stock, while the richest tenth boasted 84 percent of all shares. As a barometer for blue-collar security, the stock market was about as useful as the price of docking a yacht in Cannes. But this reality was obscured by breathless media stories about record share prices. This conflation of the stock market and the real economy aided Davos Man and his collaborator in the White House. Trump succeeded in using the stock market rally to convey a sense of American economic vigor. (Never mind that the economic boom had begun, and had added more jobs, while Obama was in office.)

The economy was Trump's rejoinder to the unending scandals that had plagued his presidency—the hush money paid to a porn star, the histrionics over the endless comings and goings within his administration, the investigations, the ceaseless lies, the bigotry, the impeachment. His claim for another term rested on the economy.

"The greatest in the world," he kept saying. "The greatest in history."

Trump's lease on the White House appeared sound. In the sweep of American presidential campaigns, an incumbent presiding over a strong economy stood an excellent chance of securing another term.

But the pandemic trashed his victory parade.

The virus first emerged in central China, in the industrial city of Wuhan. By February, it had spread to northern Italy, bringing warnings from epidemiologists that this was a truly global threat.

From Tokyo to London to New York, stock prices plummeted. By late March, the Dow Jones Industrial Average had surrendered more than one-third of its value while suffering the three worst one-day point drops in its history.

The markets were registering a plain truth about the global economy. If Chinese factories were out of commission, much of the world would soon find itself short of an astonishing array of goods. Retailers from London to Los Angeles would struggle to secure clothing, smartphones, and furniture made in China, or produced elsewhere with Chinese-made fabric, electronics, and parts. Automobile factories from Eastern Europe to Latin America would face grave difficulties purchasing needed components.

A mass slowdown of industrial production around the globe presaged weaker demand for oil and natural gas, threatening economies dependent on energy from the Persian Gulf to the Gulf of Mexico.

And China was not merely an enormous producer of goods. It was also a huge and rapidly growing purchaser. If Chinese consumers were hunkered down in quarantine rather than flocking to shopping malls and entertainment venues, that meant less demand for a vast range of goods and services—Hollywood movies, construction equipment, soybeans, iron ore, and investment banking.

As the catastrophe unfolded, central banks from the United States to the European Union unleashed unprecedented volumes of credit, pushing interest rates into negative territory to encourage consumers and businesses to spend and invest. But in the first months of the pandemic, every fresh announcement of relief triggered another jaw-dropping sell-off.

The central banks were deploying their traditional arsenal, but their weapons appeared impotent. People were not scrapping vacations and avoiding department stores because borrowing rates were too high. Spending was plunging because interaction with other humans ran the risk of death. The only way to rescue the global economy was to halt the virus; the only way to halt the virus was to choke off the economy.

For Trump, the crisis was compounded by the fact that he had initially dismissed the pandemic as a hoax, just another fake news story engineered to undermine his reelection prospects. The months that he could have used to educate the public on social distancing while testing en masse were squandered on maintaining the appearance that everything was fine, the virus was like the flu, people just had to get on with their lives.

When events rendered that stance untenable, Trump shifted strategy. The pandemic was terrible, but it was not his fault. He blamed the shortage of tests on Obama, who had been out of office for three years. He described the virus as the latest, dastardly export from China, while indulging racist tropes. He called it the "Kung flu" and the "Chinese virus," triggering an enduring wave of terror against Asian Americans.

As the virus ran rampant, Trump recast himself again, this time as a wartime president who had supposedly identified the perils earlier than anyone. He presided over daily press conferences from the White House where he dispensed confident assurances that miracle drugs were at hand; American factories were retooling at his insistence to make respirators.

His evident lack of command for basic details amplified the fear. At one point, he suggested that Americans should inject themselves with bleach to kill the virus, forcing Clorox, the prominent maker of cleaning products, to release a statement clarifying that this was a terrible idea.

Trump had spent his adult life flouting social conventions, ignoring traditional accounting, and renouncing enormous debts while never suffering meaningful consequences. His multiple bankruptcies and reputation for stiffing bankers and plumbers alike had only amplified his aura, bringing book deals and a hit television series. But the pandemic was something else altogether, the first force Trump had ever encountered that he could not simply ignore or stick on someone else. There was no credulous lender who would bail him out from his previous profligacy, entranced by his star power. The natural sphere did not care about his brand. The pandemic would deliver a comeuppance Trump could not evade.

In a single week in late March, more than 3 million Americans filed for unemployment benefits, a record that was nearly five times as many as the previous high mark. The downturn completely erased the job growth that had unfolded during Trump's presidency.

By the following month, the unemployment rate exceeded 14 percent. People were lining up for hours at food banks, sparking talk of another Great Depression. Almost overnight, Trump's reelection prospects appeared gravely endangered, placing him in uncomfortable proximity to the worst word in the Trumpian vernacular—*loser*. He was desperate to lift the siege. People had to get back to work, back to malls, back to hotels and airports and restaurants so the markets could recover.

By the middle of April, Trump indulged his trademark bombast and showmanship in announcing the formation of the Great American Revival Industry Groups, a gathering of the chief executives representing the largest companies in America. They would supposedly advise him on how to switch the economy back on.

The roster drew heavily on the ranks of Davos Men, including Dimon, Benioff, and Bezos.

"As we prepare for the next phase of this great struggle, we must also do everything in our power to restore prosperity for the American worker," Trump said at a press briefing to announce the panel. "The health and wealth of America is the primary goal."

This construction—*the health and wealth of America*—elided crucial elements that were in direct conflict. Bezos was the most obvious example. His burgeoning wealth was derived from the unprotected labors of warehouse workers.

Trump's roster of advisers included Dean Banks, CEO of Tyson Foods, the enormous meat processor. Trump would soon invoke the wartime Defense Production Act to keep American slaughterhouses in operation, even as they emerged as hot spots for the virus. Using language drafted by the meatpacking industry, he labeled these plants "critical infrastructure," which rendered the people laboring inside them essential workers.

White collar professionals were availing themselves of the web in working safely from home. But tens of thousands of slaughterhouse workers—many of them immigrants earning minimum wage—risked their lives to continue carving up pork, beef, and poultry. They labored close together on the assembly lines. They could protect their health, or they could preserve their paychecks. They could not do both.

Tyson claimed that Trump's executive action was imperative to avoid a shortage of meat. Left unmentioned was the fact that the American meat supply had become prone to shortages because Tyson and its two largest rivals had swallowed up smaller competitors. Consolidation had cut pork-processing capacity by one-fourth. This had allowed Tyson and its shareholders to reap gains through higher prices.

As was typical of Trump, the announcement was just stagecraft. Benioff had not even heard of the panel until someone told him that he was on it. The group never convened, Benioff told me, and he was never asked to provide any advice.

Trump's desperate bid to secure another term would ultimately come down to the currency he understood most—money. He adopted the pose of the magnanimous monarch, tossing trinkets at the populace. He launched negotiations with Congress to unleash a gargantuan rescue package.

In the face of a public health emergency combined with an economic unraveling, the usual political constraints on public spending were effectively suspended.

Trump was going to oversee the dispensing of trillions of dollars in the name of sparing the world's largest economy—quickly, and with minimal oversight. The United States was about to be awash in free money courtesy of the ultimate rube: the taxpayer.

Davos Man unleashed his lobbyists to position himself to get in on the festivities.

The $2.2 trillion measure Trump signed into law in late March 2020 was titled the CARES Act, for Coronavirus Aid, Relief, and Economic Security Act. It was an appropriately slippery acronym for a piece of legislation that would go down in history as a prime example of monied interests exploiting a catastrophe for elaborate gain at public expense.

The act included a major expansion of unemployment benefits—a $600 weekly payment on top of the usual checks in an effort to spur spending. Millions of American households were provided with cash grants of $1,200 to take the edge off the downturn. This approach would ultimately prove highly effective, supplying the wherewithal for families to stave off eviction, bankruptcy, and other calamities even as breadwinners lost wages and salaries. But the checks—emblazoned with Trump's own name, like a personal gift from the emperor—would not arrive for months, even as unpaid bills piled up.

Collectively, the unemployment benefits, the checks, and tax credits for companies that helped employees with student debt represented an expenditure of more than $600 billion, an enormous infusion of relief in normal times, and a key reason the downturn was not far worse for the jobless. But as the political price for this aid for regular people, every Davos Man was invited around the trough.

One item was a flat-out boondoggle—a $170 billion tax cut for real estate developers and others that was in no discernible fashion related to the pandemic. As my colleague Jesse Drucker revealed, Senate Republicans injected the provision on page 203 of the 880-page bill, making all but certain that no one would notice it until their handiwork was done. The language invited developers to deduct from their current tax bills paper losses they had incurred years earlier, well before anyone had heard of COVID-19. It had no reason for being except as a means of transferring money from the Treasury to wealthy people. Among those poised to cash in were Donald Trump and his son-in-law, Jared Kushner.

The central element of the act provided $500 billion for large companies, including $29 billion earmarked for airlines, and $17 billion for "businesses necessary for national security"—code for Boeing, the American aerospace giant.

The Treasury would administer some $454 billion in aid, pledging it as the collateral for more than $4 trillion's worth of loans that could be issued by the Federal Reserve—a convoluted but enormously consequential process that only an insider could understand.

The numbers getting thrown around day by day were already monumental, but $4 trillion was a sum that simply beggared comprehension. This was more than twice as much as all American corporations had earned collectively the previous year. Where that cash was headed and under what conditions it would be bequeathed would be heavily influenced by Trump's Treasury secretary, Steven Mnuchin.

Mnuchin resembled a comic book version of a rich guy, his perpetual smirk conjuring images of silk pajamas. His grandfather had launched a yacht club, and his father had worked on Wall Street, cracking the management ranks at Goldman Sachs. Born in 1962, he had grown up on Park Avenue and spent weekends in the Hamptons. He attended Riverdale Country School, one of the most rarefied of New York City private institutions, arriving at the lush and sprawling campus in a red Porsche. He followed in his father's footsteps—first to Yale, and then to Goldman.

Mnuchin landed in the mortgage department, soaking up knowledge that would eventually position him for his own big score. He took over a failed lender, IndyMac, sticking distressed homeowners with voluminous service fees while foreclosing en masse, flipping properties for a profit.

Removing people from their houses proved so bounteous that Mnuchin was able to pay nearly $27 million to put himself into a nine-bedroom, ten-bath manse in Bel Air to go along with his Park Avenue duplex.

When he joined the Trump campaign in 2016, assuming the

role of finance chairman, it shocked those who knew him. He lacked fund-raising experience and had evinced zero concern for any political cause. But he knew Trump as a fellow traveler in the ranks of New York real estate dealmakers. He had watched him at a rally and come away certain he could win.

Mnuchin's family was appalled by his involvement with Trump. His father's wife began reminding people that she was not Mnuchin's biological mother. After the election, Trump sought to persuade Jamie Dimon to become Treasury secretary. When Dimon turned him down, Trump settled on Mnuchin.

Awkward and reserved, Mnuchin was incapable of small talk, though he was known to break into an impersonation of Inspector Clouseau, the bumbling hero of the Pink Panther films. With his thick and blocky glasses framing his pie-shaped face, he was frequently photographed in formal wear alongside his far younger, blond wife, the Scottish actress Louise Linton.

His wife had gained infamy for her tone-deaf displays of privilege uncut by any joy-derailing self-awareness. She had once triggered an official rebuke from the Zambian government after publishing a cartoonishly insulting depiction of her year spent in the country after high school. ("I soon learned that Africa is rife with hidden danger.") On the day that the Bureau of Engraving printed the first dollar bills bearing her husband's signature, Linton vamped for the cameras in black leather gloves while she and Mnuchin held up a freshly printed sheet of money like jewels purloined in a heist. She posted a photo of herself stepping off a government jet as she accompanied Mnuchin on a visit to the federal gold depository at Ft. Knox, while using hashtags to ensure that the world recognized her Hermès and Valentino clothes. When a woman in Oregon deemed this tasteless, Linton attacked her as "adorably out of touch," while demanding gratitude for the huge taxes that she and Mnuchin selflessly paid. If Marie Antoinette had lived long enough to see Instagram, her feed would have presumably looked like this.

Now, Mnuchin, working in the employ of a president not obsessed with the niceties of process, took the lead in guiding the Fed as it distributed a cosmic sum of money.

The cash earmarked for the airlines and Boeing came with rules barring recipients from using it to pay out dividends or boost executive compensation while requiring that companies retain the bulk of their workers. But the serious money—the $4 trillion to be disbursed by the Fed with Mnuchin's counsel—came unencumbered by such conditions.

A Senate provision did seek to bar bailed-out companies from boosting executive pay while obligating them to avoid layoffs and respect collective bargaining. But the language merely required that Mnuchin "endeavor to" follow through on those details. The Fed was eager to inject cash into the marketplace immediately, making officials reluctant to impose conditions that might give executives pause in accepting the money.

Democrats in Congress were horrified by what appeared to be a monstrous slush fund controlled by the Trump administration. Still, they caved in the face of Republican arguments that further deliberation would delay relief reaching working people in the midst of an emergency. The CARES Act cleared the Senate by a tally of 96–0. The jobless were successfully deployed as hostages in the service of engorging the fortunes of Davos Man.

Democrats pretended to take solace in the fact that the spending officially came accompanied by congressional oversight. But the 2008 bailout had revealed the hollowness of this component. Congress could monitor and record what was transpiring but lacked the power to intervene and redirect money.

Within hours of signing the CARES Act, Trump asserted the power to gag the inspector general, effectively eliminating oversight. Mnuchin and the Fed had gained a clear lane to dispense more than $4 trillion largely free of supervision.

As in the bailouts that followed the financial crisis, Mnuchin and the Fed aimed to restore order by stabilizing the value of financial assets. Initially, they concerned themselves with bolstering companies whose debt was rated "investment grade," meaning it had the seal of approval from a credit rating agency. These were presumably companies that had been stable before the pandemic. But by late April, Mnuchin and Fed Chairman Jay Powell expanded the parameters to allow an especially tattered collection of companies to secure the public's charity—oil and gas enterprises that were virtually insolvent, their bonds rated as junk.

For years, speculators in the energy world had availed themselves of cheap credit left from the last crisis. Many relied on the environmentally destructive practice of fracking. Production was expensive, making the economics dependent on higher oil prices. Energy prices had fallen, turning large numbers of these dubiously conceived gambles into money losers.

Not that this prevented them from funneling wealth to shareholders. Over the previous decade, five of the largest oil and gas companies had dedicated $536 billion for dividends and share buybacks, which was far in excess of their revenues. They were going through the motions of tapping the ground for energy while sticking their funnels into more rewarding reserves—vast reservoirs of credit—and handing the proceeds to investors.

The party appeared to be ending. With the global economy in lockdown, demand had evaporated, and the market was withholding further loans. So the oil and gas industry indulged its core engineering expertise—Washington lobbying. A robust campaign obliterated the rule that rescue funds could go only to solid companies, allowing Mnuchin and the Fed to bail out insolvent polluters.

Beyond the companies themselves, Mnuchin was also rescuing financial players like Schwarzman, whose investments were losing value amid the broader alarm in the bond market.

The Blackstone leader was grateful for the bailouts.

"I'd have to give quite high grades to the economic management of this," Schwarzman said during a television appearance in April. "It's been led by the president, and fortunately for all the rest of us in society, it's going to work out well."

All the rest of us in society was a deft piece of Davos Man argot, a phrase that neatly tied together as one the interests of people laboring in Amazon warehouses, doctors attending to COVID-19 patients, the previously employed now standing in line at food banks, and a multibillionaire private equity king videoconferencing in to a television show from his Park Avenue lair.

Another major component of the CARES Act was a $349 billion scheme—later expanded to $660 billion—known as the Paycheck Protection Program. Banks distributed this money, dispensing loans to small businesses. Under the rules, much of this debt could be forgiven provided that employers avoided layoffs.

In theory, small businesses could apply directly to the government for a loan. But in reality, that was a bit like phoning your local IRS office to see if a kind staff member could maybe pop over after work to help you sort out your tax forms. The Feds lacked the people to run the program, making the government reliant on large banks to distribute the money. In determining who got loans, banks catered not to societal needs, but to their shareholders: They did business with those who tended to boost their bottom lines. Getting a loan generally required a relationship with a bank like JPMorgan Chase, which was set up to push through applications in bulk.

Jamie Dimon's bank deployed these small business loans like swag dispensed to its best customers. It indulged its "concierge service" for its longest-standing, most valuable clients, filling out their paperwork and submitting their applications. A publicly traded Indiana-based maker of sporting goods that already had a $50 million credit line from JPMorgan Chase wound up with a $5.6 million loan. Major restaurant chains, pharmaceutical companies, and hotel franchises got loans without having to do anything, while businesses that lacked an established connection with America's largest bank got free enterprise. Which is to say, very little.

Businesses owned by African Americans, Latinos, and women were largely shut out. The program would ultimately distribute 650,000 loans worth at least $150,000 each. Only 143 Black entrepreneurs received loans of that size.

Mnuchin had promised that the "overarching focus" of the program was "keeping workers paid and employed." But several major companies took the money and then fired their workers, while a parade of unsavory characters walked away with loans.

A luxury hotel in San Diego, the Fairmont Grand Del Mar, received $6.4 million but then shut down and stopped sending paychecks to hundreds of workers.

A Georgia-based biopharmaceutical company, MiMedx Group, had recently paid a $6.5 million fine to settle allegations that it had price-gouged the Department of Veterans Affairs. It had previously settled a case with the Securities and Exchange Commission over claims that it had exaggerated its revenues. Its former senior executives had been indicted by federal prosecutors in New York for accounting fraud. None of this prevented the company from qualifying for a $10 million loan under the Paycheck Protection Program.

The largest single beneficiary of the small business program was Monty Bennett, chairman of the board of a trio of Dallas-based companies that collectively controlled more than one hundred hotels, among them Ritz-Carlton resorts in St. Thomas and Lake Tahoe, Marriotts in Beverly Hills and Las Vegas, and a Hilton in New York. By the middle of March, with the hotel business decimated, shares in one of Bennett's publicly traded companies, Ashford Hospitality Trust, were down by more than

90 percent. The company was falling behind on its debt payments.

Ashford scrapped plans to pay dividends to ordinary shareholders, though it still managed to scrape together $10 million for preferred shareholders, including $2 million for Bennett and his father.

With the end near, Bennett was in a reflective mood. He penned an open letter titled "What's Wrong With America?"

"My industry and our businesses are completely crushed," he wrote. "What saddens me more is what's going on in Washington, D.C. Some politicians are too concerned whether proposed government programs help small businesses rather than 'big business,' or individuals instead of 'corporations.'"

What perverse priorities were governing the nation's capital if salt-of-the-earth real estate magnates could not jump in front of jobless people in the queue for relief? "What are all those taxes we paid supposed to provide us with anyway?" Bennett wrote. "I won't apologize for being a capitalist in America."

Bennett had donated more than $200,000 to Trump's presidential campaign and the Republican National Committee in 2016, and nearly $400,000 more to the president's reelection war chest. He swiftly did what any red-blooded American entrepreneur must in the face of challenge. He hired lobbyists.

First came Jeff Miller, who had been the finance vice chair of Trump's inaugural committee, ingratiating himself with the people in charge by bringing in nearly $3 million for the Republican National Committee and the president's reelection campaign. Bennett also engaged Bailey Strategic Advisors, which was run by another Trump rainmaker, Roy Bailey. Soon, a loophole was discovered in the Paycheck Protection Program that allowed large chains of hotels and restaurants to apply for loans provided that individual locations employed fewer than five hundred people.

Bennett's hotel empire secured $70 million's worth of loans.

But as word spread that publicly traded companies were hoovering up taxpayer funds advertised as relief for small businesses, outrage ensued. Whatever Bennett's business was, small it was not. Ashford Inc. had recorded $291 million in revenue the previous year. Bennett had taken home more than $5.6 million in total compensation.

Mnuchin adopted the mien of a person offended to have discovered gambling in Casablanca. He warned that audits would be unleashed as the administration tightened the rules of the program. Companies found to have breached the rules had two weeks to return the money or face criminal prosecution.

Bennett—apparently favoring a suite at the Ritz-Carlton over a cell in the Big House—handed back the cash. By August his companies were being probed by the Securities and Exchange Commission.

For utter shamelessness, it was difficult to top the financial players who had taken control of large swaths of American health care. Having rendered the system vulnerable to the pandemic, they exploited the resulting disaster as an opportunity to extract rescue money.

In March 2020, Steward Health Care, a chain of hospitals owned by the private equity giant Cerberus Capital, threatened to close a facility north of Philadelphia unless the state of Pennsylvania handed over $40 million. The firm, whose chairman was former vice president Dan Quayle, was in control of $43 billion's worth of investments. Its cofounder and co-CEO, Stephen A. Feinberg, boasted a net worth estimated at $1.8 billion. Yet the company insisted that it required an infusion of state relief, or the thirty thousand people of Easton, Pennsylvania, were going to lose their hospital in the middle of a pandemic.

The hospital had been founded more than a century earlier with the contributions of a local church congregation. It had remained a nonprofit until 2001 when it was purchased by a publicly traded hospital chain. Six years later, the Easton hospital's property had been sold to a real estate trust whose investors included Cerberus. The terms of the deal left the hospital paying millions of dollars a year to rent the same buildings it had previously owned.

The state threw together an $8 million lifeline. Even so, Steward informed the authorities that it was going ahead with the closure of the hospital. In June, a local nonprofit operation, St. Luke's University Health Network, stepped in to purchase the hospital and keep it running. But the new owner served notice that it refused to recognize the two unions that represented the hospital's nearly seven hundred workers, threatening layoffs.

The CARES Act included grants from the Department of Health and Human Services to compensate medical providers whose revenues had been hit by prohibitions on elective surgeries. Subsidiaries of TeamHealth—the Blackstone-owned company that had employed Dr. Lin—collected at least $2.8 million in these federal loans, according to public records compiled by Americans for Financial Reform.

One of the country's largest hospital chains, Providence Health System, secured grants exceeding $500 million, despite paying its CEO $10 million in 2018, and even as it boasted almost $12 billion in cash. The company ran a pair of venture capital funds that managed about $300 million, while transacting with private equity companies.

The Cleveland Clinic carried a reputation as one of the best institutions in the United States, an innovator known for elevating the quality of care. In the pandemic, it distinguished itself as something else—an operator on the make for bailout funds, and a Davos Man collaborator. It tapped the government for $199 million in bailout funds, even as it sat on $7 billion in cash, while generating $1.2 billion in investment returns. It had distributed $28 million to investment advisers to manage its portfolio.

In June 2020, as the pandemic spread uncontrollably through the American South and West, the Cleveland Clinic lavished special favor on one uniquely endowed money manager—the founder of Blackstone.

"Steven Schwarzman has had one of the most remarkable careers of our time," declared Cleveland Clinic's CEO, Tom Mihaljevic, as he kicked off an online event as part of a series billed "Virtual Ideas for Tomorrow." "His generosity is equally remarkable."

Mihaljevic teed up a promotional video that featured a photo montage of Schwarzman's life—his father's linen store, his childhood business mowing suburban lawns, his huddles with Presidents Obama and Trump, his ventures in China.

Schwarzman hawked his memoir, holding up the Chinese version. "I became the number one best-selling author in China," he said. He credited his success to his assiduous dedication to ethics. "You have to set a standard for integrity." He recounted how, as a Yale student, he had persuaded the New York City ballet to dispatch ballerinas to New Haven for a special performance that he organized for his classmates—a setup for a sweeping commentary on his overall achievements.

"What I've learned in life is that you can do a lot of stuff if you have a vision," Schwarzman said. "If you really beg in a convincing way, someone may take pity on you."

Throughout the American economy at that moment, tens of millions of people were in a pitiable condition. The unemployment rate remained above 11 percent. By the end of 2020, more than 23 million American workers would be set back by the pandemic—nearly 11 million officially jobless, another 7 million suffering cuts to hours and wages, and 5 million more excised from the ledger books, having given up looking for work. For every ten people who had managed to secure unemployment benefits, another three had tried but failed to navigate the bureaucracy amid an overwhelming surge of applicants.

Salvador Dominguez was among those tallied as a successful case in this grim accounting. After he lost his job selling real estate in Manhattan, he qualified for the emergency unemployment benefits under the CARES Act. But in the seventy-two days that separated his final paycheck in March 2020 from the arrival of his first unemployment compensation, he found himself borrowing from friends and relatives so he could keep paying the rent on his apartment. Lacking money for groceries, he stood in the darkness outside a gourmet Manhattan grocer after closing time, waiting for trash bags full of expired items to be deposited in a dumpster. He rooted through the discards in search of nourishment.

"It was very tough," Dominguez said. "I didn't feel alone, because I knew a lot of people like me were doing it."

Roughly one in four Americans was struggling to stay current on their bills—a figure that leapt to 43 percent among Black households and 37 percent for Latinos. Child hunger was soaring as schools remained closed, depriving low-income families of meals. These were not communities with lobbyists at their disposal.

Schwarzman, on the other hand, maintained offices in Washington that homed in on federal dollars. Blackstone's emergency room staffing company, TeamHealth, was pursuing mercy from Congress, which was again scrutinizing its business model, with some lawmakers demanding that future federal aid packages include a ban on surprise billing.

Fortunately for Schwarzman, his canny investments in lawmakers yielded valuable dividends. The chairman of the House Ways and Means Committee, Richie Neal, a Massachusetts Democrat, scotched a proposal that would have greatly restricted surprise billing via the tried-and-true legislative strategy of advancing his own, weaker bill. In place of price regulation, he substituted an arbitration system to settle billing disputes. The arbitrator would use as a reference point the rates paid in recent years—effectively locking in the jacked-up fees extracted by the private equity companies. And even that bill was delayed by a year. This was constituent service, Washington-style. Executives linked to Blackstone were Neal's largest source of campaign funds. In a written statement sent in lieu of an interview, TeamHealth characterized the resulting legislation as an acceptable compromise for all. "While imperfect, the final product was good for patients and was a significant improvement over the catastrophic proposals advanced by major insurance companies," the statement read. "Any claim that TeamHealth fought against a solution to surprise billing is completely false."

Blackstone's ultimate protection was its scale and diversification, which limited the risk to its business from any single trouble spot. As the mayhem in the marketplace drove down the values of companies, Blackstone was, in fact, positioned to snap up bargains.

"You start out buying securities that have collapsed," Schwarzman told a gathering of investors that spring. "We bought $11 billion of securities in the first two or three weeks."

That was merely the opening act. Blackstone was looking for more bargains, especially in health care.

"That's going to be an area of enormous growth," Schwarzman said. "There's always a way of making money in these types of volatile situations."

The Fed was following through on its promise to do whatever it took to right the economy by purchasing enormous quantities of government and corporate bonds. Someone would have to manage its portfolio. In a repeat of the last financial crisis, Larry Fink's firm got the gig. BlackRock gained the authority to select up to $750 billion's worth of securities for the Fed, while executing the trades.

No one could accuse BlackRock of lacking the requisite expertise. The company was by then managing $7.4 trillion in investments—a sum that exceeded the annual economic output of the United Kingdom, France, and Canada combined—giving it intimate familiarity with every crevice of the financial world.

Fink had in recent years distinguished himself as the wisest of Wall Street wise men. His counsel was valued by Democrats and Republicans alike.

But if BlackRock's role in the financial crisis of 2008 had posed a conflict of interest, its divided loyalties this time were exponentially more troubling. It had grown into an unrivaled behemoth, a company intertwined in virtually every market-place, with offices in thirty countries. BlackRock controlled at least 5 percent of the shares for 97.5 percent of the companies that traded on the S&P 500. Some two hundred financial companies, plus the Federal Reserve and the European Central Bank, used the company's Aladdin risk management system, which surveyed the markets for trouble. This placed BlackRock in the position of monitoring some $20 trillion's worth of investments, supplying it incomparable clarity on the movements of money worldwide.

As the bailouts took shape in the spring of 2020, Fink was operating behind the scenes to influence their details, while also running a company engaged in profiting from daily developments. Days before the Fed announced its foray into the bond market, he had traveled to Washington to confer with Trump and other officials on appropriate steps to stop the carnage in the marketplace. Fink spoke with Mnuchin five times during the weekend before the bailout package was unveiled. One call included Fed Chairman Powell and Larry Kudlow, Trump's primary economic adviser. People were referring to BlackRock as a fourth branch of government.

The Fed would buy corporate bonds that were already in circulation as well as new issues to ensure companies could raise money. The central bank would serve as the buyer of last resort, with BlackRock helping decide which bonds to target. That gave

Fink troubling influence over who survived and who disappeared.

In a letter to Mnuchin and Fed Chairman Powell, nine members of Congress—among them Alexandria Ocasio-Cortez, a New York Democrat, and Jesus G. "Chuy" Garcia, a Democrat from Illinois—demanded increased oversight of BlackRock's dealings with the federal government.

"BlackRock is already big," they wrote. "You must ensure that its work during this crisis doesn't cement the firm's structural importance in the global economy and our dependence on it."

Part of the central bank's buying would be focused on so-called exchange traded funds—investments made up of a basket of stocks and bonds. BlackRock was the dominant purveyor, owing to its purchase of a firm called iShares. BlackRock had bought the business from the British bank Barclays during the last crisis, paying $13.5 billion back when iShares controlled $300 billion in assets. Since then, BlackRock had grown it into a colossus that managed nearly $2 trillion.

The Fed's money was certain to land in these BlackRock-controlled funds. BlackRock itself would decide which ones and how much.

This setup violated a basic sense of fair play. In the same way that a mayor should not be able to steer a city contract to a company controlled by his family, the Davos Man overseeing taxpayer money in an emergency should presumably find some other place to park it than in his own company's funds.

In the middle of April, Fink held a conference call with stock analysts to discuss the company's most recent quarterly earnings. "BlackRock's biggest priority has been focusing on the health and safety of our employees and all their families," Fink said.

But the company had also managed to continue vacuuming up investment money. A fresh $75 billion in net inflows had poured in over the first seven weeks of the year, Fink said. Much of the money had landed in iShares.

In the ritual of the earnings call, analysts generally sucked up to power, using their opportunities to pose questions as moments to offer congratulations for another great quarter. But on this call, one analyst, Patrick Davitt of Autonomous Research, zeroed in on BlackRock's funds to pose an unusually pointed question.

"A lot of investors have been grumbling that the Fed purchasing ETFs and in particular non-investment grade ETFs, hence set some sort of bailout for BlackRock in the ETF industry more broadly," Davitt said. "What is your reaction to that?"

Fink was incensed. "I object to your—the way you framed it as a bailout," he said. "I don't even know where you're coming from with that question. I think it's insulting. There is—all the issues around what we're doing with governments is based on great practices."

BlackRock was working for the government through its consulting unit, the company emphasized, while walling off its fund management operations—meaning it was not trading on information it would gain as Uncle Sam's asset manager.

But Davos Man was constantly touting the structures his companies employed to ensure supposedly impermeable barriers separating one part of his operations from another. People who earned billions of dollars on the strength of information tended to find out what they needed to know.

The contract released by the Federal Reserve Bank of New York in March 2020 revealed that the separation between Black-Rock's consulting unit and the rest of its business was flexible. BlackRock was barred from receiving "confidential information" about the central bank's monetary policies, meaning its setting of interest rates. But BlackRock was gaining access to confidential information about the Fed's "business, economic and policy plans and strategies." It was as if a medical privacy policy barred disclosure of the patient's illness, while permitting the release of all the medicines they were taking.

The contract barred BlackRock from using confidential information to design trades for anyone other than the central bank. BlackRock staff who managed the Fed's business were "prohibited" from advising other clients in a fashion that "could be viewed as informed by the Confidential Information." But here was the punch line: That prohibition remained in place only during a two-week "Cooling-Off period."

In short, BlackRock could assign its people to handle the Fed's purchases—learning from the inside how the American central bank viewed the economy—and then, two weeks later, deploy those same employees toward managing the rest of their accounts.

When Bloomberg News dug into the numbers, it concluded that BlackRock stood to earn perhaps $48 million from its government assignment. For a company whose earnings the previous year had reached $4.5 billion, this was something like a person finding a nickel on a sidewalk. BlackRock said it was donating its services to the American taxpayer, waiving its advisory fee.

But for Fink and BlackRock, the value of deepening ties with the government and gleaning insights about the inner workings of the Fed went beyond numbers on an invoice.

At the end of May, as the Fed released the first of its reports detailing its purchases under its emergency lending operations, they showed that the central bank had spent $1.58 billion on corporate bonds via exchange traded funds. Nearly half that spending represented purchases of iShares—BlackRock's investments.

BlackRock was also benefiting from the fact that the Fed was telegraphing its designs. It planned to plunk its money into funds full of corporate bonds, so investors rushed to get in first, ahead of a virtually guaranteed increase in value. Over the first half of 2020, BlackRock saw a net influx of $34 billion in investment into the funds the Fed had purchased, an increase of 160 percent compared to the previous year.

More than anything, BlackRock, like the rest of the corporate realm, benefited from the fact that the Fed was making credit widely available. Because of the central bank's interventions, companies could borrow as needed and at low rates from the private markets, without having to submit to the unpalatable conditions that accompanied loans from some of the government's official rescue programs, such as limiting bonuses, withholding dividends, and avoiding layoffs.

Even deeply troubled companies like Boeing, whose airplanes had displayed an unfortunate tendency to fall out of the sky, were able to borrow at attractive rates. Oil prices were plummeting alongside the world economy, but ExxonMobil found takers for $9.5 billion's worth of bonds at prices only a smidgen above what the U.S. government had to pay.

Amazon, whose balance sheet was strong, set a record for lowest interest rates ever paid on a debt issue. It raised $10 billion while compensating lenders with a mere four-tenths of 1 percent.

By the end of August, the bond market had served up just shy of $2 trillion in fresh investment to corporations, the largest yearly toll in history.

This gusher of credit spared Davos Man from a cascade of bankruptcies while triggering a wealth-creating boom in the stock market, even as joblessness remained a scourge.

Pundits puzzled over this supposed disconnect. How was it possible for major companies to thrive while workers struggled to come up with the rent? But the dirty secret was that this was how American capitalism had functioned for decades, enriching Davos Man while wage earners fell backward.

CHAPTER 10

"GROSSLY UNDERFUNDED AND FACING COLLAPSE"

How Davos Man Fleeced Pensions

Mitch McConnell, master of ceremonies in the United States Senate, and devoted Davos Man collaborator, had not recently evinced grave concern over the mounting federal budget deficit.

Three years earlier, when Trump's tax cuts were on the table, McConnell dutifully rounded up the votes while perpetuating the Cosmic Lie.

"There are a whole lot of economists who think that it will pay for itself," he told the television anchor George Stephanopoulous, who graciously declined to press him to name any of these economists. "It's very likely to be a revenue producer."

That claim proved false. Less than two years after the tax cuts, the federal budget deficit had increased by more than one-fourth, reaching nearly $1 trillion.

Yet now, in April 2020, just as millions of Americans faced unrelenting hardship, McConnell was suddenly expressing horror over the runaway federal debt. Spending had to be reined in, he warned, as he opposed the latest pandemic relief bill. The wealthiest country on earth supposedly could not afford to spend more to aid a populace ensnared in a once-in-a-lifetime disaster.

"My goal from the beginning of this, given the extraordinary numbers that we're racking up to the national debt, is that we need to be as cautious as we can be," McConnell said. "We can't borrow enough money to solve the problem indefinitely."

McConnell was a legend in Washington—a dedicated practitioner of constituent service, with the caveat that his constituents were energy companies, financial institutions, defense contractors, and pharmaceutical concerns. Over a Senate career that was well into its fourth decade, he had catered relentlessly to the interests of Davos Man while extracting the lifeblood of American democracy—campaign cash.

His success is owed to his mastery of Senate procedures and his ability to instill fear within his caucus, holding the votes together above all. He is a rarity in the American capital—a career politician who appears to take pride in being liked by few. He had once been described as "a man with the natural charisma of an oyster." He wore it as a badge of honor, a sign that he was too busy worrying about the mechanics of lawmaking to press flesh.

In the give-and-take of McConnell's world, the virtues of any proposed expenditure had to be assessed through a pragmatic calculation of who wound up with the money. If the cash flowed to an industry that shared the bounty via campaign contributions, then the spending represented a prudent investment in pro-growth policies for the middle class. But if the funds went to people in no position to increase McConnell's power, then here was a reckless squandering of taxpayer dollars.

The relief bill at issue aimed to help people who were squarely in the latter camp. Democrats were proposing to send $1 trillion in federal aid to beleaguered state and local governments to prevent the layoffs of teachers, cops, and firefighters—groups that generally did not raise significant money for Republicans.

No doubt, the budget deficit was enormous. The federal government was on pace to spend almost $4 trillion more over the course of 2020 than it expected to receive in tax revenues, yielding a gap nearly twice as large as in any year since World War II. But most economists saw this as appropriate, and even imperative in the face of a colossal threat to public health and livelihoods.

Just outside San Francisco, William Gonzalez had recently written his landlord to beg for mercy. He had lost his job as an attendant at an employee cafeteria inside a hotel that was suddenly devoid of guests. His $700-a-week paycheck had become a $414 unemployment check. His wife, Sonia Bautista, had just worked her last shift as a maid at another hotel. The landlord had taken pity on his family, allowing them to pay only half of their $2,800 monthly rent, but how long would his generosity last? And how long would it take them to find new jobs? The virus appeared to have staying power.

Gonzalez and his family were foregoing heat to limit their costs. They had no money for movies or other entertainment for their fourteen-year-old son, Ricardo. They had always been careful with their bills, avoiding debt, but now they were running up credit card balances just to pay for groceries. They had recently shelled out $10 to buy masks so they could visit the unemployment office. And they were terrified by the looming loss of their health insurance benefits, which came as part of his wife's job.

"That's our biggest concern," Gonzalez told me. "We are very worried about this. What if we get sick? We can't even pay out of our pocket."

Similar fears tore at tens of millions of other American households. The government and its assortment of relief programs was the only thing preventing a full-on collapse. This was a hard truth that went back to the Depression and the seminal economist John Maynard Keynes. When the economy shut down, destroying the capacity for people to earn a living, the government had to unleash money to create demand for goods and services.

The United States was in control of its own currency, and

investors were displaying an insatiable appetite for the rock-bottom stability of American government debt, supplying the Treasury carte blanche to finance whatever spending was necessary.

Still, McConnell held firm against aid for states and local governments. This risked a repeat of the Great Recession more than a decade earlier, when the loss of housing wealth combined with the stock market rout had prompted a severe pullback in consumer spending, diminishing tax receipts. Local governments responded by slashing the ranks of teachers, cops, and other public sector workers, at once diminishing public services and further weakening their economies.

Beyond accepting joblessness and the erosion of public services in the midst of a national emergency, McConnell was blaming the victim. He claimed that cities and states were in trouble not because of the pandemic, but because of extravagant generosity toward the very people threatened with joblessness—cops, public school teachers, and other government employees.

"There's not going to be any desire on the Republican side to bail out state pensions by borrowing money from future generations," McConnell said.

If states could not manage their bills, he added, perhaps they could make use of the legal machinations frequently employed by the casino operator residing at the White House.

"I would certainly be in favor of allowing states to use the bankruptcy route," McConnell said.

That would enable state pension systems to stiff public sector workers.

In McConnell's world there was plenty of money to rescue Davos Man, but nothing left for regular working people.

In blaming rank-and-file employees for the budget problems of state and local governments, McConnell was indulging a level of cynicism that was remarkable even by his standards.

For years, so-called alternative asset managers—the benign argot for hedge funds, private equity shops, and the other pirates sailing the high seas of finance—had sought to colonize an alluring frontier strewn with diamonds: pension systems stocked with the retirement savings of state and municipal employees.

The industry had pursued this goal with flotillas laden with campaign cash and armies of lobbyists. It had carried the day by arguing that financial geniuses wielding algorithms would generate higher returns than simply putting pension money into low-cost, boring investments like index funds and government bonds.

The private equity industry had in recent years persuaded American public pension funds to entrust it with enormous sums of money. The total had climbed from $320 billion to $638 billion between 2015 and 2018.

Led by savvy opportunists like Steve Schwarzman, the industry sold itself to clients as a wealth-generating machine while exploiting the opacity of its business to impose an unending array of fees—for managing money, for looking out for risks, for monitoring positions, and for a host of ill-defined advisory services.

Davos Man courted credulous pension managers with a smorgasbord of inducements—tickets to sporting events, expensive wines, and junkets to destinations far and wide. In 2010, a manager for California's pension system—one of the largest on earth—had testified in a corruption probe that investment firms had flown him around the world on private jets, taking him to Shanghai, Mumbai, and New York for what were billed as "one on one" strategic meetings. (Nothing like a bottle of Château Margaux to focus the mind on fiduciary responsibility.)

A decade later, the ties between Schwarzman's company and the man who managed the holdings of California's pension system raised fresh questions about the propriety of their dealings. Ben Meng, the chief investment officer of the California system—by then stocked with nearly $400 billion in assets—personally owned stock in Blackstone, according to a June 2020 financial disclosure form. Three months earlier, the California pension system had entrusted $1 billion to a Blackstone fund. It was reasonable to wonder whether this transaction had been influenced by Meng's personal stake in Blackstone's performance, as opposed to the best interests of California taxpayers. Meng had also been paid between $10,000 and $100,000 for a teaching gig at the Schwarzman Scholars program at China's Tsinghua University. In August 2020, as these disclosures were excavated by the financial blog *Naked Capitalism*, Meng abruptly resigned. A state ethics probe was ongoing.

Over a fifteen-year period, private equity had sucked up $230 billion in fees from the pension funds and university endowments whose money it was managing, concluded a study by Oxford University's Said Business School. Yet the industry's returns had failed to match traditional options like index funds, which were characterized by ultra-low fees.

"This wealth transfer might be one of the largest in the history of modern finance: from a few hundred million pension scheme members to a few thousand people working in private equity," the study concluded.

No one ran a more efficient dollar-extracting machine than Schwarzman.

In recent years, Blackstone had turned itself from a methodically growing financial player into the darling of Wall Street, its share price nearly doubling over the course of 2019.

Its performance had been boosted by a gift from Schwarzman's Florida neighbor, Donald Trump.

In slashing the corporate tax rate, President Trump had enabled private equity players to ditch their previous structures as so-called partnerships—which had been set up to shield earnings from the tax collector—while converting themselves into ordinary corporations. This had unlocked a lucrative world of new investors such as mutual funds. They had previously been shut out of investing in private equity because of the complex tax filings involved in dealing with partnerships.

Blackstone's conversion to a regular corporation had produced a surge of money. By the end of 2019, with Blackstone's shares soaring, Schwarzman's net worth had climbed to $19 billion, up from $13.2 billion only eight months earlier.

Schwarzman had shared the windfall with the Republican leadership who had enabled it. McConnell's primary fundraising vehicle, the Senate Leadership Fund, was brimming with $20 million in contributions from Schwarzman alone.

At about the same time that McConnell was blaming retired public sector workers for the perilous condition of state and local finances, a lawsuit in his home state of Kentucky offered a disturbing perspective on the seamy interactions of private equity with the pension system.

The suit was filed by Kentucky's recently elected attorney general, Daniel Cameron, a Republican. He had filed it on behalf of the state's retirees, arguing that they had been cheated by Blackstone and another giant private equity company, KKR. He dropped a complaint full of damning details about how they had allegedly exploited the naivete of the state's pension overseers—a classic tale of big city bankers fleecing credulous bumpkins.

Over the previous two decades, the United States enjoyed one of the greatest bull markets in history, allowing regular people to invest in low-cost index funds and rack up terrific returns. Yet the Kentucky pension system was "grossly underfunded and facing collapse," the complaint noted. It had lost more than $6 billion since 2000, sliding from a surplus toward insolvency.

Seeking to make up lost ground while cloaking the extent of its troubles, Kentucky's pension managers bought into a pitch from Blackstone and KKR, according to the lawsuit. In 2011, the state pension system sunk more than $1.2 billion into a trio of

funds comprised of slices of other hedge funds assembled by the
two private equity giants.

Blackstone and KKR assured Kentucky officials that its
funds would yield a positive return, though they were in fact
engineered to generate exorbitant fees, the complaint alleged.
When losses resulted, the state was forced to kick in more than
$1 billion to bolster its teetering pension system. Lawmakers
came up with the money in part by cutting support for public
schools.

In its own legal filings, Blackstone asserted that the returns it
produced for the Kentucky pension system exceeded the target.

One detail in the state's complaint conveyed the sense that
Schwarzman had rolled Kentucky like a rube in a sidewalk game
of three-card monte: Schwarzman had allegedly used his private
jet to transfer cash from the taxpayers of Kentucky into his own
pockets. He had supposedly deployed the plane to fly Blackstone's agents to Kentucky for meetings, and then billed the
state for the cost of the flights. The tab had allegedly exceeded
$5 million a year.

A Blackstone spokesman called that account "totally false."

It was a devastating claim—an accusation that Schwarzman
had pillaged Kentucky's retired civil servants. He had used the
proceeds to bankroll the Davos Man collaborator who ran the Senate, who was in turn applying his power to deny aid to the people of his own state in the middle of a catastrophe.

Meanwhile, Schwarzman was about to gain another dividend
from the Trump administration.

With the country focused on the pandemic, the Labor Department quietly issued a fruitful directive: the government
cleared the path for private equity and hedge funds to begin
managing trillions of dollars' worth of retirement savings beyond government pension systems—that is, accounts managed
by companies and individuals.

Schwarzman had been seeking this change for years, correctly viewing private retirement savings as a frontier strewn with treasure.

The terse, jargon-filled directive from a little-watched arm of the federal government drew scant mention in the press. To the extent that it was covered at all, it was described in the same neutral terms that private equity companies favored—as an alternative made available for people planning for their golden years.

The regulation enabled Schwarzman and the rest of his industry to dip into a vast, as-yet-untapped reservoir of investment stocked with $8.7 trillion.

Even for Davos Man, that was a hell of a lot of money.

But other members of the billionaire tribe were not satisfied with merely profiting from the opportunities presented by an epochal disaster. They sought to exploit the pandemic as a chance to demonstrate their moral underpinnings—a useful device in the reach for fresh gains.

CHAPTER 11

"WE ARE ACTUALLY ALL ONE"

Davos Man's Words of Love

Marc Benioff was having an amazing pandemic. It was nourishing his portfolio and his soul, reminding him—teaching everyone, really—that all of humanity was just one big *ohana*.

As the world descended into lockdown, basements and bedrooms became the new offices. Those fortunate enough to be able to do their jobs remotely were working from home, while relying on technology to stay tethered to the outside world. Zoom—a videoconferencing software that, pre-COVID-19, most had never heard of—swiftly secured status as the default means of interfacing with other humans. The same forces made Benioff's company more valuable than ever.

Salesforce distributed its products via the web, so people could download them wherever they happened to be. Professionals could use the platform to collaborate in real time, even as their desks rubbed up against racks of drying underwear; as their cooped-up children, home from shuttered schools, agitated for more screen time; as Amazon delivery people interrupted their meetings to drop off fresh shipments of peanut butter, brownie mix, and other fortifications for the apocalypse.

Between late March and the middle of August 2020, Salesforce doubled in value, making the business worth more than $225 billion.

The company's founder, Benioff, was also boosting his claim to the title of most empathetic corporate chieftain.

During the first wave of the pandemic, he appeared on CNBC's *Mad Money,* hosted by Jim Cramer, Wall Street's overcaffeinated court jester. Struggling to contain his elation, Cramer introduced Benioff as a "visionary" who was proving that "business is the most powerful source for social change in America." The Salesforce chief had urged his employees to continue paying their cleaning people and dog walkers in absentia. He had pledged to avoid layoffs for at least ninety days, while calling on other companies to do the same.

"This is a moment where business has to be the greatest platform for change," Benioff said. "And that's why I've challenged CEOs all over the world to take the ninety-day pledge."

The virus was bringing people together, Benioff said, rendering obsolete the traditional divisions of wealth, class, nationality, and race.

"It doesn't discriminate," he said. "I think it's a tremendous spiritual message for us to remember. Through all of the illusions of our borders, and the illusions of our separation between us as human beings, in reality we are actually all one, and this is a tremendous moment for us to come together, as one humanity, to serve everybody, and also to express my love to all of those that are going through this horrible time."

This was a sentiment heard with growing fervor from Davos Man, the idea that the pandemic was a great unifier, a collective experience that diminished the importance of wealth disparities, racial divides, and other distinctions by reducing all of humanity to its most elemental state—one species rendered vulnerable by a virus that treated everyone equally.

The virus did indeed take up residence in any available body.

Britain's prime minister, Boris Johnson, fell ill and required hospitalization. Trump and much of his administration eventually contracted the virus. So did star athletes and Hollywood celebrities. Wealth and fame clearly afforded no inoculation.

But the dangers of the outbreak were distinctively more potent for lower-income households. African Americans and Latinos were especially exposed, given decades of systematic forms of discrimination, which left these communities more concentrated in dense neighborhoods that challenged social distancing, and more likely to be employed in low-wage service sector jobs that lacked health insurance.

During the first half of 2020 in the United States, African Americans contracted COVID-19 at nearly triple the rate of whites, while Latinos suffered even higher incidence.

American life expectancy fell by a year and a half in 2020, the steepest decline since World War II—a testament to the broad and lethal impact of COVID-19. But the drop was roughly twice as severe for Hispanics and African Americans—three years and 2.9 years respectively, compared to 1.2 years for white Americans.

The facile notion that the pandemic was an equal opportunity menace was belied by the simplest observation about who was delivering the packages, who was stocking shelves at grocery stores, and who was emptying bedpans in nursing homes, where senior citizens were dying in alarming numbers. In the United States, women, Blacks, and Latinos were prominently overrepresented in such jobs, just as they were overrepresented among the ranks of the dead.

In Britain, people of Caribbean and African descent were suffering death rates double and triple those of whites despite the country's socialized health care system, which offered free care to all.

In the townships of South Africa, in the teeming slums of

India, and in the barrios of South America, social distancing was largely impossible. People had to go to work or they went hungry.

These realities did not reflect the intrinsic nature of the coronavirus, but rather the stark inequalities of the societies in which it was spreading. Millions of economically fragile Americans were losing jobs and then getting evicted, taking refuge with friends and relatives, which increased the risk of the virus. In the twenty-seven states that lifted moratoriums on evictions over the course of 2020, people died of COVID-19 at more than one and a half times the surrounding rates. Medical workers were risking their lives to administer care. Working mothers were bearing an outsized share of the torturous responsibilities for distance learning for their children.

Benioff was speaking from his $28 million home overlooking San Francisco Bay. He would be forced to cancel Dreamforce, his beloved annual gathering. "Metallica are not playing," Benioff told stock analysts. "There's a sadness that we're not all together." Yet, there were consolations. As tens of millions of ordinary Americans lost their jobs, the value of Salesforce shares climbed, lifting Benioff's net worth from $5.8 billion to $7.5 billion by the fall of 2020.

From the South Pacific to the Caribbean, real estate agents were doing a brisk business in private islands as those with sufficient means established havens beyond reach of other humans. The private jet industry was booming. In the Hamptons—the exclusive New York–area beach preserve where Schwarzman owned an estate—dinner parties carried on as hosts screened guests with coveted instant COVID-19 tests. Meanwhile, a dearth of testing bedeviled plans to reopen New York City public schools.

The wealthiest had long sought to separate themselves from the rest of humanity. The pandemic supplied a convenient imperative to act on such instincts.

In late August—as American school districts delivered the grim news that many would not offer in-person instruction that fall—Benioff returned to Cramer's show to take a bow for having wildly exceeded Wall Street's expectations.

Salesforce had racked up more than $5 billion in revenue between April and June. A new digital dashboard that businesses could use to track the pandemic and plot their reopenings, Work.com, had grown faster than any product in the company's history. The company had just been elevated into the exclusive ranks of the Dow Jones Industrial Average, supplanting Exxon-Mobil.

Cramer's excitement verged on the level of a seizure. Exxon-Mobil was a major producer of fossil fuels, making it a leading culprit for climate change. Benioff was an environmental steward whose philanthropic efforts were planting millions of trees around the world.

"Can we conclude that *being good* actually generates great numbers?" Cramer asked.

Benioff beamed triumphantly.

"This is a victory for stakeholder capitalism," he said. "The planet is a key stakeholder."

The next day, Benioff's company quietly shared less wonderful news with a thousand members of the *ohana*. They were losing their jobs.

The term *stakeholder capitalism* had been around in various forms for many years, but it was suddenly a prominent talking point from executive suites to the conference circuit.

Klaus Schwab had used the World Economic Forum to push the concept since the 1970s, positing an updated mode of business in which the interests of companies would align with other societal concerns.

Stakeholder capitalism was supposed to represent an evolutionary leap from profit maximization.

"We need a new, better global system," Schwab declared in his 2021 book entitled, as it happens, *Stakeholder Capitalism*. "In this system, the interests of all stakeholders in the economy and society are taken on board, companies optimize for more than just short-term profits, and governments are the guardians of equality of opportunity."

At BlackRock, Fink had taken the theoretical principles discussed in Davos and injected them into the boardrooms of publicly traded corporations. In his rendering, economic inequality, climate change, and other concerns were not only legitimate areas of interest for a business, but imperative considerations for companies fully grappling with modern hazards.

In 2018, Fink captured headlines with a letter to fellow CEOs in which he warned that companies that failed to manage their businesses in this fashion would be swept aside by an inevitable reckoning. "To prosper over time, every company must not only deliver financial performance, but also show how it makes a positive contribution to society," he wrote.

In January 2020, Fink penned another letter, this one demanding that CEOs factor climate change into their plans. "Over time," he wrote, "companies and countries that do not respond to stakeholders and address sustainability risks will encounter growing skepticism from the markets, and in turn, a higher cost of capital."

The financial press christened Fink "the new conscience of Wall Street." But he wasn't calling for do-gooder charity. He was arguing for a sharpening of accounting standards to fully capture risk. In a world under assault by rising seas and turbulent weather, how safe was real estate, and what were the implications for mortgage-backed securities? With fossil fuel producers increasingly vulnerable to consumer boycotts, what was the proper valuation for oil and gas company stocks? And if a reassessment was in order, how solid were the balance sheets of the pension funds that held their shares?

Given the unrivaled pile of money that Fink managed, this was more than commentary. The investments he controlled supplied him votes at shareholder meetings. He threatened to use his power to unleash consequences on CEOs who failed to publish plans that properly addressed the risks of climate change.

"We will be increasingly disposed to vote against management and board directors when companies are not making sufficient progress," Fink wrote, underscoring the threat.

But as of early 2021, environmentalists were still waiting for follow-through that would render his pious words something more than public relations bluster.

BlackRock had joined a body called Climate Action 100+, a group of money managers that collectively controlled more than $40 trillion in investment. It aimed to force fossil fuel producers to publicly commit to plans to reduce carbon dioxide emissions. Yet BlackRock's funds held more than $87 billion's worth of shares in companies that were in the group's crosshairs, among them BP, Shell, and ExxonMobil. And BlackRock had repeatedly voted against resolutions proposed by the body seeking to impose clear targets for progress.

Following devastating brushfires in Australia in early 2020, investors in two Australian oil companies backed resolutions demanding their compliance with the emissions-reducing targets of the Paris Climate Accords. BlackRock voted against them.

In Brazil, the rain forests of the Amazon were on fire, menacing the most vital storehouse of carbon on the planet. Cattle ranchers bore much of the blame, having clear-cut vast reaches to make room for pastures. BlackRock had aggressively increased its stake in one of Brazil's largest meatpacking conglomerates.

BlackRock was negotiating to purchase a stake in a pipeline business controlled by Saudi Aramco, the world's largest oil producer. In that transaction, it was being advised by Jamie Dimon's bank.

Dimon was another leading proponent of stakeholder capitalism, having used his turn as chairman of the Business Roundtable to yield its most consequential manifestation: an updated Statement on the Purpose of a Corporation. Delivered with great ballyhoo in the summer of 2019, the statement was packaged as a revamping of the previous mode of corporate organization as distilled by Milton Friedman a half century earlier. Businesses would no longer focus solely on making money, instead balancing their duties to shareholders against their responsibilities to workers, customers, the environment, and the communities in which they operated. The heads of 181 of America's largest companies had signed the statement.

"Major employers are investing in their workers and communities because they know it is the only way to be successful over the long term," Dimon declared.

A parade of pundits hailed the Roundtable's action as a milestone. Writing in *Fortune*, the journalist Alan Murray celebrated the statement as an antidote to the forces tearing at the liberal world order, and recognition from CEOs that they had to be part of the solution.

"Something fundamental and profound has changed in the way they approach their jobs," he wrote.

Davos Man had spent decades deploying lobbyists and lawyers toward weakening the hand of the state, eviscerating regulations, and deactivating traditional antitrust concerns. The credulous embrace of the Business Roundtable statement highlighted the magnitude of his success. The billionaires had altered the view of business in the popular imagination, refashioning themselves as a source of vitality and good, in contrast to the supposed incompetence of government and other impediments to progress.

The Roundtable statement contained the implicit notion that

Davos Man could be trusted to do right by everyone, magnanimously making needed adjustments. Society did not require regulators and rules interfering with business to protect public interests like clean air or fair competition. No back-and-forth with labor unions was necessary to ensure adequate pay. The executives were benevolent masters of their domain, their virtues beyond reproach, so any counterbalancing interest could be dispensed as gratuitous impediments to their dynamism.

Later that year, the World Economic Forum delivered a Davos Manifesto that reinforced the Roundtable's elevation of stakeholder capitalism.

"Companies should pay their fair share of taxes, show zero tolerance for corruption, uphold human rights throughout their global supply chains, and advocate for a competitive level playing field," Schwab wrote in an essay published in *Time* magazine, the venerable publication that Benioff had purchased the previous year. The concept "positions private corporations as trustees of society."

In essence, addressing climate change and social injustice could be outsourced to Fink, Dimon, Benioff, and the other upstanding billionaires.

When the Forum convened in Davos in January 2020, its official theme was a "focus on establishing stakeholder capitalism." The keynote address that captured the most attention was delivered by a man not generally known for his empathy: Schwab again welcomed Donald Trump to the stage.

More than two years had passed since Trump handed out the largest package of tax cuts in American history. Trump had looked past the savage killing and dismemberment of a *Washington Post* columnist by the Saudi Arabian regime—a government courted by Fink—citing the fact that the Saudis lavished billions of dollars on American defense contractors. His administration had forcibly separated the children of undocumented immigrants from their parents at the American border. He refused to release his tax returns, undercutting transparency. And he was under trial in the Senate, having been impeached for pressuring Ukraine to pursue a probe of his soon-to-be election challenger, Joe Biden—a corruption of American foreign policy in pursuit of personal aims.

Apparently, none of this invalidated Trump's credentials as an exemplar of stakeholder capitalism.

"Congratulations for what you have achieved for your economy, but also for your society," Schwab told him. "All your politics certainly are aiming to create better inclusiveness for the American people."

Trump was delighted to play along, striking his well-honed pose as a man of the people.

"For the first time in decades, we are no longer simply concentrating wealth in the hands of a few," Trump said. "We are lifting up Americans of every race, color, religion, and creed."

The novel coronavirus would soon expose the vacuous platitudes of stakeholder capitalism.

Armed with its new statement of corporate purpose, the Business Roundtable convened a special task force to coordinate policies on COVID-19. It was cochaired by Arne Sorenson, the chief executive officer of Marriott, the largest hotel chain on earth.

Sorenson—who would die of pancreatic cancer the following year—was a regular at the Forum, though his net worth, estimated at about $121 million, made him a commoner among the billionaires. He described stakeholder capitalism as the logical extension of the principles at work in any company that was managed for the long haul.

"We will not compromise the future to deliver this quarter, period," he said on the sidelines of the Forum in January 2020. "And that means you're investing in your people, you're investing

in your communities, you're investing in these other stakeholders for whom your long-term success is very much dependent."

Two months later, Sorenson peered soberly into a camera and
recorded a video message for his employees. The pandemic presented the bleakest moment he had ever witnessed.

Marriott's 1.4 million hotel rooms were spread across 131
countries. Usually, its breadth was a strength, insulating the
company against trouble in any one region. Now, ubiquity meant
exposure to danger everywhere.

Business had plunged by three-fourths in many markets,
Sorenson said. In the United States, Marriott was furloughing
workers for at least two months, and possibly longer.

"There is simply nothing worse than telling highly valued
associates, people who are the very heart of this company, that
their roles are being impacted by events completely outside of
their control," Sorenson continued. "I wish you good health and
a sense of optimism."

Hunkered down in her apartment in South San Francisco,
Sonia Bautista and her husband, William Gonzalez—the laid-off
hotel cafeteria attendant—found optimism elusive.

For the last year, she had worked as a maid at a luxury Marriott property in downtown San Francisco, the Palace Hotel,
earning $26.44 an hour. She had already received a letter from
management informing her that she was being furloughed.

Beyond her family's mounting debts, their fears of eviction,
and the approaching expiry of their health insurance, Bautista
nursed a deep sense of injustice.

"All the executives, Sorenson and the others, they get paid
millions every year, and we just get a few dollars," Bautista told
me. "We are proud to work for Marriott. We give our soul to give
our best for our company. I try hard to make the rooms beautiful
for guests so they will come back. It's not fair. Marriott doesn't
care about us."

She and her husband were immigrants from El Salvador. They had survived a bloody civil war in the 1980s, establishing stable lives in the United States. They struggled to comprehend how, in the face of a genuine emergency, their wealthy employer could have nothing left for the people who actually did the work.

"They just say, 'We don't need you. You are on your own,'" Gonzalez said.

Marriott had earned more than $3.1 billion over the past two years. Contrary to Sorenson's talk about investing in his people, he had pursued the immediate gratification of its shareholders. He had plowed Marriott's profits plus debt toward buying more than $5 billion's worth of its own shares, leaving minimal reserves to weather the crisis that was rapidly unfolding.

This was Davos Man's standard mode. Even as Dimon campaigned for stakeholder capitalism via the new mission statement, he and the rest of the Business Roundtable endorsed share buybacks as a means of "making capital markets efficient"—finance-speak for using money to sate investors, rather than wasting it on wages.

Between 2017 and 2019, the companies that comprised the S&P 500 stock index had spent a total of $2 trillion to buy back their shares. These buybacks had sent share prices higher, enriching people like Sorenson and Dimon.

In his video message, Sorenson indulged the ritual of sacrifice. He was foregoing his salary—$1.3 million annually—in solidarity with affected workers. But he said nothing about his stock-based pay, which had exceeded $8 million the year before, or the cash incentive plan that netted him $3.5 million.

Less than two weeks later, Marriott followed through with paying out scheduled dividends, handing a fresh $160 million to shareholders—enough to employ more than five thousand maids for six months.

A few days after that, Sorenson distributed an email to

Marriott's customers updating them on the company's actions. It was housing health care professionals in its hotel rooms. It was switching on room lights at its empty properties to form heart shapes and words like *LOVE* and *HOPE*.

The Business Roundtable Statement and the Davos Manifesto were empty words. Davos Man never ran out of new management terms, or promises for transformation, or reassurances about his benevolent intent. Sorenson had been overseeing his business the same way that most publicly traded companies had been run for decades. You could call hotel maids "stakeholders" or "highly valued associates" or whatever you pleased, but when the bottom line was under attack, they became costs to be ruthlessly eliminated.

Hardly any of the signatories to the Business Roundtable's statement gained approval from their governing boards for committing to stakeholder capitalism. That fact alone laid bare that the document was really a ploy. It provided cover for Davos Man to carry on as ever while gaining kudos from collaborators.

Bolten, the Business Roundtable's president, dismissed that critique. Member companies were already governed by the principles in the statement, so a resolution was not needed.

"It did not arise from nowhere," he told me. "The statement has to be viewed as both capturing an evolution and expressing an aspiration."

That would have been a reasonable argument had the release of the statement been accompanied by a press release advertising the historic perpetuation of the status quo. Either shareholders were sacrificing to improve the lot of workers, or the statement was hollow.

But Bolten said the statement should properly be read as an obituary for short-term obsessions in corporate management. Companies had long engineered jumps in their stock prices by firing workers or eliminating benefits.

"In the long term, that's not going to serve the enterprise

well if you haven't properly taken care of all of your other stake-holders," Bolten insisted. "You cannot take care of any one of them without taking care of them all."

This was a savvy way to frame it. It was also demonstrably false. If the last half century of American capitalism had proven anything, it was that one special stakeholder—the shareholder—could prosper spectacularly at the direct expense of everyone else.

The statement that Salesforce released in late August 2020—the day after Benioff's latest exultant turn on the Cramer show—was pointedly lacking in the *ohana* vibe.

"We're reallocating resources to position the company for continued growth," it declared, a move that entailed "eliminating some positions that no longer map to our business priorities."

Benioff's ninety-day pledge had run its course, leaving him free to cut jobs as needed.

But the Salesforce CEO declared this an unfair takeaway when I spoke to him on the phone. The company was hiring in other areas, adding more than four thousand more jobs that fall, he said. And the one thousand employees affected were still on the payroll. They were being invited to apply for other positions within the company. Those who departed would take with them substantial severance packages.

Still, Benioff acknowledged the less than ideal optics of declaring the triumph of stakeholder capitalism on one day, and cutting loose one thousand employees on the next.

"Some of that is a P.R. gaffe," he said.

Salesforce employed fifty-four thousand people around the globe. "We need to make a couple of adjustments," Benioff said. "We have to be able to grow and make change or we cannot achieve our goals, which is to become a larger, much more successful company for our customers, our shareholders, and also, yes, our stakeholders."

The Forum had recently announced that its next Davos get-together, scheduled for January 2021, had been turned into a virtual gathering. Holed up in Hawaii, Benioff was bummed out about this.

"I think the world needs a Davos right now," he said. "So that everybody can get together and talk about how to move forward."

He detected my skepticism and challenged it. The Forum had been the staging ground for a global partnership that had immunized millions of children in the world's poorest countries. Environmentalists, labor advocates, and other key elements from civil society used Davos as a vital meeting point.

"Davos is not perfect, but what is the alternative?" he said. "Your premise is that companies for the most part are still acting under the guise of Milton Friedman, they are using stakeholderism as air cover, and Davos is still mostly about making money and that's why they're all going."

Pretty much, yeah.

"I totally get it," Benioff said, "because I see that aspect of it, but I also see all the other things, too, all the other conversations, all the other people, all the other things that have happened."

My depiction was incomplete, Benioff insisted. "It's definitely not totally true. Is it 50 percent? Maybe it's 60 to 70 percent. But there's definitely a wedge. And that wedge is getting bigger."

Benioff insisted that his focus on doing good could not simply be fodder for press releases, or his employees would see through it. They would go elsewhere, gravitating toward companies that were genuinely infused with social purpose.

This was reminiscent of Milton Friedman's argument that we need not worry about racial discrimination in the workplace, because the free market would prevent it. Companies that limited their access to talent would be punished. American capitalism had since demonstrated that companies could survive—could, in fact, wildly enrich their shareholders—while neglecting to make their workforces remotely representative of society.

Benioff's own company was a prime example. At Salesforce, African Americans made up less than 3 percent of the workforce and held only 1.5 percent of the leadership positions. Benioff had hired a chief equality officer, a Black executive named Tony Prophet. He found himself having to answer to employees who disdained Benioff's constant use of *ohana* as a form of cultural appropriation, while noting that Native Hawaiians, Native Americans, and Pacific Islanders collectively held less than 1 percent of the jobs.

In the first wave of the pandemic, as the virus menaced his hometown of San Francisco, Benioff had mobilized to secure protective gear for local hospitals. He called Daniel Zhang, the chief executive of Alibaba, the Chinese e-commerce giant whose founder, Jack Ma, served with him as a member of the Forum's Board of Trustees. Zhang tapped his Chinese suppliers to amass a trove of protective gear, and Benioff chartered a fleet of 747s to fly the goods from China to San Francisco.

Benioff convened a call with his fellow members of the Business Roundtable, enlisting his counterparts at other large companies to expand the effort. Salesforce dispatched a shipment to Chicago, where Walmart was waiting with a team of trucks to carry it to frontline hospitals as far away as New Orleans. United Airlines agreed to unload the planes for free.

Within weeks, Benioff and the rest of the companies had spent $25 million to deliver 50 million pieces of personal protective equipment to American institutions. He sent shipments to the United Kingdom, donating gear to the beleaguered National Health Service.

"That was very powerful, you know, that I'm able to have these relationships," Benioff told me. "I have to tell you, that I have turned those into a lot of fantastic opportunities for those companies to do well, and do good at the same time."

The scale of Benioff's company, its global presence, its operational expertise, and his personal familiarity with other CEOs had clearly yielded significant returns. Because of his efforts, vital supplies were secured in the midst of an emergency. It seemed reasonable to assume that his campaign had saved lives.

But Benioff's air bridge also begged a key question: why was the wealthiest, most powerful country on earth dependent on the charity of a profit-making software company to outfit its medical personnel with basic protection in the face of a pandemic?

Part of why individuals like Benioff could crow about giving back was because of how comprehensively they had taken to begin with. They had benefited from public goods financed by taxpayers—the schools that educated their employees; the internet, developed by publicly funded research; the roads, the bridges, and the rest of modern infrastructure, which enabled commerce—and then deployed their lobbyists, accountants, and lawyers to master legal forms of tax evasion that starved the system.

They had transferred wealth from the public to themselves by rewriting the tax code in their favor, leaving government too weak to protect the populace from the pandemic. And now they were deploying their resulting resources in the service of charity while demanding adulation.

Like every initiative championed by Davos Man, stakeholder capitalism was a voluntary undertaking, a discretionary display of generosity. Even Benioff acknowledged that some CEOs were using it to project virtue while running their companies no differently than before.

"It's a very real risk," Benioff said. "I also think we are making progress. I never said it's a revolution, but I said it's an improvement."

CHAPTER 12

"WE'RE NOT SAFE"

Davos Man and the Human Problem

Jeff Bezos also signed the Business Roundtable statement, committing to allowing "each person to succeed through hard work and creativity and to lead a life of meaning and dignity."

As the ink on his signature dried, Bezos carried on with the same cutthroat version of capitalism that had made him the wealthiest person on earth.

For years, Amazon had been the subject of stories about exploitation inside its warehouses, where low-wage workers faced unrelenting pressure to manage an overwhelming flow of packages. The pandemic dramatically intensified the strain. There were more packages than ever.

Between April and June 2020, as the first wave assailed the globe, Amazon sold 57 percent more items than it had during the same period in the previous year. In July alone, the company shipped 415 million packages.

Amazon's enormous warehouse and delivery operation initially buckled in the face of this extraordinary surge, yielding delays and consumer complaints—a grave problem for a company that cited the satisfaction of customers as justification for the incessant pressures on its workers. In a furious effort to expand capacity, the company added warehouses, renting space from Blackstone, which was investing tens of billions of dollars to purchase such facilities, cannily exploiting the growth of e-commerce.

Amazon also unleashed a hiring binge akin to a wartime mass mobilization. It added roughly five hundred thousand employees over the course of 2020, stretching its workforce to 1.3 million, roughly double the number of only two years earlier. Yet even that pace of hiring was outstripped by the sheer growth of merchandise coursing through its warehouses.

Amazon's online shopping empire long had prospered by undercutting bricks-and-mortar shops. In 2020, what physical retail outlets remained were suddenly shut or shunned as danger zones, leaving the digital realm as practically the only way for people to shop.

Demand for everything from dishwasher detergent to sweatpants was exploding. Professionals outfitting bedrooms as workspaces needed printers and computer monitors.

People forced to scrap vacations consoled themselves with new towels and bubble bath crystals. Parents filled basements with toys and stocked kitchens with baking supplies. Everyone hoarded hand sanitizer and toilet paper.

During the first half of the year, Amazon sold $164 billion's worth of goods, or more than $10,000's worth every second. Over that time, Amazon's stock price nearly doubled, turning the increases in Bezos's net worth into fodder for everyday conversation, like the batting exploits of a record-chasing baseball star, or the wind speeds of a hurricane. By the end of August, Bezos was the first human being to possess a fortune in excess of $200 billion, an increase of $87 billion since the beginning of the pandemic (which presumably helped diminish the sting of having agreed to the largest divorce settlement in history, a payout of $38 billion to MacKenzie Scott).

Before 2020 ended Bezos came to personify the rapacious

opportunism of the billionaire class who were extracting wealth from a public health emergency, at the expense of employees laboring in proximity to the virus.

This turn was largely because of a thirty-one-year-old father of three, who had simply had enough.

Christian Smalls had worked for Amazon for more than four years, starting at the company's warehouse outside Newark, New Jersey, at an entry level wage of $12.75 an hour. He began as a picker, selecting items required to fulfill orders, and placing them into bags that he deposited on a conveyor belt, bound for another team that put them into boxes.

Smalls was a natural, owing to his previous job on the graveyard shift inside a wholesale grocery distributor, where he pulled items off shelves and piled them onto pallets, forming pyramids reaching ten feet high. At that job, nearly all of his coworkers were African American men from the surrounding environs of Newark, where poverty and gang violence were constants, and jobs scarce. The supervisors were almost entirely white men. They rode around the floor on pallet jacks, hollering at workers who stopped to catch their breath.

"It was like modern-day slavery," Smalls told me. "It was like we were in the cotton fields."

Smalls had grown up middle-class, raised by a single mother who worked at a nearby hospital. He had graduated from high school and attended college in Florida, before getting homesick and dropping out. Passionate about hip hop, he had pursued a music career before relinquishing that dream to the realities of earning a living. He had married at twenty-two and began supporting his wife's son, and then their twins. When his wife started nursing school, he became the sole breadwinner.

In the fall of 2015, his mother heard about the new Amazon warehouse opening up outside Newark. She applied on his behalf. Smalls was one of the first five hundred people to be hired.

Compared to his previous warehouse, Amazon was an upgrade.

The floor was air-conditioned, and the break rooms were lined with video game consoles. He earned a promotion to supervisor after only seven months, giving him responsibility to train new hires. His pay increased to $18.50 an hour.

When Amazon opened another warehouse outside Hartford, Connecticut, Smalls was recruited to move there and initiate the new hires. He rode the Greyhound bus home to Jersey every weekend to see his wife and children, but the stress and the distance took a toll, and his marriage disintegrated. When Amazon opened another facility in New York in the fall of 2018, Smalls transferred there, accepting the night shift as the price of getting closer to home.

By then, he had sole custody of his three children, anchoring him in New Jersey. The new Amazon warehouse sat on Staten Island. Smalls did not own a car. Getting to work entailed two buses, a subway ride, and the Staten Island Ferry—a three-hour commute that was justified, though barely, by the $27 an hour he was earning for working nights.

After a few months, he managed to get back to working days. He was supervising more than three dozen people. The warehouse was humming, full of thousands of workers.

Then, in early March 2020, his employees began complaining of severe exhaustion while developing hacking coughs.

Smalls found himself glued to the television news, obsessively following the course of the pandemic.

"I'm sitting in the break room watching all this and thinking, 'What the hell are we doing to protect these workers?'"

Amazon was not supplying masks or sanitizers. It was not imposing social distancing. It was not even educating workers about the need to wash their hands.

Smalls worried about bringing the virus home to his children. When he went to human resources to express his concerns, he was told that the company was "monitoring the situation."

His employees were continuing to come to work even as some

came down with fevers. It was either that or forego their pay, because Amazon did not provide paid sick leave. The United States was one of only a handful of major economies where this was permissible, though some states legally required paid sick leave.

In Washington, the powers-that-be were claiming to have plugged this gap. As Congress approved the first wave of federal relief, House Speaker Nancy Pelosi touted the inclusion of a mandate that employers provide paid sick leave.

"We cannot slow the coronavirus outbreak when workers are stuck with the terrible choice between staying home to avoid spreading the illness and the paycheck their family can't afford to lose," she said.

But the bill that gained passage, bearing the comforting name "Families First," did little to reorder the priorities. It gave full-time workers ten days of annual paid sick leave, but it exempted companies with five hundred or more people. The bill allowed businesses with fewer than fifty employees to apply for hardship exemptions.

All told, the legislation left 80 percent of American workers facing the same conundrum: they could keep working when they got sick, or they could surrender their pay.

Under pressure, Amazon announced that it would provide up to two weeks of paid leave to employees ordered into quarantine by a doctor. Even then, some Amazon workers reported not receiving the money.

In withholding paid sick leave, Amazon was not merely exploiting a hole in American law. It was applying its corporate muscle to keeping that hole wide open. Amazon outsourced the dirty work to a host of trade associations—the U.S. Chamber of Commerce, the National Retail Federation, the National Federation of Independent Business, and the Food Marketing Institute. All reported lobbying on paid sick leave policies in the Families First Act. So did Dimon's shop, the Business Roundtable, despite its public championing of stakeholder capitalism.

When Smalls asked for time off, citing worries about his family's health, Amazon supervisors told him that he was welcome to stay home without pay. He used up his vacation time. He drained the $1,000 in his 401(k) retirement plan.

Meanwhile, he sent emails to the Centers for Disease Control, the governor, the mayor, and local media, alerting them to the fact that Amazon's Staten Island warehouse was continuing normal operations without protective measures, even as people fell ill. He heard nothing.

In the middle of March, out of cash, he returned to work. There were still no masks or sanitizer on hand, he said. Some workers were bringing in their own masks and reusing them. Some donned garbage bags as protective gowns. Many of his employees were displaying COVID-19 symptoms, he said.

When Smalls pressed human resources for the details of its COVID-19 policy, he was directed to speak to his supervisor. But his supervisor had disappeared.

"The managers were telling the employees that they were taking vacations," Smalls said. "In the middle of a pandemic. I'm like, *vacation*? They were lying to us." He assumed that managers were working from home to avoid exposure to the virus.

Not for the first time, he was struck by who was in harm's way. "The majority of the managers are white, and the workers are Black, brown immigrants," Smalls said. "Who's really being protected here?"

Concerned that some workers were staying home, Amazon began giving workers an extra $2 an hour in pay, plus double the usual rate for overtime. Smalls called it "blood money." In several states, Amazon workers earned so little that many qualified for food stamps—an effective subsidy from the taxpayer that allowed the company to pay poverty-level wages. Amazon workers were desperate, and the extra cash was an additional inducement for them to look past their fears and continue showing up.

On March 21, Bezos posted a message to Amazon's corporate website. "Dear Amazonians," it read. "This isn't business as usual, and it's a time of great stress and uncertainty."

Bezos acknowledged that people were laboring without sufficient protective gear, because Amazon—the company known as the Everything Store—could not secure it.

"We've placed purchase orders for millions of face masks we want to give to our employees and contractors who cannot work from home, but very few of those orders have been filled," Bezos wrote. "Masks remain in short supply globally and are at this point being directed by governments to the highest-need facilities like hospitals and clinics."

Bezos laid out a moral justification for keeping warehouses running, even without adequate protection. "We're providing a vital service to people everywhere, especially to those, like the elderly, who are most vulnerable," he wrote. "People are depending on us."

In other words, Smalls and his coworkers were not being pressured to risk their lives so that Bezos could purchase his next trophy residence, or further his passion to explore space. They were heroically keeping people's grandmothers safe. Moreover, the company was sharing in the sacrifice.

"We've changed our logistics, transportation, supply chain, purchasing and third party seller processes to prioritize stocking and delivering essential items like household staples, sanitizers, baby formula, and medical supplies," Bezos wrote.

Smalls could see what his team was putting into boxes. "They never changed the inventory," he said. "That was all a lie. It was the same shit—sex toys, dildos, board games, household items, clothing."

And even as Amazon laid claim to a halo, the company was profiteering off the disaster: It was jacking up prices for the very goods it was supposedly prioritizing, the watchdog group Public Citizen later revealed.

Customers could find lower-priced products from independent

vendors selling on its platform, but Amazon was dramatically marking up its own goods—the ones it promoted most aggressively.

Between April and August 2020—a period in which sixty thousand Americans a day were testing positive for the virus, filling hospitals and morgues—Amazon charged $39.99 for a pack of fifty disposable face masks that it usually sold for $4. Amazon demanded $7 for antibacterial soap that was normally $1.49.

Amazon was also hindering shipments as part of its bid to dominate the delivery business. It was penalizing suppliers who dispatched their wares to customers using competitors like Federal Express and United Parcel Service. Amazon achieved this by limiting what products could gain its coveted Prime designation—an internal seal of approval that vouched for the legitimacy of the goods and the speed of delivery.

For a merchant selling through Amazon, the value of gaining Prime status was like setting up a store in Times Square compared to hawking goods from a roadside stand in central Nebraska. During the pandemic, Amazon effectively forced merchants to use its delivery network to qualify for Prime.

The tactic worked too well. Amazon's logistics operation was swamped, yielding delays in delivery. For Bezos, keeping customers stocked in critical goods took a back seat to the quest for monopoly power.

As workers tested positive, Amazon kept these cases quiet, Smalls said. He demanded that managers alert the workforce while shutting the building down for a deep cleaning, but extracted only a promise that individual employees would be discreetly informed if they had come into contact with someone who turned out to be carrying the virus. The managers urged Smalls to play along to avoid sowing panic.

Smalls had spent his adult life working for people who had displayed indifference to his well-being. Now, he felt he was being pressured to become an accomplice in a life-threatening charade. He sat down at a table inside the cafeteria and began telling coworkers that they were in danger. People were sick, and Amazon was covering it up.

On March 25, he led a group of a dozen warehouse workers into a conference room full of general managers, disrupting their meeting with demands for protective gear and a deep cleaning. The managers said there was nothing they could do.

In response, Amazon did agree to place one employee under paid quarantine: Christian Smalls. Ostensibly sent home for health reasons, Smalls interpreted the move as an attempt to sideline his advocacy.

On March 30, Smalls returned to the warehouse, leading about fifty of his coworkers out of the building and into the sights of news cameras.

The workers stood in the parking lot in front of the long, low building, waving picket signs. "Alexa," one read—a reference to Amazon's voice-activated speaker—"Send Us Home." "Treat Your Workers Like Your Customers," proclaimed another.

Smalls wore a black bandana as a face mask as he looked directly into the cameras.

"We came out here to make a cry for help," he said. "We're not safe."

His protest went viral, bringing home the fact that Amazon's profits and Bezos's wealth were coming at the expense of vulnerable people who were usually invisible.

Two hours later, Smalls received a phone call from Amazon alerting him that he had been terminated.

The official reason: he had violated quarantine.

"I have three kids I have to take care of," Smalls said later that day. "I just lost my job because I'm speaking up for people that don't have a voice."

As word of Smalls's firing spread, Amazon employees around the country aired their own experiences, sparking union campaigns, congressional probes, and state enforcement actions.

In the Inland Empire east of Los Angeles, workers complained that Amazon was forcing them to come to warehouses even when they were sick, flouting an executive order from the governor mandating two weeks of paid quarantine.

At a warehouse outside Minneapolis, workers walked off the job after Amazon rescinded its short-lived unpaid leave policy, while also ending hazard pay. The plant employed about one thousand workers, many of them immigrants from East Africa.

By the fall of 2020, Amazon publicly confirmed that nearly twenty thousand of its workers had contracted the virus, though the company said rates of infection were much lower than in the general population. This was a classic Davos Man evasive maneuver—deploying data to project an air of authority in an effort to shut down a damaging inquiry.

As epidemiologists pointed out, Amazon's analysis was fatuous. Almost any group of employed workers was likely to be less susceptible to the virus in a comparison with the general population, which included unemployed people. The jobless tended to mix more in pursuit of work and benefits.

"It looks like someone just put a bunch of numbers together," declared one infectious disease expert, Preeti Malani.

Amazon responded to the protests not as impetus for reflection, but as a public relations crisis to be managed. At a meeting of senior executives that included Bezos, Amazon's general counsel, David Zapolsky, outlined a campaign to discredit the burgeoning labor revolt by training the spotlight on Smalls.

"He's not smart, or articulate, and to the extent the press wants to focus on us versus him, we will be in a much stronger PR position than simply explaining for the umpteenth time how we're trying to protect workers," Zapolsky wrote, in notes obtained by *Vice News*. "Make him the most interesting part of the story, and if possible make him the face of the entire union/organizing movement."

Zapolsky hailed from a middle-class, predominantly white New Jersey suburb. He had degrees from Columbia and UC Berkeley. His Facebook page displayed pictures from his hikes in alpine country, and a photo of himself posing with the civil rights hero John Lewis. Now, he was in essence arguing that Amazon's executives—largely white, and drawn heavily from Ivy League universities—should put down a rebellion from the largely Black and brown workforce by discrediting the movement as the work of an unsavory character.

Zapolsky's summary, which was circulated widely within the company, noted that his proposed attack plan garnered "general agreement" among the participants.

How did Amazon square this story with its public devotion to stakeholder capitalism? The company refused my request to put this question to a relevant executive, instead unleashing a barrage of statements attesting to its noble intentions.

"Amazon has in every way worked to protect our associates during the pandemic," read one. Smalls had been "terminated for repeatedly violating Amazon's social-distancing rules." As for Zapolsky's notes, the general counsel had spoken about many other things at the meeting, including the need to buy protective gear. His suggestion that the company focus attention on the leader of the protests had been "the result of personal frustration with the circumstances regarding Mr. Smalls." At the time of meeting, Zapolsky had not been aware of "Mr. Small's race."

The public disclosure of Zapolsky's notes confronted Amazon with a public relations disaster. Bezos announced that the company would devote the entirety of its first quarter profits— $4 billion—to hiring more workers and outfitting them with proper protective gear.

"If you're a shareholder in Amazon, you might want to take a seat, because we are not thinking small," Bezos said in late April. He was implying that Amazon's primary sin was having failed to anticipate the magnitude of the danger to its workers, an over-sight being remedied with gobs of money.

But the perils that Amazon's employees confronted stemmed from more than an unforeseen pandemic. People were sick not because of management's failure to execute an appropriate plan, but because of the plan that had been operative all along. From its inception, Amazon had been devoted to enriching share-holders through extreme vigilance against costs.

It was no coincidence that Bezos owned a collection of pala-tial residences while his employees were compelled to risk their lives inside his warehouses or jeopardize their own homes. It was a direct outgrowth of the way he ran his company, squeez-ing maximum production out of every employee while deploy-ing sophisticated methods to assess their performance. Amazon forged metrics that captured how fast individuals completed tasks, and how much time they spent doing other things like walking to the bathroom or chatting with coworkers. Bezos's obsessively systematic approach to every facet of his company made him a revered figure among the shareholder class, a case study to be analyzed at business schools.

The previous year, an activist shareholder, responding to a drumbeat of news about dreadful working conditions inside Amazon warehouses, had proposed a remedy to be put up for a vote at the next shareholder meeting. Amazon should commit to a detailed plan to protect the health and safety of its work-ers while explicitly affirming the rights of its employees to join trade unions. The shareholder sent the proposal to Zapolsky.

As the date for the shareholder meeting approached, Ama-zon sought to squelch the proposal by petitioning the Securities and Exchange Commission for permission to ignore it without a vote. The initiative was unnecessary, Amazon argued, because the company had already vowed adherence to its own Global Human Rights Principles. "We provide a clean, safe, and healthy work environment," those principles declared.

The SEC affirmed the company's logic. The initiative disappeared from the agenda.

Three days after that ruling, Amazon fired Christian Smalls.

Two weeks later, Amazon fired a pair of white-collar employees who had circulated a petition demanding that the company provide sick leave to warehouse workers.

Then, a company vice president, Tim Bray, abruptly quit, penning a blog post that described poisonous corporate values.

"Amazon treats the humans in the warehouses as fungible units of pick-and-pack potential," he wrote. "Firing whistleblowers isn't just a side effect of macroeconomic forces, nor is it intrinsic to the function of free markets. It's evidence of a vein of toxicity running through the company culture."

By late August, with Bezos's net worth above the $200 billion mark, protestors convened outside his twenty-seven-thousand-square-foot mansion in Washington, spray-painting "Protect Amazon Workers" in multihued letters in the middle of the street. They installed a faux guillotine, while demanding wealth taxes.

Bezos's reputation as a modern-day Louis XVI holed up inside the palace was soon amplified by disclosures that the company was reinforcing the moat: Amazon had posted job listings for intelligence analysts at its Global Security Operations center in Phoenix to keep tabs on "organized labor" and "activist groups." After a public uproar, Amazon deleted the postings.

Amazon was also caught producing and distributing television segments touting the company's achievements in "keeping its employees safe and healthy," while passing them off to content-hungry local television stations as real journalism.

At least eleven stations aired the packages, with their anchors reading the identical scripts word for word.

It made for a fitting tribute to stakeholder capitalism—official words of corporate empathy broadcast in unison, while the cameras cut away from protesting workers massing in Amazon warehouse parking lots.

CHAPTER 13

"THIS IS KILLING PEOPLE"

Davos Man's European Misadventure

Chiara Lepora was used to working amid catastrophe. She was a supervisor at Doctors Without Borders, the Nobel Peace Prize–winning international relief organization that provides emergency medical care in war-torn, impoverished countries like South Sudan and Afghanistan. She had most recently been deployed to Yemen, where bombs rained from the sky, forcing her to patch the limbs of children emaciated by hunger.

But Lepora was not accustomed to thinking of her home country of Italy as a disaster zone. Her assignment in the spring of 2020 was both bewildering and unexpected. She found herself stationed at a public hospital in the north of Italy, overseeing a team of doctors that was providing support to a medical system overwhelmed by the pandemic.

Lepora had been en route to her base in Dubai, returning from a trip to the United States, when she stopped to visit her family in the Italian region of Piedmont. The pandemic all but shut down air travel, leaving her stranded. Two dozen Italian colleagues were similarly stuck. So they formed their unit at the hospital in the city of Lodi, the epicenter of the initial outbreak.

Doctors and nurses were working without enough protective gear, contracting and spreading the virus as they tended to an intensive care unit full of COVID-19 patients. The beds in the unit were full, even as more patients arrived by the day, forcing doctors to decide who lived and who died.

In the four months that Lepora remained in Lodi, she came to understand that the grim shortages around her went beyond the alarming presence of the novel coronavirus.

Profit-minded interests had turned the health care system in the region of Lombardy—Italy's wealthiest—into something more like a business than a public enterprise organized to protect lives. Over decades, opportunists had privatized the system, yielding lucrative opportunities for themselves, while weakening its capacity to furnish basic medical care.

Across much of Europe, Davos Man's success in prioritizing his own financial interests over public health helped explain how the pandemic proved so deadly. Davos Man would also help himself to the European rescue funds.

In Britain, a decade of austerity weakened the vaunted National Health Service, leaving it unable to cope with COVID-19 along with the everyday medical needs of the nation.

In Sweden, years of diminished care in nursing homes—the result of a safety net weakened by tax cuts for Davos Man—condemned the elderly to a wave of death. Resources were so scarce that doctors administered comfort care, merely softening the deaths of nursing home residents, as soon as they displayed COVID-19 symptoms.

Unlike in the United States, where the vulnerabilities of a world-class medical system could be pinned directly on monied interests, Europe's tragedy was the result of a host of overlapping elements and policy decisions, with the blame less easily affixed to individuals.

Throughout Europe, national health care systems were the rule, ensuring that anyone could access medical care—a stark contrast to the United States. But the common backdrop was scarcity, the result of Davos Man's success in limiting his tax burden, combined with the injection of the profit motive.

This was the reality that Lepora absorbed in Lodi.

Desperate to economize the hospital's limited stocks of protective gear, she tried to institute a system to limit its use. The key was restricting the numbers of people entering the hospital. But that plan collided with the operations of private companies that had gained contracts to provide meals and cleaning services. They refused to limit their visits, concerned that they could be accused of breaching their contracts.

Lepora worked with the provincial health service to expand a telemedicine initiative aimed at reducing the influx of patients. Eight companies had a piece of the system, and no one was fully in charge. Some COVID-19 patients were receiving three calls a day; some were hearing from no one.

"The service rather than the patient had been put at the center of attention," Lepora told me. "If you consider profit to be the endgame of health care instead of health, some people are going to be left out."

The death rate in Europe told the story of which countries had continued to invest in public health, and which had allowed their medical systems to take a back seat to other considerations.

In Germany, the government had resisted the urging of international consultants to shrink its number of hospitals. Germany's death rate, while considerable, was less than half that in Britain and the United States during the first year of the pandemic.

In the early months of 2020, Italy was Europe's bleeding edge—the country the rest of the continent watched with a mixture of incredulity and horror, recognizing a preview of what was headed their way.

The northern Italian region of Lombardy was the hardest hit of all. Anchored by Milan, the nation's fashion and financial capital, it boasted sophisticated manufacturing along with world-class medical care. Yet its hospitals and family medical clinics were overwhelmed—the result of decades of investment that had tilted heavily toward lucrative specialties and away from primary health care.

It was a story that began in the middle of the 1990s, when the presidency of the Lombardy region was claimed by a flamboyant local politician named Roberto Formigoni.

Known widely by the moniker "Il Celeste"—the heavenly—Formigoni was a majordomo in the Fraternity of Communion and Liberation, a Catholic movement that twinned pious social conservatism with prodigious moneymaking. The organization captured interests in major hospitals throughout Lombardy, wielding its influence to restrict the availability of abortions.

Formigoni's organization was able to take control of hospitals by dint of a privatization law that he had pushed through the regional assembly. It enabled public money to be spent on private companies that provided medical care through the regional health care system. In the quarter century after the passage of the law, private hospitals seized control of 40 percent of the Lombardy market.

Privatization was sold as the means of injecting greater efficiency into the health care system as it contended with declining levels of financial support. Battered by the global financial crisis, and forced by European rules to shrink its enormous debts, Italy cut spending on medical care, after accounting for inflation, even as its population aged.

By the time the pandemic arrived, Italy was spending far less on health care than many other European countries—8.7 percent of its annual economic output, as compared to 11.7 percent in Germany, 11.2 percent in France, and 10.3 percent in Britain.

The impact on intensive care units was especially stark, with

beds in such facilities dropping from 12.5 per 100,000 inhabitants in 2012 to only 8.6 on the eve of the pandemic, as compared to 29.2 in Germany.

But not every part of health care was shrinking in Lombardy.
The privatization scheme triggered a surge of investment into
rewarding specialties like oncology and cardiac surgery, while
forsaking traditional family medicine.

At Milan's San Raffaele Hospital—one of the finest facilities
in Italy—booking an appointment as a regular user of the regional health system required calling in and sitting on hold for
nearly forty minutes, while those who paid for VIP service secured slots in forty seconds.

Among the direct beneficiaries of the marketization of
regional health care was the man who had set it in motion—
Formigoni.

Gossip magazines stalked him on lavish holidays, discover-
ing that he was enjoying jaunts on a yacht owned by his friend
Pierangelo Daccò, a lobbyist and consultant for medical facilities
in Lombardy. Over a decade, according to an eventual criminal
prosecution, Daccò supplied Formigoni with gifts and vacations
at exclusive Caribbean resorts, where he was lodged in private
villas with personal chefs, at prices reaching 80,000 euros a
week. All told, the lobbyist demonstrated his appreciation for
Formigoni's governance with 6.5 million euros' worth of treats.
In exchange, the governor had steered public spending on health
care toward Daccò's clients.

Daccò was ultimately implicated in a complex con involving
other politicians and administrators through which he raked off
much of the money and stashed it overseas. Prosecutors found
that he had bilked the regional health care system of 70 million euros. They seized his yacht, a massive wine cellar, several
houses, and more than three dozen bank accounts.

When this tawdry dealing burst into public view in the fall of
2012, the ensuing outrage ended Formigoni's reign as Lombardy's

governor—though not, remarkably, his political career. Even as he was being probed for corruption, Formigoni was elected to the Senate as a member of Silvio Berlusconi's party.

Formigoni eventually spent more than five years in prison. Daccò, who pleaded guilty to a reduced charge, served two and a half years. The hospitals at the center of the scandal passed into new hands. In 2012, the San Donato Group, the largest hospital chain in Italy, purchased the San Raffaele Group.

In the years leading up to the pandemic, officials in Lombardy sought cost savings, giving hospital managers incentive to cut stocks on items like test tubes and chemical reagents—a decision that limited the capacity for mass testing for COVID-19 when the pandemic arrived.

The managers found their own ways to profit. According to an eventual complaint from prosecutors in Milan, executives at the San Donato Group connived with their counterparts at major pharmaceutical companies, including Novartis, Eli Lilly, and Bayer, to swindle the Lombardy system through price gouging on drugs. The hospitals received the drugs at a discount, and the executives pocketed the difference—some 10 million euros—while taxpayers reimbursed the hospitals at inflated prices.

These shenanigans were not outliers, but indicators of the mindset that was driving privatization. Regional leaders were operating more like venture capitalists than public servants.

"Specializations such as hygiene and prevention, primary health care, outpatient clinics, infectious diseases and epidemiology have been considered not strategic assets, not sexy enough," said Michele Usuelli, a neonatologist in Milan who held a seat on the regional assembly, representing the center-left Più Europa Party. "That is why we have a health system very well prepared to treat the most complicated diseases, but completely unprepared to fight something like a pandemic."

Regional officials failed to use their authority to ensure that the public gained needed care. In exchange for agreeing to pay for expensive cancer treatments at newly constructed oncology centers, they could have demanded that the private owners also furnish less lucrative services like geriatric and pediatric care.

"They gave permission to the private sector to more or less open whatever they wanted," said Usuelli. "It was a complete missed opportunity to hold private companies accountable to their social responsibility."

As the first cases of COVID-19 were diagnosed in February 2020, Italy's most influential business lobby, Confindustria, urged the government to allow the factories of Lombardy to continue operating to avoid economic damage, preventing a swifter lockdown that might have limited the spread of the virus. This was especially reckless, given the links between the industrial zones of northern Italy and factories in China. Many people transited between the two countries, a vector for transmission.

Milan was a city of more than 1.3 million people. When the first wave hit, it had only five doctors expert in public health and hygiene. They were responsible for setting up a testing and contact tracing regimen. As the second wave gathered force, Lombardy's health department notified doctors that it could "no longer conduct prompt epidemiological investigations."

"Family doctors are a cost," said Filippo Anelli, president of the national federation of doctors and dentists. "If the mentality is that you need to make money from health care, the investment in community medicine looks clearly less remunerative."

Erika Conforti began her career as a family doctor in early February 2020, just in time for the pandemic. In her midthirties, fresh from residency, she had taken over a practice from a retired doctor, working out of a private office in a Milan apartment building.

She had been drawn to general practice out of a desire to help people with everyday ailments. "I love to speak with patients," she told me. "I love to spend time with them."

But as the pandemic spread, Conforti was working twelve

hours a day, and still failing to keep up with the barrage of calls and emails from patients suffering COVID-19 symptoms.

As the second wave mounted in late 2020, the region had added hospital beds, but lacked nurses and anesthesiologists. "If there's not enough people who know how to work in the hospital setting, then increasing the number of beds is pointless," Conforti said.

At her own practice, thirty patients had just tested positive for COVID-19 in a single day, while fifty more were quarantined, awaiting tests that took six days to yield results.

"I'd like to be able to contact positive COVID-19 patients at least once a day, but I just don't have the time," she said. "I'm worried that every minor distraction that I have has very serious consequences."

In Britain, Boris Johnson's administration was intent on avoiding Italy's fate. As the virus spread in the spring of 2020, the government prevented hospitals from being overrun, but at a grim cost. To free up capacity, the National Health Service diverted thousands of elderly people from hospitals to nursing homes—many of them privately run, lightly regulated, and woefully unprepared for the unfolding disaster.

Within three months of the pandemic's arrival, nursing homes in England and Wales alone had seen twenty thousand more deaths than usual.

Britain focused all resources on battling COVID-19, effectively shutting down the rest of the health care system. The resulting scarcity revealed how weak the system was before the pandemic.

In Liverpool, Simon Bowers—the doctor who had bemoaned austerity—complained that his patients with other ailments were waiting weeks and even months for treatments and tests that typically required days.

"I've written death certificates for two patients in the last week who wouldn't have died of cancer if not for COVID," Bowers told me in October. "Ten years of austerity has left the system just about coping for much of the year. The pandemic is a real perfect storm in terms of ruthlessly exposing the deficiencies of the system."

It also exposed how cronyism had trumped considerations of public health. As the government awarded emergency contracts for protective gear, ventilators, and other vital wares, it allowed politically connected businesses to exploit a secret VIP lane. Among some 1,200 contracts conferred by the central government and eventually made public—deals worth a collective $22 billion—roughly half had been secured by companies that tripped serious questions of propriety. The recipient companies were frequently run by people connected to the governing Conservative Party.

One company headed by an employee of the Board of Trade, a government body, secured a $340 million contract to furnish protective gear for medical staff. It eventually produced 50 million masks at a cost of $200 million. They proved defective and could not be used.

Meanwhile, qualified companies that lacked friends in high places were largely shut out.

As the virus mutated, turning Britain into the epicenter of a rapidly spreading variant in the first months of 2021, the country's hospital system was again threatened by a crush of cases. Again, elderly patients were shipped off to nursing homes. Again, infection rates soared.

By August 2021, the pandemic was blamed for the deaths of more than 130,000 Britons—one of the worst tolls in Europe.

Even in Sweden, the pandemic revealed the extent to which the degradation of the country's social safety net had undermined its ability to manage a public health emergency.

Like the rest of Europe, Sweden took note of the disaster in

Italy as a portent, while opting for an unorthodox response: The government counseled people to engage in social distancing, but left shops, restaurants, nightclubs, and schools open. Swedes were largely free to carry on with their lives absent rules about wearing face masks.

The government presented its strategy as a more enlightened approach. Forcing people to avoid workplaces and hunker down at home would produce joblessness and despair. The impacts of mental health ailments like depression had to be considered alongside the consequences of the coronavirus.

Around the world, those decrying pandemic restrictions seized on Sweden as an alternative model. "Without locking down, Sweden—and this is the key—has fared far better than other European countries that did lock down," declared the Fox News commentator Tucker Carlson.

There was one problem with this assessment: Sweden's strategy was a disaster.

By the summer of 2020, more than five thousand people were dead in a country of 10 million people, giving Sweden one of the worst per capita death rates on earth, and exponentially higher than in neighboring countries—twelve times worse than Norway, seven times worse than Finland, and six times the level in Denmark.

In exchange for this wave of death, Sweden had gained essentially nothing in the way of economic benefits. It was ensnared in a recession no more or less bleak than in neighboring countries, where lockdowns had been imposed.

Proponents of the government's strategy insisted that it could be fairly assessed only over the long term. But by the middle of November, a brutal second wave was again sending Swedes to hospitals at one of the fastest rates in Europe.

Nearly half of those killed by COVID-19 had been residents of nursing homes. Champions of the official strategy were implicitly dismissing their deaths as collateral damage—a stance that provoked uncomfortable memories of Sweden's experiments with extreme social engineering. As late as the 1970s, the government had imposed forced sterilizations on women deemed not socially acceptable, such as orphans and teenagers who had gotten into trouble.

Sweden's state epidemiologist, Anders Tegnell, the architect of the national strategy, was privately expressing interest in pursuing so-called herd immunity, exposing enough people to the virus to yield antibodies that would prevent further spread.

As criticism about Sweden's strategy intensified, officials began excising the elderly from the conversation. Yes, there had been a problem in the nursing homes, but otherwise Sweden was doing great. If you looked past the places where lots of people had died, not that many people had died.

But the nursing home deaths were not incidental to the story of Sweden's otherwise-masterful handling of the pandemic. They were the story itself—a direct outgrowth of Sweden's liquidation of key parts of its social safety net to free up money to hand to Davos Man while entrusting much of elder care to for-profit, private companies.

Under a series of reforms launched in the 1990s, Sweden transferred responsibility for older people from regional governments to municipal governments, while home care took precedence over a traditional reliance on nursing homes. Municipalities gained permission to contract with private companies for services. By 2020, roughly half the residents of nursing homes in the Stockholm area were living in for-profit institutions.

Part of the driver was philosophical. Sweden's leaders concluded that older people would better enjoy the last years of their lives in the comfort of their own homes, surrounded by loved ones. Private companies would design more accommodating architecture and experiences for elderly people who required an institution.

But the private companies also brought something else—an ability to squeeze costs out of the equation.

A decade of tax cuts that benefitted billionaires like the head of H&M had resulted in diminished government revenues despite the Cosmic Lie that they would pay for themselves.

Much as in the United States, for-profit nursing homes derived savings in part by downgrading staff.

"This is an undervalued part of the labor market," said Marta Szebehely, an expert in elder care at Stockholm University. "Some care workers are badly paid, badly trained, and have really bad employment conditions. And they were supposed to stop a transmission that nobody knew anything about, and without much support."

Sweden was still devoting vast sums of money to elderly care—some 3.2 percent of its annual economic output, as compared to 0.5 percent in the United States. Only the Netherlands and Norway spent more. But increasing sums were being absorbed by administrative costs and, most crucially, dividends for the shareholders of private companies.

Mia Grane knew none of this when she moved her parents into the Sabbatsbergsbyn nursing home in the center of Stockholm in the summer of 2018.

The institution was owned by Sweden's largest for-profit operator of nursing homes, Attendo. It was home to 106 residents, most of them suffering dementia. They were divided into eleven wards spread across three low-slung buildings.

Grane's mother was descending into Alzheimer's. Her father required a wheelchair. The facilities included lovely gardens used for midsummer parties.

"It was a perfect place," said Grane. "They felt at home."

But anxiety quickly replaced peace of mind as the pandemic spread.

The first case emerged in Sweden in late January. When

Grane pressed the nursing home staff for their plans to protect the residents, they treated her like a child scared of monsters.

"The people who worked there had no information," she said. "They told me, 'Everything is fine.'"

On March 3, Grane visited and took a picture of her parents in the dining room, feeling a sense that this might be her last chance to see them together.

"I thought, 'If this virus gets into this place, a lot of people are going to die,'" she said.

A few days later, she read in a local newspaper that someone in the same ward had died. She called the home in a panic to ask if the cause had been COVID-19. The staff refused to say, but they told her that her father was suffering cold symptoms. Two other people in the ward were also sick.

Inside the facility, staff were initially given no instructions on how to limit transmission, a care aide told me. Management also did not immediately supply face masks, so she used a plastic file folder and string to fashion herself a visor before she entered her ward.

The nursing team formulated an emergency plan. Staff had to be dedicated to individual wards while rigorously avoiding entering others to prevent transmission. But this design collided with the meager resources on hand. There were not enough nurses.

A geriatric nurse who was working at the home through a staffing agency typically attended to the entire facility with only one or two others during day shifts, she told me. On weekends and at night, she was frequently the only nurse on duty.

The nurse urged her supervisors to add staff to allow them to prevent the spread of the virus, she said, but they brushed her off. By the time she quit in early May, the virus had penetrated seven of the eleven wards, she said, and at least twenty residents were dead.

"The way we had to work went against everything we learned in school regarding disease control," the nurse told me. "We tried to tell them, 'This is wrong. This is killing people.' They didn't listen."

The previous year, Attendo, the company that owned the home, had tallied revenues in excess of $1.3 billion. But it had failed to stockpile adequate supplies of protective gear like masks and gowns. It had enough to comply with national guidelines, but not enough to contend with the pandemic. As the virus spread Attendo sought to buy supplies.

"It took five or six weeks to get the volumes outside of China," the company's chief executive, Martin Tivéus, told me.

The shortages inside nursing homes attested to the degree to which Sweden had been seized by the mentality of marketization. Stockpiling masks cost money. So did employing full-time nurses. Why not just rely on the web and temp agencies to deliver products and staff as needed? Limiting expenses and rewarding shareholders had taken precedence over social welfare.

"What this pandemic has done is demonstrate a number of system errors that have gone under the radar for years," said Olle Lundberg, secretary general of Forte, a health research council that was part of the Swedish Ministry of Health and Social Affairs. "We totally rely on the global production chain and just-in-time delivery. The syringes we need today should be delivered in the morning. There is no safety margin. It may be very economically efficient in one way, but it's very vulnerable."

When the care aide came down with a fever, she stayed home. But other low-wage workers at the Attendo home continued to show up. The nurse overheard several in the changing room, discussing how they had to keep working because government-furnished sick pay did not begin immediately, and did not cover all lost wages.

While the care aide lay at home recuperating, she received

a package from Attendo. Inside was a thick binder detailing instructions for managing the pandemic: how to properly put on safety gear, which she had initially lacked; how aides had to remain at least two meters removed from residents, which was impossible in caring for people with dementia.

At the nursing home, the phone rang relentlessly, with callers left on hold. Mia Grane was calling five and ten times a day. Her father had tested positive for COVID-19. She was terrified that he was being allowed to slide toward death without intervention. She urged the staff to transfer him to the hospital.

"They said, 'No one is going to be sent to the hospital,'" Grane recalled. "Those were the rules."

In Stockholm, guidelines encouraged physicians to prescribe palliative care—forgoing efforts to save lives in favor of keeping people comfortable in their final days—as soon as nursing home residents displayed COVID-19 symptoms.

The guidelines permitted doctors to proceed without so much as examining patients or conducting blood or urine tests to get information about their overall health. They prescribed morphine, cognizant that death would result within days. Experts likened it to active euthanasia, which was illegal in Sweden.

"As a physician, I feel ashamed that there are physicians who haven't done an individual assessment before they decide whether or not the patient should die," Yngve Gustafson, a professor of geriatrics at Umeå University, told me.

Doctors were adapting to scarcity. Over the previous two decades, the number of hospital beds in Sweden had dropped from 3.58 per 1,000 people to 2.1, placing the country below even Italy and the United Kingdom.

"We understood early on that we had to think very carefully about how we will benefit the most patients," Michael Broomé, a physician at an intensive care unit in Stockholm, told me. "We had to think twice about whether to put elderly people with other conditions on ventilators."

Swedish nursing homes became warehouses for people waiting to die.

At the Sabbatsbergsbyn home, the geriatric nurse was dependent upon reports logged by overworked colleagues to provide the proper care. Vital information fell through the cracks.

She was still tortured by the case of an elderly man who had been showing signs of reaching his final hours. No one had informed her of his status when she had come on duty. His family had not been told that the end was near.

"I would have gone to check on him, and maybe hold his hand to see if he was feeling anxiety or pain," the nurse said. "Maybe I would have given him morphine."

Her voice caught. "He died alone," she said.

On April 2, Grane called the nursing home and was told that her father was barely alive. He died later that day with no one by his bedside.

She begged the staff to save her mother. But she wasn't eating, and she was dehydrated. This time, Grane was at least permitted to sit in the room until the end.

Grane was wrecked by the experience. She sifted through what had happened—the confusion, the short staffing, the lack of awareness as the pandemic removed both parents from her life.

"For me, it's clear that they wanted to save costs," she told me. "In the end, it's the money that talks."

By the middle of 2021, Sweden had lost more than fourteen thousand people to COVID-19, giving it a per capita death rate far worse than its neighbors—more than triple Denmark's, and almost eight times Finland's. Attendo convened a call with stock analysts to discuss its latest earnings.

The pandemic had made Scandinavians reluctant to entrust their relatives to nursing homes. This had limited the number of "customers," said Tivéus, the CEO, yielding a "lower average occupancy compared to a year ago."

But there was better news for shareholders. The company reiterated its dividend target: 30 percent of its profits over the next three years.

As the pandemic tore at the economies of Europe, it seemed unlikely to bring out the best in a continent prone to bickering, recrimination, and tribal animosity.

Europe had never fully recovered from the economic damage left from the financial crisis less than a decade earlier. Now, an even bigger shock was playing out, threatening a wave of bankruptcies and joblessness.

The European Union was like a family in which trauma only heightened the existing dysfunction. During the crisis of the previous decade, conflict had centered on whether and how the bloc should marshal a collective relief effort, with some suggesting that it be financed by sales of so-called eurobonds backed by all member states. But Northern European countries had balked, consigning the hardest-hit nations like Greece, Spain, and Italy to unmitigated agony.

Northern European unwillingness to shoulder collective debts traditionally rested on crude stereotypes of their southern brethren. Germans were appalled by the prospect of putting their hard-earned savings on the line to allow orgiastic borrowing by Greece and Italy, where civil servants supposedly retired during their prime years, living on extravagant pensions as they reclined on the balconies of sea-facing villas.

"You cannot spend all the money on drinks and women and then ask for help," the Dutch finance minister, Jeroen Dijsselbloem, had once remarked.

These sorts of depictions skipped over the fact that Greeks actually worked longer hours than many Northern European countries. They ignored how German banks had lent aggressively to finance Mediterranean investment debacles. In limiting European relief and demanding austerity, Germany ensured that ordinary households in southern Europe would suffer years of desperation so that its own lenders could collect on their debts.

Southern Europeans had forgotten none of this. The pandemic revived their grievances, especially as the so-called Frugal Four—Austria, the Netherlands, Denmark, and Sweden—demanded that aid be extended in the form of loans that would have to be paid back by national governments.

"One can at least ask what they will do to save themselves the next time," Dutch prime minister Mark Rutte said in May 2020.

Spain's morgues were overflowing, prompting local authorities in Madrid to use an ice rink to store bodies. Italians were denied funerals amid the quarantine. Lectures about fiscal rectitude from the wealthy countries of the north had always grated. Now, they seemed a sign that European solidarity was a fraud.

But then an extraordinary consensus emerged. With uncharacteristic speed and decisiveness, European leaders ditched their budgetary strictures to yield action. The pandemic was so alarming, its potential dangers at once enormous and incalculable, that it eclipsed the usual rancor that frequently divided the nations of Europe, supplying one fundamental objective: limiting the damage. The austerity-minded governments of Northern Europe for the moment had something greater to fear than public debt, so they assented to a suspension of the rules, permitting the worst-hit countries to borrow as needed. The European Union transcended its legacy of national suspicion to forge a shared relief fund worth 750 billion euros. More significant than the sum was how the money was raised—by borrowing collectively.

In striking an agreement to sell so-called corona bonds, Europe diminished doubts about the sanctity of its union in the post-Brexit era while applying a salve toward healing foundational bitterness. It was a victory engineered by Germany and

France, the two charter members whose deadly animosities had been the impetus for the creation of the bloc. Macron had pursued as a primary target building out the next phase of the European Union. He won over a key source of opposition to collective debt, German chancellor Angela Merkel, for whom the endurance and vitality of the European Union was a legacy issue. Davos Man was happy to see an aggressive expenditure of public money, cognizant that it could be used to bail out his troubled investments in the name of protecting jobs.

Decades of widening inequality, immigration, and cuts to public services had torn at the fabric of the European Union, giving life to extremist parties that courted votes by attacking the institution. The pandemic appeared to have strengthened European solidarity while demonstrating the merits of European-style social democracy.

The United States had employed a Rube Goldberg contraption, with Mnuchin's slush fund funneled through Jamie Dimon's bank, and Larry Fink's firm buying bonds on behalf of the Fed, allowing Steve Schwarzman's private equity empire to borrow for free. All of this was supposed to trickle down through the rest of the populace.

European governments cut out the Davos Man intermediaries and stepped directly into the fray, essentially nationalizing payrolls. Instead of rescuing billionaires, they rescued workers. From Denmark to Ireland, governments agreed to pay the lion's share of wages for companies whose businesses were threatened by the pandemic provided they held on to their employees.

While the unemployment rate in the United States soared, joblessness nudged up only a tad in most of Europe through the fall of 2020.

In Britain, the shock was profound enough to end the era of austerity. In place of stern homilies about the need to live within national means, Boris Johnson called for spending with appropriate abandon. Central to this was a dramatic increase in infrastructure spending, allowing Johnson to bolster the communities in the north of England whose deteriorating fortunes had produced the revolt that had propelled him to power.

Even in Germany, where a loathing of debt amounted to a national religion, the government borrowed to finance a substantial relief program—a package of spending measures worth 750 billion euros.

But how long would the new spirit of European harmony last?

The budget rules that restricted spending by E.U. member states remained on the books. They would not be suspended indefinitely. Eventually, the bills for the rescues would be tallied, and the money would have to be paid back.

In theory, governments could raise taxes to amass what was needed. Indeed, as Britain's treasury overseer, Rishi Sunak, announced a new budget in March 2021—extending relief programs for workers through the fall—he said the bill would eventually have to be collected by lifting corporate taxes.

But Davos Man was skilled in wielding influence to deflect the burden elsewhere, raising the possibility that the debt would ultimately be paid in a fashion that had become ritual—through cuts to government services and greater burdens on rank-and-file workers. Sunak had already announced pay freezes for many government workers, while promising to "keep debt under control." Even as Prime Minister Johnson outlined proposed tax increases to finance a bolstering of the national health care system in the fall of 2021, it was clear that an outsize share would be paid by ordinary workers.

Austerity was no random faith. It was the complement to the Cosmic Lie, a value system promoted by the affluent people who benefited from it. Less public spending spelled less need for taxes—which meant more for Davos Man. And what public spending was required to pacify a restive populace could be paid for by the sacrifices of others—ordinary wage-earners, especially younger people.

Austerity might go dormant for a while, but it was never fully dead.

The relief effort in the United States was no fount of transparency. But in Britain, the treasury refused to disclose the names of the companies securing government-guaranteed loans, even as their outstanding value swelled beyond £52 billion.

Officials at the British Business Bank—a government entity that was handling the transactions—declared that allowing the public to see where its money was going would make borrowers uncomfortable, perhaps discouraging them from taking loans.

Still, the odd disclosure about such programs demonstrated that Davos Man was applying his usual prowess toward tapping the public's generosity.

Britain's treasury relied on a network of more than one hundred qualified lenders to distribute the loans. One lender, Greensill Capital, furnished £350 million's worth of government-backed loans to a collection of companies controlled by Sanjeev Gupta, an Indian-born, Cambridge-educated steel magnate with a private jet and a mansion in Wales. Those loans at least temporarily staved off disaster for both firms. Greensill had lent some £3.5 billion to Gupta's business empire over the years. That money had enabled Gupta to acquire steel and aluminum operations in the United States, Europe, and Australia, employing about thirty-five thousand people while racking up annual revenues of $20 billion.

The global economic shutdown was threatening Gupta's ability to keep making his debt payments. A default by his commercial group would be colossal—a failure large enough to take down its lender.

As subsequent disclosures made clear, Greensill was aware that the Gupta group was already behind on its payments and in serious jeopardy of sliding into bankruptcy when it used taxpayer-backed loans to help plug the gap. That should have made the company off-limits for a publicly financed rescue.

But two details transcended such mundane considerations. The Gupta group's holdings included steel mills that employed more than four thousand people in Britain, making the company's collapse a potential calamity. And its lender, Greensill, employed the former British prime minister David Cameron, paying him more than £1.2 million in annual salary and bonuses, plus stock grants that he cashed in for more than £3 million in 2019.

The following year, in March 2021, British authorities revoked Greensill's participation in the government loan program while probing the firm for allegedly breaching its rules by failing to demand adequate collateral from Gupta's companies. As Greensill's investors pulled their capital, the firm teetered toward bankruptcy. Gupta was holed up in Dubai, scrambling to raise fresh finance.

The Bank of England published a list of companies whose debt it was buying—a tab that reached £19 billion by the fall of 2020. EasyJet, a discount airline, tapped the central bank for £600 million in support, even as it outlined plans to lay off 4,500 people. Still, the company found £174 million to cover dividends for shareholders.

British Airways, the nation's largest carrier, received a £300 million infusion from the central bank, even as it outlined designs to terminate twelve thousand jobs.

Companies that had managed to avoid paying taxes to the British treasury when times were bountiful now used the crisis as an opportunity for corporate panhandling. The Agnelli family—the clan that controlled Fiat—owned a conglomerate called CNH Industrial. It had managed to secure British tax refunds exceeding £15 million between 2017 and 2019—a period in which it had relied on the hired advice of one George Osborne, the former British treasury secretary. In the midst of the pandemic, the Agnelli-owned conglomerate helped itself to £600 million in credit from the Bank of England.

But the most remarkable recipient of British public assistance was a company that regular people had likely never heard of, even as they were familiar with its holdings—Merlin Entertainment. Its portfolio included Legoland, a chain of astronomically priced amusement parks, and Madame Tussauds, famous for kitschy wax likenesses of celebrities. It operated 130 entertainment sites and 20 hotels in 25 countries, while calling itself Europe's largest visitor attraction operator. That was not a good thing to be in a pandemic.

In early April 2020, the company released a statement aimed at reassuring its bondholders that it was taking steps to cut costs while seeking public assistance. "We expect to benefit from various government measures." Later that month, Merlin released its annual report, sounding the alarm that lockdowns and social distancing measures posed "an unprecedented disruption to our business." The pandemic had resulted in "the current temporary closure of substantially all of our Attractions."

Merlin was furloughing 80 percent of its workforce worldwide. It had "implemented voluntary salary reductions," leaving one to wonder about the other options for its selfless workers. These steps had reduced its expenses by 45 percent, but it needed £12 million per month just to stay current on its debt payments.

That debt was the result of a merger completed the previous year by a deep-pocketed triumvirate—the Canadian pension fund, the billionaire family that launched Lego, and none other than Steve Schwarzman's company. They had paid a collective £6 billion to take control of Merlin. Then, they had followed the classic private equity play, using their new assets as collateral for unrestrained borrowing to finance expansion.

That strategy was in tatters. The investors were seeking £10 million a month in wage subsidies, plus £2 million a month in government support for troubled businesses.

Blackstone told me that Merlin tapped the furlough program and gained from tax relief on its shuttered properties.

"We do not believe that Merlin's employees should be arbitrarily excluded from paycheck support programs that are widely available to virtually all workers solely due to the company's private ownership," the company said.

But at the same time that Merlin was drawing on the taxpayer's generosity, Schwarzman was publicly boasting about his firm's abundant finances.

"We entered this crisis in a position of great strength," he told stock analysts.

Blackstone was sitting on $150 billion in cash and was "looking aggressively" to snap up businesses that had been knocked down to bargain bin prices. Schwarzman's company paid out more than $700 million in dividends and stock buybacks during the first quarter of 2020.

By the following year, Blackstone would use some of its hoard to purchase a majority stake in another British company—Bourne Leisure, a collection of family resorts.

The government's rescue of Merlin collided with a legal prohibition against aiding ventures that appeared to be failing—a vestige of European Union law that still applied during a transition period leading up to Brexit. By dint of its heavy debt burden, Merlin fell into the category of those at risk of collapsing.

But Merlin, the treasury, and the Confederation of Business Industry—a leading trade association—all lobbied Parliament to lift the ban on state aid, clearing the way for the government to deliver rescue funds.

Brexit had been sold to the public as a means of taking back control. Freed of the supposed European straitjacket, Britain was flexing its sovereignty, asserting the right to hand taxpayer money to Davos Man.

Months after Chiara Lepora returned to Dubai to resume her duties with Doctors Without Borders, she still struggled to make sense of how her own country—a European nation with world-class medical facilities—had so profoundly failed to protect its people from a public health emergency.

The pandemic was precisely the sort of event that had motivated humans to fashion government—a threat that wildly exceeded individual capabilities to contain. It demanded a pooling of resources, a collective battle plan, and effective execution overseen by specialists. Instead, Lepora had watched aghast as Italy suffered the sort of agony that she and her colleagues were used to seeing in the world's poorest, conflict-torn countries.

"That was definitely one of the shocking aspects for us," Lepora told me, "the idea of finding in our country, in hospitals that were very similar to the hospitals where we all started practicing medicine, the same sorts of difficulties that we are used to seeing all over the world."

But there was one crucial difference. In places like Yemen and South Sudan, the medical resources were scant, leaving populations largely dependent on outside aid organizations. In Italy—as in Europe in general—the medical know-how and facilities were both sophisticated and abundant. But they were no longer organized predominantly for the benefit of public health. That consideration operated alongside an increasingly decisive objective that frequently posed a conflict—enriching shareholders.

In incentivizing doctors to focus on lucrative specialties, Lombardy had given short shrift to basic preventative care. That limited what constituted the most basic surveillance system in a pandemic—family doctors who interacted with patients. In privatizing a host of services at its hospitals, the region produced a setup in which no one was fully in charge; in which no one was empowered to think systematically about how to respond to an emergency, rationing what protective gear was available. That was an invitation for the coronavirus to spread.

Across Europe, part of the explanation for the lethality of COVID-19 was indeed that health care services had been diminished to finance tax benefits for Davos Man. But structure was also a powerful element. When the interests of Davos Man seized primacy in the policy conversation, that relegated other concerns to secondary status. You could have the best-trained doctors, the most formidably equipped medical facilities, and access to the most advanced medicines and still fail to mount an effective response to a public health crisis.

"What we saw was really this sort of lack of centralized and integrated direction that I'm afraid is really a sign of what goes on in general in the region," Lepora told me. "The pandemic exposes all of those weaknesses."

CHAPTER 14

"IS THIS A TIME TO PROFIT?"

Davos Man Wins or People Die

It was March 2020, and nothing was breaking right for the incumbent president of the United States. As the November polls drew closer, the coronavirus was spreading across much of the country. Having failed to control the pandemic, Donald Trump was promising salvation through the development of miraculous drugs and vaccines.

"We are going to come up with some really great solutions," he declared at a rally in North Carolina. "The United States is right now ranked by far number one in the world for preparedness."

This was a preposterous claim. In dismissing the threat of the pandemic as fake news, Trump had effectively sabotaged the workings of the American public health infrastructure, leaving the United States far down whatever standings for preparedness one might imagine. As he spoke, the country was registering about two dozen new COVID-19 cases per day. By the end of the month, the number would approach twenty thousand. In an effort to engineer a comeback, he had gathered before him, in a conference room at the White House, the heads of some of the world's largest pharmaceutical companies.

The meeting included representatives from a half dozen companies that were developing vaccines, including Pfizer and Moderna. Trump took special interest in the man seated directly across the table from him—Daniel O'Day, a Davos Man aspirant who ran a biotechnology company called Gilead Sciences.

Vaccines would take many months and perhaps years to produce. Gilead was working on something immediate—a therapeutic called remdesivir. As O'Day explained it, the drug was an old antiviral that had been developed more than a decade ago for use against other coronaviruses.

"We're hoping it has effects now against COVID-19," O'Day told Trump. "We know, in vitro, that it has very high effect."

Trump cut in excitedly, as if catching word of a magical re-election potion.

"So you have a medicine that's already involved with the coronaviruses, and now you have to see if it's specifically for this," he said. "You can know that tomorrow, can't you?"

With trepidation, O'Day delivered the news that tomorrow was not a possibility.

"The critical thing is to do clinical trials," he said, detailing the tests that were underway.

Trump nodded impatiently, clearly uninterested in hearing why he had to wait for a bunch of scientists to check off formalities like human safety before he could get his hands on the elixir.

"Any response yet?" Trump asked. "When will you know if it works? I mean, you already have this medicine."

Preliminary results would be available the following month, O'Day replied. Gilead was already preparing to manufacture the drug. "We're moving as fast as we can," O'Day said.

"Get it done, Daniel," Trump implored. "Don't disappoint us, Daniel. Do you understand?"

O'Day would get it done. Though the trials would reveal that the drug was of little consequence in limiting deaths from COVID-19, and though the advent of vaccines would fail to rescue Trump's doomed presidency, remdesivir proved dramatically successful as a therapeutic for Gilead's balance sheet.

By early 2021, Trump was gone, but remdesivir was forecast to register $3 billion in sales over the course of the year.

The pharmaceutical industry was a uniquely rewarding parcel of Davos Man's preserve, a landscape teeming with delicious prey, much of it stocked by the public. Drug companies exploited research financed by taxpayers to generate marketable new drugs. Then they priced their wares to maximize returns for shareholders, frequently beyond reach of much of humanity.

The pandemic amplified the stakes, supplying the Davos Men who were running pharmaceutical companies with additional incentive to prioritize profits for shareholders over societal needs.

The global spread of the coronavirus also exposed the pitfalls of the inequality that had been widening for decades. The backlash to Davos Man's monopolization of wealth had placed belligerent nationalists like Trump in power, just as international cooperation was critically needed.

As nations struggled to secure medicines and protective gear, they confronted serious disruptions to the supply chain, resulting in part from Trump's trade war. From Europe to India, governments sought to bar exports of critical goods, threatening the availability for all.

The consequences of this spirit of rivalry intensified as vaccines became available in early 2021, bringing a new and defining form of inequality: those with access, and those without.

Davos Man's companies harnessed world-class research capabilities to yield effective vaccines in a fraction of the time most experts thought possible. But the pricing for these life-saving products left most of the world's population unable to partake.

In a nationalist free-for-all, the United States, Britain, and other advanced economies preordered many more doses than their populations needed. Poor countries were largely shut out, dependent on handouts from organizations that distributed more press releases than doses.

From South Asia to Africa to Latin America, billions of people were likely to go without vaccines for several years.

There was but one certainty: Davos Man was going to cash in.

Like many drugs, remdesivir had failed in its original incarnation. Six years earlier, Gilead had entered it into trials as a treatment for Ebola. Those tests had proved unsuccessful, leaving the product on the shelf. Then came the pandemic. Suddenly, any conceivable way to attack a virus was worth trying.

Gilead had supplied remdesivir to the authorities in China for testing as a treatment for COVID-19. A World Health Organization panel had concluded that remdesivir was "the most promising candidate" among potential therapeutics. Clinical trials had begun in the United States.

Four days after O'Day participated in the meeting at the White House, he went to Capitol Hill as part of a contingent of industry executives assembled by the leading trade association, the Pharmaceutical Research and Manufacturers of America— better known as PhRMA. At a press conference, he touted remdesivir's potential, asserting that Gilead had spent "billions of dollars trying to develop this medicine."

But he omitted mention of a crucial investor—the American taxpayer. The Centers for Disease Control, the U.S. Army, and the National Institutes of Health had all financed research projects that had laid the ground for the development of the drug.

Later that month, Gilead received another gift from the taxpayer, as the company secured approval from the Food and Drug Administration to register remdesivir as a so-called rare disease treatment. That designation brought a treasure trove of benefits—a seven-year monopoly on sales, free from the incursion of generics; tax credits for research and development costs; and a faster review time for regulatory clearance.

Congress had created this categorization in the early 1980s as a means of spurring research into diseases that afflicted so few people they might otherwise be ignored. The designation was limited to diseases that affected fewer than two hundred thousand patients. Technically, COVID-19 qualified because—at the moment of Gilead's filing—the United States had about fifty thousand cases. But this was like arguing that the beach was an unpopular destination because no one went there on the coldest day of winter. COVID-19 was in no danger of being passed over by the market. By the fall of 2020, the United States alone had registered more than 8 million cases.

"This is an unconscionable abuse of a program designed to incentivize research and development of treatments for rare diseases," declared a letter sent to O'Day from fifty-one consumer advocacy groups led by Public Citizen. "Calling COVID-19 a rare disease mocks people's suffering and exploits a loophole in the law to profiteer off a deadly pandemic."

Taxpayers had already paid for the drug through "at least $60 million in grants and innumerable contributions from federal scientists," Public Citizen noted. A broader study identified $6.5 billion's worth of federally funded projects that had contributed to remdesivir.

This was standard Davos Man operating procedure. The taxpayer had long served as the ultimate angel investor for blockbuster drugs. Between 2010 and 2019, the Food and Drug Administration approved 356 new drugs. Each was aided by public research, including $230 billion in grants from the National Institutes of Health.

On its face, this was positive. The United States possessed unsurpassed research capacities. The public was harnessing this acumen to yield lifesaving medicines. But shareholders like O'Day and his Gilead forebears were hogging the benefits.

Between 2000 and 2018, thirty-five of the largest pharmaceutical companies reported total revenues of nearly $12 trillion and profits of almost $2 trillion. They achieved these gains in part by pricing their medicines beyond reach of ordinary people. Insulins, for example, had nearly quadrupled in price over the previous decade, while multiple sclerosis drugs had risen more than fivefold. One in four Americans reported struggling to afford prescription medications.

Drug company executives tended to defend themselves against charges of profiteering by arguing that monumental gains were a requirement for developing vital medicines.

"Those who are bold and go out and innovate like this and take that risk, there needs to be more of a reward on that," Gregg H. Alton, Gilead's then vice president of corporate and medical affairs, had once declared. "Otherwise, it would be very difficult for people to make that investment."

But this notion exaggerated the degree to which drug companies were plowing their winnings into societally useful investments.

Between 2006 and 2015, eighteen large American pharmaceutical companies distributed 99 percent of their profits to shareholders via dividends and purchases of their own shares. The $516 billion they collectively lavished on shareholders exceeded the $465 billion they dedicated to research and development.

Pharmaceutical companies spent much of their money on marketing campaigns. They paid dues to trade associations like PhRMA, which, in 2019 alone, had spent a record $29 million lobbying Congress as it fought off attempts to regulate prices for prescription medicines.

Gilead was an astonishing gusher of wealth. Over the course of two decades the company's chief executive, John C. Martin, had taken home more than $1 billion in compensation, most of this haul in the form of stock grants.

These gains reflected Gilead's success as an enterprise that operated more like an investment bank than a laboratory. In 2011, Gilead paid more than $11 billion to take over an Atlanta-based biotechnology startup, Pharmasset, which had developed a promising means of treating hepatitis C. Two years later, Gilead secured the Food and Drug Administration's approval for the resulting drug, which it branded Sovaldi. It was soon selling a twelve-week course for $84,000—about $1,000 per pill.

In 2014, its first year on the market, Sovaldi racked up sales of $10.3 billion. But its price was so high that state governments—which covered much of the bill for Medicaid patients—were prescribing it only for the most serious cases. Roughly seven hundred thousand Medicaid patients suffered from hepatitis C, but less than 3 percent were able to obtain the drug.

The next year, Gilead sold nearly $14 billion's worth of another hepatitis C drug, Harvoni, which had a price tag of $94,500, for a twelve-week course.

These two blockbusters largely explained how Gilead was able to direct more than $26 billion into buying back its own shares between 2014 and 2016, just as needy patients were being priced out of affording its medicines. Gilead was exploiting tax loopholes to stash its lucre overseas, neatly avoiding taxes on nearly $10 billion in profits.

In January 2017, Gilead's then-CEO John Milligan flew to Switzerland for the World Economic Forum, where he participated in a panel discussion entitled "Rebuilding Trust in the Healthcare Industry."

The panel was moderated by Sara Eisen, a television anchor for the financial news channel, CNBC. She rattled off recent examples of pharmaceutical executives looting the public interest for private gain. There was the case of the "Pharma Bro," Martin Shkreli, a former hedge fund manager who had taken control of a drug used to treat a life-threatening parasitic infection. He increased the price from $13.50 per tablet to $750, forcing patients to spend upward of hundreds of thousands of dollars a year. A company called Theranos had touted a revolutionary blood-testing technology that had been exposed as a fraud.

These stories had "left many wondering whether there's a trust problem when it comes to health care," Eisen said as she opened the discussion. She invited her "distinguished panelists" to provide "forward thinking" on how to regain faith.

This setup adhered to the central Davos masquerade, in which every participant gets to pose as a concerned citizen. Rather than critically questioning people who had profited from a system that treated patients like suckers, Eisen invited her panel of pharmaceutical executives to offer counsel as those dedicated to Improving the State of the World.

Milligan, whose compensation that year exceeded $15 million, was asked about controversy over Gilead's pricing of hepatitis drugs. He acknowledged trouble, but cast it as a messaging problem—not the result of an exploitative business model.

"We didn't deal with it well," he said. "We didn't talk about it enough."

This was a classic Davos Man maneuver, minimizing his role in human suffering by confessing to communications mishaps, or a misunderstanding. This rendered greater communication the solution to all problems—an implicit affirmation of the very activity he was engaged in. He struck a pose of candor and even capitulation, accepting blame for the lesser crime of poor word choices, while diverting attention from far more serious issues of patients dying for a lack of affordable medicines.

Milligan portrayed Gilead as the victim of an overly complex system—one rife with insurance companies and medical providers on the make, each seeking a good deal, and unwilling to publicize the terms for fear of undercutting their bargaining position.

"There's a lack of transparency," he said. "There are always going to be opportunists."

This was like the owner of a skeevy casino bemoaning the drunkenness that accompanied gambling. Just as Schwarzman feasted on the vulnerability of emergency room patients who were unclear on the particularities of their insurance policies, Milligan's company exploited the confusion that characterized his industry. Lack of transparency was not something for Gilead to lament; it was how the company was making billions.

Gilead had applied similar shamelessness in extracting profits from the HIV epidemic. It exploited a technique developed by the Centers for Disease Control that blocked transmission of the virus. The government had patented the technique in 2015, and Gilead had used it to develop a drug, Truvada, that it was selling for $20,000 a year. Its sales had reached $3 billion in 2018, but Gilead was not paying a dime in royalties to the government, while arguing that its patent was invalid. The government eventually sued Gilead to try to collect a return.

Most of this history predated O'Day, who became CEO in December 2018. Yet almost immediately, he found himself having to answer for his new employer's unsavory reputation.

At a hearing before the House Oversight and Reform Committee in May 2019, members of Congress grilled him on the extortionate price of Truvada. There, O'Day adhered to the industry line that the world could have reasonable prices or lifesaving drugs, but not both.

"If we had lowered the prices of our medicines a decade ago, we wouldn't be sitting here with the innovations that are changing the face of HIV AIDS," O'Day said.

But business as usual was an especially perilous stance in the midst of a global pandemic. The outrage over Gilead's success in certifying remdesivir as a rare disease treatment was so potent that the company rescinded its application. O'Day soon announced that the company would donate its stockpile of remdesivir—1.5 million doses—to medical providers, gratis.

This gesture of generosity was limited. Gilead was ramping

up its manufacturing capacity, aiming to produce enough remdesivir for one million patients by the end of 2020. By then, it
would be charging for the medicine.

The National Institutes of Health soon announced results
from a clinical trial of remdesivir. The drug shortened the time
that severely afflicted patients had to remain in the hospital, but
its benefits in limiting death were minimal. Trump publicly lobbied the Food and Drug Administration to cease fiddling and
get the drug into the market. The former reality-television star
grasped that the announcement of a new drug for COVID-19
was ratings-boosting content.

"I want them to go as quickly as they can," Trump told reporters.

Two days later, the FDA cleared remdesevir on an emergency
basis. O'Day appeared with Trump at a White House press conference.

"We feel a tremendous responsibility," O'Day said. "We're
fully committed to working, Mr. President, with you and your
administration to make sure that patients in need can get this
important new medicine."

Once upon a time, the American government was in a position to guarantee that outcome. In 1989, the National Institutes
of Health declared that it would demand "reasonable" prices for
drugs produced through the aid of government research. But
the pharmaceutical industry lobbied fiercely to scrap that rule,
wielding the argument that astronomical drug prices were a requirement for innovation. Either Davos Man got paid or people
died.

In 1995, with the government led by corporate fund-raiser
par excellence Bill Clinton, and with pharmaceutical industry
contributions flowing liberally, the NIH rescinded its rule.

In freeing drug companies from the legal requirement to extend reasonable prices, the American government ratified the
triumph of Davos Man thinking. "Eliminating the clause will

promote research that can enhance the health of the American people," the NIH declared in a press release.

Five years later, members of Congress tried to revive the reasonable pricing rule with an amendment attached to a broader bill. Eight Democrats joined with Republicans to defeat it in the Senate—among them, a senator from Delaware named Joe Biden.

Two decades after that, on June 29, 2020, Daniel O'Day released a letter disclosing Gilead's pricing for remdesivir.

The medicine appeared to shorten hospital stays by an average of four days, he noted, a benefit that was worth $12,000 per patient. Gilead could, on this basis, justify charging $12,000. But the company, "with the aim of helping as many patients as possible," was selflessly leaving money on the table. It would charge governments in wealthy countries $2,340 per patient for a five-day course. Private insurance companies would pay $3,120.

By that reasoning, a toothbrush could fetch upward of $1,000, given that it could prevent root canal therapy. Gilead could have charged as little as $10 for a course of remdesivir and still made money, one analysis concluded. But that would have withheld the bounty of remdesivir from the key stakeholder— Daniel O'Day and his fellow shareholders.

The Trump administration announced that it was purchasing nearly all of the company's supply of remdesivir at its announced price and would distribute the drug to hospitals.

Across the United States, a bipartisan coalition of attorneys general representing thirty states urged the Trump administration to use its powers to invoke so-called march-in rights, permitting other companies to make generic versions of remdesivir to boost the supply and lower the price.

Gilead pronounced itself "deeply disappointed" by this questioning of its benevolence. The company urged the Trump administration to maintain "incentives for Gilead and others to continue to invest in developing much needed treatment and vaccines."

Gilead had nothing to fear so long as long as Trump remained in office.

In October 2020, the month before the presidential election, Trump contracted COVID-19, and was administered the drug—a useful bit of product placement in the final season of his show.

A rapidly spreading coronavirus operating across borders demanded international cooperation. But decades of Davos Man's plunder had sown distrust and dysfunction, elevating tribalists who viewed collaboration as a threat to national interests.

As the first wave of the pandemic swept around the world, national governments banned exports of virtually anything that could prove useful—surgical masks and gowns, raw material for pharmaceuticals, and parts for ventilators. By April 2020, nearly seventy countries had imposed such bans, including several members of the European Union. Given that raw materials and parts were drawn from a global supply chain, such barriers threatened the availability for all.

Two countries played especially critical roles in the global supply chain: India was the world's largest producer of generic drugs, from antibiotics to painkillers; Chinese manufacturers supplied India with nearly 70 percent of the raw materials for pharmaceuticals. Both were ruled by leaders who habitually stoked nationalism as a means of rallying popular support. And by the summer of 2020, these two countries were engaged in a violent border skirmish that severely curtailed their trade.

India's prime minister, Narendra Modi, was a Hindu supremacist who demonized the minority Muslim population. He sold himself to international investors as the supposed mastermind behind an economic miracle in his home state of Gujarat, while leaving out his alleged role in fomenting a massacre of Muslims there in 2002.

Intent on penetrating a marketplace that was home to more than one billion people, Davos Man joined the Modi parade.

"Wonderful to be with Prime Minister Modi in Davos," Benioff tweeted from the Forum to his one million followers in January 2018, posting a photo of himself beaming as he shook the Indian leader's hand. "The transformation of the Indian economy is very impressive. He has an open hand to business."

Never one to be outdone, Klaus Schwab used a blog post to praise Modi for presiding over a nation that possessed "a robust institutional mechanism for deftly counterbalancing pervasive diversity while projecting a single identity." His piece was published shortly after a politician from Modi's party was caught offering to pay a bounty of $1.5 million to anyone who beheaded the star and the director of a Bollywood blockbuster who had supposedly distorted a Hindu legend.

In reality, Modi distinguished himself as a ham-handed incompetent, presiding over an economic slowdown while his government doctored the books to hide the extent of joblessness.

The pandemic supplied Modi a fresh opportunity to employ nationalist machismo as a diversion from his disappointing economic performance. He restricted exports of more than two dozen medicines and raw materials, including hydroxychloroquine, an antimalarial drug that had shown initial promise as a potential treatment for COVID-19.

China's paramount leader, Xi Jinping, was intent on using the public health emergency to demonstrate his country's revived status as a superpower—self-reliant at home, and capable of supplying countries around the world with vital medicines and vaccines.

At the same time, the Trump administration seized on the pandemic as a chance to blunt China's rise by forcing American manufacturers to abandon the country.

Nearly three-fourths of the suppliers of ingredients used to make pharmaceuticals in the United States were located over-seas, including 13 percent in China. More than half of all face masks worldwide were made in China. And China was the source of 90 percent of the core chemicals used to make the raw mate-rials for a vast range of generic medicines used to treat people hospitalized with COVID-19.

Trump put his trade adviser, Peter Navarro, in charge of mobilizing American industry to produce face masks, ventila-tors, and other vital equipment. In March 2020, Navarro began preparing an executive order directing federal agencies to pur-chase drugs and protective gear from American suppliers.

Navarro claimed the order was not targeted at any particular country, but this was clearly nonsense: he had accused China of creating the novel coronavirus and intentionally unleashing it on the world.

There was logic to the idea that the United States should lessen its dependence on foreign suppliers for medicine and pro-tective gear. But it was folly to press for such an outcome in the middle of an emergency, while antagonizing the one country in position to satisfy the need.

Much of American industry was locked down. Europe was in a similar state. Having suffered the virus earliest, China was already reopening. Its factories were able to produce what the world required.

"It's not that we are buying this stuff from China that's made us vulnerable," said Chad Bown, a trade expert at the Peterson Institute for International Economics in Washington. "It's that we are buying this stuff from China, and we decided to start a trade war with them."

Even Trump appeared to grasp this. He held off on signing Navarro's order. When he finally did sign, in August, it read more like a directive to prioritize American suppliers than a prohibi-tion against foreign sources.

Nearly two decades earlier, when China was ravaged by

another coronavirus known as SARS, the American Centers for Disease Control deployed its people to Beijing to help the government contain the threat. In the years after, Chinese and American authorities pooled their expertise to help contain epidemics in Africa.

But even before COVID-19 emerged, scientific cooperation had been a casualty of the geopolitical refashioning. In the two years before the pandemic, the Trump administration steadily pulled scientists out of Beijing.

"Given the overall sentiment that any scientific research will be helping China, the United States is really trying to reduce any collaboration with China," Jennifer Huang Bouey, an epidemiologist and China expert at the RAND Corporation, told me. "That really hurts global health."

In a relentlessly dark time, vaccines were the ultimate ray of hope—the key to life returning to normal. Yet scientists cautioned that expectations were in danger of being disappointed.

In the course of medical history, the fastest a vaccine had been conceived and delivered to market was four years. No one wanted to wait that long for a fix to COVID-19. With people dying around the world, children denied access to schools, livelihoods decimated, and hunger spreading, an extraordinary effort was underway to produce vaccines as quickly as possible.

By the fall of 2020, forty-five potential candidates were undergoing clinical trials on humans around the globe, with more than ninety in some phase of testing on animals.

The urgency was appropriate, but the spirit of national rivalry was alarming. It suggested that money and power would dictate who gained access to the lifesaving creations.

Trump had underscored this threat in the first months of the pandemic with a bold move to effectively seize control of a German company that was developing a promising vaccine candidate.

The company, CureVac, was based in southwestern Germany, but also had an office in Boston. Its chief executive, Daniel Menichella, had attended the same White House gathering where Gilead's CEO had touted remdesivir.

"We believe we can develop the vaccine for COVID-19 very, very quickly," Menichella told Trump. "And we have the wherewithal to manufacture it."

Days later, Trump reportedly offered CureVac $1 billion to move its research and eventual production of its vaccine to the United States in a bid to lock up the resulting supply for Americans.

When the news broke, the company denied Trump's entreaty, and the White House insisted that it had always intended to share the fruits of any research with the world. But German officials divined the issue as a matter of national security. They crafted a counterbid that kept the company on its home soil. The company eventually produced a vaccine that was only modestly effective.

Trump's reach to capture CureVac's output resonated as a signal that governments either had to take matters into their own hands—marshaling industrial efforts to develop and manufacture vaccines—or risk watching their people die while more aggressive nations wound up with the goods.

Britain, looking past Brexit, rejected an overture from the European Union to cooperate on efforts to develop and distribute vaccines. Boris Johnson's government bet on the eventual success of a promising candidate developed at Oxford, combined with mass orders of other leading vaccines. That proved wise. Britain inoculated its people aggressively during the first months of 2021, dramatically reducing the spread of the virus, while Europe initially fumbled its own campaign through bureaucratic confusion.

Trump harnessed a little-known unit within the Department of Health and Human Services to dispense grants to companies toward speeding their vaccine development. These grants came with a vital requirement: recipients were required to supply the United States with a stockpile of any resulting vaccines. By October, various arms of the federal government distributed more than $1 billion to spur domestic production of medicines and vaccines.

The extraordinary push for vaccines soon produced three highly promising candidates—one from Pfizer in partnership with German company BioNTech, a second from Moderna, and the third from Oxford, in partnership with the Swiss-British company AstraZeneca. Russia and China produced vaccines that—while relatively less effective—helped contain the spread of the virus.

That humanity could so quickly formulate lifesaving vaccines was nothing short of miraculous. That Davos Man would largely dictate who gained access was alarming. It all but guaranteed that the world would emerge from the pandemic more unequal than ever.

Making vaccines was a relatively slow undertaking, ensuring scarcity. Limited supplies of basic elements like syringes, glass vials, and bioreactor bags along with key chemicals were certain to constrain how quickly the industry could produce supplies. The leading vaccines from Pfizer and Moderna relied on a new technology that required specialized know-how.

For pharmaceutical companies, scarcity was a benefit. They were making their products in the ultimate seller's market. Governments were desperate to procure doses and willing to pay whatever it cost.

AstraZeneca announced that it would forego profit for as long as the pandemic endured. But Pfizer continued to pursue the same model that had supplied its CEO, Albert Bourla, with a pay package reaching $21 million in 2020. The company charged as much as the market would bear.

Bourla was another signatory to the Business Roundtable's

stakeholder capitalism pledge. Yet his company was catering to shareholders above any sense of civic responsibility.

In February 2021, as vaccines began reaching humanity, Pfizer was anticipating revenues of $15 billion from its COVID-19 vaccine over the course of 2021. Only three months later, as national governments engaged in a bidding frenzy to secure vaccines, Pfizer said it expected to sell $26 billion's worth of COVID-19 vaccines before the year was done. The company anticipated that sales would continue to grow as wealthy nations amassed extra stocks of its vaccine for booster shots. It already had a deal with Canada to supply doses as far out as 2024.

Bourla was cannily playing off the governments of the wealthiest countries against one another, driving the price higher. "It was a constant negotiation," he said. "Everybody wanted it of course earlier."

He cashed in on the desperation of Israeli prime minister Bibi Netanyahu, who was eager to repair his tattered reputation in the face of multiple corruption charges. Pfizer extracted a deal to supply Israel with an enormous stock of vaccines at prices that were reportedly 50 percent higher than what the United States was paying. Israel initially vaccinated its population faster than any country on earth—though it largely denied access to Palestinians in the occupied territories.

The United States procured more vaccine doses than it needed, via contracts in which the pricing was cloaked from public view. Europe and the United Kingdom locked up more than enough doses to inoculate their populations in a series of opaque deals. The oil-rich countries of the Persian Gulf all secured substantial stocks.

By early 2021, as the worst of the pandemic ravaged the globe, people in wealthy nations could glimpse the potential outlines of an ending as vaccines reached the bloodstream. But those in poor countries were likely to wait until 2024 before their governments could get their hands on ample doses.

The Indian government promised to sell its vaccines at affordable prices to scores of countries in the name of balancing the
lopsided distribution. "India is ready to save humanity," Prime
Minister Modi declared in January 2021. But two months later,
as India absorbed one of the world's worst waves of infection—
recording more than fifty thousand new cases a day—Modi all
but cut off exports. That deprived poor countries of hundreds
of millions of doses they had expected to receive from India's
largest vaccine manufacturer, the Serum Institute. Nepal halted
its vaccine distribution, citing an inability to procure doses from
India, while Morocco and Brazil both girded for delays.

The loss of exports from India also dealt a fresh blow to an
already troubled international effort to ensure the equitable distribution of vaccines, an undertaking known as Covax.

Covax had been launched by Gavi, an immunization alliance
forged at Davos in 2000 along with the World Health Organization. It was supposed to function as a global clearinghouse
for vaccines, a rational arbiter of the world's needs, ensuring
that the most critical populations in every country—the elderly,
the infirm, frontline medical workers—received immunization
first. It was engineered to prevent the very scenario that was
unfolding: young, healthy people in the United States and Britain gaining full vaccination even as medical caregivers in sub-
Saharan Africa and South Asia continued to treat COVID-19
patients without inoculation.

Covax never had a chance. Governments from Washington
to London to Tokyo bypassed the queue to buy doses for themselves directly, while American and European pharmaceutical
companies cashed in on their creations by selling to the highest
bidder. That reduced Covax to something smaller and less promising, though still vital—an essentially charitable operation
that aimed to deliver vaccines to countries that could not afford
to buy doses on the open market. Promised contributions from

donor nations fell woefully short, even as Covax issued a flurry of announcements laying out impossible distribution targets.

"Most people in the world live in countries where they rely on Covax for access to vaccines," Mark Eccleston-Turner, an expert on infectious diseases at Keele University in England, told me. "That is an extraordinary market failure. Access to vaccines isn't based on need. It's based on the ability to pay, and Covax doesn't fix that problem."

In January 2021, the director general of the World Health Organization, Tedros Ghebreyesus, excoriated wealthy countries for hoarding vaccines.

"I need to be blunt," he said in a speech before the body's executive board. "The world is on the brink of a catastrophic moral failure, and the price of this failure will be paid with lives and livelihoods in the world's poorest countries."

His words were powerful, yet not blunt enough. The problem went beyond governments in wealthy nations monopolizing stocks of vaccines. The trouble was how these transactions were structured—with the understanding that, above all, Davos Man would get paid.

Less than two miles from the World Health Organization's headquarters in Geneva, another proceeding was underway at the World Trade Organization. Developing countries, led by South Africa and India, sought a waiver from patents protecting the vaccines, supplying them legal authority to manufacture generic versions at affordable prices. They hoped to use this threat to force the pharmaceutical companies to supply them at affordable prices.

"The question is really, 'Is this a time to profit?'" a councilor at the South African mission, Mustaqeem De Gama, told me. "We have seen governments closing down economies, limiting freedoms, yet intellectual property is seen to be so sacrosanct that this cannot be touched."

The WTO operates on consensus, meaning nothing happens unless the whole membership agrees. For months, the United States, Britain, and the European Union blocked the proposal—not out of some abstract faith in the sanctity of intellectual property, but because of the power of Davos Man. Giant companies like Pfizer financed lobbying groups like PhRMA that expertly deployed campaign cash to secure favorable policies.

The industry parried the attempt by developing countries to set aside patents by wielding a time-tested Davos Man argument: extravagant profits were inseparable from lifesaving innovation.

"The only reason why we have vaccines right now was because there was a vibrant private sector," Bourla, the Pfizer CEO, said in early 2021, leaving out another key reason: publicly financed research. "The vibrancy of the private sector, the lifeblood is the IP [intellectual property] protection."

The hollowness of that depiction was evident from a previous major argument over patent rights: the battle over access to antiretroviral drugs used to treat HIV in the 1990s. Therapies approved by American regulators in the middle of that decade yielded a plunge in deaths in the United States and Europe, where people could afford the lifesaving products. But deaths continued to soar unabated across sub-Saharan Africa for years after.

In 2001, the WTO agreed to allow pharmaceutical manufacturers to set aside patents and produce generic versions of the antiretrovirals, prompting horrified talk from the industry that incentives for research and development were being jeopardized.

Somehow, the industry survived, continuing to churn out a vast array of life-extending, money-harvesting products.

"At the time, it rattled a lot of people, like 'How could you do that? It's going to destroy the pharmaceutical industry,'" said Dr. Anthony S. Fauci, President Biden's chief medical adviser for the pandemic. "It didn't destroy them at all. They continue to make billions of dollars."

Four days after the warning from the head of the World Health Organization, Pfizer announced that it was joining Covax, making 40 million doses of its vaccine available during 2021.

"At Pfizer, we believe that every person deserves to be seen, heard and cared for," said Bourla, the company CEO, in a press release. "We share the mission of Covax and are proud to work together so that developing countries have the same access as the rest of the world."

The same access was a shameless piece of Davos Man obfuscation, a lie wrapped up as a gift to humanity. Less than two weeks later, Bourla would tell stock analysts that Pfizer was on track to deliver 2 billion doses worldwide by the end of 2021. Pfizer's sales to Covax—at undisclosed terms—represented a mere 2 percent of this production.

In early May 2021, President Biden broke with the pharmaceutical lobby and lent American support to the WTO initiative to set aside patent protections on COVID-19 vaccines. On its face, this was a stunning development. The pharmaceutical industry was especially powerful in Washington, and Biden had long leaned heavily on its contributions in financing his campaigns. But the announcement was more of a headline grabber than a meaningful alteration of reality. Europe continued to oppose the initiative, led by Germany, which was intent on protecting BioNTech's market. Just as Chancellor Merkel had prioritized the balance sheets of German banks over European solidarity during the debt crisis a decade earlier, she now gave primacy to the profits of a domestic pharmaceutical company over global public health. Biden showed no signs of applying pressure on Merkel to alter that stance.

By themselves, patent rights were of dubious value anyway. Substantially boosting the supply of vaccines required that existing manufacturers share not only the recipes for their wares but also their production processes through so-called technology transfers. Europe was supposedly in favor of that, but on a voluntary basis—a benevolent sounding construction of the status quo. Major pharmaceutical companies were at least rhetorically in favor of forging partnerships around the world, but they mostly maintained that they had already done as much as they could, exhausting the supply of factories possessing the required expertise and standards.

Some experts argued that the debate at the WTO amounted to a dangerous sideshow, like arguing over the organizational chart at the fire department during an inferno. The world's productive capacity was dominated by multinational corporations that answered to shareholders. Whether this was desirable or lamentable was a conversation best scheduled for a calmer day. Governments should simply permit companies like Pfizer to carry on unhindered and produce as much vaccine as possible. The rest amounted to a distribution problem.

But others countered that paternalistic deference to the pharmaceutical industry was precisely what had created the crisis. The pandemic was not a one-off emergency, but part of a historical continuum. From the era of colonialism through the crafting of modern trade agreements, leaders in wealthy countries tended to regard the rest of the globe as sources of raw materials to be mined and low-wage laborers to be exploited, and not as places where fairness and equality required more than nominal consideration. Coronavirus variants were already threatening new waves of infection, and booster shots would be needed—potentially for years—necessitating greater supply. Other pandemics might follow, bringing a repeat of the situation at hand. Against that backdrop, it was both immoral and unrealistic to expect that developing countries would sit and wait for wealthy benefactors to swoop in and save them from the pandemic. They had to be able to make what vaccines and medicines they needed for their own people, rather than depending on the good graces of Davos Man.

From Indonesia to Bangladesh to South Africa, pharmaceutical manufacturers professed readiness to make vaccines, if only the existing manufacturers would help them. That would not happen through magnanimous gestures or stakeholder capitalism. The woeful performance of Covax proved that.

By the middle of August 2021, Covax had delivered a mere 196 million of the 1.9 billion doses it had promised to distribute over the course of the year. Only 2 percent of Africa's 1.3 billion people had been fully vaccinated against COVID-19, compared to 62 percent in the United Kingdom, 59 percent in Germany, and 51 percent in the United States. This divide was about to be widened, as wealthy nations added to their vaccine stockpiles in anticipation of booster shots.

"As some richer countries hoard vaccines, they make a mockery of vaccine equity," declared the World Health Organization's Director for Africa, Dr. Matshidiso Moeti.

There was truth to that characterization, but it was an incomplete account. The gaping disparity in vaccine distribution was not merely reflective of which countries had the most power but also which interests retained primacy within countries. Same as ever, Davos Man was dictating the course of policy in the service of Davos Man. The result was a humanitarian tragedy in poor countries—a wave of unremitting death—along with the potential prolonging of the pandemic everywhere. So long as some countries lacked vaccines, the coronavirus was supplied a chance to yield variants that would require additional immunization. The protection of Davos Man's profits took precedence over the saving of lives.

By the summer of 2021, Biden's pledge to set aside patents on COVID-19 vaccines seemed like a distant memory. Seeking to mute the talk that the United States was doing little while most of the world suffered the worst of the pandemic, Biden announced plans to purchase 500 million doses of Pfizer vaccine and donate them to countries in need, primarily through Covax.

The donation would involve a $3.5 billion purchase of Pfizer's vaccines by American taxpayers. That price equated to about $7 a dose, compared to the $20 the company was fetching on those administered in the United States. Pfizer said this was a "not for profit" price. But outsiders were in no position to verify the veracity of that claim.

Five hundred million was an eye-catching number, yet it was only enough vaccine to fully immunize about 3 percent of the world's population. And most of those stocks would not be distributed until the middle of the following year.

Meanwhile, Pfizer was ensuring that its profits would be more robust than ever.

In its contracts with the European Union, the company raised the prices for its COVID-19 vaccine by 25 percent. In the United States, Pfizer lobbied the Biden administration to move faster to authorize booster shots, even as many scientists questioned whether the data supported that course. The spread of the so-called Delta variant in the fall of 2021 raised the prospect that boosters might indeed be required, but it was troubling that the company best positioned to profit from additional shots was the one dispensing the advice. Pfizer was telling stock analysts to expect a third more revenue from vaccine sales than previously anticipated—more than $33 billion for 2021.

The story of vaccine distribution adhered to the tale of pretty much everything.

Davos Man aspirants like Pfizer's Bourla were getting richer, while humanity remained vulnerable to the continued spread of the coronavirus, given the patchwork of protection. Poor countries were left to manage profound problems largely on their own, save for token donations and sound bites of concern from the wealthiest, most powerful people on the planet.

Many developing countries were in fact seeing their meager resources stretched further as they confronted impossible debts, and as Davos Men like Larry Fink squeezed them to pay up.

CHAPTER 15

"WE WILL GET 100 PERCENT OF OUR CAPITAL BACK"

Nobody Stiffs Davos Man

Larry Fink was in a reflective place.

Riding out the pandemic at his lodge in Aspen, Colorado, in the summer of 2020, Fink was contemplating how the global trauma could become a source of social progress.

Lockdown orders had forced employees to work from home and skip their commutes—a potentially positive development for the environment, and for family dynamics. Fink saw a rare opportunity for society to reorder its priorities.

The virus was no longer the sole source of social upheaval. A global reckoning with racial injustice was underway, triggered by the Black Lives Matter movement following the murder of George Floyd by a white cop in Minneapolis. As the protests spread that May and June, reaching more than sixty countries, they expressed widespread grievance over enduring forms of discrimination. From Africa to South Asia to Europe, people took the latest evidence of police violence against African Americans as impetus to reject repression and inequity in their own societies.

It seemed in no way incidental that communities seethed

with anger about injustice at the same time that the pandemic was destroying livelihoods. Economic inequality was widening, and skewing prominently along racial lines. The legacy of colonialism still exerted potent force, leaving people in India subject to brutal police tactics that dated back to British rule. Black South Africans were stuck in townships far removed from jobs, despite the official ending of apartheid more than a quarter century earlier.

Wealthy nations in North America and Europe were promising to aid developing countries in Asia, Africa, and Latin America while doing very little, leaving the governments of poor countries confronting the pandemic with minimal resources.

Meanwhile, Davos Man was intensifying the crisis by demanding that poor governments make good on their debts. Many developing countries were sending more money to creditors in New York, London, and Beijing than they were spending on education and health care. A summit of major economies would pledge relief by suspending debts, but it would leave out the most important player—the financial services industry.

Perched in his Rocky Mountain hideaway, Fink pointed to the global protest movement as an inflection point; a driver for the corporate transformation he had long championed.

"I do believe the impact of racial inequality is going to elevate the conversation of stakeholder capitalism even more," he declared during a virtual Global Summit convened by Black-Rock in July 2020. "And I do believe we're all going to be judged as companies, as leaders of companies, as business people, even private sector companies are all going to be judged heavily on how they are performing related to environmental issues, related to social issues."

On Zoom meetings with members of foreign governments, investors, and fellow executives, Fink sketched out visions for "the post-COVID world." Large numbers of people would continue to work from home, gaining liberation from the agita of traffic jams. Parents would have more time to spend with their children.

"We're going to make this a positive," Fink said. "I can work in Aspen, Colorado, for thirty days a year. Not so bad."

It did look appealing. Fink's virtual appearances showed him seated in what appeared to be a modernist barn punctuated by exposed wooden beams, with a forest glimpsed behind glass doors.

"There are many blessings that we're learning from the horrificness of the pandemic," Fink told stock analysts as BlackRock detailed its earnings for the third quarter of 2020.

There was the $129 billion in fresh investment that had flowed into his company's coffers. There was the windfall of time for those relieved of their commutes.

"They could spend two hours improving their health by exercising," Fink said. "They could spend two hours more in building a deeper, stronger, more resilient family."

You could view the shock of the pandemic and the wave of protests over racial injustice as indications of a global economy that was fundamentally unfair. Fink preferred to think of it as a chance to Improve the State of the World.

"Society will be better off through these processes," he said.

Yet at that very moment, Fink's own industry was exerting itself to stymie an initiative that might have allowed the poorest countries to gain relief from the pandemic.

On the other side of the world, in the Qatari capital of Doha, Mohammed Heron was awash in found time, yet in no way building a more resilient family.

He was jobless, broke, and marooned in a dormitory stuffed with other men in similar straits, separated from their wives and children by the Arabian Sea.

Three years earlier, Heron had left his village in Bangladesh on the same route toward upward mobility traced by tens of millions of South Asian migrant workers. He had ventured out in pursuit of wages that would allow him to send cash home to his family, adding meat and fish to the dinner table, while keeping his children in school.

To finance his journey, he had borrowed nearly $5,000—more than triple the annual income of the average Bangladeshi. That money paid for the recruitment agency that bought his plane ticket, secured him a work visa in Qatar, and guaranteed him a job on arrival.

His wife, Monowara Begum, had been terrified by this plan. A decade earlier, her first husband—Heron's older brother—had gone to work as a janitor in Saudi Arabia and never returned. He had been killed by a drunk driver, without consequence or compensation. The thought of sending another husband away, leaving her to raise three children alone, filled her with dread.

But the status quo was not tenable. Her family lived in a shack that was vulnerable to the torrential rains of the monsoon. Heron was lucky to earn $3.50 a day working in the surrounding rice paddies. They subsisted on a diet of rice and potatoes. Her oldest son, Hasan, was in school, where he was learning to use a computer, but tuition ran more than $70 a year.

When Heron landed in the furnace-like heat of Doha in September 2018, the recruitment agency had failed to line up a job. He looked frantically for work. After several months, he found one at a staffing company that dispatched him on a variety of assignments—cleaning offices and hotel rooms, pulling weeds from gardens, and digging ditches to lay fiber optics cable. He earned about $250 a month. The company assigned him a bunk inside a dormitory that he shared with fifteen other Bangladeshi migrant workers. Every other month, he sent home a few hundred dollars.

Heron was part of an exodus that was crucial to the fortunes of Davos Men throughout the Persian Gulf. From the oil installations of Saudi Arabia to the landscaped gardens of Kuwait, people desperate to support families in South and Southeast Asia presented an exploitable source of labor—the key element in the commercial empires forged by the wealthiest men in the region.

In Dubai, migrant workers building a Trump-branded golf course at a luxury development where villas fetched $4 million complained that the company was stiffing them on their wages—between $200 to $400 a month. Trump's partner was one of Dubai's largest developers, Damac Properties, headed by the Emirati magnate Hussain Sajwani, whose net worth was estimated at $2 billion.

At his wages, Heron would have had to work for more than six hundred thousand years to earn such a sum. Suddenly, he was earning nothing. The pandemic shut down construction and emptied hotels across Doha. Heron's employer stopped paying him. He suffered an asthma flare-up that forced him to the hospital, absorbing what was left of his cash.

When I reached him via a videoconference app in July 2020, he had not sent money home in months. He lay on his bunk for hours, using the patchy internet connection to talk with his wife and children in their village in Bangladesh.

These conversations left him feeling raw and despondent. He was supposed to be supporting his family, but now they were forced to cut back on buying food while agonizing over how they would pay their debts. His wife was begging him to come home, but he lacked the money for a plane ticket. She was urging Hasan to ditch his studies and find a job—maybe in construction, perhaps at an auto repair shop. Hasan was resisting, preferring to continue his studies at home.

"I dream that my sons will do something in their life," Heron said, struggling to remain composed. Then his WiFi cut out, and our connection was terminated.

The year before the pandemic, migrant workers worldwide had returned a record $554 billion to their home communities.

That sum was more than three times the amount distributed to poor countries by official development agencies. But as the pandemic destroyed jobs, these remittances were shrinking. Countries in South Asia and sub-Saharan Africa were suffering declines of greater than one-fifth.

This was a major reason why as many as 150 million people were at risk of falling into a state of extreme poverty, and why 265 million were on the brink of life-threatening levels of malnutrition—roughly twice as many as the year before.

The decline of remittances was intensifying the pressure on poor countries that were already struggling to come up with the cash needed to stay current on their debts to foreign creditors. Over the previous decade, Pakistan, for example, had seen its payments to foreign creditors swell from 11.5 percent of its government revenues to more than 35 percent. Less money flowing into poor countries from workers overseas was exacerbating the crisis at the worst possible time. As the virus spread, Pakistan increased spending on health care, but cut support for a range of social services as it prioritized staying current on its debts.

In Washington, the international institutions tasked with aiding countries in distress promised an extraordinary campaign.

"The World Bank Group intends to respond forcefully and massively," declared its president, David Malpass.

The same day, the managing director of the International Monetary Fund, Kristalina Georgieva, said her organization would not hesitate to tap as much of its $1 trillion lending capacity as needed to protect poor countries.

"This is, in my lifetime, humanity's darkest hour," she declared. "It requires from us to stand tall, be united, and protect the most vulnerable."

Six months later, the Fund had distributed a relative pittance—about $31 billion in emergency loans to seventy-six member states. Overall, the Fund was lending out about $280 billion, less than one-third of its total capacity. The World Bank had more than doubled its lending, but had been slow to actually distribute the money.

The G20, a summit of major economies, had forged an agreement to provide relief in the form of debt suspension. But this merely delayed loan payments, while heaping them atop outstanding balances.

And the program left out the single largest holder of debt—the global financial services industry.

By October 2020, forty-six countries—most of them in sub-Saharan Africa—had collectively gained relief from $5.3 billion in immediate debt payments. That was less than 2 percent of the total international debt payments due from developing countries that year.

The financial services industry claimed that poor countries were not actually seeking a reduction to their payments. If they asked for debt suspension, credit rating agencies would record that as a default, jeopardizing their ability to borrow in the future.

There was truth to this, but the fear of upsetting the money gods was actively fomented by the financial services industry. Leading the charge was the Institute of International Finance, a global trade association that represented more than four hundred financial companies in seventy countries.

In a letter sent to the finance ministers of the G20 in September 2020, the association's president, Timothy Adams—a regular in Davos—maintained that financial companies remained "strongly supportive of the intent" of the debt suspension initiative. Never mind that they had demonstrated this with no money whatsoever.

The most important consideration, Adams added, was that borrowing countries preserve their ability to take out more loans in the future. "If private capital is unavoidable or prohibitively expensive, how will these countries recover and attain the high growth rates needed to improve living standards?"

To which one might reasonably append another question: how exactly would these countries achieve economic growth and higher living standards if they were forced to skimp on schools and health care so they could continue making debt payments to Davos Man?

As research, experience, and common sense made clear, the best way for debt-saturated poor countries to grow was frequently to secure forgiveness from creditors on a portion of their loans. For lenders, such agreements were not charity, but rather the product of a hardheaded calculation. If governments were stuck with impossible debts, they ran the risk of defaulting. If they gained relief, they could invest in infrastructure, education, health care, and other spurs to development that would allow them to earn money needed to meet their obligations.

Adams offered assurances that private creditors were eager "to help troubled sovereign borrowers, both with short-term liquidity problems and with longer-term solvency risks."

But the association's most influential member, BlackRock, had already displayed reason to be skeptical of this depiction.

Despite his prominent championing of stakeholder capitalism, Larry Fink had personally staked out a hard line against a uniquely troubled borrower—Argentina.

In the annals of countries that had found their way to danger through exuberant borrowing, Argentina stood alone. It had defaulted on its sovereign debts no fewer than nine times.

Fink had been among a group of international investors who had bet on a supposedly foundational change. They had piled into Argentine debt, betting on the transformative powers of the new president elected in 2015, Mauricio Macri. A highly educated technocrat, he engendered hope among the investor class that he would liberate Argentina from its wrenching history as a deadbeat nation.

For much of Argentina's history, the country had been highly prosperous. Waves of European immigrants transformed the country's prodigious soils into grain farms and cattle ranches that sold their wares around the world. By 1913, the country had a higher per capita income than France.

But then came Juan Domingo Perón, the charismatic army general who assumed the presidency in 1946. He employed an authoritarian hand and muscular state power toward championing the interests of the poor, absent budgetary considerations. He and his wife, Eva Duarte—widely recognized by her nickname, Evita—would dominate Argentina's political life long after they died, inspiring waves of politicians who claimed their mantle.

Successive governments spent with abandon, financing their exploits by printing Argentine pesos, yielding hyperinflation. To put off the inevitable reckoning, they borrowed what they could from overseas while seizing hard currency from exporters.

History unspooled as a series of populist booms and busts. Governments came in on the traditional Perónist promise to rain relief on the poor, willfully ignored arithmetic, and then exited amid the resulting crisis. Neoliberal reformists intermittently claimed mandates to set everything right through fiscal rectitude, enraging the citizenry with cuts to social services.

An especially traumatic turn played out in the 1990s, as the International Monetary Fund urged Argentina to peg the value of the peso to the American dollar. This conveyed the appearance of stability, banishing volatility in the exchange rate. But it forced the government into an impossible situation. It had to promise to exchange one peso for one dollar at all times, requiring that Argentina maintain a great stash of hard currency. As the government ran out of dollars, it borrowed from the IMF, which conditioned its help on a poison pill—austerity.

As the economy slowed, investors demanded ever higher rates of interest for more loans, reinforcing the downturn. When the scheme unraveled in 2001, investors fled, and Argentina defaulted on most of its $141 billion in public debt. A veritable depression wiped out the life savings of millions of Argentines, while turning the IMF into a synonym for ruthless bastards.

Under the leadership of the husband-and-wife duo that dominated Argentina for the next decade and a half—the successive presidencies of Néstor Kirchner and Cristina Fernández de Kirchner—the economy grew, unemployment fell, and living standards rose, while poverty plunged by 71 percent. Yet by the end of Cristina's second term, Argentina's finances were tattered, and she had devolved into a symbol of the corruption scandals that dogged her presidency.

Macri presented himself as a liberator from his country's destructive cycles of populism and austerity. The former mayor of Buenos Aires, he filled the palatial ministry offices of the capital with English-speaking economists educated at elite American institutions. They promised a return to fiscal discipline—a stance that won the confidence of international investors—while vowing to assault poverty with expanded social programs.

"Macri appealed to Davos Man, because he echoed their language," Joseph Stiglitz told me. "It was all about Argentina turning a corner. It was going to be a neoliberal country."

No one was more captivated by the story than Fink.

Macri "has really shown what a government can do if it is trying to change the future of its country," the BlackRock chief declared in 2016.

Fink backed up that pronouncement with money. BlackRock was among a slew of foreign institutions that were suddenly eager to resume lending to Argentina. Macri's government sold a fresh $100 billion's worth of government bonds during the first two and a half years of his tenure, allowing him to delay planned cuts to public spending.

But a terrible drought ravaged Argentina's beef and grain exports in 2018. At the same time, the American central bank began lifting interest rates, wrapping up the extraordinary interventions of the global financial crisis. Investors took this as their cue to charge out of emerging markets and into the United States, which was suddenly paying higher returns.

The evacuation of money pushed down the value of the Argentine peso, lifting prices for imported goods like food and fuel, while ending economic growth. By June 2018, Macri was forced to turn to the IMF for a rescue package—something like asking your former kidnapper if you could crash for the night.

The Fund delivered the largest bailout in its history, a $57 billion package of loans. As ever, the Fund's money came with the requirement that Macri cut spending. He slashed subsidies for electricity, fuel, and transportation. In the middle of another bleak downturn, this was not a prescription for social harmony.

"It's a neoliberal government," Claudia Veronica Genovesi told me when I visited her in a working class suburb of Buenos Aires in April 2019. "It's a government that does not favor the people."

She and her husband earned a meager living cleaning offices. The loss of subsidies had prompted them to cease buying cooking gas. They had stopped eating beef and were diluting their *mate,* the hot drink that Argentines are constantly sipping, a fragrant infusion of dried leaves.

Outside the city of Parana, northwest of the capital, six thousand families were living in shacks on the edges of a municipal garbage dump. They waited for trash trucks to arrive, and then tore open freshly offloaded garbage bags, looking for anything they might sell to local recycling operations—shards of glass, strands of wire—or scraps of meat they could throw in a pot for dinner.

With the economy in a dire state, those jockeying for positions at the dump had doubled over recent months. A mother who had lost work as a nanny led her two-year-old daughter through the dump as she looked for discarded clothing she could sell at a sidewalk market in order to buy groceries.

The traditional course of Argentina's history suggested what would happen next: Macri would be thrown out of office and replaced by a suitably empathetic, budget-ignoring populist.

The first part held to form, as the electorate dispatched Macri in the presidential election later that year. Some wondered if the next administration would resume printing money, and perhaps even renounce Argentina's debts.

But Macri's replacement, Alberto Fernández, quickly distinguished himself as a pragmatist. He sought to negotiate a workable settlement with private creditors holding $65 billion's worth of sovereign bonds—BlackRock included—forging a deal in which they would write off some of those debts while the government affirmed its commitment to make good on the remaining balance.

He won the support of IMF officials, who signaled that they would rework the terms of the Fund's package after Argentina settled its business with its private creditors.

As Fernández began engaging Argentina's creditors early in 2020, the Fund conducted an assessment of its finances, producing a report that effectively established the parameters of a settlement. Argentina's public debt had reached nearly 90 percent of its annual economic output—an alarming level. "Substantial debt relief from Argentina's private creditors will be needed to restore debt sustainability," the Fund's managing director declared.

The Fernández government initially overplayed its hand, using the IMF's analysis as the basis for a lowball offer in which it proposed paying back less than forty cents on the dollar on its outstanding bonds. The creditors countered at seventy-five cents on the dollar, while soon dropping that to sixty cents.

The creditors were organized into three camps with differing interests, reflecting how much they had paid for their holdings and which bonds they owned—older issues that had predated the Macri government, or the newer ones sold by his administration. Given the pandemic, participants could not travel to Buenos Aires to meet in person. They convened via Zoom on group calls that included scores of creditors.

As BlackRock's chief, Fink was the de facto head of a consortium that collectively held more than a third of the bonds issued by the Macri government, supplying him effective veto power over a proposed settlement. Under the covenants of the bonds, any agreement to write down their payout had to win the support of the holders of two-thirds of their value.

Fink was clearly bitter that his wager on Macri had gone bad—a personal embarrassment. He had also concluded that the stakes were larger than one country.

With the pandemic ravaging the finances of governments throughout the developing world, Fink knew that he would find himself facing demands for debt relief from other nations. BlackRock held nearly $1 billion's worth of bonds issued by Ghana, Kenya, Zambia, Nigeria, and Senegal, all of which had borrowed heavily to finance roads connected to mining, new schools, expanded access to clean water, and health care. The pandemic had decimated their economies, depriving them of revenues needed to stay current on their debts at the same time that their services—especially medical care—were stretched thinner than ever.

Argentina would constitute a precedent. Its experience had to be unpleasant enough to deter other governments from seeking relief.

In May 2020, with talks at an impasse, the BlackRock chief phoned Argentina's economy minister, Martín Guzmán, a thirty-seven-year-old who had studied with Stiglitz at Columbia. If the government sweetened its offer to something in the range of fifty to fifty-five cents on the dollar, Fink told him, that could secure a deal.

In private conversations, Guzmán satisfied that demand. But Fink held out for more, cognizant that similar negotiations in Ecuador were headed toward a more generous payout. That stance enraged the government.

Fink felt special pressure to stem his losses in part because of the type of investor he represented. Two-thirds of the money he managed belonged to pension funds and individual retirement accounts. In decades past, bonds issued by developing countries were the province of a few big banks that specialized in so-called emerging markets. When a crisis emerged, a handful of bankers could huddle in a room with their government interlocutors and hash out a settlement. BlackRock's unrivaled scale attested to Fink's success in winning the trust of funds that oversaw the retirement savings of ordinary workers. Telling firefighters in Nebraska or teachers in England that half their money had disappeared was an option to be strenuously avoided.

In negotiations, Fink presented his interests as one and the same with those of the rest of the planet. Excessive write-offs would damage demand for government bonds throughout the developing world, he warned, as if he were doing a favor to poor countries everywhere by insisting that Argentina cough up more.

This was the same talking point that the global financial services lobby employed to justify the industry's unwillingness to take part in debt suspension. Countries had to protect their credit ratings so they could borrow again later. That Fink would wield this argument in Argentina, of all places, represented a willful denial of history. If the country's travails with default had proven anything, it was that opportunists always came back offering the next infusion of money.

The Argentines found BlackRock's negotiators arrogant and even neocolonial in their condescension. Fink's people frequently failed to show up for scheduled meetings, forcing government representatives to sit and wait. BlackRock's team marveled at the inexperience of the Argentines. They were mostly young academics like Guzmán.

As he blocked a deal, Fink claimed that he was incapable of

cutting Argentina greater slack because of his "fiduciary duty"—
another bit of Davos Man jargon deployed for its powers of protection against moral culpability. He was implying that he might
personally love nothing more than giving Argentina a break, allowing the government to finance more health care in the middle of a pandemic. But he couldn't do it, because it wasn't his
money. It belonged to the pension funds and other institutions
that had hired BlackRock to manage it.

BlackRock did indeed have a fiduciary obligation, but that
could just as easily be construed as an imperative to relieve Argentina of its unsustainable debts to decrease the odds of a default.

In one conversation with Fink, Guzmán explained that Argentina could only go so far, given that its child poverty rate was
near 50 percent. Fink said he understood, but then went on a
tirade against the IMF, whose rescue plan had failed to stabilize
Argentina. Like an angry consumer waving his warranty in the
face of a defective toaster, Fink demanded that the Fund take responsibility by writing down some of its loans. The United States
was the IMF's largest shareholder. Fink vowed to press Secretary
Mnuchin to wield his authority over the American Treasury to
push the Fund to share some of the pain.

The exchange left the Argentine minister shaken. Guzmán
seemed to be dealing with an unhinged adversary who was taking this all personally. Fink was either oblivious to the rules
of international finance or pompous enough to try to override
them. The Fund simply did not write down its loans. Mnuchin
made no such entreaty to the Fund, viewing Fink's ask as pointless.

Guzmán soon gained the public backing of his old professor, Stiglitz, who joined with another Nobel laureate, Edmund
Phelps, in calling for bondholders to accept the government's
latest proposal.

"Argentina has presented a responsible offer to creditors that reflects the country's capacity to pay," they declared in a letter, which drew the signatures of 138 economists, including Carmen Reinhart, who soon became the chief economist at the World Bank.

Fink was enraged by their letter, fuming that a bunch of professors accountable to no one had appointed themselves arbiters of justice. BlackRock and its consortium continued to hold out.

Desperate for resolution, the government increased its offer to fifty-three cents on the dollar. President Fernández pronounced this the "maximum effort," suggesting that anything beyond would leave Argentina facing an impossible burden. His position was affirmed by a fresh analysis from the IMF. The pandemic was further depleting Argentina's coffers. Argentina's ability to pay was eroding.

Fink calculated that he possessed extra leverage given how Argentina's last showdown with international creditors had played out.

For more than a decade following Argentina's 2001 default, the vulture capitalist and Davos Man Paul Singer—chief of the notorious hedge fund Elliott Management Corporation—had waged a brutal war in pursuit of repayment. He successfully sued Argentina in American courts. Then he sought to collect on the judgment by persuading a court in Ghana to order the seizure of an Argentine naval vessel that was docked off its coast. Argentina eventually settled, paying out $2.4 billion—more than tripling Singer's investment.

BlackRock intimated that an impasse would force current bondholders to dump their investments, selling out to the vulture funds. Then the Argentine government would find itself dealing not with even-keeled, reasonable people like Fink but rapacious pirates like Singer.

During one especially tendentious call, BlackRock's portfolio manager for emerging markets told Guzmán, "I will be here longer than you." His meaning was obvious to others on the call.

If the government did not take the deal, investors would simply wait, allowing the crisis to deepen, eventually taking down the administration.

Behind the scenes, BlackRock lobbied other investors to hold out, causing a schism. Beyond the optics of intimidating a government struggling with soaring poverty in the midst of a pandemic, Fink's position ran the risk of producing bigger losses. He was willing to chance that outcome in pursuit of sending a warning to other debt-saturated governments that might have ideas about not paying up.

"The BlackRock guys have gotten on the phone with a number of significant creditors," Hans Humes, president and chief investment officer at Greylock Capital Management, told me in late July 2020. "It's just insanity. It's ego. 'We're BlackRock, and we can call the shots, and we're going to show everybody who's boss.' On every level, it's a fiasco."

When I called BlackRock seeking to understand Fink's role in the summer of 2020, the company initially referred my questions to a London-based communications firm whose website described it as expert in the art of "reputation management for the investment industry." Its partners refused to speak on the record, sending a statement that offered assurances that the bondholders were motivated by concern for the welfare of the Argentine people.

My story ran in the *New York Times* on August 1. It noted that Fink had been discussed as a potential Treasury secretary in a future Biden administration; that he was a regular in Davos, and a vocal proponent of stakeholder capitalism; that he was preventing Argentina from resolving its debt crisis.

Three days later, Argentina announced that it had finally struck a deal with its creditors. The government would pay about fifty-five cents on the dollar.

The billionaire who ran the world's largest asset management company had menaced a desperate country for two pennies on the dollar. Fink had held on until the reputational damage became too great.

After the deal, BlackRock swiftly dumped much of its Argentine holdings, sending the value of outstanding bonds plummeting. By the time the bonds began recovering months later, Fink's investors were out.

Ensconced in the Rockies, Fink sounded like a man still struggling to accept a rare humiliation.

"If you are interested in Latin America, there are safer and more consistent places to invest than Argentina," Fink fumed during a virtual financial conference in late 2020. "We need to feel comfortable that we are not going to harm the money our client entrusts to us, that we can be confident that we will get 100 percent of our capital back."

This was an absurd standard. No investment came with a 100 percent guarantee, and certainly not bonds in a risky country like Argentina. Fink's characterization heightened the sense that BlackRock had overpromised the pension funds whose money it had entrusted to Argentine debt, touting the attractive returns of the country's bonds without sufficiently acknowledging the risks.

Fink's brand was his rigorous analysis and discipline. In a world of charlatans and crowd followers, he presented himself as that rare figure who did the math and reckoned with the variables. But his performance in Argentina challenged that reputation, revealing him as a Davos Man who had been mesmerized by a president who had catered to his preconceptions.

"His team didn't do their job," Stiglitz told me. "They bought into Macri, and the myth that Macri created, without doing their homework. Rather than admitting that they made a bad call, they blamed Argentina."

PART III

Resetting History

To preserve the benefits of what is called civilized life, and to remedy, at the same time, the evil it has produced, ought to be considered as one of the first objects of reformed legislation.

—THOMAS PAINE, *Agrarian Justice*, 1797

We can either have democracy in this country or we can have great wealth concentrated in the hands of a few, but we can't have both.

—U.S. SUPREME COURT JUSTICE
LOUIS BRANDEIS, 1941

CHAPTER 16

"NOT SOMEBODY WHO IS GOING TO DISRUPT WASHINGTON"

Biden Resets Davos Man's Place at the Table

Steve Schwarzman was not accustomed to being on the losing end.

Over the course of the 2020 campaign, the Blackstone chief poured more than $40 million into Republican Party organs and a war chest devoted to Trump's reelection. He was the single most important donor from the financial services industry.

His money amounted to an investment in the protection of Davos Man's palace gates—a bolstering of the walls that kept out those seeking to revoke Trump's tax cuts, close the carried interest loophole, or unleash regulators.

But it turns out that wildly mismanaging a pandemic that had killed more than 230,000 Americans by Election Day is not an especially effective way to secure a second term as president of the United States. November came, Americans went to the polls, and Donald Trump was fired.

He did not go peaceably. Trump claimed that the election had been stolen, despite no supporting evidence. He filed a flurry of frivolous legal challenges, and he bullied Republican officials in battleground states in a failed effort to overturn the results.

Then, on the January day that Congress finally certified the results, Trump incited a mob that stormed the Capitol.

The siege went down as one of the ugliest days in American history. Thousands of people—among them, cops, ex-military, and self-proclaimed white supremacists—violently overpowered a scant police presence, penetrating the chambers of the House and Senate. They vandalized congressional offices and posed for selfies while draped in American flags, exulting in their display of racism, nationalism, and rage.

In encouraging and celebrating this assault, Trump solidified his credentials as a man willing to trash the most basic norms of American democracy to retain power.

That he did not concede the race, enabling a smooth transition to the Biden administration, should not have surprised anyone who had experienced the tumultuous years of his reign. Still, Trump's behavior was so extreme—egging on a mob seeking to undermine an election—that it yielded a previously unimaginable distinction. He became the first president to be impeached for a second time, a largely symbolic yet legacy-defining act.

The public was so horrified by this brazen attack on democracy that Davos Man was compelled to finally renounce the president who had been so generous to him.

"The peaceful transfer of power is the foundation of our democracy," said Fink.

"There is no room for violence in our democracy," tweeted Benioff.

"This is not who we are as a people or a country," Dimon declared.

Even Schwarzman issued a carefully calibrated condemnation: "The insurrection that followed the President's remarks today is appalling and an affront to the democratic values we hold dear."

Note that his words did not blame Trump directly for the violence he encouraged, instead putting the onus on the mob itself. His statement also left unmentioned the people who had for years assisted Trump in gaining and maintaining power—Schwarzman himself, and the other Davos Men suddenly scrambling to disavow a presidency that had played on the worst impulses of white Americans; a presidency they had enabled and exploited as an opportunity for greater enrichment.

In the first days after the election, amid worries about the destabilizing effects of a protracted fight over the result, Schwarzman and more than two dozen other chiefs of major companies had convened on Zoom to discuss the situation. Some expressed alarm that Trump's attacks on the electoral process could be construed as an attempted coup. But Schwarzman defended Trump's right to challenge the outcome.

Schwarzman then delivered a fresh $15 million in campaign cash to a Republican war chest aligned with Mitch McConnell, ensuring ample funding for a pair of incumbent senators representing the state of Georgia. Their runoff races in January would determine which party controlled the upper chamber of Congress. Both were fierce defenders of Trump. Both had expressed support for blocking the certification of his electoral defeat in Congress—precisely what the mob had shown up to achieve.

Schwarzman had waited until the bitter end to write off his investment in a second Trump term. It was difficult to parse his eleventh-hour alarm over the sanctity of American democracy without noting that Trump was by then a spent force. He had done his part to expand Davos Man's empire, delivering tax cuts, eviscerating regulations, and opening up vast frontiers to private equity.

Schwarzman and other billionaires had stuck with him, financing his campaign, celebrating his policies, and defending his character—as Trump voiced approval for white supremacists and neo-Nazis, as he separated immigrant parents and children at the border, as my colleagues revealed that he and his family were tax cheats on a scale that could make an Italian magnate blush. The harsh judgment the billionaires trained on him following the Capitol mob came after Trump's capacity to aid them was gone.

The assault on the citadel of American democracy rendered associations with Trump radioactive, imperiling the profits of anyone viewed as his enabler. Schwarzman—like Fink—was perpetually eager to win the business of the next pension fund, the next burgeoning university endowment. Exposure as a substantial backer of a president who had incited the most malevolent attack on American soil since 9/11 ran the risk that some fund managers might withhold or even withdraw their money from Blackstone's coffers. Activists were pressuring state pension managers to do just that.

"Why would public employee pension plans continue to invest in Private Equity Corp, like Steve Schwarzman's Blackstone, who financed, benefitted from & supported Trump & coup plotters?" tweeted a union organizer, Stephen Lerner.

There was another reason that Davos Man swiftly pivoted away from the collaborator in the White House. The billionaires had no obvious reason to fear the incoming president, whose home state of Delaware was famously accommodating to corporate interests.

Biden was literally a likable Joe, a familiar and reassuring presence who possessed voluminous experience, institutional credibility, and a grasp of national and foreign policy issues. He could be relied on to unleash a serious and science-based effort to choke off the pandemic. He would presumably patch up alliances and restore American leadership as an advocate of the liberal democratic order. His presidency represented the return of traditional programming.

Throughout the campaign, restoring normalcy had been Biden's core promise. He was palatable to moderates—*electable*, was the word the politicos kept throwing around. He appealed to the sorts of blue-collar communities that had tilted for Trump four years earlier, without alienating the business interests whose contributions were required to finance his campaign.

In claiming the Democratic nomination, he had promised a return to normalcy in overtaking rivals like Bernie Sanders and Elizabeth Warren, whose own candidacies were packaged as attacks on a rigged system, and who defined themselves as enemies of the billionaire class. In Biden's formulation, Americans did not need a revolution; they needed to get rid of Trump. Seeking the former would jeopardize the latter.

"Corporate America has to change its ways," Biden had told a gathering of seventeen wealthy donors at a fund-raiser in July 2020. Yet he offered assurances that this would happen gently. "It's not going to require legislation," Biden continued. "I'm not proposing any. We've got to think about how we deal people in."

The fund-raiser was hosted by Blackstone's chief operating officer, Jon Gray, whose net worth was estimated at $4.5 billion. His involvement suggested that the firm was hedging its bets. Schwarzman might be writing fat checks for Trump, but other top Blackstone executives were cultivating access to Biden. And Biden was happy to take their money.

The previous month, Blackstone's executive vice chairman, Tony James, had hosted another Biden fund-raiser, convening thirty ultrawealthy donors.

In reassuring contributors that they need not fear legal changes on his watch, Biden might just as well have been endorsing stakeholder capitalism. The good people running private equity companies and other investment firms, who collectively dropped $3.5 million into his campaign war chest, could be counted on to share the wealth more equitably, without radical intrusions like lawmaking.

As the longtime Democratic operative Hilary Rosen put it, Biden was "not somebody who is coming in to disrupt Washington. He's coming in to heal Washington."

But normalcy raised the prospect of repeating the cycle of

disappointment and grief that had allowed Trump to take power, launching his insurgency against democracy. The norm over the last four decades was Davos Man using his money to purchase influence over the political sphere, crafting rules that allowed billionaires to keep more of their earnings. It was private equity kings like Schwarzman stripping the health care system, and Amazon applying its market power to squash competitors while exploiting workers.

What had long been the norm in American life had generated a furious backlash that had allowed a patently unqualified, would-be authoritarian to become president on the strength of a promise to destroy normalcy. The full danger of that choice had been revealed by the resulting dysfunction in American governance, which had left the richest country on earth impotent in the face of a pandemic. Now, Trump's replacement was promising to go back to normal.

This was more than a rhetorical concern. That the Oval Office would no longer serve as a venue for saluting avowed racist militants was a welcome development. That the president would not openly celebrate dictators, influence foreign policy for personal political gain, or intentionally stir up hate all constituted meaningful alterations to what had become regular fare during the Trump presidency. Still, normalcy set a low standard for change in terms of transcending the conditions that had nurtured Trumpism—that would, if left unchanged, produce further grievance that could be exploited by another opportunistic politician offering tribalism as the response to real problems.

The inequalities that defined the American economy—the legalized tax evasion, the structural racism, the erosion of labor power, and the growing impossibility of paying bills on typical wages—were realities that had long predated Trump. They would not be fixed by his removal from the White House. The movement that had propelled him to power was the continuation of forces that had been operative in the American sphere for decades.

Reagan had begun the push to dismantle government and distribute the savings via tax cuts, turning trickle-down into the central principle of economic policy. Successive administrations representing both parties had denigrated social welfare spending and catered to the shareholder class while tolerating inequality as the by-product of prosperity. Clinton had celebrated the restorative powers of cutting budget deficits, while affirming the logic that innovation required unlimited rewards. He and Obama had centered their economic designs on finance and technology, allowing Davos Man to add zeros to his net worth. They had relegated antitrust law to the history books. George W. Bush had sacrificed government on the altar of the tax-cutting gods, further gutting social programs.

Davos Man had not been some accidental beneficiary of this ideological shift. He was its driver, financing campaigns, deploying lobbyists and lawyers who promoted the Cosmic Lie, while demonstrating his supposed benevolence via philanthropy and pledges for stakeholder capitalism.

Trump had simply gone further than his predecessors, distributing an even larger bonanza of tax cuts that favored the billionaire class, while placing the state itself in the control of corporate interests.

The official word that Trump had been defeated provoked spontaneous dance parties in the streets of major American cities. But if Trump's eviction from the White House was something to celebrate, it also felt like the end in itself, and not the beginning of a fundamental refashioning. In words and deeds, Biden signaled that he was no threat to Davos Man and his dominant hold on American governance.

As he filled out his administration, Biden's selections indicated that he would seek to finesse his way through, embracing muscular stimulus for regular people, raising revenues through some additional taxes on the wealthy, but generally avoiding hard feelings with Davos Man.

Mnuchin was replaced by Janet Yellen, a respected economist who had previously headed the Fed. She brought greater concern for working people, but her financial disclosure statements also revealed affinity for Davos Man. Over the previous two years, Yellen had harvested more than $7 million in fees for speeches to corporate giants, among them Goldman Sachs, Salesforce, and Citadel, a hedge fund launched by a major Republican donor, Ken Griffin.

Yellen's deputy would be Adewale Adeyemo, who had been Fink's interim chief of staff at BlackRock.

As his secretary of health and human services, Biden selected California's attorney general Xavier Becerra, who had pressed the federal government to employ its monopoly-busting authority to override drug patents, lowering the cost of medicines. But one of Biden's closest advisers, Steve Ricchetti, previously worked as a lobbyist for major pharmaceutical companies. His brother, Jeff Ricchetti, had recently been hired by Amazon to lobby on issues connected to the pandemic, including the CARES Act.

A diverse team of economists set up shop at the White House, led by Cecilia Rouse, a respected labor economist who became the first Black person to chair the president's Council of Economic Advisers. But Biden's primary economic counselor was another BlackRock alumnus, Brian Deese. He had overseen sustainable investment strategies for Fink, making him an architect of policies that created the appearance of meaningful change while perpetuating the status quo.

In another blow to Schwarzman, the two Republican incumbent senators from Georgia were defeated, supplying Democrats a slender but crucial majority in the chamber. That gave Biden power to turn his policy proposals into law. But Davos Man's enduring influence in the political process would constrain his actions.

Even before he was inaugurated, Biden proposed a fresh $1.9 trillion in pandemic relief spending, including expanded unemployment benefits, support for beleaguered state and local governments, and cash for middle-class and low-income households. This constituted a substantial corrective to the previous rescue packages, which had concentrated on lifting asset prices.

But a rebellion from Democratic centrists prevented a key element that Biden had aimed to attach to the bill—a lifting of the federal minimum wage to $15. The minimum wage had not been increased in a dozen years. Over decades, Congress had allowed it to be steadily eroded by inflation in response to lobbying from corporate representatives like the Business Roundtable. A higher minimum wage would destroy jobs, the lobbyists warned, though the economic literature said otherwise: put more money in the pockets of workers and they would spend it, creating jobs for other people.

After accounting for inflation, the minimum wage was more than one-fourth lower than back in 1968. Though a variety of polls showed that most Americans favored lifting the minimum wage, including a majority of Republicans, Biden's proposal went down. His tenure would clearly be defined by compromise.

Whoever was in the White House, Davos Man retained his perch.

Biden's ascension and his party's control over both chambers of Congress has altered the thrust of the American handling of the pandemic and its attendant economic catastrophe. Biden has clearly been changed by the circumstances in which he assumed the presidency. He has championed a massive spending plan aimed at bolstering the nation's infrastructure and another measure that seeks to dramatically reduce poverty through the expansion of child tax credits. Instead of charting a path back to normalcy, Biden has provoked exaggerated comparisons to no less than Franklin Delano Roosevelt and his New Deal, the social safety programs inspired by the Great Depression. Biden has sought to finance his revival of muscular government by increasing corporate taxes, and by partially closing off the carried interest loophole that has long allowed private equity magnates like Schwarzman to shield their income from taxation.

In rhetoric and action, Biden speaks to those nursing a sense that American democracy has been hijacked by monied interests. But whether he would meaningfully diminish economic inequality—whether he has the stomach to upset corporate donors and the fortitude to overcome entrenched opposition— remain open questions.

If he fails to follow through, the consequences could be potentially profound. The Biden years might raise expectations for fair redress before giving way to familiar disappointment, as wages stagnate while the billionaires add to their winnings. That could wind up fertilizing the ground for an updated, more sophisticated version of Trump—someone who would pursue the traditional Republican goals of deregulation, tax cutting, and the dismantling of government while packaging this as a spur to growth; someone who would speak empathetically to the working class while serving the needs of the plutocrats; someone who would indulge the language of compassion, while solidifying the prerogatives of the privileged people who financed campaigns.

Trump is gone, but Trumpism might yet have a bright future.

Beyond the United States, entrenched political realities constrain prospects for change as countries sift through the wreckage of the pandemic.

In Britain, the arrival of an especially contagious virus variant in early 2021 again threatened to overwhelm the beleaguered national health care system, prompting the government to impose another shutdown that sent the economy back into recession. The downturn was exacerbated by Britain finally leaving the E.U., with a modest trade deal that forced exporters on both sides of the English Channel to navigate revived customs procedures. The resulting chaos at ports was at once predictable and debilitating.

Across Europe, leaders bickered over how to distribute the proceeds of the continent-wide bonds while the pandemic went on, unchecked by an initially slow vaccination drive.

The global economy appears certain to emerge from the pandemic in a more unequal state.

Here is the central problem as the world contemplates life after a public health disaster made more lethal by the predation of Davos Man: how can democratic societies attack inequality when democracy itself is under the control of the people who possess most of the money?

Absent a sudden urge on the part of billionaires to voluntarily participate in the equitable redistribution of wealth, how can communities take on entrenched economic injustice? How can they promote the sort of economic growth that holds the potential to broadly improve living standards?

These are enormous questions with no obvious answers. But solutions have to be explored. The alternative is to accept the continued degradation of democracy.

Having explored Davos Man's lair, let us now return to the rest of the human habitat.

Some communities have been experimenting with ways to expand wealth for ordinary people, reorienting public spending, and testing new forms of social insurance. These are not idealistic fantasies, but pragmatic designs on reclaiming what the world has already known—a form of capitalism that harnesses the virtues of the market system while equitably sharing the gains.

In the north of England, in a city called Preston, local leaders forged a pathway to progress that ignored Davos Man altogether.

CHAPTER 17

"THE MONEY IS RIGHT THERE IN THE COMMUNITY NOW"

Bypassing Davos Man

Like much of surrounding Lancashire county in northwest England, Preston was nurtured by the industrial revolution. Ships carried cotton from the docks of Liverpool, up the River Ribble to clattering mills that turned it into fabric. By the early twentieth century, some six hundred thousand people were employed by local textile plants. The wealth they produced erected handsome brick homes along tree-lined streets.

In recent decades, as the textile trade shifted to lower-wage countries, factories shuttered and joblessness soared. Storefronts disappeared behind boards. On downtown sidewalks, homeless people sometimes seemed to outnumber shoppers.

Local officials courted investment for a redevelopment scheme centered on a new shopping center. It would replace a central market that had devolved from a community gathering spot to a place best avoided—an area rank with the stench of fish innards, where pickpockets and drunks lurked in the alleyways.

In 2005, the local council signed an agreement with the Grosvenor Group, an international property developer with aristocratic provenance. It managed part of the $13 billion fortune controlled by the Duke of Westminster, Gerald Grosvenor. His holdings were scattered across sixty countries, from the posh London neighborhood of Mayfar to Tokyo's Roppongi district. Now, Grosvenor would turn Preston's old market into a shopping and entertainment complex.

But when the global financial crisis arrived, Grosvenor cut and ran, leaving Preston reeling, just as austerity assailed local coffers.

"It was horrific," said Matthew Brown, the leader of the Preston Council. "We were totally constrained in our ability to help people."

Brown concluded that placing faith in international developers had been an error, tethering the city's prospects to the whims of money managers with no emotional connection to the community. What Preston needed was a plan that did not depend on outsiders.

One night in March 2012, Brown went to a local pub with Neil McInroy, who headed a research institution called the Center for Local Economic Strategies, based less than an hour away in Manchester. The institute was focused on so-called community wealth building, designing ways to keep wages, tax revenues, and savings cycling through local economies. Over beers, the two men sketched out an alternative.

The plan they produced centered on local government entities transacting as much as possible with businesses in the area. When the school district needed a contractor to supply meals, it would award its business to a local company rather than a national giant. The contractor that got the work could in turn purchase meat and produce from nearby farmers. Spending would stay in Preston, to be distributed as paychecks for people who would shop in surrounding businesses, rather than filtering out to companies controlled by faraway shareholders.

What became known as the Preston model was an antidote to austerity. It did not depend upon the outcome of a national election or the assent of Davos Man. It simply required coordination among entities that were already invested in the local community.

When, in the sober light of day, Brown presented this idea to his peers on the Preston council, some concluded that he had enjoyed one pint too many. It sounded like hippie claptrap. But as austerity tore at the fabric of life, basic assumptions about governance came up for reconsideration. The traditional way of running things had produced poverty and despair, making unorthodox approaches warranted.

"There was a culture shift where they looked at these ideas in a new way," Brown told me as we sat in another neighborhood pub. "We're trying to find alternatives to the capitalist model."

Brown took the lead in organizing local institutions. The Preston government, the council for surrounding Lancashire county, the local police department, the housing authority, and a pair of nearby colleges all agreed to transact as much as possible with local businesses.

Before the scheme was unleashed, these so-called anchor institutions were directing only 5 percent of their spending within Preston and 39 percent within Lancashire county. Five years later, those numbers had swelled to 18 percent and 78 percent respectively.

The Preston model did not operate with force of law. It functioned as a social compact forged among local institutions, an understanding that they needed to consider more than the bottom line when they spent money. It was something like stakeholder capitalism run by people who actually answered to stakeholders—not through nebulous pledges like the Davos Manifesto, but via democratic elections.

The Lancashire police department had been decimated by austerity, with its ranks plunging to 2,200 from more than 3,000 a decade earlier. When the department took bids for the construction of a new police headquarters in Blackpool—a beach town known for carnival rides and alarming rates of crime—it stipulated that it would prioritize "social values." Bidders would be favored if they were local, if they hired young apprentices to boost skills, and if they recognized trade unions. The winning firm was based in Manchester, but was required to spend at least 80 percent of its budget within Blackpool.

"We believe there's a correlation between deprivation and crime," the police chief, Clive Grunshaw, told me. "If you can invest in these communities, then clearly they will benefit."

The site of the aborted shopping mall became a monument to the Preston model. The council renovated the old market, while leaving intact its original nineteenth-century steel columns. The new structure—a glass-fronted, inviting space under a high peaked roof—included a fish counter, a butcher, a pub offering local beers, and coffee outlets.

The council had leaned heavily on local tradespeople, among them John Bridge, a Preston-born architect. He used the experience as a springboard to launch his own practice. He had come to see the community's deterioration as an inflection point.

"It forced us to start looking inward," Bridge said. "We have had to think differently."

Among the people who advised Matthew Brown in Preston was an American named Ted Howard. The founder of a nonprofit called the Democracy Collaborative, Howard was a believer in the power of cooperative companies to create jobs at livable pay, even in the face of Davos Man pushing wages lower.

He and his colleagues had launched a series of cooperatives in the United States, among them a laundry service based in a low-income neighborhood in Cleveland. The company paid wages that were adequate to finance a middle-class standard of living, including health care and profit sharing. It had secured a contract to wash linens for the Cleveland Clinic, gaining this work not through charity, but via a competitive bidding process. As a cooperative, it merely had to break even. Freed from the compulsion to hand dividends to shareholders, it could afford to pay workers enough to cover their expenses while still winning business from rivals.

"The cooperatives have a real social mission, the transformation of the local community," Howard told me, "but at the end of the day they need to be financially successful."

Howard's idea had taken inspiration from the Mondragon Group, a collection of cooperative businesses in the Basque region of Spain that was the workplace for more than seventy thousand people, making it one of the ten largest employers in the country. The group owned one of Spain's largest grocery chains, a bank, and factories that exported auto parts and other components around the world.

Mondragon was governed by an agreement that the top management salary was limited to six times the wages of the lowest paid worker, as compared to a ratio of more than 300 to 1 among publicly traded companies in the United States. The laborers owned the company as partners, receiving annual shares of profit. If one business hit hard times, partners could find work at the other cooperatives.

After the global financial crisis, as the unemployment rate surged beyond 26 percent in Spain, Mondragon largely avoided job losses. When the original cooperative, a refrigerator maker, collapsed in 2013, it cost the jobs of nearly 1,900 people. But six months later, many had found new positions at partner cooperatives, and the rest had secured early retirement and generous severance packages.

Worldwide, cooperatives already employed more than 280 million people, according to the International Cooperative Alliance. The United States alone held more than thirty thousand cooperatives. They collectively controlled more than $3 trillion in assets, by one estimate.

Howard was also pursuing another promising idea that had gained traction in the United States—a consortium of forty-five nonprofit and government medical systems that operated more than seven hundred hospitals across the country. As a group, the members of the Healthcare Anchor Network spent more than $50 billion a year while managing $150 billion in assets.

Much like the Preston model, alliance members had promised to direct their spending to generate local jobs. They also pledged to turn some of their reserve funds into so-called impact investments—loans for the purchase of homes to spare low-income people from eviction, seed capital for minority-owned businesses, childcare services for the working poor. By early 2020, members had earmarked more than $300 million.

The model was especially tailored to the conditions that had long plagued American governance: the near impossibility of prying money loose from Congress, except when it involved pork barrel industries like defense, or tax cuts for Davos Man. Rather than trying to persuade Congress to finance expanded social service programs, money could be found to boost low-income communities by redirecting corporate funds that were already being spent.

The reservoir of cash was potentially vast. American hospitals and health care providers collectively expended more than $780 billion a year. They managed investment portfolios stocked with $400 billion, and they employed more than 5.6 million people. Even a slight tweak to how they directed their funds could have enormous consequences.

"Our epiphany is that one answer to the supposed scarcity of funds is that the money is right there in the community now," Howard told me. "It's in institutions that are locked in place."

Health care was especially fertile ground because of the Affordable Care Act, better known as Obamacare. It required that nonprofit hospitals produce annual assessments of their community health needs in the broadest context—including job markets, the availability of affordable housing, public transportation, and parks. They had to propose measures to improve local conditions.

That process was informed by the simple observation that poverty was a killer. People who experienced homelessness were more likely to be readmitted to hospitals after being discharged. Those without jobs did not tend to buy organic fruits and vegetables, and were less likely to shell out for gym memberships, leaving them vulnerable to a range of ailments, from heart disease to diabetes. Growing numbers of people had found themselves scrapping health insurance to finance more pressing needs like repairing cars needed to get to work.

"One in four Americans are having to make a choice between 'Do I buy milk today?' or 'Do I pay my copay to get my prescription?'" said Bechara Choucair, chief community health officer at Kaiser Permanente, a leading member of the network, citing a company survey. "'Do I pay my rent this month? Or do I pay my deductible to be able to go and get my surgery?'"

As the health care provider for 12 million Americans, Kaiser had bottom-line motivations for participation. If more people were employed in a community, that spelled more potential customers for Kaiser's services, and lower costs for providing their care.

This was the calculus that informed Kaiser's planning as it constructed a new medical center in South Central Los Angeles, where the neighborhoods of Baldwin Hills and Crenshaw converged.

The community needed far more than doctor's offices. Among its 278,000 residents—the vast majority Black or Hispanic—nearly 30 percent were officially poor. Many had not completed high school. Gang violence had long been part of local life. Former prison inmates languished in local housing projects with no means of supporting themselves. Boosting health required tackling problems that went well beyond furnishing X-ray machines and running a pharmacy.

In late 2015, Kaiser held meetings in the local community, seeking to understand the extent of the needs. What people needed most was jobs.

As Kaiser broke ground early the following year, it required that its contractor reserve 30 percent of all jobs for people living within five miles of the site. Initially, the company stumbled in trying to find appropriate candidates. It held a job fair and hardly anyone showed up. Then, the project managers ran into John Harriel, a fixture of the neighborhood known as Big John.

Harriel had grown up in the neighborhood and had run with the notorious gang the Bloods, serving five years in prison for dealing drugs. He had used that time to gain his high school equivalency and train to be an electrician, putting him in position to forge a career in the trade when he got out. He had risen to the ranks of supervisor, running teams of dozens of electricians that had erected some of the largest projects on the West Coast, including the Staples Center, home to the Los Angeles Lakers basketball team. He was active with a community organization called 2nd CALL (for Second Chance At Loving Life), which aimed to prepare formerly incarcerated people for careers that would allow them to support families.

Physically imposing and blunt, Harriel was not one for corporate-sponsored happy talk. He was especially distrustful of white outsiders who struck saintly poses as they arrived to rescue his predominantly Black community from whatever affliction was trending. As far back as elementary school, he had drawn discipline for scoffing at the notion of Santa Claus.

"I said, 'Let me get this straight,'" he told me. "'There's this fat white guy riding around in the sky delivering presents down the chimney? I don't see any chimneys in the projects.' I said, 'That's a lie. You're telling us a lie.'"

In prison, he had read African American history and chafed at the celebration of Martin Luther King Jr. by the white establishment, especially his famous "I Have a Dream" speech.

"Dreams come to people who sleep," Harriel said. "They picked the nonviolent guy with a dream."

When Kaiser approached him to seek help recruiting workers, Harriel initially smelled a publicity stunt. He demanded control over the recruitment of potential workers, having learned that turning former prison inmates into gainfully employed people was both transformational and fraught with perils.

Roughly six hundred thousand people were released from American prisons every year. The unemployment rate among the formerly incarcerated reached 27 percent. Harriel looked at that figure as both a warning and an indicator of promise. People fresh from prison were cognizant of the odds against them, which made them eager to work harder. Their paycheck was far more than a way to pay bills; it was their means of preserving their freedom.

But Harriel also understood that the average employer was not eager to hire convicted murderers or drug dealers. They had to be convinced of the merits of the people they were taking on. Those he sent out for jobs had to display the proper attitude and decorum.

"The world is looking at us," he said. "You'd rather be two hours early than two minutes late."

To say that Harriel's organization ran job training seminars was to miss the point. It helped people navigate the pitfalls of life outside prison. It ran courses in anger management and financial literacy, and provided trauma counseling. Harriel counseled Black and Latino former gang members to look their white supervisors in the eye—an action that could provoke violence in prison. He refused to send anyone out for an apprenticeship until they convinced him that they were truly dedicated.

"If someone is screwing around," he said, "I will be the first to say they should be fired."

Kaiser put Big John in charge of recruitment. He went into gang communities and knocked on doors. At the next job fair, hundreds of people showed up. Kaiser hired dozens of them, including a man named Charles Slay.

Like Harriel, Slay had grown up in the neighborhood. His mother died when he was only ten. He had been raised by his father, who worked as a mechanic. Money was perpetually tight and good jobs nonexistent. People flipped burgers or bagged groceries, but that was no pathway out of poverty. Slay signed on with an organization that offered a crude form of financial betterment. He joined the Bloods.

By the time he was fourteen, he was robbing stores at gunpoint, and ambushing people on a forlorn patch of dirt in Baldwin Village—the very place where Kaiser would construct its new campus.

By twenty-one, Slay was behind bars for killing a man in a rival gang. He completed his high school equivalency and then studied sociology. "I started thinking about the people that I robbed," he said. "I started thinking about the magnitude of my actions. How did I go from a little boy that my mother loved to a man willing to take another man's life? I started thinking about some of the things that I was lacking. I said, 'If I ever get a chance to get home, I will relish it.'"

The chance came when he was forty-eight. Back on the outside after twenty-seven years in prison, Slay moved in with his aunt. He applied to be a truck driver, but the conditions of his parole barred him from traveling more than fifty miles from home. He took a job unloading ships at a port. It paid $9 an hour with no health care.

Then he met Big John. When Kaiser began constructing its new medical center, Slay was part of the crew, working as an electrician.

"I never in my life used a power tool," he said. "The only tool I used was a gun. I feel like I've been through several lives within my time."

Slay inhabited a world that was barely connected to the American political process. Normalcy, if that was the nation's destination, did not include quality jobs in poor, predominantly Black communities.

Approaches like the Preston model and the Healthcare Anchor Network were clever adaptations to a system that was deficient—a meaningful place to start. They would keep what wealth existed inside communities, rather than sending it away to Davos Man. But lifting people out of poverty on a mass scale and restoring middle-class security would require something more comprehensive—a mechanism to transfer wealth from Davos Man to everyone else.

For centuries, social theorists, civil rights leaders, and economists have debated the most effective way to address the reality that some members of society simply lack sustenance. As the pandemic spread, threatening hundreds of millions of people with destitution, that debate took on new urgency.

One intriguing idea that had never seemed entirely practical was suddenly getting a real airing.

CHAPTER 18

"PUT MONEY IN PEOPLE'S POCKETS"

The Rise of Universal Basic Income

When I first heard about universal basic income after more than a decade writing about economics, I confess that I dismissed it as a utopian flight of fancy.

The central idea was that the government would give everyone a regular allowance to cover their essential needs. This seemed as likely to happen as Steve Schwarzman donating his real estate empire to the homeless.

But the idea had been around in various guises for centuries, and a modern version was gaining traction. In the margins of the debate over economic inequality, a handful of activists and fringe economists were championing universal basic income as a solution to problems that were impossible to disregard. Global capitalism was clearly at a crisis point. Growing numbers of people were stuck in dead-end jobs in economies around the world. The ranks of the working poor were expanding along with those who had dropped out of the workforce. With paychecks no longer a reliable source of livelihood, governments could distribute a regular allotment to all—old and young, rich and poor, healthy and infirm—ensuring that no one went without necessities like food, housing, and health care.

In the fall of 1983, a trio of researchers in Belgium had forged a collective around discussion of an idea they called *allocation universelle*. Three years later, they held an international conference that drew five dozen participants, including the British economist Guy Standing. The event yielded an institution now known as the Basic Income Earth Network, an online gathering place for those interested in the subject.

"Security is a precious asset," Standing wrote in a 2017 book on the subject, *Basic Income: And How We Can Make It Happen*. "It should be a goal of everyone who genuinely wants to build a good society rather than one that facilitates the aggrandizement of a privileged elite who knowingly gain from the insecurities of others."

Security was indeed in short supply, but basic income still struck me as an impractical goal for a political system dominated by Davos Man—a diversion from what might actually be achievable. In the United States, where the problems of the working poor were profound, anything that smacked of welfare was easy for lobbyists to defeat. And basic income was easily dismissed as a form of socialism—the ultimate idea-killing label in the world's capitalist superpower.

Then, in 2016, just as I moved to London to cover the European economy, Finland announced that it was conducting a two-year trial of a basic income scheme.

Finland was a Nordic country in which taxpayers were already financing extensive social welfare programs, making basic income a realistic aspiration. Finland was also Scandinavia's most market-oriented economy, a nation dedicated to ruthless competition in the business world. Whatever this experiment was, it could not be written off as woolly-headed socialism. Rather, it appeared to represent an attempt to reinvigorate capitalism.

I decided to go and explore Finland's experiment up close

at the same moment that a slice of the economics profession became infatuated with basic income. From Aspen to London, conferences about the future of work suddenly featured discussions on the merits of various basic income schemes. Labor had changed so fundamentally, the argument typically went, that the traditional idea of a job for every able-bodied person had gone the way of the fountain pen. Basic income would serve as a broad form of social insurance. Whatever happened—whether everyone became a part-time Uber driver, or Uber drivers were replaced by self-driving cars—people could count on sustenance.

At Davos in January 2017, Standing seemed to be everywhere. A moderator introduced him as "the moral conscience" of the Forum, based on his work on the Precariat—the growing class of people whose capacity to support themselves had been menaced by globalization.

The Precariat was growing because of excessive faith in market forces and "the commodification of everything," along with "the systematic dismantling of all institutions and mechanisms of social solidarity," Standing said. Basic income was a way to right the balance.

Davos Men like Benioff increasingly favored the idea, positing basic income as a form of compensation for how their lucrative technological innovations tended to destroy jobs. If the billionaires liked the idea, that raised the prospect that it was, like stakeholder capitalism, a calculated means to stave off a more meaningful transfer of wealth. But it also meant that basic income had greater potential to gain political support.

Chris Hughes, a Facebook cofounder, launched an advocacy and research group, the Economic Security Program, devoted to championing the idea. Its funds turned Stockton, California, a city decimated by the foreclosure crisis, into the testing ground for a basic income program.

In Kenya, a group called GiveDirectly, overseen by an assortment of credentialed academics, began distributing payments to people in nearly two hundred villages, while studying what would happen over the ensuing dozen years. Tests were planned or underway in India, South Korea, and Canada.

By 2018, another tech entrepreneur, Andrew Yang, was putting basic income at the center of an improbable presidential campaign that would attract more support than anyone predicted, promising a "Freedom Dividend" of $1,000 a month for every American adult.

Yet even as basic income had clearly captured momentum, it was still hard to get around the price tag—not necessarily on the merits, but on the prospects for political passage.

If every American were to receive $10,000 a year, the tab would run nearly $3 trillion. That was about eight times what the government was spending on existing social service programs. Washington might just as well have committed to handing out unicorns.

But realpolitik can easily turn into cynicism. Only a few years earlier, the American labor movement's "Fight for $15" campaign to double the federal minimum wage had been written off by many experts as unrealistic. That national effort had persuaded many states and localities to deliver on its goals.

And crises push out the parameters of political possibility. The pandemic jolted the usual calculus. In the name of preventing another Depression, governments from Washington to Brussels were throwing around numbers that would ordinarily seem preposterous. From unemployment benefits and wage subsidies to government-furnished health care, the bill was going to be enormous, justifying serious consideration of alternative ways to distribute public largesse.

The pandemic also reinforced the reality that, in many countries, ordinary people were but one misfortune away from catastrophe. Before the coronavirus, four in ten Americans struggled to come up with a mere $400 to deal with an unexpected event such as a car repair or fixing a broken appliance, according to a widely circulated survey from the Federal Reserve. All at once, tens of millions of Americans were suffering far worse than a blown transmission.

As the coronavirus shut down American life in 2020, garishly lit hotels in Las Vegas were empty, just as thousands of homeless people were camped out on the city's sidewalks. From Minneapolis to Madrid, shopping malls were abandoned, while food banks were packed.

European countries would pay to minimize suffering via automatic programs like unemployment insurance, housing support, and cash grants. American programs were relatively modest, but a surge of unemployment was certain to be accompanied by long-term issues that would drain taxpayers—through law enforcement and prisons, if crime spiked; via payments made to emergency rooms that attended to the tens of millions of people who lacked health insurance. Indeed, the cost of the pandemic relief programs produced in Washington—first under Trump, and then under Biden—exceeded $5 trillion by the middle of 2021.

Even among the hard-boiled pragmatists who tended to run governments, universal basic income suddenly looked like a potentially practical solution to problems that were manifest everywhere.

As a candidate, Biden had been dismissive of the idea, placing emphasis on creating quality jobs. But in May 2020, his soon-to-be vice president, Kamala Harris, then a senator from California, had sponsored a bill that looked like basic income—cash payments well above the level of the CARES Act that would last for the duration of the pandemic. Single people would receive $2,000 a month. Families would gain up to $10,000 a month.

Nancy Pelosi, the Speaker of the House of Representatives, and a proud practitioner of realism, suggested that basic income deserved a place on the public agenda.

"We may have to think in terms of some different ways to put money in people's pockets," she said. "Others have suggested a minimum income, a guaranteed income for people. Is that worthy of attention now? Perhaps so."

Pelosi was just the latest in a line of powerful figures to warm to the idea. Soon, Biden would take a step in that direction.

Throughout history, crises that revealed the pitfalls of inequality had prompted leading thinkers to embrace the notion of a government-furnished social-insurance system—a regular dollop of money for ordinary people. Some favored this concept on ethical grounds; others as a means of preventing unruly mobs from overrunning their gates.

The pandemic had laid bare the magnitude of inequality in modern times. Basic income was gaining credence as a potential solution.

Let us stipulate that there are other solutions that are also worthy of consideration.

The government could directly lift living standards by creating a federal job guarantee. Under this approach, the government would operate a job bank that would always have positions available for those in need, paying a so-called living wage— enough to finance the basics of life. When work was plentiful, the job bank would be a lonely place. When a downturn came, the government would become a mass employer in lieu of writing unemployment checks.

The job guarantee is an elegantly straightforward corrective to the dire shortage of work, and it, too, has been gaining adherents. Its greatest virtue is its broad impact on labor conditions: The government could ensure that every able-bodied person could get a job that paid a living wage. That would force all private employers to meet the standard or suffer a shortage of workers.

If Amazon failed to provide enough protective gear in the midst of a pandemic, people could take refuge at the federal employment center. Amazon would be forced to improve its treatment of workers or watch its parcels pile up undelivered.

In one swoop, the job guarantee would neatly address a pair of profound American problems—the reality that many people need work at the same time that there is much work to be done.

In major cities across the United States, highways are crumbling for lack of upkeep, public schools are deteriorating, and public transportation links need expansion as part of the battle against climate change. Meanwhile, experienced construction workers sit in unemployment offices scanning listings for jobs that pay poverty-level wages. The job guarantee could create spending power for those suffering underemployment, while laying down infrastructure that could boost economic growth for everyone via improved education and transportation.

We need not engage in some progressive version of the Cosmic Lie—pretending that these investments will pay for themselves—to justify spending what it takes. We simply need to avoid falling for the usual deficit-spending fearmongering that comes from Davos Man collaborators like McConnell, forever ready to extend the next tax cut for billionaires while crying poverty when the subject is help for regular people.

But the job guarantee confronts far tougher political obstacles than basic income. It involves the creation of a large-scale bureaucracy, while substantially increasing the role of the state in regulating pay. Basic income removes bureaucracy. Instead of forcing people to satisfy complex rules for individual aid schemes—from housing vouchers to subsidized childcare—it entails simply handing everyone a regular sum of money and allowing them to decide for themselves how to use it.

This feature has been central to basic income's appeal; the element that has allowed it to gain credibility across the political spectrum over centuries.

Half a millennium ago, Thomas More's seminal novel, *Utopia,* included the suggestion that public assistance might better deter thieves than the threat of a death sentence.

By the middle of the eighteenth century, the American revolutionary agitator Thomas Paine was advocating the creation of a national pool of money, financed via inheritance taxes on landholdings, and distributed to every adult, as a means of ensuring what we now call social justice.

Paine posited that every person was born into the world with what he referred to as a "national inheritance"—the nourishment provided by the natural sphere. Private property ownership denied some people access to the soil, which limited their ability to feed themselves.

"The most affluent and the most miserable of the human race are to be found in the countries that are called civilized," Paine wrote. "The contrast of affluence and wretchedness continually meeting and offending the eye, is like dead and living bodies chained together."

Paine was no progenitor to Marxism. His loyalties were firmly with the wealthy cultivators of the soil. But he argued that everyone was entitled to a regular allotment of money as recompense for the disruption of national inheritance. It had to be paid universally, "to every person rich or poor," so as "to prevent invidious distinctions."

If Paine were around today, he would presumably favor some form of wealth tax to finance a comprehensive system of social insurance. And he would reject philanthropy and stakeholder capitalism as untenable substitutes for a meaningful redistribution of wealth.

"In advocating the case of the person thus dispossessed, it is a right and not a charity that I am pleading for," Paine wrote. "There are, in every country, some magnificent charities established by individuals. It is, however, but little that any individual can do, when the whole extent of the misery to be relieved be considered. He may satisfy his conscience, but not his heart."

Nearly two centuries later, the Rev. Martin Luther King Jr. promoted a form of basic income as part of the movement for civil rights. He described economic inequality as a fundamental injustice, one that was inseparable from overtly racist forms of discrimination like Jim Crow laws.

"Dislocations in the market operation of our economy and the prevalence of discrimination thrust people into idleness and bind them in constant or frequent unemployment against their will," King wrote in his final book, published in 1967. "The time has come for us to civilize ourselves by the total, direct and immediate abolition of poverty."

King advocated that the government furnish an allowance that ensured that everyone could live at "the median of society," with increases tracking the standard of living. He cited an estimate from the economist John Kenneth Galbraith suggesting that such a program might run $20 billion, which was only a smidgen more than the government that year planned to spend on the futile war in Vietnam.

Milton Friedman, the godfather of shareholder maximization, also embraced a variant of basic income—negative income taxes that put cash in the pockets of the poor. Ever disdainful of government bureaucracy, he viewed cash as a far more effective form of public aid than programs run by the dreaded state.

In its modern-day incarnation, basic income has gained currency as a malleable approach that can be tailored to widely divergent conceptions of society.

Progressives like Standing envision it as a means of emancipation from the meaninglessness of low-wage work. People stuck in minimum wage jobs at fast-food restaurants could gain freedom to abandon the fryolator, going home to play with their children, make music, and dig vegetable gardens.

Labor advocates embrace basic income as a way to increase

bargaining power, enabling workers to refuse jobs at poverty-level wages.

Liberals envision basic income as a way to remove the stigma of public assistance. Instead of relying on food stamps at the grocery store while suffering the judgmental gazes of other shoppers—*Shouldn't she buy spinach instead of frozen pizza?*—poor people would receive the same steady support as everyone else.

Conservatives, like the political commentator David Frum, are drawn to basic income for its simplicity, viewing it as an all-in-one replacement for the tangle of overlapping social welfare programs that are already on offer.

And Davos Man favors universal income as a means of unburdening himself of moral responsibility for profiting off technology that threatens jobs.

"As business leaders, we have an obligation to ensure that the changes wrought by technology transcend our companies and benefit all of humanity," Benioff wrote in *Fortune* in 2017. "For those who cannot be retrained, and even those traditionally not compensated for raising a family or volunteering to help others, we need to look at universal basic income."

This sort of talk is why some economists—Stiglitz, among them—disdain basic income as an ersatz substitute for paychecks. People want to work for a living, he says. They don't want perpetual handouts.

This is true, yet his critique is premised on the narrow conception of basic income that prevails in Silicon Valley: as a permanent welfare scheme for those displaced by automation.

This dystopian picture is indeed worthy of opposition—robots doing most of the work, while redundant humans live off government-furnished scraps. But there are other ways to harness basic income toward a different vision that involves expanding employment and encouraging economic growth.

When Finland launched its trial in 2017, it was looking to

basic income not as a replacement for work, but as a means of spurring more of it.

Finland had never recovered from the global financial crisis, which had played out just as the rise of tablet computers and smartphones decimated one of the country's largest industries—commercial paper manufacturing. Nokia, the Finnish company that had once ruled mobile telephones, had failed to cash in. For a decade, the Finnish economy had grown not at all. The unemployment rate was stuck above 8 percent.

Tending to the human cost of this misfortune was expensive, because Finland's social welfare system was generous. As a share of its overall economy, Finland's spending on unemployment benefits had increased by 70 percent between 2008 and 2015.

Finland's leaders had reason to worry that their unemployment program was preventing people from moving on with their lives. As in many countries, Finland required that recipients of jobless benefits regularly visit unemployment offices to satisfy a confounding assortment of bureaucratic dictates. People had to prove that they were really looking for a job while attending training sessions. They had to continually disclose and verify their income.

Recipients were discouraged from accepting part-time jobs or launching their own businesses. Extra income risked undercutting their eligibility for benefits. So people passed up opportunities for fear of jeopardizing government support.

This was maddening to Asmo Saloranta, whose technology startup was struggling to hire workers. He was based in Oulu, a city of two hundred thousand people that no one would mistake for Palo Alto. Notched in low pine forests, only one hundred miles south of the Arctic Circle, it felt far removed from everything.

But the city had long been a hub of wireless communications—
a major outpost for Nokia, before the company faded toward
oblivion. The local unemployment rate sat above 16 percent.
Scads of creative engineers were on hand and in need of work.

Saloranta's company, Asmo Solutions, had developed a phone
charger that drew power only when the device was plugged in.
He had his eyes on a former Nokia employer who was a legend at
developing prototypes. Saloranta only needed him part-time.
He was offering 2,000 euros a month—less than the potential
hire was bringing in via unemployment benefits.

"It's more profitable for him to just wait at home for some
ideal job," Saloranta complained.

Under its basic income trial, the Finnish government planned
to randomly select two thousand people who were drawing jobless benefits and commence sending them 560 euros a month,
automatically, while exempting them from bureaucratic requirements. They would be permitted to earn money on the side.

The government was keen to see what would happen. Would
more people join startups or launch their own? How many would
pursue education that would position them for more rewarding
careers? How many would drop out of life and dedicate their
hours to vodka? The trial was as much a test of human nature as
economic policy.

Saloranta was confident the results would be positive. "It
would activate many more unemployed people," he said.

Jaana Matila was the sort of person he had in mind. When I
met her in the gray chill of an Arctic morning, she was twenty-
nine years old and in possession of three degrees in computing.
She had a borderline-obsessive interest in software. What she
did not have was a real job. She had completed three unpaid internships. She was doing a bit of freelance work, having most recently designed a website for a hair salon. Sometimes she taught
adult swimming lessons. But she had to limit these gigs lest she
imperil her 700-euro monthly unemployment check. She had

once failed to secure a receipt for one of the swim lessons. While she tracked it down, she lost her benefits for a month.

"I had to ask my boyfriend, 'Can you give me some monthly money so I can buy some food?'" she told me. She spent most of her time taking her dog on walks through the forest while trying not to think about how her skills were falling behind the constant advances of technology.

"People in a disadvantaged position, they use a major part of their cognitive ability worrying about their lives," Mikko Annala, a researcher at Demos Helsinki, a think tank, told me. "What if we have this potential there that is continuously worrying about life, about making it? What if we can get that into use by giving them something? That is a hypothesis that we should absolutely test."

This was an aspect that tended to get lost in the basic income conversation. Basic income was frequently described in shorthand as money for nothing, a dose of socialism for the masses, but Finland was testing it as a way to improve capitalism.

"Some people think basic income will solve every problem under the sun, and some people think it's from the hand of Satan and will destroy our work ethic," said Olli Kangas, who oversaw research at the Finnish government agency that administered social welfare programs. "I'm hoping we can create some knowledge on this issue."

The results of the trial three years later would not settle the argument. The sample size was so small that the findings lacked authority, while offering a little something to validate every preconception.

Those who received basic income payments were only marginally more likely to be working than those who had started off in the traditional unemployment program. But those in the trial had shown a pronounced tendency toward greater personal satisfaction and happiness. They were less likely to be depressed, sad, lonely, or stressed out.

That alone was worth something.

Finland opted not to go ahead with basic income, instead imposing stricter work requirements on recipients of unemployment—a step in the opposite direction. But elsewhere, basic income was more in vogue than ever.

In March 2021, Stockton, California, released the findings of its experiment in which it had handed out $500 a month to 125 randomly selected people for two years. There, too, recipients were less prone to depression and anxiety. And they were more likely to be employed—especially women—as the extra money financed needed childcare, clothing for interviews, and transportation.

But one key limitation was at work: Basic income appeared most politically achievable in the places where it was needed the least.

Countries that already spent heavily on social welfare programs, like Norway and Finland, could reorient their budgets to produce some version of basic income. They could do this without demanding that someone pay higher taxes, and without cutting some other program to come up with the money.

But in places like the United States and Britain, where social programs had been dramatically reduced, basic income would demand a new tax, or cuts to some other spending. History suggested how this would play out: with reductions in support for the most vulnerable people.

In the United States, the demonization of welfare by President Reagan in the 1980s had produced the so-called welfare reform signed by Clinton in the mid-1990s, which dropped support to a pittance, yielding increased poverty. Poor single mothers were required to work, even as promised increases in subsidized childcare never materialized.

In the suburbs of Atlanta, I met a nineteen-year-old single

mother who was unable to line up childcare for her infant daughter, which meant that she could not attend the job-training classes the state of Georgia required as a condition of her $235 monthly welfare check. Having lost those benefits, she was selling her body to come up with cash for diapers. Since the Clinton welfare reform, the number of poor families with children in Georgia had nearly doubled, yet the share of such families who were receiving cash assistance had plunged from 98 percent to 8 percent.

Among conservatives, basic income was appealing precisely because it would provide justification for cutting other social welfare programs. What was sold as a comprehensive form of social insurance could become a single target in the mission to dismantle government.

Beginning in the 1970s, Washington had moved away from so-called entitlement programs in which anyone who satisfied basic criteria like income had a right to public assistance. In their place came so-called block grants given to states along with the freedom to determine how to use these funds. States took this as the impetus to tighten eligibility for relief, pushing people off their welfare rolls. More fell into poverty, prompting conservatives to attack remaining programs as ineffective—grounds for further cuts.

Between 2000 and 2017, Congress cut funding for thirteen block grants that were a source of support for low-income people by more than one-third. Trump administered further reductions to help finance his tax cuts for Davos Man.

In Britain, austerity included the consolidation of multiple social programs into one all-encompassing scheme known as Universal Credit. Osborne, then running the treasury, championed this refashioning as a way to cut spending while forcing people to work.

"For too long, we've had a system where people who did the right thing—who get up in the morning and work hard—felt penalized for it, while people who did the wrong thing got re-warded," Osborne said in April 2013. "This month, we will make work pay."

Instead, Osborne engineered the reverse. Over the subsequent four years, employment edged up in low-income households in the United Kingdom, while average earnings rose by nearly 4 percent. But those gains were wiped out and then some by a 7 percent cut to state support for working age Britons, along with the elimination of tax credits for the poor. Overall, low-income people suffered a 3 percent drop in income in those years. By 2018, the share of British children who were officially poor had climbed from 27 percent to 30 percent.

Under the shift to Universal Credit, the government tightened eligibility to levels that were cruel and absurd.

In Liverpool, I met a woman with cerebral palsy who had been living on a disability check for the eight years after she lost her job answering the phones at an auto parts company. She had recently been summoned for an assessment of her continued eligibility.

The first question undercut any pretense that this was a sincere exploration of her situation: "How long have you had cerebral palsy?" From birth. "Will it get better?" No.

She was then sixty-one, and her bones were weakening. The man conducting the assessment dropped a pen on the floor and commanded that she pick it up—a test of her dexterity. Soon, a letter came informing her that she had been deemed fit for work—and, therefore, not entitled to her disability check.

"I think they were just ticking boxes," she told me.

Basic income was a catch-all phrase that meant different things depending on who was using the term. It could clearly be designed to bolster economic security, allowing people to live happier, healthier, more prosperous lives.

It could improve working conditions, boost wages, and limit

vulnerabilities to commonplace misfortunes like car trouble along with global disasters like pandemics.

But in the usage that had gained the greatest political traction—the one embraced by people like Benioff—it was an allowance proffered as justification for the status quo, a payment that indemnified Davos Man for having prospered at the expense of people in need, a substitute for billionaires submitting to meaningful sacrifices like progressive taxation.

Basic income held potential as a means of attacking inequality, but it had to be protected against hijacking by the beneficiaries of continued inequality. It had to be a complement to a robust social safety net—perhaps paired with a job guarantee—and not a substitute.

Biden gave it an important push. The $1.9 trillion stimulus spending package he signed into law in March 2021 included a provision that amounted to a version of basic income: Most American parents would receive a monthly check of $300 a month as part of an expansion of child tax credits.

That provision was authorized for only a year, but the Biden administration aimed to establish it as permanent. Researchers at Columbia University estimated that the policy could reduce child poverty by 40 percent.

Basic income had become mainstream.

"AT WAR AGAINST MONOPOLY POWER"

Davos Man Under Attack

Jeff Bezos looked vaguely annoyed. Despite his studious attempts to strike a genial pose, the tightness at the corners of his mouth betrayed him.

For more than a quarter century, he had managed to expand his business along with his personal fortune without having to justify himself to Congress. That run came to an end in a wood-paneled hearing room in the Capitol in late July 2020.

Given the continued dangers of the pandemic, he was appearing by videoconference, seated at a desk with sparsely occupied shelves behind him. His image filled a white square on a screen that was visible to the members of the House Judiciary Committee, and to millions of people watching on television.

His expression was forced, his body language uneasy, as technical glitches intermittently disrupted his audio. "Mr. Bezos," a lawmaker said at one point, "I believe you're on mute."

Next to him, in the square to the right, was Mark Zuckerberg, the founder of Facebook, another man with a lot to explain. Below them and to the left sat Tim Cook, the CEO of Apple, and Sundar Pichai, who ran Google.

Here, assembled for public interrogation, were the leaders of four companies that had achieved such unparalleled dominance that they had destroyed any meaningful concept of competition. Collectively, they possessed personal wealth in excess of $265 billion—more than the annual economic output of Finland.

The hearing had been anticipated like a prizefight. It was the culmination of a yearlong probe by the subcommittee into allegations that the four companies were prospering at the expense of American society. They had erected monopolies that were unfairly crushing competitors and ripping off consumers through higher prices, while extracting personal data without the consent of their unwitting customers. They stood accused of warping the functionality of the marketplace, stifling innovation, destroying jobs, eviscerating privacy, and wielding control of technology to redouble their supremacy.

Their Orwellian proclivities and lust for scale had been on display before anyone had heard of COVID-19, but the pandemic had enhanced their primacy. With Americans sequestered in their homes, and with the internet central to the basic dealings of commerce, the companies that controlled the digital sphere appeared to have seized modern life itself. They seemed certain to emerge from the pandemic with greater market share, and weakened competition.

Much like in the age of Robber Barons, their dominance demanded corrective action from the government. The hearing was the opening act of a process that would end with attempts to break up some of these companies into smaller pieces, in what amounted to the most sweeping assertion of antitrust authority in decades.

For months, Bezos had sought to avoid the committee like a man putting off a trip to the urologist. Talk of a subpoena had eliminated his room for maneuver. So here he was, cast uncomfortably as a leading defendant in the prosecution of a crime against representative government.

"American democracy has always been at war against monopoly power," declared the chairman of the subcommittee on antitrust, David Cicilline, a Democrat from Rhode Island, in his opening statement. "Our founders would not bow before a king, nor should we bow before the emperors of the online economy."

When Bezos got his turn to talk, he resorted to his well-honed origins story in a counterclaim for historical affirmation.

"I was born into great wealth, not monetary wealth, but it was the wealth of a loving family, a family that fostered my curiosity and encouraged me to dream big," he told the committee.

Bezos talked about his mother, how she had been a teenager when he was born. He noted that his adoptive father had come to the United States from Fidel Castro's Cuba. He described abandoning his "steady job on Wall Street" for the Seattle garage where he had started Amazon. He worked in a reference to the recently departed civil rights hero John Lewis.

Bezos was wrapping himself in the American flag as a defense against his company's systematic pillaging. Amazon was not a monopolist whose profits were extracted through labor exploitation, invasive data mining, and cosmic scale. It was a red, white and blue success story, the outgrowth of a smart idea pursued by a hardworking risk taker who had harnessed the virtues of his freedom-loving country. This was the real American narrative, he was implicitly asserting, not the diversionary nonsense about rejecting the monarchy.

"More than any place on earth, entrepreneurial companies start, grow and thrive here in the U.S.," Bezos said. "The rest of the world would love even the tiniest sip of the elixir we have here in the U.S. Immigrants like my dad see what a treasure this country is."

The interrogation that commenced would continue for more than four hours as members of the committee sought to pry into the crevices of the four businesses.

Bezos was forced to defend his company against disclosures

that it had habitually violated its own policies by examining the sales of independent merchants who sold their wares on its site, and then destroying those sellers with its own products. He had to answer questions about how Amazon had purchased a major competitor that sold diapers and then dramatically increased prices; how it tolerated sales of counterfeit products on its platform.

He suffered the withering cross-examination with a posture of patience and deference. "I appreciate that question," Bezos said repeatedly. "I don't know the answer to that question," was another phrase that gained a vigorous workout. "I don't remember that at all," he said at one point, while carefully adding words of pacification. "I would like to understand it better."

His tone suggested that he was laboring to stifle his exasperation, offering a reminder that Bezos was accustomed to demanding answers from others, and not the other way around. Pressed to explain what he had done to investigate claims that Amazon was abusing companies that sold on its platform, he said: "It's not as easy to do as you would think."

His ultimate defense could be boiled down to this: Amazon was giving the people what they wanted.

"Customer obsession has driven our success," he said.

This was a hardwired Davos Man maneuver, the assertion that had enabled generations of American corporate chiefs to vanquish efforts to constrain their monopoly power going all the way back to the Robber Barons.

Davos Man used this argument—in combination with copious campaign contributions, and energetic lobbying—to persuade Washington to look the other way while he completed increasingly audacious mergers, manipulated financial markets, and exploited working people. He was doing right by the customer. No harm, no foul.

In placing consumers at the center of the action, Davos Man cast other incarnations of humanity—workers, tenants, people desiring clean air—as impediments to the public interest. Consumers were aligned with shareholders: both benefited from ruthlessness in the pursuit of lower costs. Which made Davos Man an agent of good, and anything that added cost—from regulations to collective bargaining—the enemy of progress.

Such depictions typically involved the selective harnessing of data. Bezos had come prepared. He told the panel that Amazon's sales amounted to less than 1 percent of a global retail market worth $25 trillion a year, and less than 4 percent of the retail realm in the United States. The committee countered by focusing on the relevant space—American e-commerce. There, Amazon controlled nearly three-fourths of the market, giving it the power to dominate the terms of trade.

As the hearing broke up, the airwaves and Twittersphere filled with talk that a comeuppance was at hand. Big Tech was encountering the Fist of God—the federal government intervening to protect the marketplace.

"It's rare to see Congress cover itself in glory," declared Matt Stoller, a leading critic of federal acquiescence in the rise of monopoly power, "but believe it or not, that's what happened."

Yet the day after the hearing, Amazon reported the most bountiful earnings in its history. Between April and June—the worst of the first wave of the pandemic—it had recorded a profit of $5.2 billion, double the level of the previous year. Its stock price immediately leapt by 5 percent, indicating that those in control of money were more impressed by Amazon's market dominance than the threats from Congress to cut it down to size.

The scrutiny of the technology giants was shaping up as a crucial test of the rules that would apply in the global economy after the pandemic. Would they still be written by and for Davos Man? Or would the concerns of ordinary people gain a hearing?

There were myriad reasons to imagine that Amazon and the other technology titans really were in for a sustained offensive.

The subcommittee's investigation had been that rare flower in Washington—a bipartisan undertaking. Both the Justice Department and the Federal Trade Commission had launched probes of Amazon, along with Facebook and Google.

Biden would take office the following year, advancing the push. In March 2021, he placed two crusading legal scholars in prime positions to attack the power of the Silicon Valley goliaths.

Lina Khan had served as an aide to the House Judiciary Committee as it probed the companies hauled before Congress. Biden appointed her to a seat on the Federal Trade Commission, which was certain to be at the center of any attempts to hold the tech giants to account. And after Khan gained Senate confirmation, Biden elevated her to the chair of the commission, putting the agency in her hands. He selected another sworn enemy of monopoly power, Tim Wu, for a post at the White House, giving him a seat on the National Economic Council.

On the other side of the Atlantic, Amazon was facing antitrust enforcement, following the filing of formal charges by the European Commission in November 2020. German authorities were investigating Amazon for manipulating prices. In France, a court had barred Amazon from shipping nonessential items, citing the need to protect warehouse workers, and prompting the company to shutter its operations for several weeks.

But all this governmental action was chasing a moving target. Amazon was getting bigger just as many of its competitors were struggling. Italians had set aside their traditional disdain to embrace Amazon as the means of summoning pasta, wine, and toys to their door. In France, the reimposition of a lockdown in the fall of 2020 provoked outrage from small businesses and merchants. They had to close, but Amazon was always open, making the crisis a chance for the American colossus to add to its hold on the market.

By March 2021, European authorities were struggling to

make sense of the algorithms Amazon employed on its site, challenging their efforts to mount a case.

For nearly half a century, the billionaires had monopolized the spoils of economic growth by looting democracy itself. They had manipulated the process of passing laws, crafting budgets, and regulating industries. Their predation had generated a powerful backlash. The public interest appeared to be reasserting itself, reaching for the levers of control. But an arsenal of lobbyists, lawyers, and accountants would have a lot to say about the outcome before history could be written. Davos Man was nothing if not relentless. He was playing for keeps.

The billionaires had mastered a recipe for moral alchemy, passing off what was lucrative for them as beneficial for society, even as the evidence mounted that they were accumulating their wealth at the direct expense of the rest of the populace.

And when the resulting anger built to cataclysmic proportions, threatening the liberal democratic order and globalization—the underpinnings of their affluence—they had conjured up novel ways to pretend to make amends, to placate the aggrieved without sacrificing anything of great value. They had erected philanthropic foundations to broadcast their benevolence. They had concocted stakeholder capitalism to display their empathy. They had adopted the language of change without yielding power to labor movements, regulators, activist shareholders, or other groups that actually had a stake in what transpired.

The flaying in Congress was a ritual, though perhaps a prelude to meaningful policy change.

Meanwhile, business went on.

The campaign to redress monopoly power in Washington represented the revival of a spirit that went all the way back to the founding of the nation.

In the usual account of American history, the Boston Tea

Party of 1773 was a revolt against unjust taxation. A faraway monarch in England unfairly squeezed his colonial subjects through exorbitant taxes. In protest, patriots ransacked an incoming shipment of British tea, hurling it into Boston Harbor.

But the Tea Party was really an uprising against monopoly power. The patriots were enraged that the British Crown had allowed the East India Company to sell tea directly to the American colonies, instead of working through a network of local distributors. Rather than a reaction to high taxes, the revolt was actually sparked by a reduction of taxes. The Crown had lowered levies on the East India Company's imports of tea from Asia, reinforcing its monopolistic grip on the tea drinkers of the American colonies.

The history that has unspooled in the two and a half centuries since has been rife with battles over the justice of monopoly power. Laborers, small businesses, and farmers have frequently mobilized to restrain the avaricious tendencies of the largest, most deeply financed American conglomerates.

During the last three decades of the nineteenth century, the monopolists gained the upper hand. Much as Bezos would later seize the promise of the internet, industrialists like John D. Rockefeller and J. P. Morgan exploited advances in technology—the railway locomotive, the steamship, the telegraph—to integrate the West into the rest of the American economy. They dominated finance, transportation, steelmaking, electrical production, and oil distribution, buying off politicians to win access to land, and brutally crushing labor movements that sought a greater share of the gains.

These were the Robber Barons—Davos Man's forebears. Anger over their rapacious ways delivered Woodrow Wilson to the White House in 1913, bearing a mandate to tame and democratize industry. He took aim at the dominant industrialists, introducing the Federal Trade Commission, a body created to combat monopoly power.

But Wilson's project met its demise as the United States entered World War I. The war effort demanded steel, coal, munitions, and other fruits of industry, elevating efficiency to primacy above all other considerations. The next president, Warren Harding, adopted the same stance as Joe Biden a century later: he promised "a return to normalcy." He handed the Treasury to the tycoon who had helped finance his campaign—Andrew Mellon.

Mellon was invested in nearly every crevice of American industry, from oil and gas to steel and glass-making. He used his position to block antitrust enforcement, defenestrating the Federal Trade Commission. In a best-selling book, *Taxation: The People's Business,* he indulged an early iteration of the Cosmic Lie, arguing that taxing the rich posed a "menace for the future." Amid the robust economic growth of the mid-1920s, the industrialists claimed public validation.

In an oft-repeated pattern, the industrialists overplayed their hand. Through a wave of mergers, a handful of companies came to dominate steel and automobile manufacturing along with the distribution of food. Farmers and workers paid the price through lower wages and crop prices. By 1928, nearly one-fourth of all income in the United States was flowing into the coffers of the most affluent 1 percent.

Wealthy Americans plowed their winnings into all manner of speculation—from real estate to the stock market—driving prices to levels bearing no connection to fundamentals, and creating the conditions for the market crash that began the Great Depression.

Soaring joblessness, commonplace calamity, and rage toward the industrialists laid the ground the presidency of Franklin Delano Roosevelt and the New Deal leveling policies that he championed. He unleashed the power of the state to constrain monopolists, introduced the most progressive income tax regimen on earth, and directed the proceeds to finance public spending that spurred a broad-based economic revival.

"The measure of the restoration lies in the extent to which we apply social values more noble than mere monetary profit," Roosevelt declared in his first inaugural address, in March 1933. "The joy and moral stimulation of work no longer must be forgotten in the mad chase of evanescent profits."

Previously, as the governor of New York, Roosevelt had wrangled with Mellon over his grip on the steel industry, and with Morgan over his control of the electrical supply. As president, Roosevelt sicced his Justice Department on the Robber Barons, prosecuting them for corruption and tax evasion. He reinvigorated the Federal Trade Commission, which sued to break up monopolies. He helped farmers keep their land by establishing a government system that offered cut-rate mortgages. These policies prepared the ground for a sustained period of economic growth whose benefits were widely shared.

Yet again, foreign conflict—this time, the Cold War—gave the plutocrats a shot at resurrection. The global competition for supremacy with the Soviet Union elevated the importance of efficiency and industrial might above all, while tainting state power. Business lobbies depicted regulatory authority as akin to the totalitarian menace of Communism. In their rendering, big business was heroic and representative of American ideals, juxtaposed against the Leninist hand of government.

As Matt Stoller reveals in his seminal history of American monopoly power, *Goliath,* this was as much a triumph of ideas as an exercise in brute market force. "Co-opting the rhetoric of liberty was essential in persuading Americans who had been raised on populist suspicion of centralized power," he writes.

That did not happen by accident. The glorification of the unhindered market and the denigration of regulatory authority was insinuated into the workings of American democracy by a band of true believers headquartered at the University of Chicago—the hothouse for neoliberalism.

The Chicago school, whose disciples included Milton Friedman, relentlessly attacked the New Deal as antithetical to American freedom. One figure produced by this movement would lay down the infrastructure for Davos Man's dominance—Robert Bork, a legal scholar whose subversive ideas about antitrust were critical to the rise of commercial giants like Amazon.

Bork, who served as solicitor general in the Nixon administration, would describe the University of Chicago as a breeding ground for an intellectual revolution. "A lot of us who took the antitrust course or the economics course underwent what can only be called a religious conversion," he said years later. "It changed our view of the entire world."

Traditional conceptions of American antitrust law regarded scale as inherently dangerous. A company that was too big and deeply financed had the power to prey on smaller competitors, putting them out of business by dropping prices, and then raising them once it had the market to itself. It could corner the supply of raw materials, suffocating rivals. A prodigious scholar, Bork argued that these ideas were not only wrong, but anathema to the free market—a shackling of productive power that would limit innovation.

In Washington, think tanks and lobbying organizations financed by major corporations spread the gospel that scale was a virtue. The American Enterprise Institute—a conservative think tank launched in the late 1930s to attack the New Deal— hired Bork as an antitrust policy adviser. Major companies, among them Chase Manhattan, U.S. Steel, and Pfizer, financed research by Bork and other Chicago school apostles, attacking traditional conceptions of antitrust. The Business Roundtable convened in 1972 to promote the idea that corporations left to their own devices were good for society. The Roundtable took direct aim at the Federal Trade Commission.

The movement would achieve a substantial victory in 1975, as Congress invalidated so-called fair-trade laws that had allowed manufacturers to set the prices for their finished goods. These laws—in force in many states—had been a fixture of the New Deal. They had been crafted to protect manufacturers and local distributors against predatory forms of discounting by national chains that dropped prices below profitability to destroy competitors and seize the marketplace.

In signing the repeal of fair-trade laws in December 1975, President Gerald Ford endorsed the logic of the Chicago school: The laws were costing consumers $2 billion a year through higher prices. A range of goods—from prescription drugs to televisions—would become cheaper.

The elimination of free-trade laws cleared the path for Walmart, the discount empire that came to dominate retail, its very name synonymous with the hollowing out of American downtowns. Walmart was the logical extension of the Chicago school unleashed on the business landscape—an enterprise meticulously organized to supply customers with the lowest prices, without consideration for the attendant social costs.

Three years after the lifting of fair-trade laws, Bork produced *The Antitrust Paradox*, an influential book that made explicit the concept that would dominate American thinking on corporate behavior for decades after.

"The only legitimate goal of antitrust is the maximization of consumer welfare," Bork wrote.

With this formulation, Bork dismissed the generations-old American struggle to restrain the forces of monopoly, reducing the consideration of corporate conduct to one simple test: What was the impact on consumer prices? If shoppers benefited, nothing else mattered.

By 2000, wages throughout American retail had been reduced by $4.5 billion a year as a result of Walmart driving down pay and decimating competitors. This was a neat transfer of wealth

from working people to shareholders—one justified by the benefits for the consumer. Shoppers needed those low prices, because
they were increasingly working at places like Walmart. A feed-
back loop of diminishing living standards for American workers
turned Walmart's founders into the richest family in the land.

"It wasn't that Republicans gained political power, and implemented Bork's philosophy, though that happened," writes
Stoller. "It was that Bork convinced not just the right wing but
the left that antitrust, and more broadly democracy, as practiced
in the middle of the twentieth century was not only inefficient,
but countered the dictates of natural economic systems and science itself."

Bill Clinton, raised in Walmart's home state of Arkansas and
educated at Yale Law School, where he studied with Bork, presided over an unrestrained wave of corporate mergers. He lifted
strictures on banking, setting the stage for the financial crisis of
2008. He deregulated telecommunications, allowing cable and
telephone companies to fashion dominant conglomerates, and
preparing the path for Google, Facebook, and the other modern-
day monopolists.

Their dominance over advertising, which decimated local
journalism, tripped no antitrust alarms under the concept formulated by the Chicago school, because Google and Facebook
were giving away their products. The consumer was paying nothing, even as American democracy itself was under assault from a
replacement of fact-based journalism by fake news.

Corporate scale became celebrated in American life, infused
with a national worship of technology and innovation, enabling
Bezos and the rest of the Davos Men to reconstitute the market
power enjoyed by their forebears.

This was the reality most in need of rectification, argued Lina
Khan, the legal scholar selected by Biden to oversee a reinvigorated Federal Trade Commission. At thirty-two, she became
the youngest person to ever head the agency. She was both an

iconoclast and an advocate for returning to deeper-set American traditions.

"The current framework in antitrust—specifically its equating competition with 'consumer welfare,' typically measured through short-term effects on price and output—fails to capture the architecture of market power in the twenty-first century marketplace," Khan had written in a widely admired *Yale Law Journal* article published in 2017. "In other words, the potential harms to competition posed by Amazon's dominance are not cognizable if we assess competition primarily through price and output. Focusing on these metrics instead blinds us to the potential hazards."

In the four years after her critique was published, Amazon grew more powerful than ever, and Khan gained a perch to challenge the company's dominance.

An epic battle was taking shape as lawmakers and regulators from Washington to Brussels took on Bezos and the other Davos Men.

The ending was far from clear.

For the moment, critics of monopoly power appeared to have momentum. But Davos Man was skilled at drawing strength from attacks on his power, using them to project the appearance of change, while carrying on with business as usual.

For Davos Man, the battle over monopoly power would determine the future of his corporations.

Another fight was hitting even closer to home—a reinvigorated campaign to force the wealthy to pay their fair share in taxes.

CHAPTER 20

"TAXES, TAXES, TAXES. THE REST IS BULLSHIT."
Making Davos Man Pay

Rutger Bregman was supposed to say something uplifting and affirming about universal basic income, a subject on which he had written a book. This was why the Forum organizers had invited him to Davos, and why he had been selected as a panelist at a session held on the last day of the annual meeting in January 2019.

The session was titled "The Cost of Inequality." It began with a slick, scene-setting video produced by the host of the event, *Time* magazine.

"As the gap between rich and poor gets wider, the costs of inequality are adding up," a narrator intoned. The screen displayed images of popular examples—Britain Brexiting, France rocked by Yellow Vest protests, homelessness in the United States, anger in the townships of South Africa. "Governments, corporations, and individuals are all being asked what they will do to tilt the global economy in a more equitable direction."

Bregman, a thirty-year-old historian from the Netherlands, was attending Davos for the first time, and he was beleaguered by the experience—the masquerade of billionaires agonizing over how to solve problems that were eminently solvable.

He was asked for his thoughts on how to get people out of poverty, a setup for his talk about basic income. But he took the question in an unanticipated direction, producing an answer that went viral.

"I hear people talk in the language of participation and justice and equality and transparency, but then, I mean, almost no one raises the real issue," Bregman said. "Tax avoidance. The rich just not paying their fair share. I mean, it feels like I'm at a firefighter's conference and no one's allowed to speak about water."

That line drew laughter from the audience, but also some eye-rolling. Under the unspoken code of the Forum, panelists were welcome to speak critically about almost anything—inequality, unaffordable drug prices, fossil fuels emissions—but implicating participants for the problem was verboten. In the central pretense of Davos, everyone was Committed to Improving the State of the World, so every problem reflected complexity, or the elusiveness of solutions—but certainly not gluttony on the part of the people in the room.

Bregman was accusing the billionaires of hypocrisy on a scale responsible for mass poverty and despair—a striking breach of decorum. Invited inside Davos Man's lair, he was lecturing the inhabitants on their failure to live up to their own lofty rhetoric.

"I mean, ten years ago, the World Economic Forum asked the question: what must industry do to prevent a broad social backlash," Bregman continued. "It's very simple: just stop talking about philanthropy, and start talking about taxes."

A couple of days earlier, Michael Dell, the technology billionaire and another signatory to the Business Roundtable stakeholder capitalism pledge, had been asked at another Davos panel whether he supported attempts to lift the top tax rate in the

United States from 37 percent to 70 percent. He had argued against an increase by pointing to his philanthropic efforts.

"I feel much more comfortable with our ability as a private foundation to allocate those funds than I do giving them to the government," Dell said.

This was Davos Man's standard evasive maneuver in the face of a predatory challenge to his wealth: Dell was arguing that philanthropy obviated the need for taxes.

The previous year, 2018, the twenty wealthiest Americans had collectively contributed $8.7 billion, which was both a large amount of money, and a mere 0.81 percent of their wealth.

Politicians like Elizabeth Warren and Bernie Sanders were proposing wealth taxes as a means of securing revenue to finance ideas like universal health care and subsidized childcare. A 6 percent wealth tax applied to fortunes larger than $1 billion would have netted $63 billion from the twenty richest people—more than seven times their reported philanthropic contributions. Not even the most generous, Warren Buffett and Bill Gates, approached the 6 percent mark. Dell had given less than the average—$158 million, or 0.6 percent of his $27.6 billion fortune.

Not content to exaggerate his altruism, Dell indulged a corollary of the Cosmic Lie: he was against taxes reaching 70 percent not because he preferred to keep his money but out of social concern.

"I don't think it would help the growth of the U.S. economy," Dell said. "Name a country where that's worked. Ever."

This was clearly intended as a rhetorical question, but the panelist seated to his left, the economist Erik Brynjolffson, immediately blurted out an answer.

"The United States," he said. "From about the 1930s through about the 1960s, the tax rate averaged about 70 percent. At times, it was up as high as 95 percent. And those were actually pretty good years for growth."

At his own panel, Bregman recounted this anecdote as proof that the billionaires were pontificating about economic inequality, while refusing to do anything to address it.

"This is not rocket science," he said. "We can talk for a very long time about all these stupid philanthropy schemes, we can invite Bono once more, but, come on, we've got to be talking about taxes, and that's it. Taxes, taxes, taxes. All the rest is bullshit."

You may have watched this scene already. People shared a video clip of it widely on social media, because it resonated as a rare bit of truth-telling amid the self-aggrandizing that dominates Davos. Yet equally striking was what came after.

The moderator of the session, *Time*'s editor in chief Edward Felsenthal, turned to another panelist, Jane Goodall—the world's foremost expert on chimpanzees—to solicit her opinion on why humans had not solved inequality. He addressed her as a naturalist accustomed to thinking about the characteristics of species.

"What's lacking in the brain?" Felsenthal asked Goodall. "Why can't we get there? What is it about us that we see, we see the solution, and the urgency, but we can't get there?"

Felsenthal was prostrating himself in submission to the species that was dominant on the local terrain—Davos Man.

Inequality was in large part the result of the billionaire class mobilizing lobbyists to avoid taxes while writing economic policy in their favor. But Felsenthal—a regular at the Forum, and under the employ of a magazine recently purchased by Benioff—was implying that everyone was doing their level best, that inequality was the result of something other than the billionaires plundering the democratic process. It was, instead, the manifestation of a mysterious evolutionary problem worthy of discussion by an expert on primates.

Goodall played along.

"The most intellectual creature that's ever walked on this

planet, destroying its only home, destroying the environment, and causing all these inequalities in our societies—what's gone wrong?" she asked. "We've broken the link between intellect and wisdom."

As a question of policy, reducing economic inequality is not terribly complicated. It's just exceedingly difficult as a political objective. The government needs to reapportion wealth so that ordinary people regain a meaningful stake in society. But those who possess wealth have mastered how to use it to manipulate democracy, preventing a fair distribution.

Davos Man has consistently defeated efforts to increase his tax burden by deploying variants of the Cosmic Lie—arguing that wealth trickles down, that attempts to tax and redistribute it destroy incentives for entrepreneurs to invest and hire.

The Cosmic Lie has been a political winner for reasons that go beyond campaign contributions for Davos Man collaborators like Macron and McConnell. The concept of trickle-down rests on appealing assumptions about human nature, and the heroic achievements of individuals as juxtaposed against the faceless, joy-killing operations of government.

The fantasy of the Cosmic Lie is especially alluring for Americans because of how we tend to view our own character. It exerts a pull on our reverence for our supposed frontier identity, and the enduring myth of Horatio Alger-style upward mobility.

As he campaigned for Trump's tax cuts in 2017, Jamie Dimon trotted out the usual argument—that corporations relieved of their tax burdens would use the extra money to build factories, expand operations, and increase pay. "That connection is real," Dimon told the journalist William D. Cohan. "It's indirect. I can't prove it to you, but I know it's true." He was voicing the same sentiment that has guided American economic policy going back to Reagan.

But sentiment is no longer relevant. For more than four decades, humanity has tested the merits of such assumptions through an elaborate, open-air experiment. We have allowed Davos Man to dominate, and the results are in: Cutting taxes on the wealthy has proved disastrous for the vast majority of ordinary people. It has not promoted growth. It has not yielded increased wages for rank-and-file workers. It has largely produced more wealth for the people who already had most of it.

An expansive study of tax cuts for the wealthy in eighteen large economies around the world found that they widened economic inequality while producing no additional economic growth or jobs. Just one part of the equation actually came to pass—life kept getting sweeter for Davos Man.

Since 1980, the share of all income in the United States that has flowed to those whose incomes are in the top 1 percent has nearly doubled, growing from 10 percent to 19 percent. Over the same four decades, the share received by those in the bottom half has dropped from 20 percent to 13.5 percent.

Though the United States is an extreme case, the same general trend holds throughout much of the wealthy world. In Italy, the top 10 percent increased its share of national income from 24 percent to 33 percent between 1980 and 2017, while the bottom half saw its share fall from 27 percent to 21. In Britain, France, and even Sweden, Davos Man has engineered a milder version of this same picture.

These four decades have exposed the Cosmic Lie as such, while revealing what we may call the Big Truth: the real sources of broad, socially beneficial economic growth are the same elements that achieved success during the first three decades after World War II—public investments in education, health care, and infrastructure.

When the government applies its money toward ensuring that people are healthier, better educated, and able to move about and communicate with one another, the entrepreneurial world can then deliver the vibrancy that Davos Man loves to celebrate. The result is innovation and new businesses that hire people, purchasing goods and services from one another, as the economy expands.

But public education, health care, and infrastructure require money. Davos Man has looted national treasuries, leaving governments in most major economies chronically underfunded. That has left them short of the resources needed to promote growth, which has enhanced the value of other strategies to win votes, such as demonizing immigrants.

This is a structural reality that cannot be solved with sexy ideas about the next technological breakthrough, or lectures to working people about their need to retrain themselves to seize the day. It will not be fixed by waiting for Davos Man to deliver on his promise of stakeholder capitalism, or whatever fresh branding he applies to demonstrate his sensitivity.

Narrowing inequality requires tinkering with the formulas that determine who receives the benefits of economic growth. It's in good measure about the tax code.

Davos Man has created a robust industry devoted to gaming whatever tax regime the politicians design—accountants, lawyers, and financial wizards on every shore, strategizing over how to classify money, and where to move it to share as little as possible with the authorities. The fact that salaried American workers now pay a larger percentage of income to the government than their billionaire employers is a testament to the formidable expertise of this industry. It reflects how wealthy people have cannily exploited an archaic tax code. Davos Man has prospered in large part by figuring out how to get wealthier without generating much of the thing that the United States taxes—income.

Most of us cannot avoid paying taxes for the simple reason that the bulk of what we owe is transparently tabulated, removing opportunities for creative accounting. Whether we work as dishwashers or college professors, our employers calculate our income taxes and withhold them from our pay, along with our contributions to Social Security, turning them over to the authorities. If we own a home, our property taxes are typically folded into our mortgage payments. And if we fail to pay, the local taxing authority literally knows where we live and is empowered to seize our property.

We pay sales taxes when we shop—an exceptionally regressive form of taxation. As a percentage of their income, a person filling their car with gas on the way to their job at an Amazon warehouse will inevitably pay more in sales taxes than Jeff Bezos.

Davos Man has relied on tax havens scattered from Switzerland to the Caribbean to stash away some $7.6 trillion—8 percent of all the household wealth in the world—according to one estimate. Most of this money has been officially undeclared, meaning it is beyond the purview of tax authorities.

In the United States, the top earning 1 percent of all households hide more than one-fifth of their income from the tax authorities, according to one study. The nonpartisan Congressional Budget Office concluded that between 2011 and 2013, Americans successfully evaded $381 billion's worth of taxes.

Davos Man's tolerance for the legal risks of mischief has been enhanced by his knowledge that the American taxing authorities have been gutted. Between 2010 and 2017, budget cuts reduced the number of Internal Revenue Service auditors by one-third, severely diminishing the agency's capacity to pursue tax evaders. Audits of households making more than $1 million a year have fallen by nearly three-fourths in recent years, while inspections of major corporations have dropped by more than half.

In an age of theatrical hand-wringing over budget deficits, here is an easy source of revenue. Every dollar spent to boost enforcement at the IRS results in six additional dollars in tax collections. Davos Man simply does not want to pay.

The problem of tax injustice goes well beyond hidden treasure and rule breaking. Davos Man has designed the tax system as a special preserve for his interests.

In the United States, federal taxes revolve around income, which means that they hit regular people much harder than billionaires. Jeff Bezos has long earned a base salary of $81,840 a year—roughly as much as the typical California elementary school teacher. His extraordinary wealth comes from the shares he owns in Amazon, a roughly 10 percent stake that was worth more than $160 billion at the end of 2020.

Even as those shares increased by more than $100 billion over the previous two years, that appreciation resulted in no taxes. Bezos was liable only when he sold stock and turned his paper increase into money, triggering capital gains taxes. And even then, Bezos and the rest of the billionaire class have managed to shrink their tax burden. Since the early 1980s, Congress—spurred on by corporate-financed lobbyists—has dropped the highest capital gains tax rates from 35 percent to 20 percent.

Davos Man has also embraced stock repurchases by publicly traded companies to limit his tax burden. Until the early 1980s, that practice was barred by regulators as a form of stock manipulation. Companies that wanted to shower goodies on shareholders had to distribute dividends—cash payments that recipients were forced to disclose as income, paying taxes accordingly. But Reagan entrusted the Securities and Exchange Commission to a longtime Wall Street executive, John Shad. He legalized the practice, opening the way for share buybacks. That gave executives a way to lift share prices while sparing shareholders additional taxes.

Not coincidentally, the executives of corporations have reworked their compensation packages so they are paid predominantly in stock. Three decades ago, the average CEO of an American publicly traded company received 42 percent of their compensation in the form of salary, and only 19 percent in stock grants and stock options. By 2014, their salary had dropped to a mere 13 percent of their pay, while stock and stock options had more than tripled, reaching 60 percent.

The systematic campaign by the wealthiest people to limit their tax bills has worked with remarkable efficiency. When ProPublica published insights gleaned from a secret trove of federal tax documents in June 2021, the details affirmed the audacity of the undertaking. In both 2007 and 2011, Bezos had managed to pay zero in federal taxes. Others who had achieved this distinction included Tesla founder Elon Musk and the billionaire magnates Carl Icahn, George Soros, and Michael Bloomberg.

The one moment when billionaires must pay taxes on their wealth is death. Even then, Davos Man has limited the hit to his heirs. Congress has dropped the top estate tax rate from 77 percent in 1976 to below 40 percent, while IRS enforcement actions have almost disappeared.

This was the context for attempts by Warren and Sanders to institute a wealth tax. Their proposals took as inspiration the simple fact that rich people can always find ways to evade taxation focused on income.

Warren advocated a 2 percent annual tax on fortunes greater than $50 million, and 3 percent above $1 billion—a measure that would hit about seventy-five thousand American families. Sanders proposed a lower starting point—a 1 percent annual tax on fortunes greater than $32 million, with increases reaching to 8 percent for those whose wealth exceeded $10 billion.

Both candidates relied on the advice of a now-famous pair of French economists at the University of California, Berkeley, Gabriel Zucman and Emmanuel Saez. They estimated that Sanders's proposal could raise $4.35 trillion over a decade, giving the government the ability to furnish universal health care and childcare, while expanding affordable housing. Warren claimed that her proposal would raise $3.75 trillion, though many experts put the number lower.

Davos Man reacted to these proposals as if the Bolsheviks were at the gates.

Schwarzman said a wealth tax would prompt billionaires to flee the United States. "They would leave," he said in October 2019. "People who would come here to start businesses wouldn't come, because the success would be taxed away."

Jamie Dimon warned that a wealth tax was beyond the administrative capacities of the United States.

"A wealth tax is almost impossible to do," Dimon said in September 2020. "I'm not against having higher tax on the wealthy. But I think that you do that through their income as opposed to, you know, calculate wealth which becomes extremely complicated, legalistic, bureaucratic, regulatory, and people find a million ways around."

Behind this thicket of words was the reality that a wealth tax would result in Dimon paying a great deal more to the government. The previous year, he had taken home compensation worth $31.5 million. That included $6.5 million in salary and cash bonus, which was subject to income taxes, and $25 million in stock-based pay, which entailed no immediate taxes. His net worth was estimated at $1.8 billion.

You did need a supercomputer to crack the relevant arithmetic: Even if Dimon were forced to pay 100 percent tax on his salary and bonus, surrendering it in entirety to Uncle Sam, that would come to $6.5 million. A mere 1 percent tax on his wealth would run $18 million.

Davos Man was staking his case against wealth taxes on the claim that his wealth was so vast and impenetrable that no one would ever be able figure out what it was all worth. Government auditors would have to assign values to his Giacometti sculptures, cellars full of aged Madeira, and custom jewelry. They would have to reckon with the worth of his sports cars, helicopters, bespoke wardrobes, and exotic animals. The process would be rife with abuse—an invitation for billionaires to undervalue their assets as a means of evading taxes.

Wealth taxes would no doubt require that the IRS expand its ranks and upgrade its capabilities, but this had to happen in any event. Davos Man's warning was perverse: Don't try to tax us or make the system fairer, because we will cheat in any scenario. Give up and accept the status quo along with our kind promises for stakeholder capitalism and philanthropy.

One wealthy American who favored wealth taxes, the venture capitalist Nick Hanauer, came up with an ingenious idea to guard against rich people undervaluing their assets. Whatever worth they put down on paper, the government should retain the right to buy any asset at its listed value, auctioning off the goods for public benefit. A billionaire who claimed that their Maserati had depreciated to a mere $5 would watch it driven away.

Many American economists were suspicious of wealth taxes, noting that other countries had opted to scrap their own versions after collections proved disappointing.

It was true that between 1990 and 2017, the number of countries with wealth taxes dropped from twelve to four. A major reason for their disappearance was the one cited by Macron in lifting France's version—because a person could simply move to Belgium. But this was a poor reason for opposing wealth taxes in the United States. The American tax code was unique in that it did not care whether people resided in Toledo or Tokyo. Americans had to pay their taxes regardless. The only way out was to renounce citizenship, and even then the government collected a hefty exit tax.

European wealth taxes tended to set the applicable threshold much lower than what Sanders and Warren were proposing. The wealth tax in Spain kicked in at only 700,000 euros. A retired butcher living on a modest pension could see their apartment

rise in value above that threshold and suddenly face unaffordable levies, forcing them to sell their home to come up with the
money. That was indeed a problem, and it explained why European wealth taxes were bedeviled by exemptions.

But this had little relevance for Americans with upward of
$50 million. If Schwarzman had to sell one of his residences,
or a Van Gogh painting, or a Gulfstream jet to amass the cash
for his required wealth taxes, it was hard to see how this would
damage the American economy.

A lot of the opposition to wealth taxes amounted to a reflex-
ive defense of the status quo—not just from obvious beneficiaries like Dimon, but from supposedly neutral people whose egos
and reputations were invested in years of often-wayward policy
influence.

Larry Summers had been Treasury secretary in the Clinton
administration, and then President Obama's chief economic adviser. He was withering in his critique of wealth taxes, even attacking the professional credentials of proponents.

"It's a riverboat gamble with the future of the American
economy in terms of what it means for our continued prosperity," Summers said in a debate with Saez in October 2019.

Two decades earlier, Summers had sounded equally shrill
warnings about the supposed perils of regulating the trading of
derivatives. He and the then chairman of the Federal Reserve,
Alan Greenspan, had shut down an effort to impose rules on
such transactions by claiming that they would frighten away investors. Money would flee New York for more accommodating
marketplaces like London.

That view triumphed. Unregulated derivatives trading carried on, eventually contributing to the worst financial crisis
since the Great Depression.

Now, Summers was warning that if American lawmakers
exercised their taxing authority, they risked upsetting wealthy

people, which might damage the economy for everyone. The pain would trickle down.

Summers portrayed wealth taxes as inherently counter to the American spirit of solidarity. They were "an approach that has as its center pitting workers against companies," he said, and "some Americans against other Americans, rather than focusing on cooperatively making the investments we need to compete and have the stronger economy that's necessary for everybody's prosperity to go up."

This was quintessential Davos Man thinking. Everyone's prosperity would rise together, which meant there was no need for anyone to sacrifice. Whereas making the wealthy uncomfortable, questioning their magnanimity, risked unforeseen calamities. Davos Man had to be appreciated or everyone suffered.

Summers's depiction was dismissive of the previous four decades of experience—experience that he had helped engineer.

Millions of working people already viewed themselves as pitted against their companies—people like Christian Smalls, who had to choose between his well-being and his paycheck in a formulation that delivered more wealth to Bezos, and Ming Lin, whose job security at Schwarzman's empire rested on his keeping silent in the face of a dangerous contributor to a pandemic. Americans were already at odds with other Americans in an economy defined by scarcity. Wealth taxes would indeed involve formidable logistical challenges, but they were designed with solidarity in mind. They align the interests of 99.9 percent of taxpayers against the 0.1 percent whose outlandish wealth has come at the expense of public health, economic security, and the sanctity of democracy itself.

In the Senate, Warren has resurrected her wealth tax proposal, while Sanders is in charge of the Budget Committee, supplying a powerful perch to advance the issue.

Polls show that wealth taxes are highly popular, drawing support from about two-thirds of Americans.

Biden has not been a supporter of wealth taxes. Yet, in piecemeal fashion, his policies have aimed to significantly increase the tax burden on the richest Americans. To pay for his spending plans, he is seeking to roughly double the highest tax rate on capital gains—those paid on investments—lifting it to nearly 40 percent, while increasing estate taxes. He has proposed spending an additional $80 billion on IRS enforcement over the next decade, an increase of roughly two-thirds, while stepping up the agency's authority to stamp out tax evasion. The White House has said this would produce an extra $700 billion in tax revenues, money that would finance childcare programs and education.

The Biden administration has also persuaded other major economies to establish a global minimum corporate tax rate of at least 15 percent in an effort to stamp out tax havens, reducing the incentive for multinational companies to hopscotch the world in pursuit of a better deal. That rate is far too low to end the shenanigans that have allowed companies like Salesforce to pay nothing, but it's a beginning.

None of this will happen easily. Davos Man will again mobilize his wealth toward preventing the will of the people.

At stake is no less than the justice of the American system. Everything else is bullshit.

"OUR CUP RUNNETH OVER"

Other people could tally the dead. Steve Schwarzman was too busy counting the money.

"Blackstone was a huge winner coming out of the global financial crisis," Schwarzman boasted during a virtual gathering in December 2020, as the pandemic's worldwide death toll neared 2 million. "I think something similar is going to happen now."

Schwarzman's own winnings were already in hand. He took home more than $610 million in compensation over the course of the year—a 20 percent increase from 2019—in a testament to the enriching powers of a public health catastrophe.

Blackstone was deriving half of its earnings from real estate. At a time when ordinary people were struggling to make their housing payments, and as businesses fell behind on commercial leases, Schwarzman was crowing about the riches that flowed from jacking up rents in a pandemic.

"We pick the good neighborhoods, if you will," Schwarzman said, singling out his major purchases of warehouses. "We're the largest owner of real estate in the private world, and that asset class has boomed, with huge increases in rents."

Even the bad news had a way of yielding fresh riches. As Biden pressed to increase capital gains taxes—no doubt, a bummer—many business leaders were eager to sell their assets to get out ahead of higher payments to the government. That meant that Blackstone was presiding over a buyer's market.

"It's really like an avalanche now of opportunities," Schwarzman said at another virtual gathering. "People want to sell things before their taxes are much higher."

Benioff capped off 2020 with the $28 billion takeover of Slack, a messaging platform for businesses. It was all about laying down the infrastructure that allowed employees to work from anywhere—a status enhanced by the pandemic.

"Wow, what a quarter," he declared as he returned to Jim Cramer's TV show in December 2020. "I feel very excited and motivated on everything that we need to do to double the company once again."

Thanks to taxpayer-financed rescues that were initially designed to bolster financial assets, Jamie Dimon was again positioned to emerge from a disaster in a stronger position. His bank's revenues from trading were on track to reach nearly $6 billion over the last three months of the year—a record pace—supplying him cash to take over other companies.

"It might be software," he said. "It might be something overseas. We're open-minded."

He was in the process of opening a new headquarters in Paris stocked with bankers moved from post-Brexit Britain. This movement of high-finance refugees amounted to a victory for Macron.

Dimon's board soon gave him approval to resume buying back stock, approving some $30 billion for that purpose.

"Our cup runneth over," he told stock analysts in April 2021. "We're earning a tremendous sum of money."

What was striking about the exultations of Davos Man was how they came uncut by acknowledgments of the contrast between his overflowing coffers and the surrounding calamity. The billionaires appeared to have internalized their own propaganda—the story of trickle-down and stakeholder capitalism, and their dedication to Improving the State of the World.

A year into the pandemic, the coronavirus had killed more than half a million Americans, while more than 78 million people had lost jobs. Over the same period, American billionaires—a group numbering fewer than seven hundred people—had gained a collective $1.3 trillion in wealth. This was in large part because stock markets had ended 2020 at record highs.

"I think we're going to continue to see the market be strong in 2021," Larry Fink declared, as BlackRock revealed that managed assets had ballooned past $8.6 trillion.

In Britain, George Osborne, the Davos Man collaborator who imposed austerity, quit his consulting gig at BlackRock to take a position at a London investment bank. The firm had tallied profits of £17.9 million in 2020, while paying zero in taxes. "I'm proud to be joining this first-rate team," Osborne said.

Celebrations of robust earnings had failed to translate into the selfless giving for which the billionaire class so enthusiastically congratulated itself. Over the course of 2020, philanthropic contributions had totaled about $2.6 billion, the smallest figure since 2011.

Jeff Bezos stood alone. He had earned enough money to transcend the ordinary constraints of living on planet Earth.

On a Tuesday morning in July 2021, only a few weeks removed from handing over day-to-day control of Amazon to his successor, Bezos climbed aboard a rocket ship in a tiny town in West Texas and blasted into space.

He was not the first billionaire to reach the heavens. Richard Branson, the famously adventurous overseer of the Virgin airline and entertainment empire, had beaten him there by nine days. Even so, Bezos's eleven-minute inaugural journey represented both the realization of his boyhood fantasy and the culmination of his obsession to construct a private space company.

He was savoring the milestone. After returning to Earth, still sporting his blue space suit, Bezos donned an absurdly oversize cowboy hat as he addressed the media.

He thanked the two thousand inhabitants of Van Horn, Texas, for hosting the proceedings, and then he expressed his gratitude to a much larger group of human beings.

"I also want to thank every Amazon employee, and every Amazon customer, because you guys paid for all this," Bezos said. "So, seriously, for every Amazon customer out there and every Amazon employee, thank you from the bottom of my heart."

This exultation captured international attention as a marker of the degree to which billionaires like Bezos had become unmoored from the rest of the human experience. The company he had built stood accused of mass labor exploitation and ruthless market predation. He had personally become a symbol of grand-scale, if legal, tax evasion. Yet the monumental winnings he had extracted from Amazon—from modern life—had allowed him to catch a glimpse of the Earth from more than sixty miles above the ground, which he was celebrating not just as a personal triumph but as an advance for all of humanity.

Three years earlier, Bezos had described his quest to reach space as part of a grand aspiration for his species in the face of declining resources on its home planet.

"I'm thinking of a time frame of a couple of hundred years," Bezos had said. "Take the scenario where you move out in the solar system. The solar system can easily support a trillion humans. And if we had a trillion humans, we would have a thousand Einsteins and a thousand Mozarts and unlimited, for all practical purposes, resources and solar power."

Bezos was rightfully admired as a visionary, his thinking unbounded by conventional limitations. That he was contemplating human progress long after he would be around to enjoy it was in some ways inspiring. Yet there was no end of human problems demanding solutions in the here and now, problems for which Bezos was personally implicated. His company had exposed workers to extraordinary pressures and perils, helping him amass an unrivaled fortune, and now he was thanking those same employees for advancing a mission whose hypothetical rewards would be accrued long after they were all dead.

Bezos had reportedly poured $5.5 billion into his space company. That was enough to save 38 million people from starvation, according to World Food Program estimates—not two centuries forward, but right now. It was twice as much money as Covax was seeking in its bid to vaccinate 2 billion people against COVID-19, in a pandemic that was by no means over. It was money that could have funded paid sick leave for Amazon's employees.

Down on the ground, people were mired in their terrestrial concerns: bills to pay, children to raise, traffic to navigate on their way to stultifying jobs. Bezos preferred to contemplate the Earth from high above.

"It felt so serene and peaceful," he said. "And the floating, it's actually much nicer than being in full-on gravity."

Over the course of my journalism career, I've frequently been struck by how people tend to view economics in fatalistic terms, accepting the notion that unfathomable wealth alongside mass scarcity is essentially inevitable, and beyond the power of democracy to alter. To pass as a sophisticated person in the twenty-first century often seems to require being resigned to the futility of controlling the forces operating across borders—the capital flows, the technology, the multinational corporations. It means accepting the triumph of Davos Man over the public interest.

But that is not really sophistication; it is cynicism. Deference to the inevitable supremacy of the billionaire class amounts to a renunciation of our historical legacy, a failure to realize that humanity has been here before.

Americans stared down the Robber Barons, using democracy

to fashion an effective response to the injustice of one select group monopolizing the gains of capitalism. Britain reacted to the trauma of the Depression by constructing a social welfare model that shared the gains of its industrial might. Even as France and Sweden have seen their social democratic values diluted, they retain status as exemplars of societies that have figured out how to harness the merits of the market system while still attending to collective interests. For all of its problems—and they are many—Italy is a showcase of human potential, from the arts to engineering to modern medicine.

The challenges of the current crisis of inequality may be greater this time, because Davos Man possesses especially advanced tools to preserve the status quo by undermining collective action. Social media distorts the information stream, while companies wield surveillance technology and data collection in the service of political aims. Amazon's fake television spots attest to its refined tactics in preventing worker solidarity. Benioff, Fink, and Dimon have excelled at drawing accolades for turning business into a vehicle for progressive change while profiting mightily off the status quo. Around the globe, extremist political parties that provoke tribal hatred divert the electorate from accountability for Davos Man's plunder.

The point is not that the billionaires are puppeteers in a master conspiracy; it is that Davos Man thrives amid confusion, conflict, and suspicion. The billionaires exploit governance that is compromised by discord and dysfunction as an opportunity to profiteer absent the usual checks and balances.

But democracy is itself a powerful tool—a system of governance that guarantees nothing and is forever vulnerable to being hijacked by organized interests, yet contains within it the mechanism by which the public can realize its own interests.

Many of the world's most meaningful problems are, at root, issues of unfair economic distribution. Human beings have developed extraordinary capacities in our brief time on earth. We have harnessed science to coax unprecedented volumes of food from the soil, applied medical know-how to tame disease, pioneered inventive forms of housing and transportation, while conjuring novel means of keeping boredom at bay.

In ways both profound and prosaic, this is surely the greatest time to be alive in the history of civilization, an era of multiplying solutions to problems once considered unsolvable, ubiquitous, tedious, and fatal.

Davos Man would have us believe in the false binary choice at the heart of his grift—that we either accept globalization as we have known it for decades, or we throw in our lot with Luddites operating in the thrall of backward ideas. This frame is not only false but dangerous. It invites those who have not shared in the benefits of globalization to demand its opposite—nationalism, nativism, parochialism, and ignorance. If globalization run by Davos Man for the betterment of Davos Man gives way to the destruction of globalization and the pursuit of tribal interests, the world will be poorer, more violent, and less able to summon the cooperation needed to solve the most complex problems, from pandemics to climate change.

The lethal spread of COVID-19 and the appalling lack of preparedness were clearly symptomatic of how globalization has been run without required supervision, enabling unchecked shareholder demands to make the world susceptible to dangers.

But we need not choose between allowing Steve Schwarzman to exploit the American health care system or having no health care at all. We can purchase the wares that Amazon delivers to our doors while still demanding that its workers receive sick pay. We can use the software that entrepreneurs like Marc Benioff provide, and at the same time tax them to finance the schools that train their engineers.

We can tap the genius of our brightest research minds, who have cracked the code on a vaccine for COVID-19, and also demand value for taxpayers who financed the research, ensuring the availability of these lifesaving inventions for all.

We can run global capitalism in a way that preserves its capacity for innovation and prosperity without handing all the rewards to Davos Man.

Fukuyama was wrong, arrogant, and even colonialist when he declared the end of history, as if American primacy and its version of capitalism represented the highest order of human development. But he was not crazy in his reverence for the market system. Global capitalism is indeed the most advanced form of economic organization. It promotes the inspiration and exchange of groundbreaking ideas that have extended and improved life. It produces more wealth, which is a hell of a lot better than the alternative.

What capitalism lacks is an inherent mechanism that justly distributes the gains. That is the responsibility of government, operating under a democratic mandate. That Davos Man has convinced us to believe otherwise, accepting horrific levels of inequality as part and parcel of modern times, has imperiled faith in the legitimacy of democracy itself. The resulting anger has tapped into the worst aspects of human nature, supplying oxygen to hate-inspired movements, while giving rise to fantastical conspiracy theories. Facts and science have been devalued.

Society has been so poisoned by bitterness and grievance that governance sometimes seems impossible.

The idea that the defining characteristics of human experience—where we live, how much health care we receive, the quality of our schools, and the abundance of food on our tables—should be entrusted solely to the unsentimental workings of the market will, with any luck, one day look as insane as burning witches at the stake or applying leeches to attack disease. That this idea achieved the status of truth among broad slices of the populace amounts to a form of collective madness. But it did not gain command of the policymaking levers by accident. This thinking was promoted by people in charge of money, spread by academics compensated by finance companies, and disseminated by a public relations machine working for multinational corporations. It is an idea that has enabled Davos Man to add to his wealth, while justifying his station as the fruits of a system that rewards virtue. In truth, even as he is prone to wax poetically about the magic of free markets, Davos Man is not really interested in that concept, or any ideological position. He propagates market fundamentalism when that serves as justification for things he craves—weakened regulations, diminished taxes, and license for monopoly power. We have not had free markets. We have had markets manipulated by the most powerful interests for their profit at society's expense. We have had welfare for billionaires and rugged individualism for everyone else.

Davos Man's greatest triumph has been insinuating into public discourse the notion that anyone who opposes his monopolization of wealth is antibusiness, as if forcing Schwarzman and Bezos to pay higher tax rates than their secretaries would be akin to turning suburban subdivisions into people's communes. That idea must be revealed for what it is—not merely a lie, but the foundational lie for the pillaging of capitalism itself.

History never ended, but history needs to be reset. Capitalism must be reshaped to extend the bounty to far more people.

In the popular narrative, the billionaires were—by the middle of 2021—under attack. They faced antitrust probes in multiple nations, a new American president empowered to revive fairness, and an international push to eradicate tax havens. But Davos Man was expert at weathering outrage, projecting his rhetorical admission of injustice as evidence of change, which meant that those on the other side of the divide—the 7.7 billion people around the globe who fell short of being billionaires—were going to have to fashion a meaningful strategy to right the balance.

To survey the last few decades of the global economy is to understand that the lopsided distribution of gains will not be rectified through voluntary acts of benevolence from the handful of people who control most of the wealth. It will not unfold through stakeholder capitalism, or whatever formulations emerge from the idea labs of communications consultants.

It can happen only through the exercise of democracy—by unleashing strategies centered on boosting wages and working opportunities, by erecting new forms of social insurance, by reviving and enforcing antitrust law, by modernizing the tax code to focus on wealth.

None of this will be easy. But absent substantial economic redistribution, the very concept of democracy is endangered. This is the inescapable truth of recent times, from the Trump era, to Brexit, to the wave of illiberalism sweeping the globe.

It is a story that is in no way over, a force still gathering strength. When people are deprived of the material for stable lives, they take refuge in traditional privileges—tribal identities, and fantasies of glorious futures enabled by reclaiming what they view as theirs. They become susceptible to simplistic explanations peddled by demagogues who weaponize democracy itself. The result is chaos, anger, and instability. No one wins except the people who have already won.

Launching an era in which Davos Man no longer writes the rules is not a radical step. It is the restoration of what advanced economies knew in the first decades after World War II—a far-from-perfect time, yet a period of collective progress.

Democracy has been warped by the billionaire class, its workings tilted toward private islands, offshore bank accounts, and secret meetings in Davos convened to plot the next insider deal.

Reclaiming power from Davos Man requires no insurrection or revolution of ideas. It demands the thoughtful use of a tool that has been there all along: democracy.

ACKNOWLEDGMENTS

This book owes its existence to my extraordinary fortune in working for the *New York Times*. Not many newsrooms are so devoted to deep and immersive field reporting that they encourage writers to follow their stories to every corner of planet Earth. In urging me to think globally about widening economic inequality and its social consequences, my editors supplied the time and resources to do just that.

One uniquely gifted editor was instrumental in this undertaking: Adrienne Carter, a masterful framer of stories and an all-around wonderful person, guided much of the early reporting that eventually led to this book.

Supreme gratitude to Dean Baquet and Joe Kahn for updating the *Times* for the digital era while advancing its vital mission, and for bringing me back to the fold after several years in self-imposed exile. Many thanks to publisher A. G. Sulzberger and his unwavering faith in journalism as a core element of democracy—something we used to take for granted; not anymore.

The business section has long been my home at the *Times*. Much appreciation to Dean Murphy for welcoming me back while dispatching me to London, where I was lucky to be based during the reporting and writing of this book. Huge thanks to current business editor Ellen Pollock, whose irreverence, skill, and knack for finding journalistic buried treasure keeps life interesting. Rich Barbieri, my editor during the pandemic years, brings sharp eyes, wisdom, and grace to everything. Thanks to then–business editor Larry Ingrassia for bringing me aboard more than a dozen years ago, and for looking out for me ever since.

Thanks to my colleagues on the Europe-based international business team, led by the unflappable Kevin Granville, among them Adam Satariano, Eshe Nelson, Geneva Abdul, Jack Ewing, and Stanley Reed. I'm grateful for collaborations with talented and dedicated business correspondents and editors around the world: Carlos Tejada, Ashwin Seshagiri, David Enrich, Phyllis Messinger, Kevin McKenna, Patricia Cohen, Keith Bradsher, Alexandra Stevenson, Vikas Bajaj, Pui-Wing Tam, Renee Melides, Roe D'Angelo, Justin Swanson, and David Schmidt.

The international desk has been my second home during my London years, guided by the infectiously enthusiastic Michael Slackman. I'm thankful for the friendship and wise counsel of Jim Yardley, who runs our London operation with aplomb and who included me in projects that eventually provoked this book. I learned firsthand why Kyle Crichton is celebrated as a legendary editor. Many thanks to the stellar team of editors on the foreign desk in London and New York, among them Greg Winter, Kim Fararo, Suzanne Spector, Kirk Kraeutler, Laurie Goodstein, Marc Santora, and Richard Pérez-Peña. And thanks for the ambitious thinking and healthy skepticism of senior editors in the mothership: Matt Purdy, Alison Mitchell, Philip Pan, and Rebecca Blumenstein. Susan Chira exited the building, but my appreciation carries on.

David Segal, a terrific friend and virtuoso storyteller, graciously read and improved an early draft. I am much obliged for the incisive critiques of other friends and colleagues who read pieces of the book at various stages: Jesse Eisinger, Mark Leibovich, David Sirota, Liz Alderman, Emma Bubola, and Jesse Drucker.

This book reflects indispensable contributions from stringers and researchers in myriad countries: Andrew Perez in the United

States; Eloïse Stark in France; Christina Anderson and Erik Augustin Palm in Sweden; Giulia Alagna, Riccardo Liberatore, and Aaron Maines in Italy; Claudia Witte in Switzerland; Daniel Politi in Argentina; Rachel Chaundler in Spain; and Mari-Leena Kuosa in Finland.

A great joy of working at the *Times* is appearing on *The Daily* podcast, where some of the concepts in this book were sharpened by resident geniuses Lisa Tobin and Michael Barbaro.

I have shamelessly appropriated insights, mined contacts, and exploited the local savvy of *Times* correspondents around the globe, among them Hannah Beech, Jason Horowitz, Steven Erlanger, Matt Apuzzo, Jeffrey Gettleman, Dan Bilefsky, Danny Hakim, Stephen Castle, Hari Kumar, Choe Sang-Hun, Joanna Berendt, Jason Gutierrez, Karan Deep Singh, Sui-Lee Wee, Katrin Bennhold, Patrick Kingsley, Alissa Rubin, Declan Walsh, Abdi Latif Dahir, Gaia Pianigiani, Andrew Higgins, Ellen Barry, Elizabeth Paton, Raphael Minder, and Carlotta Gall.

Thanks to Katie Thomas, Apoorva Mandavili, Rebecca Robbins, and Matina Stevis-Gridneff, for fruitful collaborations on vaccine nationalism.

My Davos fondue gang—Rana Foroohar, Adi Ignatius, Anya Schiffrin, and John Gapper—helped maintain my tether to reality during a decade of Forums.

Writing a book about the global economy entails constantly diving into subjects about which many people know far more than you. I am grateful for the wisdom and patience of the economists, political analysts, lawyers, historians, bankers, activists, and other experts whose work (and even play) I have shamelessly interrupted to pose questions ranging from simplistic to naive.

On globalization and international trade, I have benefited greatly from conversations with Joseph Stiglitz at Columbia University, Adam Posen and Chad Bown at the Peterson Institute for International Economics (PIIE), Ian Goldin at Oxford University, Pietra Rivoli at Georgetown University, Brad Setser at the Council on Foreign Relations, Richard Kozul-Wright at the United Nations Development Program, Meredith Crowley at the University of Cambridge, Swati Dhingra at the London School of Economics, Ben May at Oxford Economics, and Willy Shih at Harvard Business School. Thanks to the wise and generous Keith Rockwell at the World Trade Organization. And thanks to Gady Epstein for provocative discussions about China in the world.

On the operations of the European Union and the eurozone, I am indebted to Jacob Funk Kirkegaard and Nicolas Veron at PIIE, Christian Odendahl at the Centre for European Reform, Angel Talavera at Oxford Economics, Maria Demertzis at Bruegel, Kjersti Haugland at DNB Markets, Peter Dixon at Commerzbank, and the data wizards at Eurostat and the Organisation for Economic Cooperation and Development.

On the story of the Italian economy, many thanks to Nicola Borri at Libera Università Internazionale degli Studi Sociali, Nadia Urbinati at Columbia University, and Servaas Storm at Delft University of Technology.

In decoding the inscrutable absurdities of Brexit, I owe a debt to William Wright at New Financial, Mujtaba Rahman at Eurasia Group, and Sam Lowe at the Centre for European Reform. On the lasting consequences of British austerity, many thanks to Barry Kushner, for opening up the wonderful city of Liverpool, and Matthew Brown, for helping me navigate Preston. Thanks to Jonathan Davies at De Montfort University, Mary-Ann Stephenson at the Women's Budget Group, and Paul Johnson at the Institute for Fiscal Studies.

On the rise of inequality in France, I'm grateful for my conversations with Agnès Bénassy-Quéré at the Economic Analysis Council in Paris, Amandine Crespy at the Free University of Brussels, Philippe Askenazy at the French National Center for Scientific Research, and Louis Maurin at French Inequality Watch.

On the diminution of the Swedish social safety net, much appreciation for Marten Blix at the Research Institute of Industrial Economics in Stockholm, Carl Melin at Futurion, Annika Wallenskog at the Swedish Association of Local Authorities and Regions, and Andreas Johansson Heino at Timbro. On all matters Nordic (and on other vital subjects, including the locations of ice cream parlors from Helsinki to Santa Monica), I'm grateful for the counsel and connections of Ambassador Derek Shearer.

On the consequences of privatization and financialization in health care, many thanks to Simon Bowers in Liverpool; Michele Usuelli and Chiara Lepora in Milan; and Joacim Rocklöv, Torbjörn Dalin, and Michael Broomé in Sweden. I'm especially indebted to the scholarship of Eileen Appelbaum at the Center for Economic and Policy Research in Washington and Zack Cooper at Yale University.

On the subject of international support for poor countries during the pandemic, many thanks to Adnan Mazarei at PIIE, Scott Morris at the Center for Global Development, Lidy Nacpil at the Asian People's Movement on Debt and Development, Jayati Ghosh at Jawaharlal Nehru University, and Tim Jones at the Jubilee Debt Campaign.

In digging into the pharmaceutical industry and vaccine distribution, I'm grateful for conversations with Selva Demiralp at Koc University in Istanbul, Clare Wenham and Ken Shadlen at the London School of Economics and Political Science, Simon Evenett at the University of St. Gallen in Switzerland, and Mark Eccleston-Turner at Keele University.

Thanks to Chuck Reid in Holland, Michigan, for keeping me in touch with the realities of manufacturing. Ted Howard schooled me in the ways of cooperatives and community wealth building. Many thanks to Mustafa Qadri, for opening up the world of migrant laborers.

On the subject of universal basic income, I'm indebted to Guy Standing at the School of Oriental and African Studies, Olli Rehn in Helsinki, Olli Kangas at the Social Insurance Institution of Finland, Heikki Hiilamo at Helsinki University, Mikko Annala at Demos Helsinki, Natalie Foster at the Economic Security Project, and former Stockton, California, mayor Michael Tubbs.

On questions around taxation, I'm grateful for the help of Gabriel Zucman at the University of California, Berkeley. Thanks to Matt Stoller for his clarifying book on the history of American monopoly power. And thanks to Brad Stone for his seminal work on Amazon, and to Aaron Glantz for his important book on the foreclosure crisis. Thanks to Rob Johnson at INET for his highly useful podcast.

Every writer deserves an agent like Gail Ross, whose ferocious smarts, encouragement, and agility were vital to this project from inception. Thanks to Shannon O'Neil, for elevating the proposal.

At Custom House, the superb Peter Hubbard immediately grasped the central point, and then skillfully guided the manuscript toward what it was meant to be. Many thanks to Molly Gendell for calmly and patiently turning the manuscript into a book.

My father, Arnold Goodman, left us as I was beginning to conceptualize this book. My wanderings were first inspired by his love of maps, his immaculately penned postcards, and his stories from his travels with my mother, Elise Simon Goodman—still intrepid after all these years.

This book was conceived and written during the worst days of the pandemic. Our bigger kids, Leo and Mila, were locked down at home for months while struggling with distance learning, yet their irrepressible curiosity, focus on social justice, and demands for diversion sustained us all in a bleak time. Our baby boy, Luca, was born in the middle of the madness and immediately lived up to his name: bringer of the light. My oldest daughter, Leah, who completed her college studies in London during the pandemic, reminded me why stories matter. Emma Small and Nicol Koderova were there for us in the thick of things, lifelong honorary members of the family.

My partner, Deanna Fei, sacrificed too much for this book, contending with my absences, setting aside her own writing, and heroically attending to a household awash in every conceivable form of need, while still administering a rigorous and crucial edit. There are no words to acknowledge her contributions. I can only say thank you, and I owe you—for this, for our family, and for the brilliance you shine on everything.

Can you thank a city park in acknowledgments? The Hampstead Heath was my refuge during lockdown, a portal to a better place.

NOTES

PROLOGUE: **"THEY WRITE THE RULES FOR THE REST OF THE WORLD"**

4   *philanthropic contributions fell:* Sissi Cao, "Billionaires Made Record Profit, Donated Record Lows in 2020," *Observer,* January 5, 2021, https://observer.com/2021/01/billionaires-philanthropy-record-low-2020-bezos-elon-musk.

6   *The collective fortune:* Tom Metcalf, "Dalio, Dimon and 117 Other Billionaires to Descend on Davos," Bloomberg, January 17, 2020.

12   *the wealthiest 1 percent:* Matt Bruenig, "Top 1% Up $21 Trilion. Bottom 50% Down $900 Billion," People's Policy Project, June 14, 2019, https://www.peoplespolicyproject.org/2019/06/14/top-1-up-21-trillion-bottom-50-down-900-billion.

12   *corporate executives have:* Lawrence Mishel and Julia Wolfe, "CEO Compensation Has Grown 940 Percent Since 1978," Economic Policy Institute, August 14, 2019, https://www.epi.org/publication/ceo-compensation-2018.

12   *ten richest people:* Justinas Baltrusaitis, "World's Top Ten Billionaires Worth More Than Poorest 85 Countries Combined," LearnBonds, May 15, 2020, https://learnbonds.com/news/top-10-richest-people-worth-more-than-85-poorest-countries-gdp.

12   *Had income in the United States:* Carter C. Price and Kathryn A. Edwards, "Trends in Income from 1975 to 2018," Rand Corporation, https://www.rand.org/pubs/working_papers/WRA516-1.html.

CHAPTER 1: **"HIGH UP IN THE MOUNTAINS"**

22   *A half century earlier:* Lawrence Mishel and Julia Wolfe, "CEO Compensation Has Grown 940% Since 1978," Economic Policy Institute, August 14, 2019, https://www.epi.org/publication/ceo-compensation-2018.

22   *University of California at Berkeley economists:* Emmanuel Saez and Gabriel Zucman, *The Triumph of Injustice: How the Rich Dodge Taxes and How to Make Them Pay* (New York: W.W. Norton & Co., 2019), Chapter One.

22   *In Britain, the average worker:* William Wright and Christian Benson, "The Crisis of Capitalism—A Summary," New Financial, November 2019, https://newfinancial.org/report-the-crisis-of-capitalism.

27   *Goldin had coauthored a prescient book:* Ian Goldin and Mike Mariathasan, *The Butterfly Defect: How Globalization Creates Systemic Risks, and What to Do About It* (Princeton, NJ: Princeton University Press, 2014).

29   *the wealthiest person in Asia:* Mukesh Ambani, *Forbes* profile, https://www.forbes.com/profile/mukesh-ambani/#26a95919214c.

29   *The company's promotional literature:* Amanda DiSilvestro, "The 6 Greatest Benefits of CRM Platforms," Salesforce.com website, https://www.salesforce.com/crm/benefits-of-crm.

30   *Benioff has literally written the book:* Marc Benioff and Karen Southwick, *Compassionate Capitalism: How Corporations Can Make Doing Good an Integral Part of Doing Well* (Franklin Lakes, NJ: Career Press, 2004).

31   *"the reason we're doing software":* Mark Leibovich, "The Outsider, His Business and His Billions," *Washington Post,* October 30, 2000, p. A1.

31   *"I've always believed that technology":* Marc Benioff and Monica Langley, *Trailblazer: The Power of Business as the Greatest Platform for Change* (New York: Random House, 2019), A New Direction.

31   *"I have been very fortunate":* Interview on *Charlie Rose,* November 29, 2011.

32   *in the company of his golden retriever:* Benioff, *Trailblazer,* op. cit., Chapter Three.

32   *He was rhapsodic about Dreamforce:* Ibid., Chapter Four.

32   *"It's a four-day opportunity":* Ibid.

32   *"During those endless Sundays":* Ibid., Chapter One.

32   *He was also struck:* Ibid., 38.

33   *Less than four years later:* Ibid., Prologue.

33   *special relationship with the boss:* Leibovich, op. cit.

33   *"the hugging saint":* Benioff, *Trailblazer,* op. cit., Prologue.

33   *"In your quest to succeed":* Ibid.

34   *"Doing well by doing good":* Ibid.

34   *When the state of Indiana:* Jena McGregor, "This Tech CEO Is Taking a Real Stand Against Indiana's 'Religious Freedom' Law; Salesforce.com's Marc Benioff Has Launched an All-Out Campaign Against the New Law," *Washington Post,* March 27, 2015.

34 *a stance that put him crosswise:* Jillian D'Onfro, "The Controversial San Francisco Homeless Tax That Pitted Tech Billionaires Marc Benioff and Jack Dorsey Against Each Other Passes," CNBC, November 7, 2018, https://www.cnbc.com/2018/11/07/san-francisco-proposition-c-homeless-tax-passes.html.

34 *The new taxes were likely:* Maya Kosoff, "Billionaires Jack Dorsey and Marc Benioff Spar over How to Solve Homelessness," *Vanity Fair Hive,* October 12, 2018, https://www.vanityfair.com/news/2018/10/billionaires-jack-dorsey-and-marc-benioff-spar-over-how-to-solve-homelessness.

35 *zero in federal taxes:* Matthew Gardner, Lorena Roque, and Steve Wamhoff, "Corporate Tax Avoidance in the First Year of the Trump Tax Law," Institute on Taxation and Economic Policy, December 16, 2019, https://itep.org/corporate-tax-avoidance-in-the-first-year-of-the-trump-tax-law.

35 *accounting hocus-pocus:* Chris Colin, "The Gospel of Wealth According to Marc Benioff," *Wired,* December 11, 2019, https://www.wired.com/story/gospel-of-wealth-according-to-marc-benioff.

35 *the Treasury opened up a loophole:* Matthew C. Klein and Michael Pettis, *Trade Wars Are Class Wars: How Rising Inequality Distorts the Global Economy and Threatens International Peace* (New Haven, CT: Yale University Press, 2020), Chapter One.

35 *Clinton's Treasury bestowed this gift:* Ibid.

35 *So-called profit shifting:* Kimberly A. Clausing, "Profit Shifting Before and After the Tax Cuts and Jobs Act," *National Tax Journal* 1233–1266 (2020), UCLA School of Law, Law-Econ Research Paper No. 20-10, June 3, 2020, 73(4), available at SSRN https://ssrn.com/abstract=3274827 or http://dx.doi.org/10.2139/ssrn.3274827.

35 *Benioff's individual compensation:* Salesforce, 2019 proxy statement, p. 39, https://s23.q4cdn.com/574569502/files/doc_financials/2019/664082_Salesforce_Proxy_bookmarked.pdf.

37 *Benioff credited Schwab:* Benioff, *Trailblazer,* op. cit., Chapter Ten.

38 *Einstein had given a presentation:* Nick Paumgarten, "Magic Mountain," *The New Yorker,* March 5, 2012.

38 *"High up in the mountains":* Schwab and Vanham, op. cit., 11.

38 *The first iteration:* Paumgarten, op. cit.

39 *"The anxiety of exclusion pervades":* Ibid.

41 *"We do not welcome them":* Ibid.

43 *The company elevated Klaus Schwab:* Julia Flynn and Steve Stecklow, "Transparency Eludes Founder of Davos Forum," *Wall Street Journal,* January 27, 2000.

44 *Xi used his turn at the podium:* Peter S. Goodman, "In Era of Trump, China's President Champions Economic Globalization," *New York Times,* January 18, 2017, p. A1.

46 *"We cannot evade it":* Andrew Carnegie, "The Gospel of Wealth," *North American Review,* June 1889.

CHAPTER 2: "THE WORLD THAT OUR FATHERS IN WORLD WAR II WANTED US TO LIVE IN"

48   *a sixth grader in Houston:* Brad Stone, *The Everything Store: Jeff Bezos and the Age of Amazon* (New York: Little, Brown and Co., 2013), Prologue.

48   *as a single twentysomething:* Stone, op. cit., Chapter One.

51   *"The peoples of the earth":* Address by the Honorable Henry Morgenthau Jr. at the closing plenary session of the Bretton Woods conference, July 22, 1944, accessed by Fraser at the Federal Reserve Bank of St. Louis, https://fraser.stlouisfed.org/files/docs/historical/eccles/036_17_0004 .pdf.

51   *Half of the world's manufactured wares:* Tony Judt, *Postwar: A History of Europe Since 1945* (New York: Penguin Books, 2005), Chapter Five.

52   *Tax rates exceeding 70 percent:* Chrystia Freeland, *Plutocrats: The Rise of the New Global Super-Rich and the Fall of Everyone Else* (New York: Penguin Books, 2012), Chapter One.

52   *The trade organization conceived:* Klein and Pettis, op. cit., Chapter One.

52   *By 2000, the volume of trade:* Meredith Crowley, "An Introduction to the WTO and GATT," Federal Reserve Bank of Chicago, *Economic Perspectives,* 27, 4th, no. 4 (November 2003): 43.

52   *the advent of so-called container shipping:* Klein and Pettis, op. cit., Chapter One.

53   *Milton Friedman set the revolution in motion:* Milton Friedman, "The Social Responsibility of Business Is to Increase Its Profits," *The New York Times Magazine,* September 13, 1970.

54   *Students at business schools were marinated:* For a useful summation of this history, see Sam Long, "The Financialization of the American Elite," *American Affairs* 3, no. 3 (Fall 2019), https://americanaffairsjournal.org /2019/08/the-financialization-of-the-american-elite/.

55   *Under the terms of its entry:* A comprehensive examination of the negotiations that produced China's accession deal can be found in Paul Blustein's book, *Schism: China, America and the Fracturing of the Global Trading System* (Waterloo, Ontario, Canada: Centre for International Governance Innovation, 2019).

56   *In one single year:* Jesse Eisinger, Jeff Ernsthausen, and Paul Kiel, "The Secret IRS Files: Trove of Never-Before-Seen Records Reveal How the Wealthiest Avoid Income Tax," ProPublica, June 8, 2021, https://www .propublica.org/article/the-secret-irs-files-trove-of-never-before-seen -records-reveal-how-the-wealthiest-avoid-income-tax.

59   *China's share of world steel production:* Zhiyao Lu, "State of Play in the Chinese Steel Industry," China Economic Watch, Peterson Institute for International Economics, July 5, 2016.

59   *the shock inflicted by Chinese imports:* David H. Autor, David Dorn, and Gordon H. Hanson, "The China Shock: Learning from Labor Market Adjustment to Large Changes in Trade," National Bureau of Economic Re-

search Working Paper No. 21906, January 2016, https://www.nber.org/papers/w21906.

60   *top tenth of Chinese households:* Thomas Piketty, Li Yang, and Gabriel Zucman, "Capital Accumulation, Private Property, and Rising Inequality in China, 1978–2015," *American Economic Review,* 109, no. 7 (July 2019), https://www.aeaweb.org/articles?id=10.1257/aer.20170973.

62   *Trump's trade war:* Adam S. Posen, "The Price of Nostalgia," *Foreign Affairs,* May–June 2021.

62   *"The fetishization of manufacturing jobs":* Ibid.

62   *the company paid out $31 million:* United States Steel Corp., Form 10-K Filed with Securities and Exchange Commission for Fiscal Year Ended December 31, 2016, https://www.ussteel.com/sites/default/files/annual_reports/USS%20Form%2010-K%20-%202016.pdf.

63   *a $1.5 million salary:* Securities and Exchange Commission Schedule 14A, Proxy Statement for United States Steel Corp., March 14, 2017.

63   *the economist Jeff Faux:* Jeff Faux, "PNTR with China: Economic and Political Costs Greatly Outweigh Benefits," Economic Policy Institute, Briefing Paper No. 94, April 1, 2000, https://www.epi.org/publication/briefingpapers_pntr_china.

63   *Clinton declared in 2000:* Remarks by Bill Clinton to the Johns Hopkins University Paul H. Nitze School of Advanced International Studies, March 8, 2000, as cited in James Mann, *The China Fantasy: How Our Leaders Explain Away Chinese Repression* (New York: Viking, 2007), 174.

64   *A Chinese journalist:* Peter S. Goodman, "Yahoo Says It Gave China Internet Data; Journalist Jailed Tracing E-mail," *Washington Post,* September 11, 2005, p. A30.

64   *JPMorgan Chase handed out internships:* Ned Levin, Emily Glazer, and Christopher M. Matthews, "In J.P. Morgan Emails, a Tale of China and Connections: Firm's Hiring of Son of Chinese Government Official Has Drawn Scrutiny from U.S. Authorities Investigating Hiring Practices of Several Big Banks," *Wall Street Journal,* February 6, 2015.

64   *A Chinese sovereign wealth fund:* Stephen A. Schwarzman, *What It Takes* (New York: Simon & Schuster, 2019), Chapter Twenty.

65   *Chinese Communist Party leaders:* Bethany Allen-Ebrahimian, "The Moral Hazard of Dealing with China," *The Atlantic,* January 11, 2020.

65   *as a graduation speaker:* Ibid.

66   *In Denmark:* OECD.Stat, Net Replacement Rates in Unemployment, https://stats.oecd.org/Index.aspx?DataSetCode=NRR.

67   *"I have always been academically smart":* Franklin Foer, "Jeff Bezos's Master Plan," *The Atlantic,* November 2019, https://www.theatlantic.com/magazine/archive/2019/11/what-jeff-bezos-wants/598363.

67   *At Miami Palmetto Senior High School:* Luisa Yanez, "Jeff Bezos: A Rocket Launched from Miami's Palmetto High School," *Miami Herald,* August 6, 2013.

67   *"Einstein was there":* Mark Leibovich, "Child Prodigy, Online Pioneer;

Amazon.com Founder Bezos Hires Great Minds. But Will It Matter?" *Washington Post,* September 3, 2000, p. A1.

67 *Bezos hatched the idea:* Stone, op. cit., Chapter One.

68 *3 million books in print:* Ibid.

68 *Job interviews entailed:* Leibovich, op. cit.

68 *He emulated Walmart's dominance:* Stone, op. cit., Chapter Three.

68 *loyalty card stamped:* Ibid.

68 *He had chosen the city:* Stone, op. cit., Chapter Two.

68 *pay for parking:* Stone, op. cit., Prologue.

68 *"The reason we are here":* Stone, op. cit., Chapter Three.

68 *"We need to apply":* Stone, op. cit., Chapter Six.

69 *"Are you lazy":* Ibid.

69 *For an Amazon executive:* Stone, op. cit., Chapter Eleven.

69 *"If Marxist revolutionaries":* Foer, op. cit.

69 *the seventeen executives:* Ibid.

70 *"The idea was always":* Peter de Jonge, "Riding the Perilous Waters of Amazon.com," *The New York Times Magazine,* March 14, 1999.

70 *Amazon actively recruited Chinese suppliers:* Jon Emont, "Amazon's Heavy Recruitment of Chinese Sellers Puts Consumers at Risk," *Wall Street Journal,* November 11, 2019.

70 *"Amazon isn't happening":* Stone, op. cit., Prologue.

71 *Amazon applied its muscle:* Brad Plumer, "Here's What Amazon Lobbies for in D.C.," *Washington Post,* August 7, 2013.

71 *Amazon was employing twenty-eight lobbyists:* Alec MacGillis, *Fulfillment: Winning and Losing in One-Click America* (New York: Farrar, Strauss and Giroux, 2021), 86–87.

71 *It had leveraged its status:* Renee Dudley, "Amazon's New Competitive Advantage: Putting Its Own Products First," ProPublica, June 6, 2020.

72 *Even as Amazon raised pay:* Conor Sen, "Still Worried About Inflation? Keep an Eye on Amazon," Bloomberg, April 30, 2021.

75 *Less than a third of his support:* Nicholas Carnes and Noam Lupu, "The White Working Class and the 2016 Election," Cambridge University Press, May 21, 2020.

75 *The counties that had absorbed:* Andrea Cerrato, Francesco Ruggieri, and Federico Maria Ferrara, "Trump Won in Counties That Lost Jobs to China and Mexico," *Washington Post,* December 2, 2016.

CHAPTER 3: **"SUDDENLY, THE ORDERS STOPPED"**

77 *"Agnelli is Fiat":* Arbër Sulejmani, "Gianni Agnelli—Juventus' Uncrowned King of Italy," Juvefc.com, January 24, 2017.

77 *"He wore his tie askew":* "The Best Dressed Men in the History of the World," *Esquire,* August 20, 2007.

78 *The impressive haul:* Ettore Boffano and Paolo Griseri, "Il tesoro nascosto dell'Avvocato," *La Repubblica,* June 11, 2009.

79 *The papers exposed:* Paolo Biondani, Gloria Riva, and Leo Sisti, "Barilla,

Corallo e Margherita Agnelli: I tesori dei vip d'Italia sono all'estero," *L'Espresso,* June 29, 2018.

79   *the strict rules of the currency:* Servaas Storm, "How to Ruin a Country in Three Decades," Institute for New Economic Thinking, April 10, 2019, https://www.ineteconomics.org/perspectives/blog/how-to-ruin-a -country-in-three-decades.

81   *HSBC's banking operations:* Paolo Biondani, "Quello scudo fiscale in regalo agli evasori," *L'Espresso,* February 12, 2015, https://espresso.repubblica .it/attualita/2015/02/12/news/quello-scudo-fiscale-in-regalo-agli -evasori-1.199228.

81   *evasion of European value-added taxes:* "Italians Are Europe's Worst Tax Cheats (Again . . .)," *Local,* September 7, 2016, https://www.thelocal .it/20160907/italians-europe-vat-tax-evasion-dodge-again.

82   *Marchionne demanded an immediate infusion:* Marco Capobianchi, *American Dream: Cosi Marchionne ha salvato la Chrysler e ucciso la Fiat* (Rome: Chiarelettere, 2014).

82   *money to expand abroad:* Ibid.

83   *establishing itself in the United Kingdom:* "Fiat Says Ciao to Italy as Chrysler Merger Is Approved," *Automotive News,* August 1, 2014, https://www .autonews.com/article/20140801/COPY01/308019978/fiat-says-ciao-to -italy-headquarters-as- chrysler-merger-is-approved.

83   *the highest-paid CEO in Italy:* Gianni Dragoni, "Industriali battono banchieri: ecco i 50 manager più pagati in Italia nel 2017," *Il Sole 24 Ore,* November 25, 2018, https://www.ilsole24ore.com/art/industriali -battono-banchieri-ecco-50-manager-piu-pagati-italia-2017-AEy YvKmG.

83   *77 percent of Italians:* Richard Wike, Laura Silver, and Alexandra Castillo, "Many Across the Globe Are Dissatisfied with How Democracy Is Working," Pew Research Center, April 29, 2019, https://www.pewresearch.org /global/2019/04/29/many-across-the-globe-are-dissatisfied-with-how -democracy-is-working.

86   *A textile workforce:* Data from Prato office of Confindustra, Italy's largest industrial trade association.

87   *he employed a team of trendspotters:* Sarah Forbes Orwig, entry on Amancio Ortega, Encyclopaedia Britannica, https://www.britannica.com /biography/Amancio-Ortega.

87   *Zara sold its wares:* Suzy Hansen, "How Zara Grew into the World's Largest Fashion Retailer," *The New York Times Magazine,* November 9, 2012.

87   *a fortune estimated at $55 billion:* "Forbes World's Billionaire List: The Richest in 2020," https://www.forbes.com/billionaires.

88   *supplying Persson with wealth:* Ibid., "#84 Stefan Persson," https://www .forbes.com/profile/stefan-persson/#2242fb925dbe.

90   *nighttime raids on the plants:* Guy Standing, *The Precariat: The New Dangerous Class* (London: Bloomsbury, 2011), Chapter One.

90   *"an Islamic caliphate":* Shaun Walker, "Matteo Salvini; Vote for Nationalists to Stop European Caliphate," *Guardian,* May 2, 2019, https://

www.theguardian.com/world/2019/may/02/matteo-salvini-vote-for
-nationalist-parties-stop-islamic-caliphate.

90 *"ethnic cleansing":* Eric Sylvers, "Italy Far-Right Leader Gets Boost," *Wall Street Journal,* May 30, 2018.

CHAPTER 4: **"OUR CHANCE TO FUCK THEM BACK"**

94 *"I sat him down":* Jenny Johnston, "George Osborne: Why I'm Ready to Be Mr Nasty," *MailOnline,* October 3, 2009.

95 *people on trading floors in London:* Peter S. Goodman, "'Brexit' Imperils London's Claim as Banker to the Planet," *New York Times,* May 12, 2017, p. A1.

101 *"He looks permanently pink":* Andy Beckett, "The Real George Osborne," *Guardian,* November 28, 2011.

101 *"I want to be rich":* Patricia Crisafulli, *The House of Dimon: How JPMorgan's Jamie Dimon Rose to the Top of the Financial World* (New York: John Wiley & Sons, Inc., 2009), Chapter Three.

101 *His grandfather had arrived:* Duff McDonald, *Last Man Standing: The Ascent of Jamie Dimon and JPMorgan Chase* (New York: Simon & Schuster, 2010), Chapter One.

101 *the family name:* Crisafulli, op. cit., Chapter Three.

102 *Dimon spent most of his youth:* McDonald, op. cit., Chapter One.

102 *His family home:* Keith Flamer, "The Secret History of Park Avenue's 'Gothic' Grande Dame (And Its $16 Million Penthouse Project)," *Forbes,* October 22, 2015, https://www.forbes.com/sites/keithflamer/2015/10/22 /the-secret-history-of-park-avenues-gothic-grande-dame-and-its-16 -million-penthouse-project/?sh=4863977fc93d.

102 *He and his two brothers:* Aaron Glantz, *Homewreckers: How a Gang of Wall Street Kingpins, Hedge Fund Magnates, Crooked Banks, and Vulture Capitalists Suckered Millions Out of Their Homes and Demolished the American Dream* (New York: William Morrow, 2019), Chapter Eighteen.

102 *Their homes in Greenwich:* Crisafulli, op. cit., Chapter Three.

102 *Weill had grown up:* McDonald, op. cit., Chapter Two.

102 *Weill offered him a summer job:* Crisafulli, op. cit., Chapter Three.

102 *Weill denied Dimon a place:* Ibid.

103 *He persuaded JPMorgan Chase:* Duff McDonald, "The Heist," *New York,* March 21, 2008.

103 *"Don't do anything stupid":* McDonald, *Last Man Standing,* op. cit., Chapter Four.

103 *"We do not yet know":* Roger Lowenstein, *The End of Wall Street* (New York: Penguin Books, 2010), Chapter Seven.

103 *the largest Ponzi scheme:* Erik Larson and Christopher Cannon, "Madoff's Victims Are Close to Getting Their $19 Billion Back," Bloomberg, December 8, 2018.

103 *"too good to be true":* Jesse Eisinger, *The Chickenshit Club: Why the Justice Department Fails to Prosecute Executives* (New York: Simon & Schuster, 2017), 234.

103   *The bank shielded management:* Ibid., 234–36.

104   *Paulson soon rushed to Capitol Hill:* Adam Tooze, *Crashed: How a Decade of Financial Crises Changed the World* (New York: Penguin Books, 2018), Chapter Seven.

105   *"Counter to what most people think":* Hugh Son, "Dimon Says JP Morgan's Actions During '08 Crisis Were Done to 'Support Our Country,'" CNBC, September 14, 2018.

105   *the five largest banks:* Robert B. Reich, *The System: Who Rigged It, How We Fix It* (New York: Knopf, 2020), Chapter Three.

105   *spa treatments:* Brian Ross and Tom Shine, "After Bailout, AIG Execs Head to California Resort," ABC News, October 7, 2008.

106   *"Be careful how you make those statements":* Eamon Javers, "Inside Obama's Bank CEOs Meeting," *Politico,* April 3, 2009, https://www.politico.com/story/2009/04/inside-obamas-bank-ceos-meeting-020871.

106   *His Justice Department failed:* Eisinger, *Chickenshit Club,* op. cit.

107   *to buy back their stock:* Edward Yardeni, Joe Abbott, and Mali Quintana, "Corporate Finance Briefing: S&P 500 Buybacks & Dividends," Yardeni Research, Inc., August 21, 2020; as cited in William Lazonick and Matt Hopkins, "How 'Maximizing Shareholder Value' Minimized the Strategic National Stockpile: The $5.3 Trillion Question for Pandemic Preparedness Raised by the Ventilator Fiasco," Institute for New Economic Thinking, July 2020, https://www.ineteconomics.org/research/research-papers/how-maximizing-shareholder-value-minimized-the-strategic-national-stockpile-the-5-3-trillion-question-for-pandemic-preparedness-raised-by-the-ventilator-fiasco.

107   *Over the course of those ten years:* Chuck Collins, Omar Ocampo, and Sophia Paslaski, "Billionaire Bonanza 2020: Wealth Windfalls, Tumbling Taxes, and Pandemic Profiteers," Institute for Policy Studies, April 23, 2020, https://ips-dc.org/wp-content/uploads/2020/04/Billionaire-Bonanza-2020.pdf.

108   *Dimon's compensation:* "JP Morgan Doubles CEO Jamie Dimon's Salary Despite Billions in Fines," Associated Press, published in the *Guardian,* January 24, 2014, https://www.theguardian.com/business/2014/jan/24/jp-morgan-jamie-dimons-salary-billions-fines.

108   *"I think a lot of it was unfair":* "JPMorgan CEO Dimon Says Government Cases Were 'Unfair,'" Reuters, January 23, 2014, https://www.reuters.com/article/us-jpmorgan-dimon/jpmorgan-ceo-dimon-says-government-cases-were-u nfair-idUSBREA0M0PL20140123.

108   *Dimon called the rules "anti-American":* Tom Braithwaite, "Dimon in Attack on Canada's Bank Chief," *Financial Times,* September 26, 2011.

108   *losses that exceeded $6 billion:* Renae Merle, "The 'London Whale' Trader Lost $6.2 Billion, but He May Walk Off Scot-Free," *Washington Post,* April 13, 2017, https://www.washingtonpost.com/business/economy/the-london-whale-trader-lost-62-billion-but-he-may-walk-off-scot-free/2017/04/12/14b3836a-1fb0-11e7-be2a-3a1fb24d4671_story.html.

114   *"preference as a business":* "Nissan Statement: UK Should Remain in EU,"

press release on Nissan website, February 24, 2016, http://nissaninsider
.co.uk/nissan-it-makes-sense-for-uk-to-remain-in-eu.

116   *only to "professional investors"*: European Commission, Directive on
Alternative Investment Fund Managers: Frequently Asked Questions,
Memo 10/572, November 11, 2010, https://ec.europa.eu/commission
/presscorner/detail/fr/MEMO_10_572.

116   *One hundred executives:* William Schomberg and Guy Faulconbridge,
"Hedge Fund Managers Crispin Odey and Paul Marshall Say Brexit Would
Help London," Reuters, April 29, 2016.

116   *hedge fund manager Crispin Odey:* "Rich List 2020," *Sunday Times* (London),
https://www.thetimes.co.uk/sunday-times-rich-list#TableFullRichList.

116   *"Cluckingham Palace":* Harriet Dennys, "City Diary: Crispin Odey's Chick-
ens Come Home to (a Luxury) Roost," *Telegraph*, September 25, 2012,
https://www.telegraph.co.uk/finance/comment/citydiary/9563587
/City-Diary-Crispin-Odeys-chickens-come-home-to-a-luxury-roost.html.

116   *contributed nearly £900,000:* Caroline Mortimer, "Brexit Campaign
Was Largely Funded by Five of UK's Richest Businessmen," *Independent,* April 24, 2017, https://www.independent.co.uk/news/uk/politics
/brexit-leave-eu-campaign-arron-banks-jeremy-hosking-five-uk-richest
-businessmen-peter-hargreaves-a7699046.html.

117   *hedge fund manager Paul Marshall:* "Rich List 2020," *Sunday Times* (London); ibid.

CHAPTER 5: "IT HAD TO EXPLODE"

120   *"For our society to get better":* Michel Rose and Sybille de La Hamaide,
"Macron Urges the French to Value Success, Rejects 'President of the
Rich' Tag," Reuters, October 15, 2017, https://uk.reuters.com/article
/uk-france-politics/macron-urges-the-french-to-value-success-rejects
-president-of-rich-tag-idUKKBN1CK0TG.

121   *"We believe that this presidency":* Sophie Fay, "Larry Fink: 'I See a Strong
Europe in the Years to Come," *L'Obs,* June 28, 2017, https://www.nouvelobs
.com/economie/20170628.OBS1352/larry-fink-je-vois-une-europe-forte
-dans-les-an nees-qui-viennent.html.

122   *"It's nice to be wanted":* William Horobin, "In Shift, France to Speed Tax
Cuts," *Wall Street Journal* (Europe Edition), July 13, 2017, p. A4.

122   *Nearly half of his campaign funds:* Sylvain Tronchet, Julie Guesdon, and
Cellule investigation de Radio France, "Half of Emmanuel Macron's Campaign Funded by Major Donors," Radio France, May 3, 2019, https://
www.franceculture.fr/politique/comment-800-grands-donateurs-ont
-finance-la-moitie-de-la-campagne-demmanuel-macron.

123   *one of the three wealthiest people:* Forbes list of billionaires, accessed August 5, 2020, https://www.forbes.com/profile/bernard-arnault
/#505b73e066fa.

123   *Arnault's yacht:* Laura Craik, "The Fabulous World of Bernard Arnault,"
Times (London), January 27, 2013.

123 *"Emmanuel Macron's program":* Bernard Arnault, "Pourquoi je vote Emmanuel Macron," *Les Echos,* May 5, 2017, https://www.lesechos.fr /2017/05/pourquoi-je-vote-emmanuel-macron-1115472.

124 *Arnault's accountants had made:* Monique Pinçon Charlot and Michel Pinçon, *Le Président des ultra-riches* (Paris: Zones, 2019), Chapter Two.

124 *"What you call tax fraud":* Interview with Mediapart and BFM-TV, April 15, 2018, https://www.youtube.com/watch?v=mt0as7x-kfs.

124 *He took several trips to London:* Antton Rouget, Mathilde Matthieu, Mathieu Magnaudeix, and Martine Orange, "Macron Leaks: The Secrets of an Extraordinary Fundraising Operation," *Mediapart,* May 21, 2017, https://www.mediapart.fr/journal/france/210517/macron-leaks-les -secrets-dune-levee-de-fonds-hors-norme?onglet=full.

125 *"If we want to avoid this fragmentation":* Peter S. Goodman, "Europe Is Back. And Rejecting Trumpism," *New York Times,* January 24, 2018, p. B3.

126 *"If I cannot explain to people":* Ibid.

126 *less than 10 percent of the French workforce:* OECD.Stat, trade union density data, https://stats.oecd.org/Index.aspx?DataSetCode=TUD.

126 *contracts lasting less than a month:* Analysis of government data provided by Philippe Askenazy, a labor economist at the French National Center for Scientific Research in Paris.

127 *One in five young people:* OECD.Stat, youth unemployment rate data, https://data.oecd.org/unemp/youth-unemployment-rate.htm.

127 *he divided the unions:* James McAuley, "Macron Could Succeed Where Other French Presidents Failed on Labor Reform," *Washington Post,* September 2, 2017, p. A8.

127 *like Nordic-style free enterprise:* Peter S. Goodman, "Nordic-Style Designs Sit at Heart of French Labor Plan," *New York Times,* October 26, 2017, p. B1, https://www.nytimes.com/2017/10/26/business/france-labor -reform-economy-macron.html.

127 *lowering it by 70 percent:* Anne-Sylvaine Chassany, "Macron Slashes France's Wealth Tax in Pro-business Budget," *Financial Times,* October 24, 2017.

128 *Economic inequality was nowhere near:* The World Bank, World Development Indicators: Distribution of Income or Consumption, http://wdi .worldbank.org/table/1.3.

128 *Only Denmark, Sweden, and Belgium:* Orsetta Causa and Mikkel Hermansen, "Income Redistribution Through Taxes and Transfers Across OECD Countries," OECD Economics Department Working Papers No. 1453, July 22, 2019, p. 11.

128 *Between 1983 and 2015:* Bertrand Garbinti, Jonathan Goupille-Lebret, and Thomas Piketty, "Income Inequality in France, 1900–2014: Evidence from Distributional National Accounts (DINA)," Wealth & Income Database, Working Paper Series No. 2017/4, April 2017, revised January 2018, https://wid.world/document/b-garbinti-j-goupille-and -t-piketty-inequality-dynamics-in-france-1900-2014-evidence-from -distributional-national-accounts-2016.

128 *dramatic reduction in inequality:* Facundo Alvaredo, Lucas Chancel, Thomas Piketty, Emmanuel Saez, and Gabriel Zucman, World Inequality Report, 2018, p. 95.

128 *explosive strikes:* Eleanor Beardsley, "In France, The Protests of May 1968 Reverbate Today—and Still Divide the French," National Public Radio, May 29, 2018, https://www.npr.org/sections/parallels/2018/05 /29/613671633/in-france-the-protests-of-may-1968-reverberate-today -and-still-divide-the-french.

129 *barely 20 percent of national spending:* O. Causa and M. Hermansen, "Income Redistribution through Taxes and Transfers Across OECD Countries," *OECD Economics Department Working Papers,* No. 1453, OECD Publishing, Paris, 2017, https://doi.org/10.1787/bc7569c6-en.

129 *Macron pledged to slash the tax rate:* Simon Jessop and Inti Landauro, "France Lures Private Equity with Post-Brexit Tax Break," Reuters, November 2, 2018.

130 *nursing feelings of betrayal:* Jacques Monin, Radio France Investigation Unit, February 21, 2019, https://www.francetvinfo.fr/economie /transports/gilets-jaunes/l-histoire-secrete-de-la-reforme-de-l-isf-elle -a-ete-precipitee-sous-la-pression-deconomistes-et-de-grands-patrons _3199431.html.

130 *secretly met the president:* Ibid.

130 *Lifting the wealth tax:* Henry Samuel, "Paris Overtakes London in the Super-Rich League as the 'Macron Effect' Lures the Wealthy to City of Light," *Telegraph,* September 6, 2018.

130 *the one hundred wealthiest people:* Report from MM. Vincent Eble and Alberic de Montgolfier, on behalf of Senate Finance Committee, October 9, 2019, https://www.senat.fr/notice-rapport/2019/r19-042-1-notice.html.

130 *The year before its abolition:* Askenazy, op. cit.

130 *Among the beneficiaries:* Mathilde Mathieu, "Macron Caught by His ISF," *Mediapart,* May 31, 2016, https://www.mediapart.fr/journal/france /310516/macron-rattrape-par-son-isf?onglet=full.

131 *bill for makeup services:* James McAuley, "French President Macron Has Spent $30,000 on Makeup Services in Just 3 Months," *Washington Post,* August 25, 2017, https://www.washingtonpost.com/news/world views/wp/2017/08/25/french-president-macron-has-spent-30000-on -makeup-services-in-just-3-months.

131 *For his fortieth birthday:* Adam Sage, "Emmanuel Macron Living Like a King, Critics Taunt After 'Lavish' Birthday Party," *Times* (London), December 18, 2017.

131 *new set of 900 dinner plates:* Adam Nossiter, "Let Them Eat on Fancy Plates: Emmanuel Macron's New China," *New York Times,* June 15, 2018, p. A5.

131 *new swimming pool:* Kim Willisher, "From Plates to Piscine: Now Macrons Want a Presidential Pool," *Guardian,* June 21, 2018, https://www .theguardian.com/world/2018/jun/21/from-plates-to-piscine-now -macrons-want-a-presidential-pool.

131   *"truckload of cash on social programs":* Vincent Michelon, "Video: Emmanuel Macron: 'On met un pognon de dingue dans les minima sociaux," LCI, June 13, 2018, https://www.lci.fr/politique/emmanuel-macron-on-met-un-pognon-de-dingue-dans-les-minima-sociaux-video-2090364.html.

131   *"stop messing around":* Alissa J. Rubin, "That's 'Mr. President' to You: Macron Scolds French Student," *New York Times,* June 20, 2018, p. A5, https://www.nytimes.com/2018/06/19/world/europe/france-president-macron.html.

133   *rubber bullets and tear gas:* Alissa J. Rubin, "Macron Inspects Damage After 'Yellow Vest' Protests as France Weighs State of Emergency," *New York Times,* December 2, 2018, p. A10, https://www.nytimes.com/2018/12/01/world/europe/france-yellow-vests-protests-macron.html?action=click&module=inline&pgtype=Article&region=Footer.

133   *reversed course:* Adam Nossiter, "France Suspends Fuel Tax Increase That Spurred Violent Protests," *New York Times,* December 5, 2018, p. A6.

134   *"One can always do better":* Adam Nossiter, "Macron, Chastened by Yellow Vest Protests, Says 'I Can Do Better,'" *New York Times,* April 26, 2019, p. A11.

136   *"between nationalists and globalists":* Geert De Clercq, "France's Le Pen Launches EU Campaign with Appeal to 'Yellow Vests,'" Reuters, January 13, 2019, https://uk.reuters.com/article/uk-france-politics-farright/frances-le-pen-launches-eu-campaign-with-appeal-to-yellow-vests-idUKKCN1P70RK.

136   *typical French worker was retiring at sixty:* "France Economy: Risking the Rage of the Aged," *Economist Intelligence Unit,* September 14, 2019.

137   *"the Wizard of Oz":* Suzanna Andrews, "Larry Fink's $12 Trillion Shadow," *Vanity Fair,* March 2, 2010.

139   *BlackRock had worked:* Katrina Brooker, "Can This Man Save Wall Street?" *Fortune,* October 29, 2008.

139   *He told Paulson and Geithner:* Henry M. Paulson, Jr., *On the Brink: Inside the Race to Stop the Collapse of the Global Financial System* (New York: Hachette, 2013), Chapter Five.

139   *the solidity of Lehman Brothers:* Andrew Ross Sorkin, *Too Big to Fail: The Inside Story of How Wall Street and Washington Fought to Save the Financial System—and Themselves* (New York: Penguin Books, 2009), Chapter Seven.

140   *a gaping conflict of interest:* Liz Rappaport and Susanne Craig, "BlackRock Wears Multiple Hats," *Wall Street Journal,* May 19, 2009, https://www.wsj.com/articles/SB124269131342732625.

140   *"Our clients trust us":* Ibid.

140   *regular at San Pietros:* Sorkin, op. cit.

140   *Macron hosted Fink:* Luc Peillon and Jacques Pezet, "Est-il vrai que Macron a rencontré le groupe BlackRock, spécialisé dans les fonds de pension?" *Liberation,* September 12, 2019, https://www.msn.com/fr-fr/actualite/france/est-il-vrai-que-macron-a-rencontr%C3%A9-le-groupe-blackrock-sp%C3%A9cialis%C3%A9-dans-les-fonds-de-pension/ar-BB

XZWcc?ocid=sf&fbclid=IwAR0MPKkgRDwGIYdP_jLlvuvRtmenK3vm0
yRzpSuA5mQyeu7NoZKq9SdKw.

140 *His schedule included a dinner with Fink:* Sophie Fay, "Larry Fink, the $5.4 Trillion Man," *L'Obs*, June 28, 2017.

140 *BlackRock helped organize a summit:* Odile Benyahia-Kouider, "Comment L'Elysée a déroulé le tapis rouge au roi de Wall Street," *Le Canard Enchaîné*, October 26, 2017.

141 *he collected more than £600,000:* Jill Treanor and Rowena Mason, "Buy, George? World's Largest Fund Manager Hires Osborne as Adviser," *Guardian*, January 20, 2017.

141 *moving perhaps one thousand jobs:* Stephen Morris and Richard Partington, "Brexit: HSBC May Move 20% of Its London Banking Operations to Paris, Chief Executive Stuart Gulliver Says," *Independent*, January 18, 2017, https://www.independent.co.uk/news/business/news/brexit-latest-news-hsbc-bank-move-20-cent-fifth-london-banking-operations-paris-chief-executive-stuart-gulliver-a7532711.html.

141 *"At the center of our mission":* Chad Bray, "Former Top British Official to Join BlackRock as an Adviser," *New York Times*, January 20, 2017.

142 *5 percent of French savings:* Liz Alderman, "A Wall Street Giant Is Fueling Anticapitalist Fervor in France," *New York Times*, February 15, 2020, p. A1.

143 *protestors stormed BlackRock's office:* Ibid.

143 *"We deplore the fact":* Ibid.

CHAPTER 6: "EVERY STONE I LOOKED UNDER WAS A BLACKSTONE"

146 *"The financialization of housing":* Letter to Schwarzman from Surya Deva, Chair-Rapporteur of the Working Group on the issue of human rights, and Leilani Farha, Special Rapporteur on adequate housing, United Nations, March 22, 2019, https://www.ohchr.org/_layouts/15/WopiFrame.aspx?sourcedoc=/Documents/Issues/Housing/Financialization/OL_OTH_17_2019.pdf&action=default&DefaultItemOpen=1.

147 *Swedish women to work:* Marten Blix, *Digitalization, Immigration and the Welfare State* (Cheltenham, U.K.: Edward Elgar Publishing, 2017), 19.

148 *"Frugality drives innovation":* Brian Smale, "Bezos on Innovation," *Bloomberg Businessweek*, April 17, 2008.

148 *miners put stock in the Nordic Model:* Peter S. Goodman, "The Robots Are Coming, and Sweden Is Fine," *New York Times*, December 28, 2017, p. A1, https://www.nytimes.com/2017/12/27/business/the-robots-are-coming-and-sweden-is-fine.html.

154 *flying economy class:* Robert D. McFadden, "Ingvar Kamprad, IKEA Founder Who Built a Global Empire Through Thrift, Dies at 91," *New York Times*, January 29, 2018, p. A1.

154 *secondhand clothes:* Giulia Crouch, "Father of Flat-Pack 'Stingy' IKEA Founder Ingvar Kamprad, Worth £54billion, Was as Cheap as His Furniture, Bought Clothes in Flea Markets and Drove a 20-Year-Old Volvo," *Scottish Sun*, January 28, 2018, p. 20.

154   *showing up unannounced:* McFadden, op. cit.

154   *participation in a fascist group:* Ibid.

155   **"His philosophy throughout the years":** Johan Stenebo, *The Truth About IKEA: The Secret Behind the World's Fifth Richest Man and the Success of the Flatpack Giant* (United Kingdom: Gibson Square, 2010), Chapter Nine.

155   **"symbolic sums":** Ibid.

155   *Kamprad returned home:* Jens Hansegard, "IKEA Founder to Return Home," *Wall Street Journal Europe,* June 28, 2013, p. 20.

155   *reduction in government revenue:* Blix, op. cit., 25.

155   *slashing public spending:* Claes Belfrage and Markus Kallifatides, "Financialisation and the New Swedish Model," *Cambridge Journal of Economics* 2018, 882.

156   *average rate of unemployment:* Gregg M. Olsen, "Half Empty or Half Full? The Swedish Welfare State in Transition," *Canadian Review of Sociology and Anthropology,* May 1, 1999.

156   *inflation spread:* Andreas Bergh, "The Swedish Economy," *Milken Institute Review,* January 1, 2017.

156   *Sweden's central bank lifted interest rates:* Blix, op. cit., 24.

156   *unemployment rate was above 8 percent:* Olsen, op. cit.

156   *the government slashed public sector jobs:* Ibid.

156   *Sweden reduced job training:* Ibid.

156   *they would pay for themselves:* Blix, op. cit., 26.

156   *8,700-acre country estate:* Dan Alexander, "Meet the 10 Billionaire Tycoons Who Rule Their Countries' Economies," *Forbes,* March 14, 2014.

156   *an entire English village:* Tristan Cork, "Swedish Clothes Tycoon Adds Historic Estate to Portfolio," *Western Daily Press,* March 19, 2013, p. 8.

157   *8,500-acre manor:* Murray Wardrop, "Swedish H&M Boss Stefan Persson 'to Buy Entire Hampshire Village,'" *Telegraph,* May 24, 2009.

157   *Incomes in Sweden were widening:* Jon Pareliussen, Christophe Andre, Hugo Bourrousse, and Vincent Koen, "Income, Wealth and Equal Opportunities in Sweden," OECD Economics Department Working Papers, No. 1394, OECD Publishing, Paris, https://www.oecd-ilibrary.org/economics/income-wealth-and-equal-opportunities-in-sweden_e900be20-en.

157   *poverty doubled:* Ibid., 11.

157   *one in four young adults:* Anneli Lucia Tostar, "Young Adults and the Stockholm Housing Crisis: Falling Through the Cracks in the Foundation of the Welfare State," Master's Thesis, Royal Institute of Technology, 7.

157   **"I grew up in the middle-class suburbs":** Stephen A. Schwarzman, *What It Takes* (New York: Simon & Schuster, 2019), Prologue (Made, Not Born).

158   **"I'm a very happy man":** Ibid., Chapter One.

158   **"that will make a great difference":** Ibid., Chapter Two.

158   *started at the lowest rungs:* David Carey and John E. Morris, *King of Capital: The Remarkable Rise, Fall, and Rise Again of Steve Schwarzman and Blackstone* (New York: Crown Publishing, 2010), Chapter Seven.

158   *her family's Park Avenue apartment:* Schwarzman, op. cit., Chapter Two.

158   *cultivated a bond:* Ibid.

159 *poster child, Michael Milken:* Laurie P. Cohen, "About Face: How Michael Milken Was Forced to Accept the Prospect of Guilt," *Wall Street Journal,* April 23, 1990, p. A1.

160 *he paid $37 million:* James B. Stewart, "The Birthday Party," *The New Yorker,* February 4, 2008.

160 *neighbors in the building:* Aaron Glantz, *Homewreckers,* op. cit., Chapter Five.

160 *"I love houses":* Stewart, op. cit.

160 *$78 billion in assets:* Ibid.

160 *shield $3.7 billion in income:* David Cay Johnston, "Blackstone Devises Way to Avoid Taxes on $3.7 Billion," *New York Times,* July 13, 2007.

161 *spending $3,000 on groceries:* Henny Sender and Monica Langley, "Buyout Mogul: How Blackstone's Chief Became $7 Billion Man—Schwarzman Says He's Worth Every Penny; $400 for Stone Crabs," *Wall Street Journal,* June 13, 2007, p. A1.

161 *full-length portrait of the birthday boy:* Stewart, op. cit.

161 *guests included:* Michael Flaherty, "Blackstone CEO Gala Sign of Buyout Boom," Reuters, February 14, 2007.

161 *"a celebration with six hundred people":* Schwarzman, op. cit., Chapter Nineteen.

161 *dressed up as Marie Antoinette:* Glantz, op. cit., Chapter Eleven.

161 *"We are the rich":* Ibid.

162 *"I don't feel like a wealthy person":* Stewart, op. cit.

162 *"the Blackstone bill":* Alec MacGillis, "The Billionaire's Loophole," *The New Yorker,* March 7, 2016.

162 *Another bill in the House:* Stewart, op. cit.

162 *nearly $5 million on lobbying:* MacGillis, "The Billionaire's Loophole," op. cit.

162 *Schumer deployed a novel means:* Ibid.

163 *auctions held on courthouse steps:* Glantz, op. cit., Chapter Twelve.

163 *"Once we fixed up the houses":* Schwarzman, op. cit., Chapter 22.

164 *Invitation invited them to pay:* Michelle Conlin, "Uneasy Living: Spiders, Sewage and a Flurry of Fees—The Other Side of Renting a House from Wall Street," Reuters, July 27, 2018, https://www.reuters.com/investigates/special-report/usa-housing-invitation.

164 *celebrated the bond issue:* Glantz, op. cit., Chapter Seventeen.

164 *more than doubling its initial stake:* Patrick Clark, "Blackstone Exits Single-Family Rental Bet Slammed by Warren," Bloomberg, November 21, 2019.

165 *a leading Swedish investment bank:* "Enskilda Securities and the Blackstone Group to Cooperate on North American/Scandinavian M&A," *Business Wire,* October 11, 1995.

165 *Jacob Wallenberg:* Richard Milne, "Meet the Wallenbergs," *Financial Times,* June 5, 2015.

165 *Blackstone plunked down $287 million:* "Blackstone Obtains All Approvals for Purchase of 32% Interest in Sweden's D Carnegie & Co," *SeeNews Nordic,* August 25, 2016.

165   *upped its stake:* Stephanie Linhardt, "The Direct Approach," *The Banker,*
       May 1, 2018.

166·   *Blackstone sold its stake:* "Real Estate Firm Vonovia Buys Majority Stake
       in Sweden's Hembla for $1.26 Billion," Reuters, September 23, 2019.

166   *"unwavering focus on its tenants":* Anthon Näsström, "Blackstone Sells
       Its 61 Percent Stake in Hembla to Vonovia," *Nordic Property News,* Sep-
       tember 23, 2019.

CHAPTER 7: "THEY ARE NOW LICKING THEIR LIPS"

169   *Three-fourths of the benefits:* "Corporate Tax Cut Benefits Wealthiest,
       Loses Needed Revenue, and Encourages Tax Avoidance," Center on
       Budget and Policy Priorities, https://www.cbpp.org/research/federal
       -tax/corporate-tax-cut-benefits-wealthiest-loses-needed-revenue-and
       -encourages-tax.

169   *Americans earning between:* Reconciliation Recommendations of the
       Senate Committee on Finance, Congressional Budget Office, November
       26, 2017, https://www.cbo.gov/system/files/115th-congress-2017-2018
       /costestimate/reconciliationrecommendationssfc.pdf.

169   *"When you put all these pieces together":* Peter S. Goodman and Patricia
       Cohen, "It Started as a Tax Cut. Now It Could Change American Life," *New
       York Times,* November 30, 2017, p. A1.

171   *as steel prices climbed:* Don Lee, "Trump's Steel Tariffs Were Supposed
       to Save the Industry. They Made Things Worse," *Los Angeles Times,* Octo-
       ber 29, 2019, https://www.latimes.com/politics/story/2019-10-29/steel
       -industry-faces-a-bleaker-future-than-when-trump-moved-to-rescue-it.

172   *his access to Trump and President Xi:* Michael Kranish, "Trump's China
       Whisperer: How Billionaire Stephen Schwarzman Has Sought to Keep
       the President Close to Beijing," *Washington Post,* March 13, 2018.

172   *Fink also served as a go-between:* Lingling Wei, Bob Davis, and Dawn Lim,
       "China Has One Powerful Friend Left in the U.S.: Wall Street," *Wall Street
       Journal,* December 2, 2020.

172   *"There may be retaliation":* Victor Reklaitis, "Jamie Dimon Says Trump's
       Tariff Plan Is 'the Wrong Way' to Tackle Trade Problems," *MarketWatch,*
       March 8, 2018.

173   *a $250,000 gift to his inauguration:* Michela Tindera, "The Majority of Don-
       ald Trump's Billionaire Donors Didn't Give to His 2016 Campaign," *Forbes,*
       May 15, 2020, https://www.forbes.com/sites/michelatindera/2020/05/15
       /the-majority-of-donald-trumps-billionaire-donors-didnt-give-to-his
       -2016-campaign/#33c57b404340.

174   *This was what $9 million could buy:* Laura M. Holson, "Camels, Acrobats
       and Team Trump at a Billionaire's Gala," *New York Times,* February 14, 2017,
       https://www.nytimes.com/2017/02/14/fashion/stephen-schwarzman
       -billionaires-birthday-draws-team-trum p.html.

175   *"That was then":* Robert Schmidt and Ben Brody, "Dimon's Challenge:
       Making Staid CEO Club a Lobbying Power," Bloomberg, March 14, 2017.

175   *"America's outdated tax system"*: Business Roundtable television adver-
      tisement, "Slowest Recovery," August 4, 2017, https://www.youtube.com
      /watch?v=UwjiuZihT4U.

176   *"Not only will this tax plan pay for itself"*: Kate Davidson, "Treasury Sec-
      retary Steven Mnuchin: GOP Tax Plan Would More Than Offset Its Cost,"
      Wall Street Journal, September 28, 2017.

176   *University of Chicago surveyed:* IGM Economic Experts Panel, the Uni-
      versity of Chicago Booth School of Business, November 21, 2017, http://
      www.igmchicago.org/surveys/tax-reform-2.

176   *Two years after the tax cuts:* Peter Cary, "Republicans Passed Tax Cuts—
      Then Profited," Center for Public Integrity, January 24, 2020, https://
      publicintegrity.org/inequality-poverty-opportunity/taxes/trumps-tax
      -cuts/republicans-profit-congress.

176   *companies used their windfall:* Matt Egan, "Corporate America Gives Out
      a Record $1 Trillion in Stock Buybacks," *CNN Business,* December 17,
      2018, https://edition.cnn.com/2018/12/17/investing/stock-buybacks
      -trillion-dollars/index.html.

176   *a record $1.3 trillion in dividends:* Cary, op. cit.

177   *more than triple the total earnings:* Sarah Anderson, "How Wall Street
      Drives Gender and Race Pay Gaps," Inequality.org, March 26, 2019,
      https://inequality.org/great-divide/wall-street-bonus-pool-2019.

177   *"The economy is ripping"*: Jordan Novet, "Salesforce CEO Marc Benioff:
      The Economy Is 'Ripping,'" CNBC, September 25, 2018.

178   *"The survival of our entire civilization"*: Peter Baker and Peter S. Good-
      man, "Trump and Davos: Not Exactly Best Friends, but Not Enemies Ei-
      ther," *New York Times,* January 25, 2018, p. A1.

CHAPTER 8: "THEY ARE NOT INTERESTED IN OUR CONCERNS"

185   *Americans spent $3.8 trillion:* Rabah Kamal, Daniel McDermott, Gior-
      lando Ramirez, and Cynthia Cox, "How Has U.S. Spending on Healthcare
      Changed over Time?" Peterson-KFF Health System Tracker, https://www
      .healthsystemtracker.org/chart-collection/u-s-spending-healthcare
      -changed-time/#item-start.

185   *emergency rooms were uniquely attractive:* Eileen Appelbaum and Rose-
      mary Batt, "Private Equity and Surprise Medical Billing," Institute for New
      Economic Thinking, September 4, 2019, https://www.ineteconomics.org
      /perspectives/blog/private-equity-and-surprise-medical-billing#_edn12.

185   *"an immense opportunity"*: Schwarzman, op. cit., Chapter 10.

185   *more than $833 billion:* Eileen Appelbaum and Rosemary Batt, "Private
      Equity Buyouts in Healthcare: Who Wins, Who Loses?" Institute for
      New Economic Thinking, March 25, 2020, https://www.ineteconomics
      .org/perspectives/blog/private-equity-buyouts-in-healthcare-who-wins
      -who-loses.

186   *"the same value-extraction strategy"*: Eileen Appelbaum, "How Private
      Equity Makes You Sicker," *The American Prospect,* October 7, 2019.

187   *roughly one of every three:* Appelbaum and Batt, op. cit.

187   *This resulted in charges:* Zack Cooper, Fiona Scott Morton, and Nathan Shekita, "Surprise! Out-of-Network Billing for Emergency Care in the United States," National Bureau of Economic Research, Working Paper 23623, July 2017, p. 4, https://www.nber.org/papers/w23623.

187   *hassled by collection agents:* Wendi C. Thomas, Maya Miller, Beena Raghavendran, and Doris Burke, "This Doctors Group Is Owned by a Private Equity Firm and Repeatedly Sued the Poor Until We Called Them," ProPublica, November 27, 2019, https://www.propublica.org/article/this -doctors-group-is-owned-by-a-private-equity-firm-and-repeatedly-sued -the-poor-until-we-called-them.

188   *"These higher payment rates":* Cooper, Morton, and Shekita, op. cit. 3.

188   *billed at out-of-network rates:* Ibid., 54.

188   *one-third increase:* Ibid., 23.

188   *more than $28 million:* Margot Sanger-Katz, Julie Creswell, and Reed Abelson, "Mystery Solved: Private-Equity-Backed Firm Are Behind Ad Blitz on 'Surprise Billing,'" *New York Times,* September 14, 2019, p. B3.

189   *170 hospitals shuttered:* Andrew W. Maxwell, H. Ann Howard, and George H. Pink, "Geographic Variation in the 2018 Profitability of Urban and Rural Hospitals," NC Rural Health Research Program, April 2020.

189   *a range of services:* Kathleen Knocke, George H. Pink, Kristie W. Thompson, Randy K. Randolph, and Mark Holmes, "Changes in Provision of Selected Services by Rural and Urban Hospitals Between 2009 and 2017," NC Rural Health Research Program, April 2021.

190   *924,000 hospital beds:* American Hospital Association data.

190   *twenty-five metropolitan areas:* Reed Abelson, "When Hospitals Merge to Save Money, Patients Often Pay More," *New York Times,* November 14, 2018, p. B1.

190   *more than twenty thousand beds:* Carl Campanile, Julia Marsh, Bernadette Hogan, and Nolan Hicks, "New York Has Thrown Away 20,000 Hospital Beds, Complicating Coronavirus Fight," *New York Post,* March 17, 2020, https://nypost.com/2020/03/17/new-york-has-thrown-away-20000 -hospital-beds-complicating-coronavirus-fight.

190   *emergency field hospital in Central Park:* Ron Lee, "Emergency Hospital Being Constructed in Central Park," *Spectrum News,* NY1, March 29, 2020.

190   *Local morgues had run out of space:* Alan Feuer and Andrea Salcedo, "New York City Deploys 45 Mobile Morgues as Virus Strains Funeral Homes," *New York Times,* April 2, 2020, https://www.nytimes.com/2020/04/02 /nyregion/coronavirus-new-york-bodies.html.

190   *Hospitals that served more than 100 million:* Lauren Leatherby, John Keefe, Lucy Tompkins, Charlie Smart, and Matthew Conlen, "'There's No Place for Them to Go': I.C.U. Beds Near Capacity Across U.S.," *New York Times,* December 9, 2020.

192   *many slashed pay:* Lev Facher, "Amid Coronavirus, Private Equity-Backed Company Slashes Benefits for Emergency Room Doctors," *STAT,* April 1,

2020, https://www.statnews.com/2020/04/01/slashes-benefits-for-doctors
-coronavirus.

192 *more than $8.5 million in total compensation:* Steve Twedt, "UPMC
CEO Compensation Jumps to $8.54 Million," *Pittsburgh Post-Gazette,*
May 17, 2019, https://www.post-gazette.com/business/healthcare
-business/2019/05/17/UPMC-compensation-Jeffrey-Romoff-8-54
-million/stories/201905170111#:~:text=UPMC%20President%20and%20
CEO%20Jeffrey,increas e%20from%20the%20previous%20year.

192 *publicly dismissing the threat:* Matt Stoller, "Why Does a Hospital Monopoly Want to Re-Open the Economy?" BIG (newsletter), May 9, 2020,
https://mattstoller.substack.com/p/why-does-a-hospital-monopoly-want.

CHAPTER 9: **"THERE'S ALWAYS A WAY OF MAKING MONEY"**

195 *Roughly half of all American households:* Patricia Cohen, "We All Have
a Stake in the Stock Market, Right? Guess Again," *New York Times,* February 9, 2018, p. B1, https://www.nytimes.com/2018/02/08/business
/economy/stocks-economy.html.

196 *the Dow Jones Industrial Average:* Liz Frazier, "The Coronavirus Crash
of 2020," *Forbes,* February 11, 2021, https://www.forbes.com/sites
/lizfrazierpeck/2021/02/11/the-coronavirus-crash-of-2020-and-the
-investing-lesson-it-taught-us/?sh=37b5f02346cf.

199 *language drafted by the meatpacking industry:* Michael Grabell and Ber-
nice Yeung, "Emails Show the Meatpacking Industry Drafted an Executive Order to Keep Plants Open," ProPublica, September 14, 2020, https://
www.propublica.org/article/emails-show-the-meatpacking-industry
-drafted-an-executive-order-to-keep-plants-open.

199 *risked their lives to continue carving up pork:* Jane Mayer, "How Trump Is
Helping Tycoons Exploit the Pandemic," *The New Yorker,* July 20, 2020.

200 *Consolidation had cut pork-processing capacity:* Jen Skerritt, "Tyson
Foods Helped Create the Meat Crisis It Warns Against," Bloomberg, April
29, 2020.

201 *language invited developers:* Jesse Drucker, "Bonanza for Rich Real Estate Investors, Tucked Into Stimulus Package," *New York Times,* March 27,
2020, p. B8.

202 *grandfather had launched a yacht club:* Glantz, op. cit., Chapter Three.

202 *the mortgage department:* Glantz, op. cit., Chapter Seven.

202 *nine-bedroom, ten-bath manse:* Ibid.

203 *he knew Trump as a fellow traveler:* Ibid.

203 *Mnuchin's biological mother:* James B. Stewart and Alan Rappeport, "Steven Mnuchin Tried to Save the Economy. Not Even His Family Is Happy,"
New York Times, August 31, 2020, p. A1.

203 *When Dimon turned him down:* Ibid.

203 *impersonation of Inspector Clouseau:* Ibid.

203 *"Africa is rife with hidden danger":* Louise Linton, "How My Dream Gap
Year in Africa Turned into a Nightmare," *Telegraph,* July 1, 2016.

204 *unencumbered by such conditions:* Jeff Stein and Peter Whoriskey, "The U.S. Plans to Lend $500 Billion to Large Companies. It Won't Require Them to Preserve Jobs or Limit Executive Pay," *Washington Post,* April 28, 2020, https://www.washingtonpost.com/business/2020/04/28/federal -reserve-bond-corporations.

204 *the language merely required:* Michael Grunwald, "The Corporate Bailout Doesn't Include the Limits Democrats Promised," *Politico,* April 2, 2020, https://www.politico.com/news/2020/04/02/coronavirus-corporate -bailout-deal-161374.

204 *the power to gag the inspector general:* Josh Wingrove and Saleha Mohsin, "Trump Claims Power to Gag Watchdog Overseeing Virus Stimulus," Bloomberg, March 28, 2020, https://www.bloomberg.com/news/articles /2020-03-28/trump-claims-power-to-gag-watchdog-overseeing-virus -stimulus?sref=12wQtvNW.

205 *Energy prices had fallen:* Matt Phillips and Clifford Krauss, "American Oil Drillers Were Hanging On by a Thread. Then Came the Virus," *New York Times,* March 21, 2020, p. B5.

205 *dividends and share buybacks:* Clark Williams-Derry, Kathy Hipple, and Tom Sanzillo, "Living Beyond Their Means: Cash Flows of Five Oil Majors Can't Cover Dividends, Buybacks," Institute for Energy Economics and Financial Analysis, January 2020, https://ieefa.org/wp-content /uploads/2020/01/Living-Beyond-Their-Means-Five-Oil-Majors-Cannot -Cover-Dividends_January-2020.pdf.

205 *obliterated the rule:* Gregg Gelzinis, Michael Madowitz, and Divya Vijay, "The Fed's Oil and Gas Bailout Is a Mistake," Center for American Progress, July 31, 2020, https://www.americanprogress.org/issues/economy /reports/2020/07/31/488320/feds-oil-gas-bailout-mistake.

205 *financial players like Schwarzman:* Jesse Eisinger, "The Bailout Is Working—for the Rich," ProPublica, May 10, 2020.

206 *"quite high grades":* Interview with Schwarzman on *Mornings with Maria,* Fox Business, April 7, 2020, https://www.facebook.com/watch /?v=1062782480764306.

206 *"concierge service":* Emily Flitter and Stacy Cowley, "Banks Gave Richest Clients 'Concierge Treatment' for Pandemic Aid," *New York Times,* April 2, 2020.

206 *Indiana-based maker of sporting goods:* Jessica Silver-Greenberg, David Enrich, Jesse Drucker, and Stacy Cowley, "Large, Troubled Companies Got Bailout Money in Small-Business Loan Program," *New York Times,* April 27, 2020, p. A1.

207 *Only 143 Black entrepreneurs:* Transcript of House Financial Services Subcommittee on Diversity and Inclusion, Hearing on Access to Capital for Women-and-Minority-Owned Businesses During the New Coronavirus, July 9, 2020, accessed via CQ Transcriptions.

207 *luxury hotel in San Diego:* Peter Whoriskey, "Given Millions from PPP, Some Firms Fail to Keep Workers," *Washington Post,* July 28, 2020, p. A20.

207 *None of this prevented the company:* Silver-Greenberg, Enrich, Drucker, and Cowley, op. cit.

208 *managed to scrape together $10 million:* Konrad Putzier, "Dallas Hotel Owner Is Biggest Beneficiary of Coronavirus Loan Program," *Wall Street Journal,* April 22, 2020.

208 *"our businesses are completely crushed":* Monty Bennett, "What's Wrong With America?" Medium, March 22, 2020, https://medium.com /@AshfordCEO/whats-wrong-with-america-30bbad18aded.

208 *Bennett had donated:* Federal Election Commission campaign disclosures, https://www.fec.gov/data/receipts/individual-contributions/?committee _id=C00618389&contributor_name=bennett%2C+monty&two_year _transaction_period=2016&two_year_transaction_period=2018&two _year_transaction_period=2020&min_date=01%2F01%2F2015&max _date=12%2F31%2F2020.

208 *First came Jeff Miller:* Lachlan Markay, "Trump Donor Hired Trump-Tied Lobbyists, Then Raked In Coronavirus Relief Cash," Daily Beast, April 23, 2020, https://www.thedailybeast.com/the-top-covid-relief-recipient -hired-trump-tied-lobbyists-weeks-before-getting-aid.

208 *Bailey Strategic Advisors:* Ibid.

208 *loophole was discovered:* David McLaughlin, Patrick Clark, and Ben Brody, "Luxury Hotelier Who Backed Trump Wins Big in Small-Business Aid," Bloomberg, April 23, 2020.

208 *Bennett's hotel empire:* Jeanna Smialek and Kenneth P. Vogel, "Hotelier's Push for $126 Million in Small-Business Aid Draws Scrutiny," *New York Times,* May 2, 2020, p. A1.

209 *$291 million in revenue:* Ashford, Inc., 2019 Annual Report, p. 146, https://s1.q4cdn.com/428793312/files/doc_financials/2019/ar/2019 -Annual-Report.pdf.

209 *Bennett had taken home:* U.S. Securities and Exchange Commission, Schedule 14A (proxy statement), Ashford, Inc., April 1, 2020, http:// d18rn0p25nwr6d.cloudfront.net/CIK-0001604738/508b422b-272f -4cfd-9353-d6fedaae60f5.html#NC10008218X1_DEF14A_HTM_TE.

209 *two weeks to return the money:* Alan Rappeport, "Treasury Vows to Re-coup Virus Relief Aid Claimed by Big Companies," *New York Times,* April 29, 2020, p. A1.

209 *his companies were being probed:* Konrad Putzier, "Texas Hotelier Monty Bennett's Companies Under SEC Investigation," *Wall Street Journal,* August 3, 2020.

209 *a chain of hospitals:* Brian Spegele and Laura Cooper, "As Coronavirus Cases Climbed, Private-Equity-Owned Hospital Faced Closure," *Wall Street Journal,* April 26, 2020.

210 *paying millions of dollars a year:* Ibid.

210 *stepped in to purchase the hospital:* Brian Spegele, "Hospital That Was Private-Equity Backed Sold to Local Health Network," *Dow Jones Institutional News,* June 3, 2020.

210 *refused to recognize the two unions:* Kurt Bresswein, "'We Are Out': Some

Easton Hospital Employees Are Being Replaced by St. Luke's Staff," le highvalleylive.com, June 17, 2020, https://www.lehighvalleylive.com /easton/2020/06/we-are-out-most-easton-hospital-employees-are-being -replaced-by-st-lukes-staff.html.

210 *secured grants exceeding $500 million:* Jesse Drucker, Jessica Silver-Greenberg, and Sarah Kliff, "Wealthiest Hospitals Got Billions in Bailout for Struggling Health Providers," *New York Times,* May 26, 2020, p. A1.

210 *tapped the government for $199 million:* Ibid.

211 *"What I've learned in life":* Schwarzman appearance at Cleveland Clinic, Virtual Ideas for Tomorrow, June 23, 2020, https://www.youtube.com /watch?v=dO93WgowPl8.

211 *By the end of 2020:* "Top Charts of 2020: The Economic Fallout of Covid-19," Economic Policy Institute, December 18, 2020, https://www.epi.org/pub lication/top-charts-of-2020-the-economic-fallout-of-covid-19.

211 *For every ten people:* Ibid.

211 *those tallied as a successful case:* Peter S. Goodman, Patricia Cohen, and Rachel Chaundler, "European Workers Draw Paychecks. American Workers Scrounge for Food," *New York Times,* July 4, 2020, p. A1.

212 *one in four Americans was struggling:* Kim Parker, Rachel Minkin, and Jesse Bennett, "Economic Fallout from Covid-19 Continues to Hit Lower-Income Americans the Hardest," Pew Research Center, September 24, 2020, https://www.pewresearch.org/social-trends/2020/09/24 /economic-fallout-from-covid-19-continues-to-hit-lower-income -americans-the-hardest.

212 *a ban on surprise billing:* Kristina Peterson and Julie Bykowicz, "Congress Debates Push to End Surprise Medical Billing," *Dow Jones Institutional News,* May 14, 2020.

213 *Neal's largest source of campaign funds:* Akela Lacy, "Effort to Take On Surprise Medical Billing in Coronavirus Stimulus Collapses," The Intercept, December 8, 2020, https://theintercept.com/2020/12/08/surprise -medical-billing-neal-covid.

213 *"always a way of making money":* Schwarzman at Bernstein's 36th Annual Strategic Decisions Conference, May 27, 2020, transcript posted on Seeking Alpha, https://seekingalpha.com/article/4350994-blackstone-group-inc -bx-ceo-steve-schwarzman-presents-bernsteins-36th-annual-strategic.

214 *some $20 trillion's worth of investments:* Graham Steele, "The New Money Trust: How Large Money Managers Control Our Economy and What We Can Do About It," American Economic Liberties Project, November 23, 2020; Alexander Sammon, "The Dawn of the BlackRock Era," *The American Prospect,* May 15, 2020.

214 *Days before the Fed announced:* Dawn Lim and Gregory Zuckerman, "Big Money Managers Take Lead Role in Managing Coronavirus Stimulus," *Wall Street Journal,* May 10, 2020.

214 *Fink spoke with Mnuchin five times:* Jeanna Smialek, "Top U.S. Officials Consulted with BlackRock as Markets Melted Down," *New York Times,* June 25, 2021, p. A1.

214 *One call included Fed Chairman Powell:* Ibid.

214 *fourth branch of government:* Annie Massa and Caleb Melby, "In Fink We Trust: BlackRock Is Now 'Fourth Branch of Government,'" *Bloomberg Businessweek,* May 21, 2020.

215 *"BlackRock is already big":* Letter to Mnuchin and Powell from Members of Congress, April 22, 2020, https://chuygarcia.house.gov/sites /chuygarcia.house.gov/files/Congressional%20Letter%20to%20Fed%2 0Treas%204_22.pdf.

216 *"I object to your":* BlackRock, Inc. (BLK) CEO Larry Fink on Q1 2020 Results—Earnings Call Transcript, April 16, 2020, transcript posted on Seeking Alpha, https://seekingalpha.com/article/4338041-blackrock-inc -blk-ceo-larry-fink-on-q1-2020-results-earnings-call-transcript.

217 *two-week "Cooling-Off period":* Contract between BlackRock Financial Management, Inc. and the Federal Reserve Bank of New York, as amended May 11, 2020, and June 29, 2020, and emailed on February 4, 2021, https://www.newyorkfed.org/medialibrary/media/markets/SMCCF_ Investment_Management_Agreement.pdf.

217 *perhaps $48 million:* Massa and Melby, op. cit.

217 *Nearly half that spending:* Christine Idzelis, "BlackRock Rakes in Big Portion of Fed's ETF Investments," *Institutional Investor,* June 1, 2020.

217 *investors rushed to get in first:* Katherine Greifeld, "Traders Pour $1 Billion into Biggest Credit ETF to Front-Run Fed," Bloomberg, March 24, 2020.

217 *net influx of $34 billion:* Cezary Podkul and Dawn Lim, "Fed Hires Black-Rock to Help Calm Markets. Its ETF Business Wins Big," *Wall Street Journal,* September 18, 2020.

218 *Even deeply troubled companies:* Joshua Franklin and David Shepardson, "Boeing Raises $25 Billion in Blowout Debt Sale, Eschews Government Aid," Reuters, April 30, 2020, https://uk.reuters.com/article /uk-boeing-debt/boeing-raises-25-billion-in-blowout-debt-sale-eschews -government-aid-idUKKBN22C3SL.

218 *ExxonMobil found takers:* Joshua Franklin, "Exxon Raises $9.5 Billion to Load Up on Cash While Debt Market Still Open to New Deals," Reuters, April 13, 2020, https://www.reuters.com/article/us-exxon-mobil-debt /exxon-raises-9-5-billion-to-load-up-on-cash-while-debt-market-still -open-to-new-deals-idUSKCN21V269.

218 *It raised $10 billion:* Molly Smith, "It's a Borrower's Bond Market as Amazon Gets Record Low Rates," Bloomberg, June 2, 2020.

218 *largest yearly toll in history:* Joe Rennison, "US Corporate Bond Issuance Hits $1.919tn in 2020, Beating Full-Year Record," *Financial Times,* September 2, 2020.

CHAPTER 10: "GROSSLY UNDERFUNDED AND FACING COLLAPSE"

219 *"a whole lot of economists":* McConnell on *This Week with George Stephanopoulos,* ABC News, December 3, 2017, https://abcnews.go.com/Politics /week-transcript-12-17-sen-mitch-mcconnell-rep/story?id=51533836.

220 *"My goal from the beginning of this"*: Burgess Everett, "McConnell Slams Brakes on Next Round of Coronavirus Aid," *Politico*, April 21, 2020, https://www.politico.com/news/2020/04/21/mcconnell-slams-brakes -coronavirus-aid-199890.

220 *"natural charisma of an oyster"*: Gail Collins, "Just Steele Yourselves," *New York Times*, March 6, 2009.

220 *on pace to spend almost $4 trillion more:* David J. Lynch, "Record Debt Load Poses Risk of 'Fiscal Tipping Point,'" *Washington Post*, April 19, 2020, p. A1.

222 *"I would certainly be in favor"*: Carl Hulse, "McConnell Says States Should Consider Bankruptcy, Rebuffing Calls for Aid," *New York Times*, April 23, 2020, p. A14.

223 *The total had climbed:* "Public Pension Funds Investing in Private Equity," *Private Equity & Venture Capital Spotlight* (June 2018): 12.

223 *unending array of fees:* Eileen Appelbaum and Rosemary Batt, "Fees, Fees and More Fees: How Private Equity Abuses Its Limited Partners and U.S. Taxpayers," Center for Economic and Policy Research, May 2016, https:// cepr.net/images/stories/reports/private-equity-fees-2016-05.pdf.

223 *strategic meetings:* Evan Halper, "CalPERS Investment Staff Receive Luxury Travel, Gifts from Financial Firms," *Los Angeles Times*, August 19, 2010, https://www.latimes.com/archives/la-xpm-2010-aug-19-la-me -calpers-20100819-story.html.

224 *personally owned stock:* Justin Mitchell, "CalPERS CIO Meng Resigns amid Questions over Personal Investments," *Buyouts*, August 6, 2020.

224 *A state ethics probe:* "CalPERS Won't Hire a New CIO Until Next Year," Chief Investment Officer, August 2, 2021, https://www.ai-cio.com/news /calpers-wont-hire-a-new-cio-until-next-year.

224 *the industry's returns had failed to match:* Ludovic Phallipou, "An Inconvenient Fact: Private Equity Returns & the Billionaire Factory," University of Oxford, Said Business School, Working Paper, July 15, 2020, available at SSRN, https://papers.ssrn.com/sol3/papers.cfm?abstract_id =3623820.

224 *"This wealth transfer"*: Ibid.

224 *converting themselves into ordinary corporations:* Greg Roumeliotis, "Blackstone to Switch from a Partnership to a Corporation," Reuters, April 18, 2019, https://www.reuters.com/article/us-blackstone-group -results/blackstone-to-switch-from-a-partnership-to-a-corporation -idUSKCN1RU196.

225 *Schwarzman's net worth:* Antoine Gara, "Blackstone Now More Valuable Than Goldman Sachs and Morgan Stanley amid the Coronavirus Chaos," *Forbes*, March 5, 2020, https://www.forbes.com/sites/antoinegara /2020/03/05/blackstone-overtakes-goldman-sachs-and-morgan-stanley -amid-the-coronavirus-chaos/?sh=6a28e89d400f.

227 *$8.7 trillion:* Eileen Appelbaum, "CEPR Statement on New Labor Department Guidance Allowing Risky Private Equity Investments in Workers' 401(k) Accounts," Center for Economic and Policy Research, June 4, 2020,

https://cepr.net/cepr-statement-on-new-labor-department-guidance
-allowing-risky-private-equity-investments-in-workers-401k-accounts.

CHAPTER 11: **"WE ARE ACTUALLY ALL ONE"**

229 *"It doesn't discriminate":* Benioff on *Mad Money,* CNBC, April 8, 2020, https://www.cnbc.com/video/2020/04/08/salesforce-ceo-on-90-day-no -layoff-pledge-three-phase-virus-outl ook.html.

230 *During the first half of 2020:* Richard A. Oppel Jr., Robert Gebeloff, K. K. Rebecca Lai, Will Wright, and Mitch Smith, "The Fullest Look Yet at the Racial Inequity of Coronavirus," *New York Times,* July 5, 2020.

230 *American life expectancy fell:* Elizabeth Arias, Betzaida Tejada-Vera, Farida Ahmad, and Kennetrh D. Kochanek, "Provisional Life Expectancy Estimates for 2020," Centers for Disease Control and Prevention, National Vital Statistics System, Report No. 015, July 2021, https://www .cdc.gov/nchs/data/vsrr/VSRR015-508.pdf.

231 *In the twenty-seven states:* Kathryn M. Leifheit, Sabriya L. Linton, Julia Raifman, Gabriel Schwartz, Emily A. Benfer, Frederick J. Zimmerman, and Craig Pollack, "Expiring Eviction Moratoriums and COVID-19 Incidence and Mortality," November 30, 2020, prepublication paper available at SSRN, https://papers.ssrn.com/sol3/papers.cfm?abstract_ id=3739576.

231 *"Metallica are not playing":* Benioff, call with analysts to discuss quarterly earnings, August 25, 2020, transcript posted on Seeking Alpha, https:// seekingalpha.com/article/4370780-salesforce-com-inc-s-crm-ceo-marc -benioff-on-q2-2021-results-earnings-call-transcript?part=single.

231 *lifting Benioff's net worth:* Salesforce Form 8-K, filed with U.S. Securities and Exchange Commission, March 27, 2020, https://www.sec.gov /ix?doc=/Archives/edgar/data/1108524/000110852420000018/crm -20200327.htm.

231 *brisk business in private islands:* Jamie Smyth, "Wealthy Buyers Snap Up 'Safe Haven' Private Islands to Flee Pandemic," *Financial Times,* July 24, 2020.

231 *private jet industry:* Tanya Powley and Claire Bushey, "Wealthy Switch to Private Jets to Avoid Coronavirus," *Financial Times,* July 25, 2020.

231 *In the Hamptons:* Alyson Krueger, "Rapid Testing Is the New Velvet Rope," *New York Times,* August 16, 2020, p. ST1.

232 *"victory for stakeholder capitalism":* Benioff on *Mad Money,* CNBC, August 25, 2020, https://www.cnbc.com/2020/08/25/salesforces-marc -benioff-claims-a-victory-for-stakeholder-capitalism.html.

233 *"We need a new, better global system":* Klaus Schwab, *Stakeholder Capitalism: A Global Economy That Works for Progress, People, and the Planet* (Hoboken, NJ: John Wiley & Sons, Inc., 2021), 171.

233 *"To prosper over time":* Laurence D. Fink, Annual Letter to CEOs, January 2018, http://www.corporance.es/wp-content/uploads/2018/01/Larry -Fink-letter-to-CEOs-2018-1.pdf.

233 *"companies and countries that do not respond"*: Laurence D. Fink, "A Fundamental Reshaping of Finance," Letter to CEOs, January 2020, https://www.blackrock.com/corporate/investor-relations/larry-fink-ceo-letter.

233 *"new conscience of Wall Street"*: Leslie P. Norton, "Blackrock's Larry Fink: The New Conscience of Wall Street?" *Barron's*, June 23, 2018.

234 *"We will be increasingly disposed"*: Ibid.

234 *more than $87 billion's worth of shares:* Patrick Greenfield and Jasper Jolly, "BlackRock Joins Pressure Group Taking on Biggest Polluters," *Guardian*, January 10, 2020.

234 *brushfires in Australia:* Attracta Mooney, "BlackRock Accused of Climate Change Hypocrisy," *Financial Times*, May 17, 2020.

234 *Brazil's largest meatpacking conglomerates:* Robert Mackey, "How Larry Fink, Joe Biden's Wall Street Ally, Profits from Amazon Cattle Ranching, a Force Behind Deforestation," The Intercept, August 30, 2019.

234 *pipeline business controlled by Saudi Aramco:* Davide Barbuscia and Hadeel Al Sayegh, "Saudi Aramco and BlackRock, Others, Discussing Deal Worth over $10 Billion," Reuters, October 13, 2020.

235 *"Something fundamental and profound"*: Alan Murray, "America's CEOs Seek a New Purpose for the Corporation," *Fortune*, August 19, 2019, https://fortune.com/longform/business-roundtable-ceos-corporations-purpose.

236 *"Companies should pay their fair share"*: Klaus Schwab, "What Kind of Capitalism Do We Want?" *Time*, December 2, 2019.

236 *looked past the savage killing:* Mark Landler, "In Extraordinary Statement, Trump Stands with Saudis Despite Kashoggi Killing," *New York Times*, November 21, 2018, p. A1.

237 *"We will not compromise the future"*: Arne Sorenson, interview with Bloomberg TV in Davos, January 21, 2020, https://www.bloomberg.com/news/videos/2020-01-21/marriott-international-ceo-sorenson-on-corporate-stakeholders-culture-video?sref=12wQtvNW.

238 *"There is simply nothing worse"*: "A Message to Marriott International Associates from President and CEO Arne Sorenson," March 20, 2020, https://www.youtube.com/watch?v=SprFgoU6aO0.

239 *$2 trillion to buy back their shares:* Matt Phillips, "The Stock Buyback Binge May Be Over. For Now," *New York Times*, March 25, 2020, p. B4.

240 *Hardly any of the signatories:* Lucien Bebcuk and Roberto Tallarita, "The Illusory Promise of Stakeholder Governance," *Cornell Law Review*, July 1, 2020.

241 *"reallocating resources"*: Aaron Tilley, "Salesforce Notifies Some Staff of Job Cuts," *Dow Jones Institutional News*, August 26, 2020.

243 *less than 3 percent of the workforce:* Rosalie Chan, Benjamin Pimentel, Ashley Stewart, Paayal Zaveri, and Jeff Elder, "The Tech Industry Has a Terrible Track Record on Diversity. Here's How 17 Companies That Spoke Out Against Racism This Week Say They Plan to Improve," *Business Insider*, June 6, 2020.

243 *form of cultural appropriation:* Austin Weinstein, "Salesforce's Hawaii

Obsession Provokes Debate over Appropriation," Bloomberg, September 28, 2018.

CHAPTER 12: **"WE'RE NOT SAFE"**

245   *57 percent more items:* Karen Weise, "Amazon Hires at a Record Clip: 1,400 Per Day," *New York Times,* November 28, 2020, p. A1.

245   *the company shipped 415 million packages:* Frank Holland, "Amazon Is Delivering Nearly Two-Thirds of Its Own Packages as E-commerce Continues Pandemic Boom," CNBC, August 13, 2020.

246   *roughly five hundred thousand employees:* Matt Day, "Amazon Will Hire 75,000 Logistics Workers in Latest Hiring Binge," Bloomberg, May 13, 2021.

246   *double the number of only two years earlier:* Weise, op cit.

246   *a fortune in excess of $200 billion:* Michelle Toh, "Jeff Bezos Is Now Worth a Whopping $200 Billion," *CNN Business,* August 28, 2020, https:// edition.cnn.com/2020/08/27/tech/jeff-bezos-net-worth-200-billion-intl -hnk/index.html.

249   *The United States was one of only a handful:* Jody Heymann, Hye Jin Rho, John Schmitt, and Alison Earle, "Contagion Nation: A Comparison of Paid Sick Day Policies in 22 Countries," Center for Economic and Policy Research, May 2009, https://cepr.net/documents/publications/paid-sick -days-2009-05.pdf.

249   *"We cannot slow the coronavirus outbreak":* Pelosi Statement on Introduction of the Families First Coronavirus Response Act, March 11, 2020, https://pelosi.house.gov/news/press-releases/pelosi-statement-on -introduction-of-the-families-first-coronavirus-response-act.

249   *companies with five hundred or more people:* U.S. Department of Labor, Summary of Families First Coronavirus Response Act, https://www.dol .gov/agencies/whd/pandemic/ffcra-employee-paid-leave.

249   *workers reported not receiving the money:* Caroline O'Donovan, "Amazon Says Employees Quarantined by a Doctor Will Get Paid, but So Far Many Say They Haven't," BuzzFeed News, April 11, 2020, https://www .buzzfeednews.com/article/carolineodonovan/amazon-workers-not -getting-quarantine-pay.

249   *Amazon outsourced the dirty work:* Amazon, 2019 U.S. Political Contribution and Expenditure Policy and Statement, https://s2.q4cdn .com/299287126/files/doc_downloads/governance/2019-Political -Expenditures-Statement.pdf.

251   *"Dear Amazonians":* "A Message from our CEO and Founder," Amazon blog, March 21, 2020, https://blog.aboutamazon.com/company-news/a -message-from-our-ceo-and-founder.

252   *Amazon charged $39.99:* Alex Harman, "Prime Gouging: How Amazon Raised Prices to Profit from the Pandemic," Public Citizen, September 9, 2020, https://www.citizen.org/article/prime-gouging.

252   *Amazon's logistics operation was swamped:* Ron Knox and Shaoul Suss-

man, "How Amazon Used the Pandemic to Amass More Monopoly Power," *The Nation*, June 26, 2020.

254 *flouting an executive order:* Sam Levin, "Revealed: Amazon Told Workers Paid Sick Leave Doesn't Cover Warehouses," *Guardian*, May 7, 2020, https://www.theguardian.com/technology/2020/may/07/amazon-warehouse-workers-coronavirus-time-off-california.

254 *warehouse outside Minneapolis:* Chris Mills Rodrigo, "Amazon Workers Protest Termination of Unlimited Unpaid Time Off Policy," The Hill, April 27, 2020.

254 *many of them immigrants from East Africa:* Matt Day, "Amazon Covid-19 Outbreak in Minnesota Was Worse Than Local County," Bloomberg, June 30, 2020.

254 *rates of infection were much lower:* Daniel Uria, "Amazon Says Nearly 20,000 Workers Have Tested Positive for COVID-19," United Press International, October 1, 2020, https://www.upi.com/Top_News/US/2020/10/01/Amazon-says-nearly-20000-workers-have-tested-positive-for-COVID-19/2551601595828.

254 *Amazon's analysis was fatuous:* Spencer Soper, "Amazon Study of Workers' Covid Is Faulted over Lack of Key Data," *Bloomberg News,* October 6, 2020.

254 *"someone just put a bunch of numbers together":* Ibid.

254 *"He's not smart, or articulate":* Paul Blest, "Leaked Amazon Memo Details Plan to Smear Fired Warehouse Organizer: 'He's Not Smart or Articulate,'" Vice News, April 2, 2020, https://www.vice.com/en_us/article/5dm8bx/leaked-amazon-memo-details-plan-to-smear-fired-warehouse-organizer-hes-not-smart-or-articulate.

255 *"general agreement" among the participants:* Ibid.

256 *sophisticated methods to assess their performance:* Jodi Kantor, Karen Weise, and Grace Ashford, "The Amazon That Customers Don't See," *New York Times,* June 15, 2021.

256 *an activist shareholder:* David Sirota, "Amazon & Trump Agency Blocked Worker Safety Initiative Amid Pandemic," *TMI,* May 1, 2020, https://sirota.substack.com/p/scoop-amazon-and-trump-agency-blocked.

257 *The initiative disappeared:* Ibid.

257 *"fungible units of pick-and-pack potential":* Tim Bray, "Bye Amazon," a blog post, May 4, 2020, https://www.tbray.org/ongoing/When/202x/2020/04/29/Leaving-Amazon#p-3.

257 *faux guillotine:* Emily Kirkpatrick, "There's Now a Guillotine Set Up Outside Jeff Bezos's Mansion," *Vanity Fair,* August 28, 2020, https://www.vanityfair.com/style/2020/08/jeff-bezos-guillotine-protest-amazon-workers.

257 *job listings for intelligence analysts:* Robert Hackett, "After Public Outcry, Amazon Deletes Listings for 2 Intelligence Jobs That Involved Tracking 'Labor Organizing Threats,'" *Fortune,* September 1, 2020, https://fortune.com/2020/09/01/amazon-anti-union-jobs-tracking-labor-organizing-threats-jeff-bezos.

257 *touting the company's achievements:* Nicolas Reimann, "Amazon Sent out a Scripted News Segment, and 11 Stations Aired It," *Forbes,* May 26, 2020, https://www.forbes.com/sites/nicholasreimann/2020/05/26/amazon-sent-out-a-scripted-news-segment-and-11-stations-aired-it/#51b7d878 48b9.

CHAPTER 13: **"THIS IS KILLING PEOPLE"**

261 *40 percent of the Lombardy market:* Andrea Sparaciari, "San Raffaele: dopo l'inchiesta sulla truffa da 10 milioni, scoppa il caso dei bilanci segreti. E per salvarsi chiama Maroni," *Business Insider Italia,* July 2, 2020, https://it.businessinsider.com/san-raffaele-inchiesta-truffa-da-10-milioni-sbilanci-segreti-maroni/amp.

261 *Italy was spending far less on health care:* OECD.Stat, Health expenditure data, 2019, https://stats.oecd.org/Index.aspx?ThemeTreeId=9.

261 *impact on intensive care units:* Rapporto Sanita 2018, 40 Anni del Servizio Sanitario Nazionale, p. 16, https://programmazionesanitaria.it/_progsan/2018/SSN40-Rapporto.pdf.

262 *Milan's San Raffaele Hospital:* Stefano Colombo, "Quanto ci vuole a prenotare una visita medica in Lombardia? Dipende da quanto potete pagare," The Submarine, June 29, 2020, https://thesubmarine.it/2020/06/29/prenotare-visita-lombardia-attesa.

262 *gifts and vacations at exclusive Caribbean resorts:* Gianluca Di Feo and Michele Sasso, "Formigoni re delle Antille," *L'Espresso,* April 19, 2012, https://espresso.repubblica.it/palazzo/2012/04/19/news/formigoni-re-delle-antille-1.42330.

262 *70 million euros:* "Processo Maugeri, '70 milioni die euro tolti ai malati per i sollazzi di Formigoni,'" *il Fatto Quotidiano,* September 20, 2016, https://www.ilfattoquotidiano.it/2016/09/20/processo-maugeri-70-milioni-di-euro-tolti-ai-malati-per-i-sollazzi-di-formigoni/3046192.

262 *seized his yacht:* Luigi Ferrarella and Giuseppe Guastella, "Maugeri, sequestrati yacht, immobili, denaro e vino pregiato per oltre 60 milioni di euro," *Corriere Della Sera,* July 16, 2012, https://milano.corriere.it/milano/notizie/cronaca/12_luglio_16/san-raffaele-sequestro-2011024259999.shtml.

263 *counterparts at major pharmaceutical companies:* Andrea Sparaciari, "San Raffaele: dopo l'inchiesta sulla truffa da 10 milioni, scoppa il caso dei bilanci segreti. E per salvarsi chiama Maroni," *Business Insider Italia,* July 2, 2020.

264 *Italy's most influential business lobby:* Jason Horowitz, "The Lost Days That Made Bergamo a Coronavirus Tragedy," *New York Times,* November 30, 2020, p. A1.

264 *"Family doctors are a cost":* Peter S. Goodman and Gaia Pianigiani, "Why COVID Caused Such Suffering in Italy's Wealthiest Region," *New York Times,* November 21, 2020, p. B1.

265 *twenty thousand more deaths:* Talha Burki, "England and Wales See 20,000 Excess Deaths in Care Homes," *Lancet,* May 23, 2020.

266 *secret VIP lane:* Jane Bradley, Selam Gebrekidan, and Allison McCann, "Waste, Negligence and Cronyism: Inside Britain's Pandemic Spending," *New York Times,* December 17, 2020.

267 *"Without locking down":* Tucker Carlson monologue, "Are Coronavirus Lockdowns Working?" Fox News, April 22, 2020, https://www.youtube .com/watch?v=MuuA0azQRGQ.

267 *Sweden had gained essentially nothing:* Peter S. Goodman, "Sweden Has Become the World's Cautionary Tale," *New York Times,* July 8, 2020, p. A1.

267 *again sending Swedes to hospitals:* Jon Henley, "Swedish Surge in Covid Cases Dashes Immunity Hopes," *Guardian,* November 12, 2020.

268 *pursuing so-called herd immunity:* Jon Henley, "Sweden's Covid-19 Strategist Under Fire over Herd Immunity Emails," *Guardian,* August 17, 2020, https://www.theguardian.com/world/2020/aug/17/swedens-covid-19 -strategist-under-fire-over-herd-immunity-emails.

269 *Only the Netherlands and Norway:* "Key Issues in Long Term Care Policy," OECD, https://www.oecd.org/els/health-systems/long-term-care.htm.

272 *hospital beds in Sweden:* OECD data on hospital beds, https://data.oecd .org/healtheqt/hospital-beds.htm.

274 *"money on drinks and women":* Silvia Amaro, "Dijsselbloem Under Fire After Saying Southern Europe Wasted Money on 'Drinks and Women,'" CNBC, March 22, 2017.

275 *Germany ensured that ordinary households:* Joseph E. Stiglitz, *The Euro: How a Common Currency Threatens the Future of Europe* (New York: W. W. Norton & Co., 2018), 201–3.

275 *"One can at least ask":* Peter Conradi, "EU Plans for Virus Bailouts Rejected by 'Frugal Four' States," *Sunday Times* (London), May 24, 2020.

275 *Spain's morgues were overflowing:* Al Goodman, Laura Perez Maestro, Ingrid Formanek, Max Ramsay, and Ivana Kottasova, "Spain Turns Ice Rink into a Morgue as Coronavirus Deaths Pile Up," CNN, March 24, 2020, https://edition.cnn.com/2020/03/24/europe/spain-ice-rink-morgue -coronavirus-intl/index.html.

275 *Italians were denied funerals:* Jason Horowitz and Emma Bubola, "Italy's Coronavirus Victims Face Death Alone, with Funerals Postponed," *New York Times,* March 17, 2020, p. A1.

275 *borrowing collectively:* Matina Stevis-Gridneff, "E.U. Adopts Groundbreaking Stimulus to Fight Coronavirus Recession," *New York Times,* July 22, 2020, p. A1.

276 *the lion's share of wages:* Peter S. Goodman, Patricia Cohen, and Rachel Chaundler, "European Workers Draw Paychecks. American Workers Scrounge for Food," *New York Times,* July 4, 2020, p. A1.

276 *Boris Johnson called for spending:* Peter S. Goodman, "With a Torrent of Money, Britain Takes Aim at Coronavirus and Austerity," *New York Times,* March 12, 2020, p. A18.

277   *measures worth 750 billion euros:* Peter S. Goodman, "Europe's Leaders Ditch Austerity and Fight Pandemic with Cash," *New York Times,* March 26, 2020, p. A6.

277   *"keep debt under control":* Andrew Atkinson and David Goodman, "U.K. Budget Deficit Narrows to Almost Half of Pandemic Level," Bloomberg, August 20, 2021.

278   *British Business Bank:* Michael Pooler and Robert Smith, "Treasury Under Fire over Disclosure Silence on Virus Loans," *Financial Times,* August 24, 2020.

278   *£350 million's worth of government-backed loans:* Ibid.

278   *That money had enabled Gupta:* John Collingridge, "Follow the Money? It Isn't Easy in Sanjeev Gupta's Empire," *Sunday Times* (London), March 15, 2020.

278   *Greensill was aware:* BBC Panorama, August 9, 2021.

279   *paying him more than £ 1.2 million:* Ibid.

279   *revoked Greensill's participation:* Mark Kleinman, "Greensill Stripped of Government Guarantee on Loans to Steel Tycoon Gupta," Sky News, March 1, 2021, https://news.sky.com/story/greensill-stripped-of-government-guarantee-on-loans-to-steel-tycoon-gupta-12233039.

279   *EasyJet, a discount airline:* "Coronavirus: EasyJet Plans up to 4,500 Job Cuts," BBC, May 28, 2020, https://www.bbc.co.uk/news/business-52830665.

279   *dividends for shareholders:* "Easyjet Seeks State Loans—But Pays Stelios £60 Million," *Times* (London), March 20, 2020.

279   *£300 million infusion:* Philip Georgiadis, "BA to Drop Controversial 'Fire and Rehire' Plan for Thousands of Staff," *Financial Times,* September 16, 2020.

280   *credit from the Bank of England:* Simon Duke, "Big Beneficiaries of COVID-19 Loan Scheme Paid No Corporation Tax," *Times* (London), June 6, 2020.

280   *"We expect to benefit":* Merlin Entertainments Limited, COVID-19 Update Statement, April 7, 2020, http://northeurope.blob.euroland.com/press-releases-attachments/1206630/Publication-COVID-19-Update-Statement-_2020-04-07.pdf.

280   *"substantially all of our Attractions":* Merlin Entertainments Limited, 2019 Annual Report, Exhibit A, http://northeurope.blob.euroland.com/press-releases-attachments/1219498/Publication-Announcement-2019-Annual-Report-Other-Information-_2020-04-24.pdf.

280   *it needed £12 million per month:* Merlin Entertainments, 2019 Annual Report, p. 38, https://www.merlinentertainments.biz/media/3068/merlin-entertainments-annual-report-and-accounts-2019.pdf.

281   *"We entered this crisis":* Chibuike Oguh, "Blackstone's First-Quarter Profit Rises but Coronavirus Weighs," Reuters, April 23, 2020.

281   *sitting on $150 billion:* Heather Perlberg, "Steve Schwarzman Sees Virus Wiping $5 Trillion From GDP," Bloomberg, April 7, 2020.

CHAPTER 14: "IS THIS A TIME TO PROFIT?"

285 *"Get it done, Daniel":* "Remarks by President Trump and Members of the Coronavirus Task Force in Meeting with Pharmaceutical Companies," March 2, 2020, video via C-Span, https://www.c-span.org /video/?469926-1/president-trump-meeting-pharmaceutical-executives -coronavirus.

287 *World Health Organization panel:* "Informal Consultation on Prioritization of Candidate Therapeutic Agents for Use in Novel Coronavirus 2019 Infection," World Health Organization, R&D Blueprint, January 24, 2020, p. 9, https://apps.who.int/iris/handle/10665/330680.

287 *"trying to develop this medicine":* Biopharmaceutical response to COVID-19, PhRMA press event, March 6, 2020, https://www.youtube .com/watch?v=e951H8uSesM.

287 *all financed research projects:* Kathryn Ardizzone, "Role of the Federal Government in the Development of GS-5734/Remdesivir," Knowledge Ecology International, Briefing Note 2020:1, https://www.keionline.org /BN-2020-1.

288 *"an unconscionable abuse":* Letter to Daniel O'Day from consumer advocacy groups, March 25, 2020, https://www.citizen.org/wp-content /uploads/Letter-from-50-groups-to-Gilead-renounce-remdesivir-orphan -drug-claim.pdf.

288 *$60 million in grants:* Ibid.

288 *$6.5 billion's worth:* Ekaterina Galkina Cleary, Matthew J. Jackson, Zoe Folchman-Wagner, and Fred D. Ledley, "Foundational Research and NIH Funding Enabling Emergency Use Authorization of Remdesivir for COVID-19," Center for Integration of Science and Industry, Bentley University, preprinted paper, https://www.medrxiv.org/content/10.1101/20 20.07.01.20144576v1.full.pdf+html.

288 *ultimate angel investor:* Ekaterina Galkina Cleary, Matthew J. Jackson, and Fred D. Ledley, "Government as the First Investor in Biopharmaceutical Innovation: Evidence from New Drug Approvals 2010–2019," Institute for New Economic Thinking, Working Paper No. 133, August 5, 2020, https://www.ineteconomics.org/uploads/papers/WP_133-Cleary-et-al -Govt-innovation.pdf.

289 *revenues of nearly $12 trillion:* Ibid.

289 *nearly quadrupled in price:* Mary Caffrey, "JAMA: List Prices for Key Drugs More Than Doubled over 10-Year Period," *JAMA,* March 3, 2020.

289 *One in four Americans:* Deb Chaarushena and Gregory Curfman, "Relentless Prescription Drug Price Increases," *JAMA,* March 3, 2020.

289 *"Those who are bold":* William Lazonick, Matt Hopkins, Ken Jacobson, Mustafa Erdem Sakinç, and Öner Tulum, "U.S. Pharma's Financialized Business Model," Institute for New Economic Thinking, Working Paper No. 60, July 13, 2017, https://www.ineteconomics.org/uploads/papers /WP_60-Lazonick-et-al-US-Pharma-Business-Model.pdf.

289   *99 percent of their profits:* Ibid.

289   *a record $29 million:* Jessie Hellmann, "PhRMA Spent Record-High $29 Million on Lobbying in 2019," The Hill, January 22, 2020, https://thehill .com/policy/healthcare/479403-phrma-spent-record-high-29-million -lobbying-congress-trump-administration.

289   *$1 billion in compensation:* Lazonick et. al., op. cit.

290   *the most serious cases:* Olga Khazan, "The True Cost of an Expensive Medication," *The Atlantic,* September 25, 2015, https://www.theatlantic .com/health/archive/2015/09/an-expensive-medications-human -cost/407299.

290   *less than 3 percent:* Staff report from United States Senate Committee on Finance, "The Price of Sovaldi and Its Impact on the U.S. Health Care System," December 2015, p. 82, https://www.finance.senate.gov/imo/media /doc/1%20The%20Price%20of%20Sovaldi%20and%20Its%20Impact%20 on%20the%20U.S.%20Health%20Care%20System%20(Full%20Report) .pdf.

290   *exploiting tax loopholes:* William Rice and Frank Clemente, "Gilead Sciences: Price Gouger, Tax Dodger," Americans for Tax Fairness, July 2016, https://americansfortaxfairness.org/files/ATF-Gilead-Report-Finalv3 -for-Web.pdf.

292   *not paying a dime in royalties:* Christopher Rowland, "An HIV Treatment Cost Taxpayers Millions. The Government Patented It. But a Pharma Giant Is Making Billions," *Washington Post,* March 26, 2019.

292   *"If we had lowered":* Transcript of hearing before the Committee on the Oversight and Reform, U.S. House of Representatives, May 16, 2019, Serial No. 116–24, https://www.congress.gov/event/116th-congress/house -event/LC64021/text?s=1&r=55.

293   *its benefits in limiting death:* "NIH Clinical Trial Shows Remdesivir Accelerates Recovery from Advanced COVID-19," NIH News Release, April 29, 2020, https://www.nih.gov/news-events/news-releases/nih-clinical -trial-shows-remdesivir-accelerates-recovery-advanced-covid-19.

293   *"as quickly as they can":* Joseph Walker, "U.S. Explores Emergency-Use Approval for Gilead Drug After Study Found It Helped Recovery from COVID-19," *Wall Street Journal,* April 29, 2020.

293   *"a tremendous responsibility":* "Remarks by President Trump in Announcement on Remdesivir," White House, May 1, 2020, https://www .whitehouse.gov/briefings-statements/remarks-president-trump -announcement-remdesivir.

293   *"reasonable" prices for drugs:* Tinker Ready, "NIH to Watch Drug Prices After AZT 'Mistake,'" *HealthWeek,* September 25, 1989.

293   *the NIH rescinded its rule:* Warren E. Leary, "U.S. Gives Up Right to Control Drug Prices," *New York Times,* April 12, 1995, p. A23.

293   *"Eliminating the clause":* National Institutes of Health, Public Health Service, news release, April 11, 1995, https://www.ott.nih.gov/sites/default /files/documents/pdfs/NIH-Notice-Rescinding-Reasonable-Pricing -Clause.pdf.

294 *a senator from Delaware:* Roll Call Vote, 106th Congress—2nd Session, Vote Number 168, June 30, 2000, https://www.senate.gov/legislative/LIS/roll_call_lists/roll_call_vote_cfm.cfm?congress=106&-session=2&vote=00168#position; as cited in Ryan Grim and Aída Chávez, "How the Senate Paved the Way for Coronavirus Profiteering, and How Congress Could Undo It," The Intercept, March 2, 2020.

294 *"as many patients as possible":* "An Open Letter from Daniel O'Day, Chairman & CEO Gilead Sciences," *Business Wire,* June 29, 2020.

294 *Gilead could have charged:* Melanie D. Whittington and Jonathan D. Campbell, "Alternative Pricing Models for Remdesivir and Other Potential Treatments for COVID-19," Institute for Clinical and Economic Review, May 1, 2020.

294 *so-called march-in rights:* Manojna Maddipatla and Michael Erman, "State Attorneys General Urge U.S. to Let Other Firms Make Gilead COVID-19 Drug," Reuters, August 4, 2020, https://uk.reuters.com/article/us-health-coronavirus-remdesivir/state-attorneys-general-urge-u-s-to-let-other-firms-make-gilead-covid-19-drug-idUKKCN250248.

295 *nearly seventy countries:* Data from Global Trade Alert project at the University of St. Gallen in Switzerland.

295 *the world's largest producer:* Forum Bhatt, "India-China Standoff Threatens to Disrupt World's Biggest Exporter of Generic Drugs," Bloomberg, July 2, 2020.

296 *Schwab used a blog post:* Klaus Schwab, "India's Opportunity in a Multiconceptual World," World Economic Forum, January 9, 2018, https://www.weforum.org/agenda/2018/01/india-opportunity-in-a-multiconceptual-world.

296 *offering to pay a bounty:* Vidhi Doshi, "Indian Politician Offers $1.5M Bounty for Beheading of Top Bollywood Star Deepika Paukone," November 21, 2017, https://www.independent.co.uk/arts-entertainment/films/news/india-bollywood-beheading-bounty-deepika-padukone-padmavati-surajpal-amu-sanjay-leela-bhansali-hinduism-offence-a8066566.html.

297 *13 percent in China:* Testimony of Janet Woodcock, Director, Center for Drug Evaluation and Research, Food and Drug Administration, Department of Health and Human Services, before the Subcommittee on Oversight and Investigations, Committee on Energy and Commerce, U.S. House of Representatives, December 10, 2019, https://www.congress.gov/116/meeting/house/110317/witnesses/HHRG-116-IF02-Wstate-WoodcockMDM-20191210.pdf.

297 *the source of 90 percent:* Interview with Rosemary Gibson, health care expert at the Hastings Center, April 6, 2020.

297 *he had accused China:* "White House Adviser Navarro Lashes Out at China Over 'Fake' Test Kits," Reuters, April 27, 2020, https://www.reuters.com/article/us-health-coronavirus-usa-china-idUSKCN2292S8.

297 *He held off on signing:* Jeff Stein, Robert Costa, and Josh Dawsey, "White House Aides Torn over Trade Hawk's Proposal as President Trump Weighs Action on China," *Washington Post,* April 29, 2020.

297 *prioritize American suppliers:* Maegan Vazquez, "Trump Signs 'Buy American First' Pharma Executive Order," CNN Wire, August 6, 2020.

299 *offered CureVac $1 billion:* Katrin Bennhold and David E. Sanger, "U.S. Offered 'Large Sum' to German Company for Access to Coronavirus Vaccine Research, German Officials Say," *New York Times,* March 16, 2020, p. A12.

299 *They crafted a counterbid:* Ibid.

299 *an overture from the European Union:* "Coronavirus: UK Rejects Chance to Join EU's COVID-19 Vaccine Scheme," *Euronews,* October 7, 2020, https://www.euronews.com/2020/07/03/coronavirus-uk-considering -whether-to-join-eu-s-vaccine-scheme-as-race-is-on-to-secure-sup.

300 *to spur domestic production:* U.S. Department of Health and Human Services press release, October 13, 2020, https://www.hhs.gov/about /news/2020/10/13/trump-administration-expands-manufacturing -capacity-cytiva-components-covid-19-vaccines.html.

301 *In February 2021:* Hannah Kuchler, "Pfizer Expects $15bn in COVID Vaccine Revenue This Year," *Financial Times,* February 2, 2021.

301 *$26 billion's worth of COVID-19 vaccines:* Rebecca Robbins and Peter S. Goodman, "Pfizer Reaps Hundreds of Millions in Profit from COVID Vaccine," *New York Times,* May 5, 2021, p. B1.

301 *a deal with Canada:* Ibid.

301 *"a constant negotiation":* Stephanie Baker, Cynthia Koons, and Vernon Silver, "Inside Pfizer's Fast, Fraught, and Lucrative Vaccine Distribution," *Bloomberg Businessweek,* March 4, 2021.

301 *the desperation of Israeli prime minister:* Ibid.

301 *50 percent higher:* Ibid.

301 *denied access to Palestinians:* Reality Check, "COVID-19: Palestinians Lag Behind in Vaccine Efforts as Infections Rise," BBC, March 22, 2021, https://www.bbc.co.uk/news/55800921.

301 *more vaccine doses than it needed:* Megan Twohey, Keith Collins, and Katie Thomas, "With First Dibs on Vaccines, Rich Countries Have 'Cleared the Shelves,'" *New York Times,* December 16, 2020, p. A6.

302 *"ready to save humanity":* Geeta Mohan, "India Ready to Save Humanity with 2 Made in India COVID Vaccines, Says PM Modi," *India Today,* January 9, 2021, https://www.indiatoday.in/india/story/india-ready-to -save-humanity-with-2-made-in-india-covid-vaccines-says-pm-modi-17 57390-2021-01-09.

302 *all but cut off exports:* Jeffrey Gettleman, Emily Schmall, and Mujib Mashal, "India Cuts Back on Vaccine Exports as Infections Surge at Home," *New York Times,* March 26, 2021, p. A7.

302 *That deprived poor countries:* Ibid.

302 *halted its vaccine distribution:* Ibid.

303 *"The world is on the brink":* WHO Director-General's opening remarks at 148th session of the Executive Board, January 18, 2021, https:// www.who.int/director-general/speeches/detail/who-director-general-s -opening-remarks-at-148th-session-of-the-executive-board.

303 *"'Is this a time to profit?'"*: Peter S. Goodman, "One Vaccine Side Effect: Global Economic Inequality," *New York Times*, December 26, 2020, p. A1.

304 *"IP [intellectual property] protection"*: Peter S. Goodman, Apoorva Mandavilli, Rebecca Robbins, and Matina Stevis-Gridneff, "What Would It Take to Vaccinate the World Against COVID?" *New York Times*, May 16, 2021, p. A1.

304 *"It didn't destroy them"*: Ibid.

305 *"We share the mission"*: Pfizer press release, January 22, 2021, https://www.pfizer.com/news/press-release/press-release-detail/pfizer-and-biontech-reach-agreement-covax-advance-purchase.

305 *Pfizer was on track:* Pfizer, Inc., Earnings Call Transcript for Q4 2020, February 2, 2021, transcript posted on Seeking Alpha, https://seekingalpha.com/article/4402872-pfizer-inc-pfe-ceo-dr-albert-bourla-on-q4-2020-results-earnings-call-transcript.

305 *broke with the pharmaceutical lobby:* Thomas Kaplan, Sheryl Gay Stolberg, and Rebecca Robbins, "Taking 'Extraordinary Measures,' Biden Backs Suspending Patents on Vaccines," *New York Times*, May 6, 2021, p. A1.

307 *Covax had delivered:* Maria Cheng and Lori Hinnant, "Rich Nations Dip into COVAX Supply While Poor Wait for Shots," Associated Press, August 14, 2021, https://apnews.com/article/joe-biden-middle-east-africa-europe-coronavirus-pandemic-5e57879c6cb22d96b942cbc973b9296c.

307 *Only 2 percent:* Abdi Latif Dahir, "Booster Shots 'Make a Mockery of Vaccine Equity,' the W.H.O.'s Africa Director Says," *New York Times*, August 20, 2021, p. A10.

307 *"a mockery of vaccine equity"*: Ibid.

308 *a $3.5 billion purchase:* Megan Specia, Sharon LaFraniere, Noah Weiland, and Michael D. Shear, "Addressing the Global Vaccine Shortage, Biden Cites 'Our Humanitarian Obligation to Save as Many Lives as We Can,'" *New York Times*, June 10, 2021.

308 *a "not for profit" price:* Ibid.

308 *the company raised the prices:* Donato Paolo Mancini, Hannah Kuchler, and Mehreen Khan, "Pfizer and Moderna Raise EU Covid Vaccine Prices," *Financial Times*, August 1, 2021.

308 *more than $33 billion:* Ibid.

CHAPTER 15: **"WE WILL GET 100 PERCENT OF OUR CAPITAL BACK"**

313 *a Trump-branded golf course:* Peter S. Goodman, "Late Wages for Migrant Workers at a Trump Golf Course in Dubai," *New York Times*, August 27, 2017, p. B4.

313 *migrant workers worldwide:* "World Bank Predicts Sharpest Decline of Remittances in Recent History," World Bank, April 22, 2020, https://www.worldbank.org/en/news/press-release/2020/04/22/world-bank-predicts-sharpest-decline-of-remittances-in-recent-history.

314 *a state of extreme poverty:* World Bank data, updated October 7, 2020, https://www.worldbank.org/en/topic/poverty/overview.

314 *life-threatening levels of malnutrition:* "COVID-19 Will Double Number of People Facing Food Crises Unless Swift Action Is Taken," World Food Program, April 21, 2020, https://www.wfp.org/news/covid-19-will -double-number-people-facing-food-crises-unless-swift-action-taken.

314 *Pakistan, for example:* Jubilee Debt Campaign, Debt Data Portal, https:// data.jubileedebt.org.uk.

314 *a relative pittance:* Peter S. Goodman, "How the Wealthy World Has Failed Poor Countries During the Pandemic," *New York Times,* November 2, 2020, p. B1.

315 *World Bank had more than doubled:* Julian Duggan, Scott Morris, Justin Sandefur, and George Yang, "Is the World Bank's COVID-19 Crisis Lending Big Enough, Fast Enough? New Evidence on Loan Disbursements," Center for Global Development, Working Paper 554, October 2020, https://www.cgdev.org/publication/world-banks-covid-crisis-lending -big-enough-fast-enough-new-evidence-loan-disbursements.

315 *immediate debt payments:* Iolanda Fresnillo, "Shadow Report on the Limitations of the G20 Debt Service Suspension Initiative: Draining Out the Titanic with a bucket?" European Network on Debt and Development, October 14, 2020, https://www.eurodad.org/g20_dssi_shadow _report.

315 *"If private capital is unavoidable":* Letter from Timothy Adams, president and CEO of the Institute of International Finance, to finance minister of Saudi Arabia Mohammed Al-Jadaan, September 22, 2020, https://www .iif.com/Portals/0/Files/content/Regulatory/IIF%20Letter%20to%20 G20%20on%20DSSI%20Sept%202020.pdf.

316 *"troubled sovereign borrowers":* Ibid., https://www.iif.com/Portals/0 /Files/content/Regulatory/IIF%20Letter%20to%20G20%20on%20D SSI%20Sept%202020.pdf.

317 *higher per capita income:* Vito Tanzi, *Argentina from Peron to Macri: An Economic Chronicle* (Bethesda, Maryland: Jorge Pinto Books, 2018), Chapter One.

317 *Argentina defaulted:* Todd Benson, "Report Looks Harshly at I.M.F.'s Role in Argentine Debt Crisis," *New York Times,* July 30, 2004, p. W1.

318 *"trying to change the future":* Larry Fink at event hosted by Americas Society/Council of the Americas, June 29, 2016, https://www.youtube .com/watch?v=TM_MC2Fj-JI.

319 *the largest bailout in its history:* Jason Lange and Hugh Bronstein, "IMF Increases Argentina Financing Deal to $56.3 Billion," Reuters, October 26, 2018, https://uk.reuters.com/article/us-argentina-imf/imf-increases -argentina-financing-deal-to-56-3-billion-idUKKCN1N02GK.

320 *"Argentina's private creditors":* "Argentina: Technical Assistance Report-Staff Technical Note on Debt Sustainability," International Monetary Fund, Western Hemisphere Department, March 20, 2020, https://www.imf.org /en/Publications/CR/Issues/2020/03/20/Argentina-Technical-Assistance -Report-Staff-Technical-Note-on-Public-Debt-Sustainability-49284.

321　***$1 billion's worth of bonds:*** Elkon financial data platform, cited in "Under the Radar: Private Sector Debt and the Coronavirus in Developing Countries," a paper from several aid organizations including Oxfam, October 2020, https://www.oxfam.org/en/research/under-radar-private-sector-debt-and-coronavirus-developing-countries.

323　***"Argentina has presented":*** Hugh Bronstein, "Nobelist Stiglitz, Economists from 20 Countries Back Argentina in Debt Showdown," Reuters, May 6, 2020.

324　***fresh analysis from the IMF:*** "IMF Staff Technical Statement on Argentina," International Monetary Fund, Press Release No. 20/228, June 1, 2020, https://www.imf.org/en/News/Articles/2020/06/01/pr20228-argentina-imf-staff-technical-statement.

324　***an Argentine naval vessel:*** Jacob Goldstein, "Why a Hedge Fund Seized an Argentine Navy Ship in Ghana," National Public Radio, October 22, 2012, https://www.npr.org/sections/money/2012/10/22/163384810/why-a-hedge-fund-seized-an-argentine-navy-ship-in-ghana?t=1604295241384.

324　***paying out $2.4 billion:*** Gregory Zuckerman, Julie Wernau, and Rob Copeland, "After 15 Years, a Bond Trade Now Pays Off," *Wall Street Journal*, March 2, 2016.

325　***fifty-five cents on the dollar:*** Scott Squires and Jorgelina Do Rosario, "Argentina Bonds Rally After $65 Billion Restructuring Deal," Bloomberg, August 4, 2020.

326　***"100 percent of our capital back":*** "BlackRock's Fink Says Argentina Won't Soon Regain Investor Trust," *Buenos Aires Times,* November 6, 2020, https://www.batimes.com.ar/news/economy/blackrocks-fink-says-argentina-wont-soon-regain-investor-trust.phtml.

CHAPTER 16: **"NOT SOMEBODY WHO IS GOING TO DISRUPT WASHINGTON"**

331　***Schwarzman defended Trump's right:*** Andrew Edgecliffe-Johnson and Mark Vandevelde, "Schwarzman Defended Trump at CEO Meeting on Election Results," *Financial Times,* November 14, 2020.

333　***"It's not going to require legislation":*** Press pool report for Biden fundraiser, July 20, 2020.

333　***"coming in to disrupt Washington":*** Annie Linskey and Sean Sullivan, "Biden's Still Locked in a Bitter Fight. But the Jockeying Is Already Underway for Jobs in His Would-Be Administration," *Washington Post,* November 1, 2020.

336　***including the CARES Act:*** Brian Schwartz, "Amazon Hires Lobbyist Brother of Biden White House Counselor," CNBC, December 28, 2020.

337　***more than one-fourth lower:*** David Cooper, "Raising the Federal Minimum Wage to $15 by 2024 Would Lift Pay for Nearly 40 Million Workers," Economic Policy Institute, February 5, 2019, https://www.epi.org/publication/raising-the-federal-minimum-wage-to-15-by-2024-would-lift-pay-for-nearly-40-million-workers.

CHAPTER 17: "THE MONEY IS RIGHT THERE IN THE COMMUNITY NOW"

342   *Five years later:* Data compiled by Center for Local Economic Strategies.

344   *more than 300 to 1:* Lawrence Mishel and Jori Kandra, "CEO Compensation Surged 14% in 2019 to $21.3 Million," Economic Policy Institute, August 18, 2020, https://www.epi.org/publication/ceo-compensation-surged-14-in-2019-to-21-3-million-ceos-now-earn-320-times-as-much-as-a-typical-worker.

344   *$3 trillion in assets:* Steven Deller, Ann Hoyt, Brent Hueth, and Reka Sundaram-Stukel, "Research on the Economic Impact of Cooperatives," University of Wisconsin Center for Cooperatives, 2009, https://resources.uwcc.wisc.edu/Research/REIC_FINAL.pdf.

348   *the formerly incarcerated:* Lucius Couloute and Daniel Kopf, "Out of Prison & Out of Work: Unemployment Among Formerly Incarcerated People," Prison Policy Initiative, July 2018, https://www.prisonpolicy.org/reports/outofwork.html.

CHAPTER 18: "PUT MONEY IN PEOPLE'S POCKETS"

352   *"a precious asset":* Guy Standing, *Basic Income: And How We Can Make It Happen* (London: Pelican, 2017).

353   *a basic income program:* Peter S. Goodman, "Free Cash to Fight Inequality? California City Is First in U.S. to Try," *New York Times,* June 3, 2018, p. BU1.

355   *survey from the Federal Reserve:* "Report on the Economic Well-Being of U.S. Households in 2018," Board of Governors of the Federal Reserve System, May 2019, https://www.federalreserve.gov/publications/2019-economic-well-being-of-us-households-in-2018-dealing-with-unexpected-expenses.htm.

355   *up to $10,000 a month:* Rob Berger, "Does Joe Biden's Choice of Kamala Harris Signal Support for a $2,000 Monthly Stimulus Check?" *Forbes,* August 12, 2020.

355   *"We may have to think":* Nancy Pelosi, interview on MSNBC, April 27, 2020, https://www.msnbc.com/stephanie-ruhle/watch/pelosi-says-guaranteed-income-may-be-worth-considering-amid-coronavirus-hardships-82606661627.

356   *has been gaining adherents:* See, for example, Pavlina R. Tcherneva, *The Case for a Job Guarantee* (Cambridge, U.K.: Polity Press, 2020).

358   *"The most affluent":* Thomas Paine, "Agrarian Justice," 1797, accessed via Wikisource, https://en.wikisource.org/wiki/Agrarian_Justice.

358   *"it is a right":* Ibid.

359   *"The time has come":* Martin Luther King Jr., *Where Do We Go from Here: Chaos or Community?* (Boston: Beacon Press, 1967), as cited in Jordan Weissman, "Martin Luther King's Economic Dream: A Guaranteed Income for All Americans," *The Atlantic,* August 28, 2013.

359   *might run $20 billion:* Ibid.

360   *"As business leaders"*: Marc Benioff, "How Business Leaders Can Help Narrow Income Inequality," *Fortune*, January 17, 2017.

361   *Finland's spending*: OECD.org, public unemployment spending.

363   *They were less likely*: Tera Allas, Jukka Maksimainen, James Manyika, and Navjot Singh, "An Experiment to Inform Universal Basic Income," McKinsey & Company, Public and Social Sector Practice, September 2020, https://www.mckinsey.com/~/media/McKinsey/Industries/Public%20 and%20Social%20Sector/Our%20Insights/An%20experiment%20to%20 inform%20universal%20basic%20income/An-experiment-to-inform -universal-basic-income-vF.pdf.

364   *Finland opted not to go*: Peter S. Goodman, "Finland Has Second Thoughts About Giving Free Money to Jobless People," *New York Times*, April 24, 2018.

364   *Stockton, California, released the findings*: Annie Lowrey, "Stockton's Basic-Income Experiment Pays Off," *The Atlantic*, March 3, 2021.

364   *subsidized childcare*: Peter S. Goodman, "Cuts to Child Care Subsidy Thwart More Job Seekers," *New York Times*, May 24, 2010, p. A1.

365   *the job-training classes*: Peter S. Goodman, "'Back at Square One': As States Repurpose Welfare Funds, More Families Fall Through Safety Net," HuffPost, June 19, 2012, https://www.huffingtonpost.co.uk/entry /breakdown-tanf-needy-families-states_n_1606242?ri18n=true.

365   *poor families with children*: Ibid.

365   *Congress cut funding*: Isaac Shapiro, David Reich, Chloe Cho, and Richard Kogan, "Trump Budget Would Cut Block Grants Dramatically, Underscoring Danger of Block-Granting Social Program," Center on Budget and Policy Priorities, March 28, 2017, https://www.cbpp.org/research /federal-budget/trump-budget-would-cut-block-grants-dramatically -underscoring-danger-of.

366   *"we will make work pay"*: Andrew Osborn, "Osborne Tries to Limit Welfare Overhaul Fallout," Reuters, April 2, 2013, https://www.reuters .com/article/uk-britain-politics-welfare/osborne-tries-to-limit-welfare -overhaul-fallout-idUKBRE9310N920130402.

366   *low-income people suffered*: Pascale Bourquin, Robert Joyce, and Agnes Norris Keiller, "Living Standards, Poverty and Inequality in the UK: 2020," Institute for Fiscal Studies, p. 15, https://ifs.org.uk/uploads/R170 -Living-standards-poverty-and-inequality-in-the-UK-2019-2020%20 .pdf.

366   *the share of British children*: Ibid., p. 20.

367   *American parents would receive*: Jason DeParle, "In the Stimulus Bill, a Policy Revolution in Aid for Children," *New York Times*, March 8, 2021, p. A1.

367   *reduce child poverty*: "Child Poverty Drops in July with the Child Tax Credit Expansion," Center on Poverty & Social Policy at Columbia University, August 20, 2021, https://www.povertycenter.columbia.edu/news -internal/monthly-poverty-july-2021.

CHAPTER 19: **"AT WAR AGAINST MONOPOLY POWER"**

369   *attempts to break up:* Cecilia Kang and David McCabe, "House Lawmak-
       ers Condemn Big Tech's 'Monopoly Power' and Urge Their Breakups," *New
       York Times,* October 7, 2020, p. B1.

372   *"It's rare to see Congress":* Matt Stoller, "Congress Forced Silicon Valley
       to Answer for Its Misdeeds. It Was a Glorious Sight," *Guardian,* July 30,
       2020.

373   *the filing of formal charges:* Adam Satariano, "Amazon Charged with Anti-
       trust Violations by European Regulators," *New York Times,* November 11,
       2020, p. B5.

373   *a court had barred Amazon:* Sam Schechner, "Amazon to Reopen French
       Warehouses After Deal with Unions," *Wall Street Journal,* May 16, 2020.

373   *Italians had set aside:* Adam Satariano and Emma Bubola, "Pasta, Wine
       and Inflatable Pools: How Amazon Conquered Italy in the Pandemic,"
       New York Times, September 28, 2020, p. B1.

373   *the reimposition of a lockdown:* Liz Alderman, "'We Want to Open!'
       French Shopkeepers Revolt Against Orders to Close," *New York Times,* No-
       vember 4, 2020, p. B3.

375   *The Crown had lowered levies:* Matt Stoller, "The Boston Tea Party Was a
       Protest Against Monopoly," *BIG,* July 1, 2019, https://mattstoller.substack
       .com/p/the-boston-tea-party-was-a-protest.

375   *During the last three decades:* Matt Stoller, *Goliath: The 100-Year War
       Between Monopoly Power and Democracy* (New York: Simon & Schuster,
       2019), Chapter One.

375   *introducing the Federal Trade Commission:* Ibid.

376   *a "menace for the future":* Ibid.

376   *Farmers and workers paid:* Ibid.

376   *nearly one-fourth of all income:* Emmanuel Saez, "Striking It Richer: The
       Evolution of Top Incomes in the United States," Technical Notes 201506,
       World Inequality Lab, 2015, as cited in Stoller, *Goliath,* op. cit.

377   *"The measure of the restoration":* First Inaugural Address of Franklin D.
       Roosevelt, March 4, 1933; via Lillian Goldman Law Library, Yale Law
       School, https://avalon.law.yale.edu/20th_century/froos1.asp.

377   *Roosevelt had wrangled:* Stoller, *Goliath,* op. cit., Chapter Four.

377   *Roosevelt sicced his Justice Department:* Ibid., Chapter Six.

377   *"Co-opting the rhetoric of liberty":* Ibid., Chapter Nine.

378   *"It changed our view":* Edmund W. Kitsch, "The Fire of Truth: A Remem-
       brance of Law and Economics at Chicago, 1932–1970," *Journal of Law and
       Economics* 26, no. 1 (April 1983): p. 183, as cited in Stoller, *Goliath,* op. cit.,
       Chapter Nine.

378   *The American Enterprise Institute:* Stoller, *Goliath,* op. cit., Chapter Nine.

378   *financed research by Bork:* Ibid.

378   *The Business Roundtable convened:* Ibid., Chapter Thirteen.

379   *The laws were costing:* Eileen Shanahan, "'Fair Trade' Laws Coming to an
       End," *New York Times,* December 13, 1975.

379   *"maximization of consumer welfare":* Robert H. Bork, *The Antitrust Paradox: A Policy at War with Itself* (New York: Basic Books, 1978), 7.

379   *wages throughout American retail:* David Moberg, "How Wal-Mart Shapes the World," *The American Prospect,* April 19, 2011, https://prospect.org /power/wal-mart-shapes-world/.

380   *"It was that Bork convinced":* Stoller, *Goliath,* op. cit., Chapter Fifteen.

381   *"In other words":* Lina M. Khan, "Amazon's Antitrust Paradox," *The Yale Law Journal,* 126, no. 3 (January 2017), https://www.yalelawjournal.org /note/amazons-antitrust-paradox.

CHAPTER 20: "TAXES, TAXES, TAXES. THE REST IS BULLSHIT."

384   *the twenty wealthiest Americans:* Analysis of 2018 Forbes 400 Richest People in America and Forbes America's Top 50 Givers, conducted by Gabriel Zucman.

384   *more than seven times:* Ibid.

386   *"It's indirect":* William D. Cohan, "'I Can't Prove It to You, But I Know It's True': Jamie Dimon Puts His Faith in Trump's Tax Plan," *Vanity Fair,* December 8, 2017.

387   *An expansive study:* David Hope and Julian Limberg, "The Economic Consequences of Major Tax Cuts for the Rich," London School of Economics, December 16, 2020, http://eprints.lse.ac.uk/107919.

387   *the share of all income:* World Inequality Database, Income Inequality, USA, 1913–2019, https://wid.world/country/usa.

387   *In Italy, the top 10 percent:* Ibid.

389   *stash away some $7.6 trillion:* Gabriel Zucman, *The Hidden Wealth of Nations: The Scourge of Tax Havens* (Chicago: University of Chicago Press, 2013).

389   *one-fifth of their income:* John Guyton, Patrick Langetieg, Daniel Reck, Max Risch, and Gabriel Zucman, "Tax Evasion at the Top of the Income Distribution: Theory and Evidence," National Bureau of Economic Research, Working Paper 28542, March 2021, https://www.nber.org/papers /w28542.

389   *evaded $381 billion's worth of taxes:* "Trends in the Internal Revenue Service's Funding and Enforcement," Congressional Budget Office, July 2020.

389   *Between 2010 and 2017:* Paul Kiel and Jesse Eisinger, "How the IRS Was Gutted," ProPublica, December 11, 2018, https://www.propublica.org /article/how-the-irs-was-gutted.

389   *households making more than $1 million:* "Millionaires and Corporate Giants Escape IRA Audits Again in FY 2020," TRAC, Newhouse School of Communications and Whitman School of Management, Syracuse University, March 18, 2021, https://trac.syr.edu/tracirs/latest/641.

389   *Every dollar spent:* Richard Rubin, "IRS Enforcement Spending Yields $6 for Every $1, Lew Says," Bloomberg, May 8, 2013.

390   *He legalized the practice:* Emily Stewart, "Stock Buybacks, Explained,"

Vox, August 5, 2018, https://www.vox.com/2018/8/2/17639762/stock-buybacks-tax-cuts-trump-republicans.

391 *while stock and stock options:* Alex Edmans, Xavier Gabaix, and Dirk Jenter, "Executive Compensation: A Survey of Theory and Evidence," National Bureau of Economic Research, Working Paper 23596, July 2017, p. 152, https://www.nber.org/system/files/working_papers/w23596/w23596.pdf.

391 *a secret trove:* Jesse Eisinger, Jeff Ernsthausen, and Paul Kiel, "The Secret IRS Files: Trove of Never-Before-Seen Records Reveal How the Wealthiest Avoid Income Tax," ProPublica, June 8, 2021, https://www.propublica.org/article/the-secret-irs-files-trove-of-never-before-seen-records-reveal-how-the-wealthiest-avoid-income-tax.

391 *Congress has dropped:* Saez and Zucman, op. cit., Chapter Three.

392 *"They would leave":* Julia La Roche, "Steve Schwarzman: A Wealth Tax Would Make Businesses Up and Leave," Yahoo Finance, October 14, 2019, https://finance.yahoo.com/news/blackstone-ceo-steve-schwarzman-on-wealth-tax-201228998.html.

392 *"A wealth tax is almost impossible":* Yen Nee Lee, "Jamie Dimon Says He's OK with Higher Taxes on the Rich, but Wealth Tax Is Almost Impossible,'" CNBC, September 23, 2020, https://www.cnbc.com/2020/09/23/jp-morgans-jamie-dimon-on-taxing-the-rich-donald-trumps-tax-cuts.html.

393 *the number of countries:* "The Role and Design of Net Wealth Taxes in the OECD," OECD Tax Policy Studies, Paper No. 26, 2018, p. 11, https://read.oecd-ilibrary.org/taxation/the-role-and-design-of-net-wealth-taxes-in-the-oecd_9789264290303-en#page3.

394 *"It's a riverboat gamble":* Larry Summers and Emmanuel Saez on *On Point*, WBUR, October 23, 2019, https://www.wbur.org/onpoint/2019/10/23/wealth-tax-democrats-warren-sanders.

394 *Summers had sounded:* Peter S. Goodman, "Taking Hard New Look at a Greenspan Legacy," *New York Times*, October 9, 2008, p. A1.

395 *"pitting workers against companies":* Summers and Saez, op. cit.

396 *roughly double the highest tax rate:* Robert Frank, "Wealthy May Face Up to 61% Tax Rate on Inherited Wealth Under Biden Plan," CNBC, May 3, 2021, https://www.cnbc.com/2021/05/03/wealthy-may-face-up-to-61percent-tax-rate-on-inherited-wealth-under-biden-plan.html.

396 *$80 billion on IRS enforcement:* Jim Tankersley and Alan Rappeport, "Biden Seeks $80 Billion to Beef Up I.R.S. Audits of High-Earners," *New York Times*, April 28, 2021, p. A1.

396 *a global minimum corporate tax rate:* Alan Rappeport, "Finance Ministers Meet in Venice to Finalize Global Tax Agreement," *New York Times*, July 10, 2021, p. B1.

CONCLUSION: **"OUR CUP RUNNETH OVER"**

397 *"We pick the good neighborhoods":* Schwarzman at Goldman Sachs U.S. Financial Services Virtual Conference, December 9, 2020, transcript

posted on Seeking Alpha, https://seekingalpha.com/article/4393944
-blackstone-group-inc-bx-ceo-stephen-schwarzman-presents-goldman
-sachs-u-s-financial-services.

398 *"It's really like an avalanche"*: Brian Chappatta, "Schwarzman Sees 'Avalanche' of Opportunities from Tax-Hike Risk," Bloomberg, June 23, 2021.

398 *"Wow, what a quarter"*: Benioff on *Mad Money,* CNBC, December 1, 2020, https://www.cnbc.com/2020/12/01/marc-benioff-slack-is-one-step-in-salesforces-path-to-double-revenue.html.

398 *"It might be software"*: Michelle F. Davis, "Dimon Asks Bankers to Call Him with Their M&A Ideas for JPMorgan," Bloomberg, December 8, 2020.

398 *"Our cup runneth over"*: JPMorgan Chase & Co., 1Q21 Financial Results, Earnings Call Transcript, April 14, 2021, https://www.jpmorganchase.com/content/dam/jpmc/jpmorgan-chase-and-co/investor-relations/documents/quarterly-earnings/2021/1st-quarter/1q21-earnings-transcript.pdf.

399 *the coronavirus had killed:* Zachary Parolin, Megan Curran, Jordan Matsudaira, Jane Waldfogel, and Christopher Wimer, "Monthly Poverty Rates in the United States During the COVID-19 Pandemic," Center on Poverty & Social Policy, School of Social Work, Columbia University, Poverty and Social Policy Working Paper, October 15, 2020, https://static1.squarespace.com/static/5743308460b5e922a25a6dc7/t/5f87c59e4cd0011fabd38973/1602733471158/COVID-Projecting-Poverty-Monthly-CPSP-2020.pdf.

399 *gained a collective $1.3 trillion:* Chuck Collins, "Updates: Billionaire Wealth, U.S. Job Losses and Pandemic Profiteers," Inequality.org, February 24, 2021, https://inequality.org/great-divide/updates-billionaire-pandemic.

399 *"I think we're going to"*: Kevin Stankiewicz, "CEO of World's Largest Money Manager Sees Stocks Rallying in 2021 but Not as Much as Last Year," CNBC, January 14, 2021, https://www.cnbc.com/2021/01/14/blackrocks-fink-stocks-to-rally-in-2021-but-not-as-much-as-last-year.html.

399 *"I'm proud to be joining"*: Rupert Neate and Simon Murphy, "Former Chancellor George Osborne to Become Full-Time Banker," *Guardian,* February 1, 2021.

399 *totaled about $2.6 billion:* Sissi Cao, "Billionaires Made Record Profit, Donated Record Lows in 2020," *Observer,* January 5, 2021.

400 *"I also want to thank"*: Blue Origin Jeff Bezos Post-Flight Press Conference Transcript, July 20, 2021, https://www.rev.com/blog/transcripts/blue-origin-jeff-bezos-post-flight-press-conference-transcript.

400 *"a couple of hundred years"*: Mathias Döpfner, "Jeff Bezos Reveals What It's Like to Build an Empire—And Why He's Willing to Spend $1 Billion a Year to Fund the Most Important Mission of His Life," *Business Insider,* April 28, 2018.

401 *Bezos had reportedly poured:* Kevin T. Dugan, "Everything to Know About

Tuesday's Blue Origin Space Launch with Jeff Bezos," *Fortune,* July 19, 2021.

401   *That was enough to save:* Joe McCarthy, "Jeff Bezos Just Spent $5.5B to Be in Space for 4 Minutes. Here Are 7 Things That Money Could Help Solve," Global Citizen, July 20, 2021, https://www.globalcitizen.org/en/content /jeff-bezos-space-flight-money-better-uses.

INDEX